MAIN BHI CHOWKIDAR

(Loss of Truth)

MANOJ KUMAR KAUSHAL

INDIA • SINGAPORE • MALAYSIA

Notion Press

Old No. 38, New No. 6
McNichols Road, Chetpet
Chennai - 600 031

First Published by Notion Press 2019
Copyright © Manoj Kumar Kaushal 2019
All Rights Reserved.

ISBN 978-1-64546-621-5

Chapter 1

THE CASE OF THE LOST BOUNTY/THE NATION THAT DID NOT WANT TO KNOW

I am Manoj Kumar Kaushal from Kotlan Kalan, Una, Himachal Pardesh. I have served in the Indian Military Intelligence for eighteen years. Due to a medical emergency in the family, I had to take retirement in 2009 from the service. However, right before the retirement, I encountered and confronted something for which I am still fighting for. This is a story of that incident that has not ceased to haunt the lives of people who formed a crucial part of the story's uncovering and those to whom justice was denied when they sought it almost a decade ago. The story unfolds in Guwahati, Assam, in 2006 where I was posted until 2009. During my tenure there, I headed many secret operations and build a reliable and very efficient network of investigators and secret agents. This network of agents and informers would fill me in with information that was secret and completely offhand to many public servants and government officials. Even after my retirement, I continued to receive information that was relevant to the well being of the nation from my informers. Having left the service, I would direct the informers and the information to the Army personnel, C.I.D, or the Crime Branch. And that's what I did, when I received the information about which this book is about. The information which begin as a simple straightforward case transformed into an open-ended, inconclusive, and disturbing tale of human greed, organizational chaos, Red Tapism, and bureaucratic ambiguity. That tale still goes on and hasn't ended.

On May 10th, 2014, I receive a phone call from one of my informers, Jiten Kalita, on my mobile number, and following is the conversation I have with Jiten:

Kalita: Hello Sir, how are you?

Manoj Kumar: Hello Kalita, I am fine, you say how are you?

Kalita: I am fine. I wanted to give you some important information. Is it possible for your to come to Guwahati?

Manoj Kumar: What is it? I'll share this information with the Army Intelligence at Guwahati.

Kalita: There is a Kali Temple at a tea estate by the name of Rani Tea Garden. A basement has been discovered under this temple which has been used to store Rs. 300 crore, 300 Kg gold, and two AK47 rifles. Please come to Guwahati or inform an Army officer at the earliest.

Manoj Kumar: Ok. Go to the Narangi camp and meet the Army intelligence officer there at the earliest. But tell me how did you come to know about all of this?

Kalita: Actually, we have got hold of the diary of either the owner or the manager of that tea estate which had mentions of all that was stashed away in that basement and other things. We have also verified that there is a basement underneath the temple by going and checking the specific area.

Manoj Kumar: Ok. Go and meet the officer.

After this conversation, I was not able to talk to him much or very frequently because I was still having a hard time processing all that information. The thought of such enormous amount of money stashed away like that was as incredulous to me as it would be to any other individual.

As the days progressed and my touch-points in Guwahati started to fade away, I came to know that with my informer, there were five to six more men with him who in the hope of getting their share from the government became involved with the case. They wanted to hand over the cash and gold to the government and make a decent living from the reward they would receive. The names of those men are as follows: Hitesh Kalita, Mrinal Das, Bolen Kalita, Din Vandhu Alias Niranjan Kalita, Satyajeet Das, Dipen Nath.

Chapter 2

In those days, Punjab Regiment 9 was on duty in Assam. My informer, at my behest, went to meet Major Rana who was then preparing to going on course. Upon hearing the informer's elaboration on the incident, Major Rana sent Lieutenant Sanjay with the informer on to the site where the bounty was stashed. My informer took the Lieutenant to the basement and also pointed out to him area that was slightly dug out. The informer even told the Lieutenant that, "Sir, it is better you have the bounty taken out as soon as possible otherwise it will be stolen." To this Lieutenant Sanjay replied, "Our Company Commander Major Arappa will return on 1ˢᵗ June and then we will have the bounty taken out." To be on top of this case completely and to have the bounty handed over to the government officials at the earliest, my informer and his colleagues decide to go to the Crime Branch, Guhawati. There they meet Inspector Chhetri. From there they go on to meet Major Gautam Vishwas at Narangi Camp (Army Intelligence). And as they are coming back from the last meeting, one of the men accompanying of the informer, Hitesh Kalita, leaves them to meet one of his old friends Dinesh Das urf Baskar Das who stayed near the landmark Rani Tea Garden. Kalita does not take anyone else with him. There is a woman named, Manju Aurang, was also part of Hitesh Kalita's group and who also stays near the Rani Tea Garden.

After a couple of days after the meetings, my source, Jiten Kalita, along with the Crime Branch prepares to extract the secret bounty. They plan to start the process in the morning itself, however, my informer's friends who had been running around with him for days show no interest in taking part in the excavation. Bolen Kalita told him that he can not go with them. my source went to Hitesh Kalita's house to get him, he was asleep. Albeit, my source wakes him up and gets him ready to go to the site but with a lot of difficulty. And when Mrinal Nath is called to ask about his whereabouts, he responds, "You go ahead as I won't be able to join you but do keep my share with you." This kind of behavior confuses my informer as he cannot make sense of what is going on? Anyway, they head to the site where the treasure is stored and are shocked at what they encounter. They find the entire basement dug out and empty. This means that someone had already taken out all the bounty before my informer and the crime branch could reach that place. Encountering this unexpected turn of events, my informer as well as the Crime branch decide to return from the site. My informer also drops Hitesh Kalita at Rangia and returns to home, despondent and dejected.

However, the same evening, the news Channel Day 365 starts showing news of this event – the case of the lost bounty. The news channel is playing this story on repeat and the reporters who are covering this story are Vinay and Girdhar Kalita. My source's friend, Hitesh Kalita is shown narrating the entire story including the value and worth of the bounty that is 300 Crore rupees in cash and gold weighing 300 kg along with an AK56. Further, Hitesh Kalita seems to be informing that this entire bounty was taken out. As he is telling this to the reporters, his accomplice Dinesh Das corroborates his version by also affirming that, the entire stash of good was stolen from this underground cellar.

PHOTOS OF MEDIA COVERAGE BY CULPRITS

As this news is playing, my informer, Jiten Kalita, informs me over the phone that whatever is being shown on the TV is true and someone has actually run away with the cash and gold. I tell him to take photos and make recordings of the news that is being shown on the TV regarding this heist. It was also very odd that none of the other channels, except for Day 365, was playing this news. I immediately guessed that this was no coincident but a planned heist. So I told Jiten, my informer to ensure that he does not lose contact with his partners/friends. However, they suddenly started avoided him and gradually disappeared from Assam. Hitesh Kalita eloped to Patna, Bolen Kalita and Mrinal Nath simply disappeared and there whereabouts were unknown. None of my informers partners were taking calls on their respective phones. However, as my informer had already recored the news coverage and also taken pictures. We had decent evidence to prove that the cash and the gold were actually stolen from the underground cellar. Baffled but determined to solve this riddle, I told my informer, Jiten Kalita that I am coming to Assam on 10th June by air.

On 10th, 2014 I took the Jan Shatabdi to Delhi from Una and from there took a flight to Guhawati. At the Guhawati airport, I was received by Jiten and a man named Satyajit Das. Satyajit Das was related to Mrinal Nath and was sent to spy on us, as we later came to know. Satyajit never came back. After staying here for two days, I shifted to the Kayarna Devi guest house. During this stay we worship Maa Kamakhya.

POTOTOCOPY OF GATE TICKET

Jiten was in touch with Hitesh Kalita and the latter told him that he will return after 16th June, 2014. As time passed, Jiten Kalita was able to speak with Dinesh Das too but he did not disclose anything about the cash or the Gold.

Chapter 3

After 16th June, as informed, Hitesh Kalita returns from Patna. I disguise myself as a temple priest and go to meet him. He gives me a cold shoulder and is not very welcoming. Suddenly, I spot an Air ticket and some packets of almonds and cashews. My suspicion that Hitesh is involved in the heist is further fortified. We speak for almost two hours and head back to our room in the guest house. As we reach our room, Jiten Kalita receives a phone call from Hitesh who is furious at him and asks Jiten, "Why did you get pandit Manu to his house?" Following that call, he breaks all contact with Jiten. Before meeting Hitesh, Jiten and I had also met Dinesh on 13th June. I had met Dinesh as a business man and Dinesh, just like, Hitesh, does not want to associate with us and keeps his distance. Considering the events as they unfolded before us, it was pretty clear to us that the cash and jewelry has been stolen by these boys but we also reckoned that these young men could not have executed such a heist all alone. Then, I thought to myself, going to the local police may not prove very fruitful and it would be better if I contact the Delhi Crime Branch, whose name and prestige is well-known. I contacted the Crime Branch in Delhi and spoke to Mr. Amarpal. We sent all the evidence we had, including the recordings and the photographs of the coverage and asked him to come to ground zero, at the earliest. At first he was suspicious but after listening and looking at the telling evidence and our persuasive accounts of what had transpired, Mr. Amarpal finally agreed to come down to Assam. However, Mr. Amarpal kept delaying his visit to Assam for a week after our conversation with him in which he had promised that he would come. He completely left us in hanging with hope that he will be coming to Assam. Meanwhile, we put pressure on Dinesh to reveal the entire heist to us and we even make him hear the recording of conversation with Crime Branch. We even urge him to become a government witness so that he is not implicated in the case but he doesn't agree. By now, twenty days pass and there's not even a single message from Delhi. Finding no breakthrough, I book a reservation on the North East train and on 30th June 2014, head back to Una. Just an hour of sitting in the train and I receive a call from Dinesh. To my shock, I answer the phone and hear him threatening me, "If you return here again, we'll cut you in pieces."

Not getting fazed by his empty threats I retort, "One can die in an accident too. I have served in the army and I am not scared of your threats. Though, I am certain that you and your friends have stolen the cash, jewelry, and the arms. Now I'll come back for sure so you better stay alert." During this Hitesh Kalita was also with him. I also remembered that while staying at the Kamakhaya Guest House, I met J.P. Dubey, Vinay Bhagat, and Dharampal Sharma from Delhi, who had come there to pay their homage at a temple. I had narrated the entire incident to them and had got them on my side too.

As I reach Delhi, I get in touch with Mr. Dharampal Sharma and take him with me to meet Surinder Manav. Mr. Manav knew Master ji, who was a teacher to the Rajnath Singh, the honorable Home minister of the country. Master ji further makes meet Kharak Bahadur Singh, the PA to Rajnath Singh, who works at the latter's home. Master Ji requests Kharak Bahadur Singh to pay special attention to Manoj's matter as it is in the best interest of the nation. After receiving Kharak Bahadur Singh's convincing affirmation on the matter, we leave. We eagerly wait for the office of the Home Ministry to send an appropriate response. However, to our surprise, a week passes and there is no reply despite the fact that we had left a letter in writing at the Home Minister's office, narrating the incident. Discouraged and dejected at the indifference of the government, I decide to think of a new approach to resolve this matter.

Chapter 4

I come back to Una and here I meet up with a member of the BJP Yuva Morcha, Mr. Sumit. He gets me in touch with Anurag Thakur, a member of the parliament, who gives us an appointment to meet him. I meet Anurag Thakur at his house. I recounted the entire incident and the subsequent occurrences to Anurag Thakur and requested him to look into the matter. After patiently hearing me out, he assured me that he will take this matter to the Home Ministry and definitely work toward solving this crime. I handed the copy of the letter that I had marked to the Home ministry and ended our meeting. Feeling encouraged and hopeful that something may come to fruition, I set toward my home.

PHOTOCOPY OF LETTER

Letter to Rajnath Singh (Home Minister)

To

The Home Minister

India

New Delhi,

Respected Sir,

I am Manoj Kumar Kaushal and I belong to the village of Lower Kotla, Takka Road, Una. I have served in the secret service of the Indian Army for 18 years.

I retired from Assam in 2009 and till today I have connections and a well spread network in Assam. About two months ago, I received a phone call from one of my informers in Assam who informed me about an enormous amount of treasured buried in a cellar underneath a Kali Temple in a tea estate called Rani Tea Garden near Guwahati Airport in Assam. The treasure found included Rupees 300 Crore, 3 quintal gold biscuits, and 2 AK47s. He requested me to appeal to the army to help solve this case.

I told him to meet the Army intelligence officer in Guwahati. My informer along with his friends went to meet the Army personnel who agreed to dig out the cellar for the treasure on 1st June 2014. However, my informer's friends thought that if the army takes the entire treasure then they will not get anything and hence on the night of 31st May 2014, they went and dug out the entire money, gold, and 2 AK47s. The group that committed this crime is now absconding.

The news was also covered in the local media but the police is still in the dark about who committed this crime. I know that the entire bounty is with the boys who accompanied my informer to the army. Till now these boys have only divided one box with among themselves, the remaining two have been kept at someone's house.

It is my humble appeal to you to please ensure that this enormous amount of Rupees 300 Crore and 300 Kg Gold is retrieved from these men and used for the endeavors that will help in the progress of the nation. I implore you to involve a top-level crime agency in this investigation. I will fully cooperate with the agency that takes this case and offer all my help in making sure that the money and the gold are retrieved.

Thank you.

Yours Sincererly,

Manoj Kumar Kaushal

(Lower Kotla, Takka Road

Una, Himachal Pardesh

Pin: 174303

Phone: 9418604126, 9816169403

Vinay Kumar Bhagat

Dharmapal Sharma

Jiten Kalita

AFTER SOME DAYS MY MP ANURAG THAKUR SENT ME COPY OF LETTER WITTEN TO HOME MINISTER

Photocopy of the Letter by Anurag Thakur to Mr. Rajnath Singh

Anurag Singh Thakur

Member of the Lok Sabha

14, Janpath

New Delhi – 110001

Telephone – 011–23782365

Fax – 23782368

Respected,

Mr. Rajnath Singh

Subject: With regard to the investigation in the case of the missing treasure of Rupees 300 Crore, 300 Kg Gold Biscuits, and 2 AK47 rifles.

This is to request you to please observe Mr. Manoj Kumar Kaushal's who belongs to Lower Kotla, Takka Road, Una – 174303, Himachal Pardesh, documents attached with this letter which prove that he has served the Indian Army's intelligence bureau for almost 18 years. His service in the department has enabled him to have contacts in the secret organization and a widespread network of informers. From his reliable resources he received information that a massive treasure constituting Rupees 300 Crores, 300 Kg Gold biscuits, and 2 AK47 rifles were found in a cellar underneath the Kali Goddess temple in Rani Tea Garden estate, 6 KM from the Guwahati airport. This treasure which was stolen by a group of men in a systematic and strategic way. It is requested that this case is thoroughly investigated and the treasure which was buried under the temple is retrieved and the culprits are deservingly punished. We request you to kindly get the bounty back and have it deposited in the national treasury.

In my personal opinion, this a matter of great concern, therefore, I humble insist that this case is investigated by the highest authorities as per your directive initiative.

With respect and best wishes,

Documents Attached: Manoj Kumar Kaushal's credentials.

Sh. Rajnath Singh

Respected Home Minister,

Government of India

New Delhi

On 8 August 2014, I receive a call on my mobile – 9816169403 – from Assam A Landline Number 0361233074. On the phonehe told me that he is Rajindra Mahapatra from Intelligence Burue Guwahati and have received a letter from the MP of our state and would like to know the name of the men involved in the incident. I told them that I'll come to Assam and inform tell them the names and the location from where the cash and gold were found. They agree. After talking to them, I felt elated at the action taken and also felt proud of our crime-fighting system's intolerance toward crimes. I was proud of my nation for assuring that justice is served and crimes are resolved.

I started my prep to go to Assam and also called Mr. Jai Prakash Dubey and told him how the IB contacted me for the case and are ready to take action. He got two Rajdhani tickets for 10th August 2014. On the morning of 10th August 2014, I took the Jan Shatabdi from Una and reached the New Delhi Railway Station.

PHOTOCOPY OF TICKETS

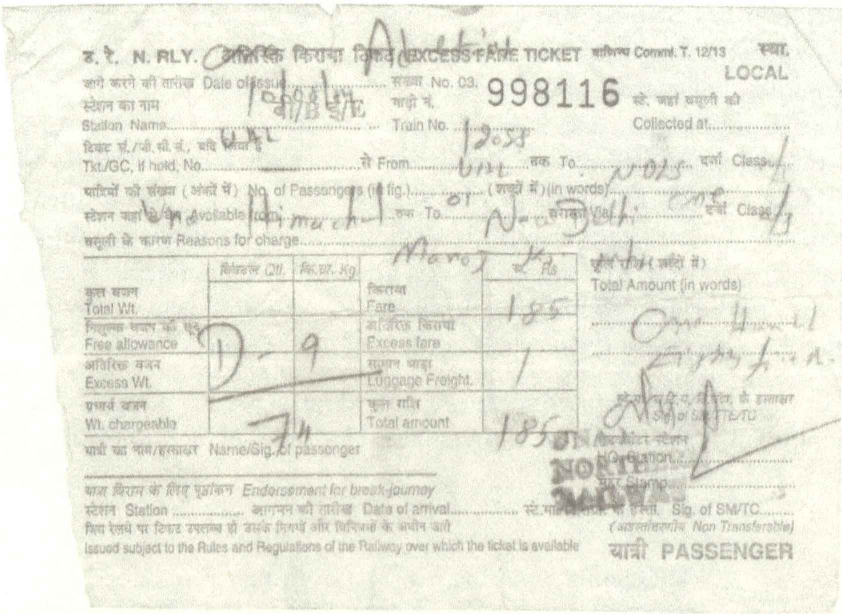

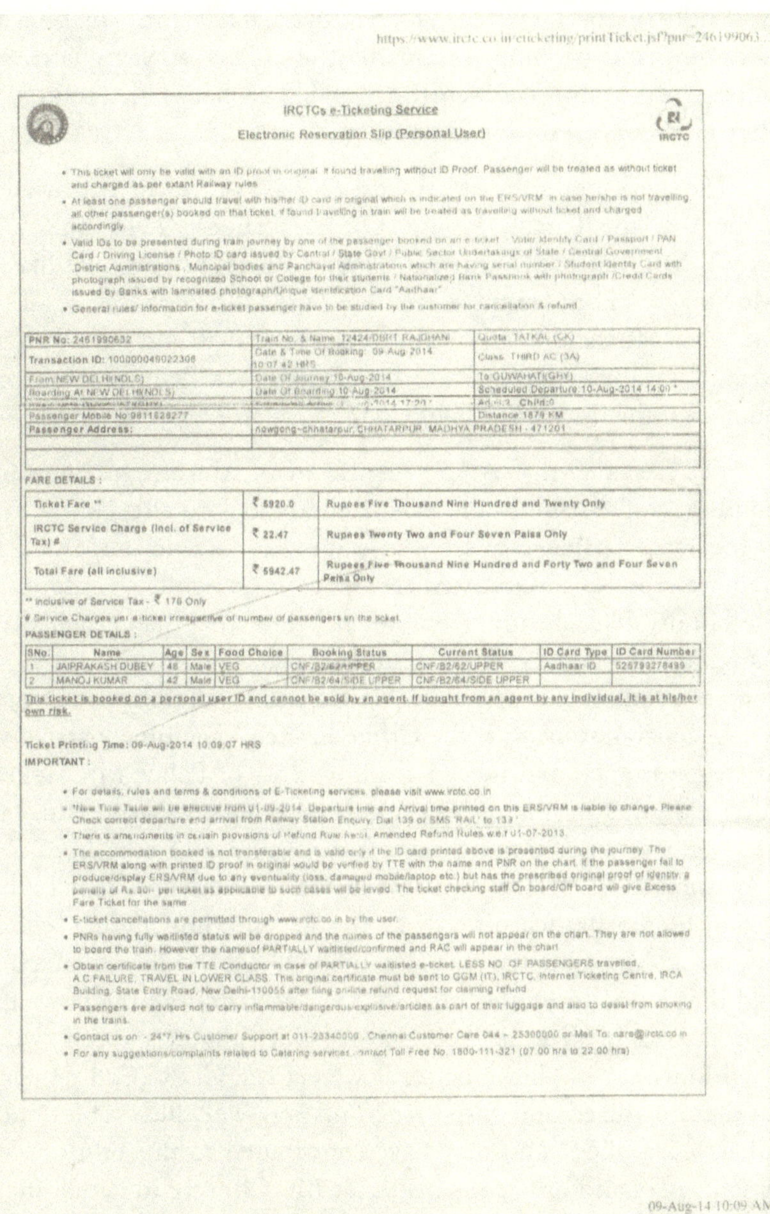

Our train to Assam was at 17:00 and the ticket was with Mr. Dubey. In an adventurous turn of event, Mr. Dubey could not make it in time for the train. Stuck in a horrible traffic Jam, he arrived at the station very late. I requested the TT to let me board the train but he bluntly refused.

At 17:00 sharp, I saw Mr. Dubey, who has a limp in one of the legs, screaming and running toward the train. The railway guard saw this and stopped the train. We were finally able to board the train to Guhawati after much uncertainty and panic.

The next day, on 11th August 2014, we reach Guhawati and book a room at the Circuit House. On 12th August 2014, the day after our arrival, Mr. Mahapatra sent Mr. Singh to meet us. Here I'd like to mention Mr. Singh's phone number at the time, 8822865738. I also spoke to Mr. Mahapatra and told him that today we can go and pay our homage at the Mata Kamakhya temple to which he agreed. Mr. Rajindra Mahapatra's phone number at the time was 9864033038.

The next day that is 13th August, 2014 Mr. Singh comes to our guest house in a Tata Sumo and take Kalita and I to the Crime Branch. This is the same Crime Branch whose officials had accompanied my source, Kalita to the Kali Mandir where the cash and gold were found. However, the bounty had already been stolen before they had reached the temple. As we are on the way to the Crime Branch, I point out to Mr. Singh that you are taking us to the police. He responds, "all our operations are carried out in collaboration with the Crime Branch." We finally arrive at the office of Crime Branch and meet Superintendent of Police Mr. Sudhakar Singh. After narrating to him the entire turn of events, we waited for his response. He begins by questioning my source Kalita and asks him, "Why didn't you come to us before?" To this Kalita informs him that he had taken a few of Crime Branch officials to the site of crime among whom a certain inspector, Mr. Chhetry was also present. Mr. Sudhakar Singh is satisfied and then turns to us and suggests that let's arrest all the boys involved and also asks us to give us their names. Not fully convinced with this idea, I tell him that it will be better if we get the CDR (Call details record) of all those involved and suspected. This way we will be able to know about other accomplices who may have contributed to this crime. Mr. Sudhakar Singh agrees and orders his inspector Mr. Chhetry to get all the call details out by the next day and order to given call details to me. After handing over them the phone numbers of all the suspects we return to the Circuit House. The following day Mr. Singh calls me and informs that we will also get the call details and let you know who all are involved. I agree with him and say, "Very well, please go ahead and do it." On the fifth day after our meeting Inspector Mr. Chhetry emails me some call detail records.

The moment I saw those call details I was stunned into silence. It not only contained phone numbers of the suspect boys but also of some policemen. I was outraged to know that all that cash and gold which was the property of the nation had been flinched by the police! Trying to wrap my head around this new astonishing detail, I pause and think of what to do next. I decide not to inform the IB that I have received the call detail records. The very next day, Mr. Singh calls me and says I have the call details but there is no intrinsic connection at all among the details. I tell him that we will come to you and show you all the connections that exist in those call details. To which he replies, "We cannot show you the call details." Surprised and agitated, I reply, "How can you say this? We have come all the way from Himachal and you are trying to avoid us." Not saying much beyond this, he only says, "I am compelled." After this conversation, I call Mr. Singh the next day and I find out that he has been transferred to some other station. I call the office and they inform me that they will call me when they require my input but for now Mr. Singh is being relocated to some other station. I try calling Mr. Singh's mobile number 8822865738 but it is switched off. And to date that number is switched off. I look at one of the call details a bit thoroughly and find out that it contains the details of an IB official, Rajendra Ji. He is also the one who was running away from us. I also informed him the present location of the gold before starting our journey. and he disclosed the plan and they changed the location of the gold on 11 August midnight . The investigation carries on from 23:00–1:30 a.m. in the night as disclosed by the call details of Budiram Mukhtyar.

No one from IB calls or sends any message. Rajendra Mahapatra too does not pick our calls. I lose all hope of a breakthrough One day in circuit guest house, we are caught off guard when a few people to meet Mr. Dubey. Before them a lady had also come to meet Mr. Dubey. As soon as the lady is about to leave the guest house, the reporter of Day 365, Girendhar Kalita asks on camera that who is this lady and what was she doing in Mr. Dubey's room? Igniting it as a scandal the reporter calls the office of Chief Minister, the In-charge of the guest house and gets our booking cancelled. This terrible incident and fake accusations make it certain that there are many who want us to quit this case. However, instead of being scared or discouraged we are further inspired to make sure that the bounty is recovered and justice is served.

We leave that guest house and shift to two rooms put up for rent by the Kamakhya temple priest. We did not want anyone to know about our whereabouts. Our mobiles were recording during this peried and book a ticket back to Delhi to meet my MP. Mr. Dubey continues to be in Guwahati along with my source Kalita.

PHOTOCOPY OF RAILWAY TICKET TO NEW DELHI

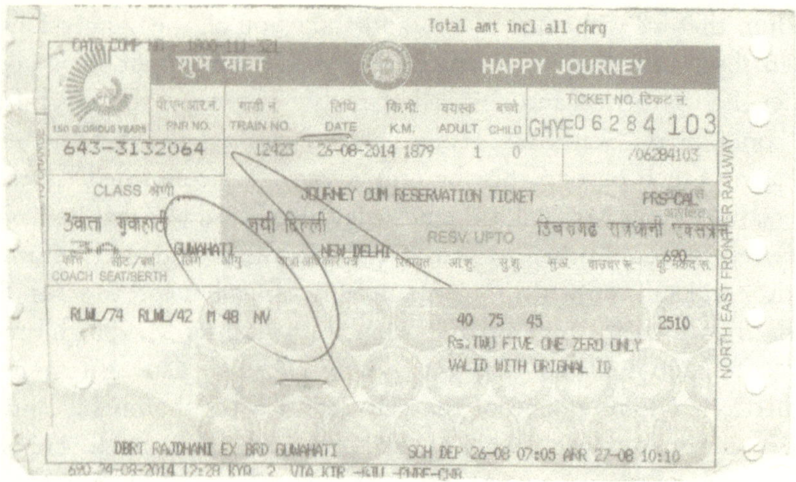

On 27th August, 2014 I reach Delhi and along with Mr. Dharampal I head to Rajnath Singh's house. There I met IPS Sudhir and gave him a letter which said that the IB in Guwahati is not offering assistance in solving the case. I tell him the matter is of serious magnitude and it will be better if a special team from Delhi is assigned this case. The IPS, Mr. Sudhir, asks me to give him the letter and assures that it is now on them to get the job done and my job is over. After this meeting I head to the BJP office and meet my MP Anurag Thakur. Anurag Thakur makes a phone call to the Home Ministry and speaks to the OSD of Rajnath Singh, B.K. Singh. After speaking over the phone, he sends me to B.K. Singh. I take Mr. Dharampal along to meet B.K. Singh. When at the office of Home Ministry, Mr. B.K. Singh makes us meet the Joint Director of IB, Mr. Manoj Yadav. We explain the entire incident along with all the twists and turns of the event. After hearing us he made us meet the Joint Secretary of North East, Mr. Shambhu Singh. That day was 27th August, 2014. I am pasting the handwritten post-it on which Mr. Manoj Yadav gave us Mr. Shambhu's reference. We go to meet Mr. S.N. Singh who after listening to the state of affairs, phones the IGP of Law and Order unit, S.N. Singh and informs him that Mr. Manoj will come to them and he must arrest all the boys a involved in this crime with my help. He also gave us a letter to give it to him. Mr. Manoj Yadav given His Office contact Number 01123092452 for further conecction. That letter was completely pan sealed. I left that meeting encouraged and fully heartened again. I was sure now that we will be able to recover all the money and the gold.

HAND WRITING OF JOINT DIRECTOR IB MANOJ YADAV

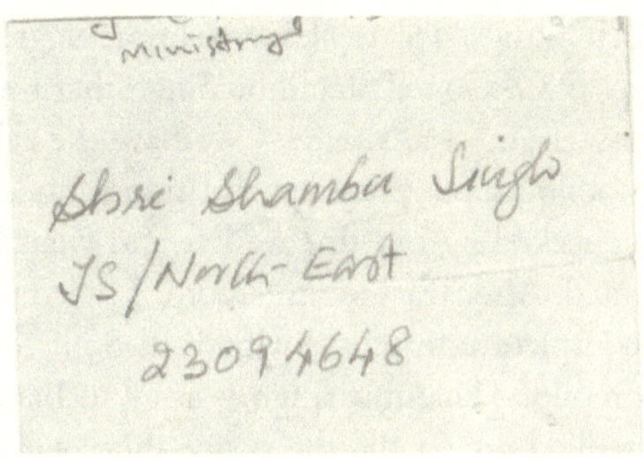

Before going back to Guwahati, I go to my house in Himachal and spend two days there. On the third day, Dharampal and I take the Rajdhani to Guwahati and reach our destination the next day. Once in Guwahati, the next step was to meet S.N. Singh the IGP of Law and Order. So four of us, Mr. Dubey, Mr. Dharampal, Mr. Vinay Bhagat, and I go to the Law and Order office and meet Mr. S.N. Singh. We reveal to him the crime, the unfolding, and the current state of affairs along with our ordeal of receiving any assistance. He notes down everything on a piece of paper (the handwritten note by S.N. Singh is pasted below:) Then he calls the SP of Crime Branch, S.P. Sudhakar Singh and orders him to handle the case. To everyone's surprise, the S.P. Sudhakar Singh refuses to take this case. Then he called on ASP Tiwari to handle this case but ASP Tiwari too expressed his discomfort and eventually refused to handle this case. By this time, it gets very awkward and I break my silence by informing ASP Tiwari about the reporter Vinay Kalita. To this Mr. Tiwari replies, "He roams around in dilapidated sandals." I understood that these officers are avoiding this case and I remembered how I had communicated this to Manoj Yadav in Delhi, the Joint Director of IB that the police will not help in this case. Meanwhile, the IGP of Law and Order, Mr. S.N. Singh offered us some tea and snacks and told us to come to the office the next day. We return to our guest house.

After getting the rooms and settling in, all four of us went to the Law and Order office to meet S.N. Singh. Mr. Singh was not in his chair so we waited for his return. After an hour of our waiting he returns. He sits on his chair and without acknowledging our presence, begins to light a cigarette unsuccessfully. By this time, I realize that there will not be any investigation happening anytime soon and especially not by these officials. As I was thinking all this, he (Mr. S.N. Singh) bursts into shouting and anger. He says, "I feel like beating your source black and blue." Stunned and also angry, I try to control my the hurt and the pain that this comment causes me and in a neutral tone, ask him why is he saying such things. He replies even more aggressively, "Am I your servant? Bloody Army JCO! Go tell Shambhu Singh that I will not do anything. What will you do now, huh?" I answered, "We have the call detail records and also the details of mobile money transfers and transactions. I will go to Delhi and get all of these checked." After this we left and went back to our rooms, tensed and disappointed. After reaching the room, I called up Mr. Manoj Yadav and told him our complete interaction with IGP S.N. Singh. After listening to us, Manoj Yadav replies, "Shambu Singh is away to Bangladesh, you should meet the DGP." I replied saying the the police there will not do anything to help us and that we are returning to Delhi and will meet him.

HANDWRITTING OF IGP LOW AND ORDER S.N. SINGH

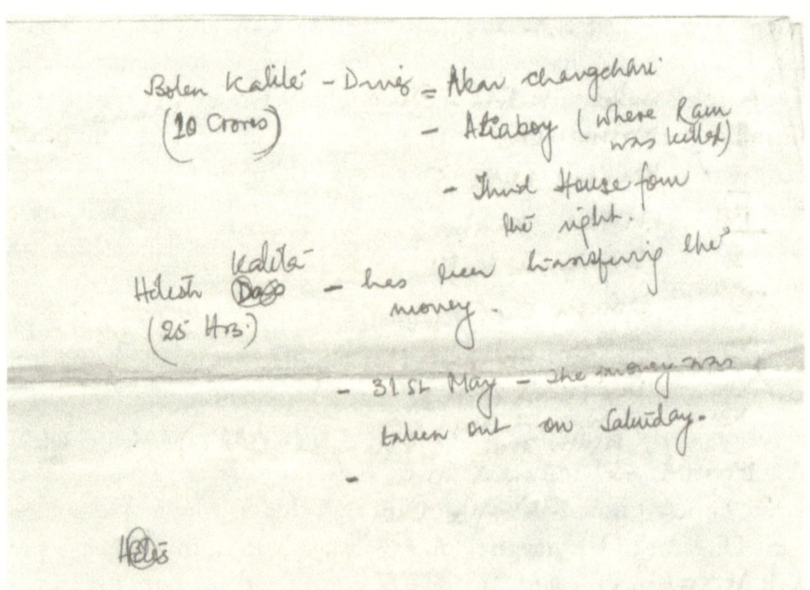

We booked our tickets to Delhi the next day and took the Rajdhani back to Delhi. We immediately wanted to set up a meeting with Manoj Yadav but it was not possible. Mr. Yadav refused to meet us. Then we tried to get in touch with B.K. Singh, the OSD to the home minister. Even he did not show any interest in meeting us and kept avoiding us by making excuses fpr the day saying, "he has gone to dropping the Home Minister to the airport who is traveling to Bangladesh." We had lost all hope by then and returned to our respective home towns and cities. After some time it comes to my notice that Mr. Manoj Yadav took posting to Guwahati Intelligence Burue. I Understood that why he get this posting.

In month of September 2014 I Met My M.P. Anurag Thakur aaat Amb Una along with my sorce Jiten Kalita. I told him about no any progresss on the matter. He gave me a number of his known CBI Joint Director Rajib Singh. The Number was 03323348713. I contact on Phone with Mr. Rajib Singh and said all about the Matter. Hi gave me direction that Meet to B.K. Singh OSD Home Minisiter and release order for me for the enquiry. I Knew that B.K. Singh will not meet me and I never contact Mr. Rajib Singh.

Chapter 5

At the time when I was pursuing this case, my wife, who had a failed kidney, was undergoing dialysis.

PHOTOCOPY OF MY FAMILY DURING DYLASIS

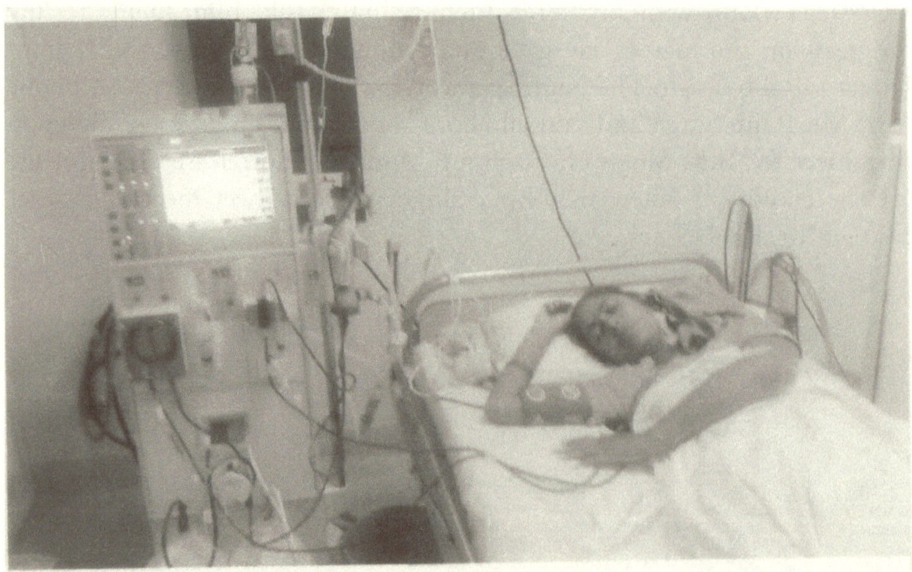

1. Due to my divided attention and my absence from home, I was not able to take much care of her either. My entire family was suffering due to my wife's medical condition at the time but I was not able to attend to her or the rest of the family because I was fully immersed in solving this case and hellbent on ensuring that the bounty reaches the national treasury. One day as I was idling at home, I decided to write another letter to the Home Ministry saying that the IB team is not appearing to be of any use and it will be better if a CBI team takes up this case.

2. Letter to the Home Ministry for CBI Team

To

The Home Ministry

Indian Government

New Delhi

Subject: Requesting the involvement of CBI in the investigation of disappearance of Rupees 300 Crore and 300 Kg gold, and 2 AK47s.

Respected Sir,

I am Manoj Kumar Kaushal and I belong to the village of Lower Kotla, Takka Road, Una. I have served in the secret service of the Indian Army for 18 years.

I retired from Assam in 2009 and till today I have connections and a well spread network in Assam. About two months ago, I received a phone call from one of my informers in Assam who informed me about an enormous amount of treasured buried in a cellar underneath a Kali Temple in a tea estate called Rani Tea Garden near Guwahati Airport in Assam. The treasure found included Rupees 300 Crore, 3 quintal gold biscuits, and 2 AK47s. He requested me to appeal to the army to help solve this case.

I told him to meet the Army intelligence officer in Guwahati. My informer along with his friends went to meet the Army personnel who agreed to dig out the cellar for the treasure on 1ˢᵗ June 2014. However, my informer's friends thought that if the army takes the entire treasure then they will not get anything and hence on the night of 31ˢᵗ May 2014, they went and dug out the entire money, gold, and 2 AK47s. The group that committed this crime is now absconding.

The news was also covered in the local media but the police is still in the dark about who committed this crime. I know that the entire bounty is with the boys who accompanied my informer to the army. Till now these boys have only divided one box with among themselves, the remaining two have been kept at someone's house.

It is my humble appeal to you to please ensure that this enormous amount of Rupees 300 Crore and 300 Kg Gold is retrieved from these men and used for the endeavors that will help in the progress of the nation. I implore you to involve a top-level crime agency in this investigation. I will fully cooperate with the agency that takes this case and offer all my help in making sure that the money and the gold are retrieved.

We have the names, home addresses, and the phone numbers of all the boys who were involved in the heist. However, no one is ready to help us in this. Also, you, through the IB officers, had us informed that you have obtained the CDR (Call detail records) of those boys but because IB did not have the man power or arresting power, no progress was made.

I profoundly request you once again to get the CBI involved in the investigations of this case. We will be highly grateful to you.

Deep gratitude.

Yours Sincerely,

Manoj Kumar Kaushal

Jai Prakash Dubey

Vinay Bhagat

Dharampal Sharma

Jiten Kalita

The Home Ministry responded to this letter saying that the CBI does not fall under the purview of Home Ministry. The letter I received from the department of Home Ministry was written on 22nd September 2014.

COPY OF HOME MINISTRY LETTER

F.No.24013/1/Orissa/2014-CSR.III
Government of India
Ministry of Home Affair

NDCC-II Bldg., Jai Singh Road, New Delhi.
Dated 22 September.2014

To,

Principal Secretary,
Home Department,
Govt. of Orissa,
Orissa Secretariat,
Bhubeneshwar – 751001

Subject: Representations for redressal of grievances regarding law & order and related matters – Forwarding of.

Sir,

I am directed to forward herewith ~~nine~~ *Eight* representations (as per enclosed Annexure). in original, received from various aggrieved persons. relating to various grievances and complaints.

2.   Since 'Police and 'Public Order' are State subjects under the Seventh Schedule to the Constitution of India. it is the responsibility of the concerned State Government to prevent. detect. register and investigate crime and prosecute the criminals involved through the machinery of its law enforcement agencies. and hence. you may take action on the representation. as deemed appropriate.

3.   So far as the request of some of the petitioners for CBI enquiry of their cases is concerned. it may please be kept in view that the Union Government cannot. suo-moto. entrust to the Central Bureau of Investigation (CBI). the investigation of an offence which has taken place in a State. unless the State Govt. proposes and gives its consent under Section 6 of the DSPE Act. 1946 for extension of jurisdiction of CBI in respect of that offence. Further, the Ministry of Home Affairs has no administrative jurisdiction over CBI, which comes under the control of the Ministry of Personnel, PG & Pensions, Department of Personnel & Training. The Ministry of Personnel, PG & Pensions, Department of Personnel & Training. may be approached if it is desired to hand over any case to CBI.

4.   A reply may please be sent to the petitioner.

Yours faithfully,

(V. Mahalingam)
Section Officer (CSR.III)
Tel: 23438141

Encl: Annexure

Copy to all Petitioners/applicants
(As per list enclosed)

List – Odisha
Date-19.09.14

S. No.	Name & Address of Petitioner	Subject	Date of Petition	Computer No.
1	Sh. Bibhuti Bhusan Tripathy National Informatice Centre Assam State Centre, Assam Secretariat, P.O. Assam Sachivalaya, Guwahati-781006	Unauthorized constructions within 500meters of high-tide line lying within coastal regularity zone at puri	06.08.14	325591
2	Sh. S.K. Safik Mohhamad President- Help Line, Arad Bazar, Balasore	Safe guard the tax- payers or loot the Govt. tax	04.06.14	326457
3	Sh. Yusuf Khan & Others R/o. Vill & Post- Jashipur, Dist- Mayeer Bhanj (Orissa)	Encroach ment of masjid property by the land grabbers in Connivance with tehsildar	02.08.14	324426
4	Smt. Kalpana Jena R/o. 44- Satyanagar Bhubaneswar, Odisha	Complaint against Mr. Pramod Panda and his superior Mr. B.K. Sharma	Nil	297155
5	Sh. Manoj Kumar Kaushal R/o.Vill- Loar Kotala Takka Road, Una, Himachal Pradesh	Reg. Army Intelligent agency	Nil	304061
6	Sh. Sudarshan Behera S/o. Lt. Sh. Indramani Behera Vill- Nandakishorepur, P.O Kumudajoypur, P.S- Mahanga, Dist- Cuttack, Odisha	My requirement your request to honorable Chife Minister of Odisha Mr. Navin Pattanayak to finance me Rs 2,00000/- as an aid the following causes	07.08.14	337944
7	Sh. Jolly vishes President revolutionary Jantha Party All India Commettee, Jolly Vishes Tower, Thonacad P.O, Cheriyanad, Chengannur, (VIA), Alleppey (Dist), Kerala	Complaint against Neigh bower	15.08.14	337301

I was hopeful because I remembered that we had written letters to CBI director, P.M. Modi, and Jitendra Singh.

3. Letter to Dr. Jitender Singh

To

Dr. Jitender Singh

Ministry of Personnel

Ministry of personal and training

Indian Government

New Delhi – 110001

Subject: Application to request and arrest the culprits involved in stealing Rupees 300 Crore, 300 Kg Gold, and 2 AK47s after filing the F.I.R/R.C. Also requesting to retrieve the bounty and get it deposited in the national treasury.

Respected Sir,

It is our (1) Manoj Kumar Kaushal, Address: Lower Kotla, Takka Road, Una, Himachal Pardesh (2) Jai Prakash Dubey, Address – Block D, #2044, Palm Vihar, Gurgaon (3) Dharampal Sharma, Address: R.J.D.F – 99/147, Street Number 41 B, Shaadnagar, Palm Colony, New Delhi – 45.

This is to bring to your notice that the people mentioned above and I have been spending our personal resources of time, effort, and money in order to bring back the stolen treasure so that it can be utilized in the growth and development of the nation. We hope that we not only receive the due cooperation from the crime branch of the nation, that is the C.B.I but also the Indian government who as per country's financial guidelines can retrieve the Gold and the money that was buried it the cellar at the Rani Tea Garden and add it to the national treasury.

The heist took place in Assam, 6 km from the Guwahati airport at the Rani Tea Garden. The tea garden had a Kali Temple underneath which there was a cellar. The door to the cellar was found to be under the statue of Goddess Kali. In the cellar was found Rupees 300 Crore, 3 quintal gold, and 2 AK47s.

The boys who stole the money are about 13 in number. There names are as follows:

1. Hitesh Kalita

2. Budikhura Mukhtiya

3. Deepak Das

4. Bolen Kalita

5. Abhijit Deka

6. Jitu Mani Das

7. Manju Urang

8. Dinesh Dag/Das

9. Giasudin Ahmed

10. Mrinal Das

11. Binod Kalita

12. Pravin Musahari

13. Nur Ahmed

These men obtained informal details of the treasure through Mridul's diary in March and using that information stole the entire dividend and the gold after a period of 1.5/2 months. They searched the area and conducted a full recce of the field before stealing Rupees 300 Crore, and 3 quintal Gold biscuits and the rifles.

This information was given to Manoj Kumar Kaushal who had served in the Army intelligence for 18 years before taking voluntary retirement in the year 2009. He had a secret informer from Assam, Jiten Kalita who is a resident of Assam and was also part of the group that orchestrated this heist but is now in touch with Mr. Kaushal and us. The above mentioned amount and Gold is with the men whose names have been listed above. The photograph of the temple and the cellar is attached herewith.

We also found that the above group was sending the money through internal bank transfer nationally and internationally. We have a copy of the transfers as well which is attached with this document.

The above mentioned group, after the heist on 31st May 2014, used their phones to divide and hide the bounty at different places. We have their call records which we will present whenever they are asked. I am attaching a copy of a few call records for your attention. Please see attachment #3.

The treasure was accumulated and belonged to Mridual Bhattacharya who was the director of the Assam Tea Garden association. Mridul Bhattacharya used to give a ransom to the ULFA terrorists against security and protection. For this he used to collect money from other tea estate and garden owners and smuggle gold from Burma. At the end of four years he had Rupees 300 Crores and 300 Kg Gold and 2 AK47 rifles in his cellar which he had built under the Kali Goddess temple. He was noting the details of this collection in a diary which belonged to his manager. The said manager disappeared in 2010 and is still missing today. Mridual Bhattacharya and his wife lost their lives in 2012 in a tragic accident. In 2014, when this information reached the boys, they stole the entire treasure.

We have been trying to recover this treasure so that it can be deposited in the national treasure, where it rightfully belongs. However, we have not received any help or assistance from the concerned authorities instead we have been hitting one wall after the other. This complaint letter is being presented to the Prime Minister so that this case can be resolved.

We implore the your person to kindly look into the above mentioned matter and take some action. The nation will be directly impacted by the decision that higher authorities take in this matter and hence we request you to keep the wellbeing of the country in mind while deciding on the fate of this case. We also request you to register a F.I.R/R.C with the C.B.I and assign this case to an honest and conscientious C.B.I officer who will not only bring the perpetrators to the court of law but also retrieve the treasure that belongs to the nation. We would like to see this treasure deposited in the national treasury and us awarded with the dividend that the Indian government deems right.

Thanking you.

Yours Sincerely,

Manoj Kumar Kaushal

Jai Prakash Dubey

Dharapal Sharma

I wrote this letter on 29th September 2014. Out of these, 2 letters were addressed to Ranjit Singh, the director of CBI and the office of PM Modi.

During the month of October 2014 I received a letter from my M.P. Anurag Singh with the response of Home Minister.

Photocopy of My M.P. Anurag Thakur Reply.

4. Reply by Sh. Anurag Singh Thakur

Anurag Singh Thakur

Member of the Lok Sabha

14, Janpath

New Delhi – 110001

Dated: 25th October 2014

Dear Sh. Kaushal Ji,

Kindly see the attached letter, sent on 30th July, 2014 to Mr. Rajnath Singh, the Home Minister for your reference. I am also attaching the response sent by honorable Mr. Rajnath Singh, Home Ministry, Government of India, New Delhi – 110001, received on 5th August 2014 for your observation.

With Best Wishes,

Sh. Manoj Kumar Kaushal

Gram: Lower Kotla,

Takka Road,

Una – 174303

Zila: Una, Himachal Pradesh

Yours Sincerely,

(   )

Anurag Thakur

5. Response from Rajnath Singh

Rajnath Singh

Home Minister

India

New Delhi – 110001

H.M.P – 323527

05 Aug. 2014

Dear Sh. Thakur Sahib,

I have received your letter dated 30th July 2014 in which you had requested to initiate investigation in the case of the missing treasure and 2 AK47 rifles that were found near the Guwahati Airport.

I am getting this matter looked into.

Regards,

Sh. Anurag Thakur

Member of Parliament (Rajya Sabha)

14, Janpath

New Delhi – 110001

Yours,

(   )

Rajnath Singh

But I was disappointed from Ministry of home because because something was going wrong.

I got a letter from Ministery of Personnel and Training on 20th November 2014. Once again, I was hopeful. The letter from Ministry which under CBI comes,aid, "We have forwarded your request to CBI's CGO complex."

COPY OF LETTER OF MINISTRY OF PERSONAL AND TRAINING

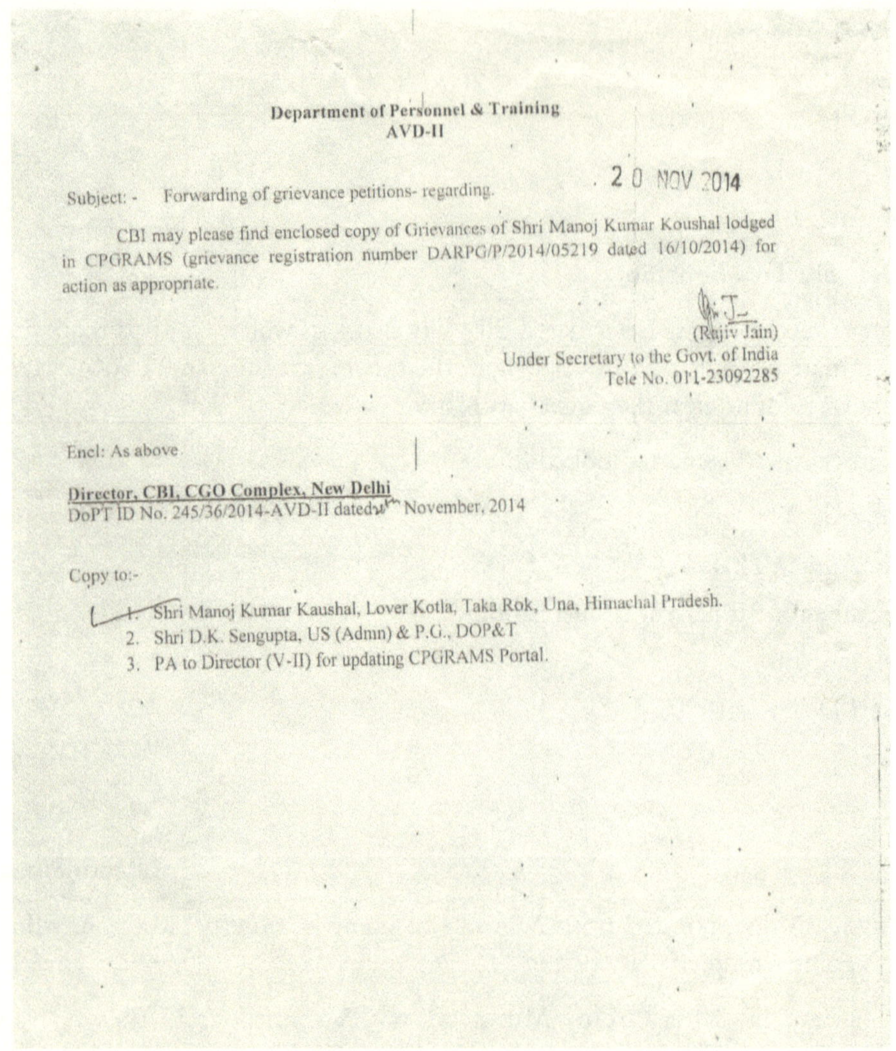

Department of Personnel & Training
AVD-II

Subject: -   Forwarding of grievance petitions- regarding.

20 NOV 2014

CBI may please find enclosed copy of Grievances of Shri Manoj Kumar Koushal lodged in CPGRAMS (grievance registration number DARPG/P/2014/05219 dated 16/10/2014) for action as appropriate.

(Rajiv Jain)
Under Secretary to the Govt. of India
Tele No. 011-23092285

Encl: As above

Director, CBI, CGO Complex, New Delhi
DoPT ID No. 245/36/2014-AVD-II dated   November, 2014

Copy to:-

1. Shri Manoj Kumar Kaushal, Lover Kotla, Taka Rok, Una, Himachal Pradesh.
2. Shri D.K. Sengupta, US (Admn) & P.G., DOP&T
3. PA to Director (V-II) for updating CPGRAMS Portal.

I immediately wrote a letter of thanks to our M.P. Anurag Thakur and requested him to initiate the investigation process at the earliest possible.

COPY OF THANKS LETTER TO MY MP ANURAG SINGH

Later on, I faxed a copy of the letter to the Director Ranjit Sinha requesting him to meet me immediately as I have many proofs showing that a heist did take place at the Kali Mata temple and which can help you solve this case. However, I did not receive any reply. I had now lost all my faith in the justice system and the system of our country. I could not believe that this was the status of our law and order units where, even after contacting the highest officials, neither justice nor investigation were assured. The people who did meet us, took all the information and broke all contact. They even stopped responding to any follow up requests and completely stopped all communications with us as if we were their sworn enemies. The nation's Home Minister sent a letter to our M.P. Anurag Thakur stating that he investigating the matter.

During the time the CM of Assam at the time, Mr. Gogoi was visiting Delhi along with his PA, Mr. Vipul Gogoi. I gave a letter to them also, requesting them to do something in the matter but even they were of no help. By now my spirit was completely broken as I could not see even a single ray of hope and was constantly reminded of PM Modi's words that, "we need to let go of the 'nothing will change' attitude." Following this philosophy, I had come too far, almost to the point of no return. All the CDR (Call details records) were with me but there were no takers for them. Frustration and dejection had sunk in and I realized that these government officials were supposedly working for the nation and drawing their salaries, but in actuality they were simply masters of their own will. I, on the contrary, a former soldier was spending my own money in order to make sure that these enemies of the state, the plotters behind the heist, are deservingly punished. However, even the CBI officials refused to meet me. Having lost all my faith, and almost all of my money, because of the investigative operations of our nation and its Ministries, I contemplated of abandoning this case. By this time, my monthly installments against the home loan I had taken had not been deposited, my homegrown business had reached the shutdown stage and were barely meeting our with the pension I was receiving. On top of all this, I was usually away from family and hence could not be there for them regularly and even during some momentous occasions. I was full of anger at the fact that how can we ever think of tackling the black money stashed in foreign states when we cannot even take care of the black money right at home! There was no optimism or hope left in me and I realized the the country's government officials are not worth their salt.

During this I catch a screenshot of counting money from the culprit facebook page

PHOTO

The entire 2014 went by in this pursuit but I could not accomplish anything. The power of money was not only immense but unsurpassable. The bounty, including money and wealth, that was hidden constituted a huge sum – 300 Crore rupees, 300 Kg Gold, and 2 AK47s. These figures were revealed by the men themselves who had later stolen it. I had all their videos and their calling details but nobody in the country, the law and order unit, or the government was ready to take them from me. Any representative whether it belonged to the police, the government or a ministry, who would get in touch with me would take all the information and disappear. The role of the executive bodies of the country was over in this case. I knew that they would not move a muscle to bring the perpetrators to law and I was completely directionless in my mind and did not know what to do next. Suddenly, I remembered that there is one more official body that I have not contacted; the Judiciary, the Indian Judicial system.

Chapter 6

I started listening to the PM Modi's address on "Man ki Baat" in which he said we have let go of our cynical and pessimistic attitude that forces us to think that nothing can change the status quo. This helped me gain my confidence and resilience back. I was once again determined to take this case to its rightful conclusion. However, by this time, all my friends had left this pursuit thinking that nothing can be done about it now. Nevertheless,

I now thought of seeking the support of the Judicial body. The very first thing I did was contact the prominent and a highly qualified Supreme Court Lawyer, Prashant Bhushan. I got an appointment with him at his home. I remember it was a Thursday and I was fasting. Over juice we discussed the entire matter and the other struggles I faced following the revelation of the heist. I gave him all the information and requested him to fight this case as I did not have money enough to hire a Supreme Court lawyer. I heard that Prashant Bhushan is very helpful and philanthropic but, even Mr. Bhushan did not agree to my requests and began to avoid me. Once again, my pleas were rejected and I returned to Una.

A few days later I came to know about Mr. Suresh Sharma who was a Patiala House court lawyer from Una and who had shifted base to Delhi. I got hold of his phone number and contacted him. I spoke to him and narrated to him the series of events. Upon hearing the turn of events that had taken place, he assured me that he will help me. He informed me that one of his friend's son is Supreme Court lawyer and that he will speak to him regarding this case. I was grateful to him and hopeful of getting a good lawyer for this case. As promised, Mr. Suresh Sharma got me in touch with Jaspreet Singh Rai and gave me his address- B-244, Greater Kailash, New Delhi. He also provided me his mobile number: 98107-25372. I spoke to Mr. Jaspreet Singh Rai and got an appointment with him. I met Advocate Jaspreet Singh Rai in 2015 and informed him about the entire case. I also handed him all the documentation I had accumulated over the year. I also enquired about his fee but he said, "It is alright, we'll talk about it later.

First let's just focus on preparing all the paperwork." After this discussion, he started preparing the documents and toward the end of 2015, he filed the case in which 13 people were made party along with the centre and the state. On 13th April 2016, our case was registered. Apart from pursuing the case in court, I was continuing to write emails to the Home Ministry which included the DRI HQ, the SIT committee set up to tackle black money, and the retired CBI official, Mr. Joginder Singh.

Chapter 7

MY CRIMINAL WRIT PETTION: SYNOPSIS & LIST OF DATES

Aug.' 1992   The Petitioner joined army in August 1992 as a soldier and in 1995 joined Military Intelligence.

1995 to 2009   The Petitioner has served in several sectors i.e. from 1995 to 1997 the Petitioner was in Pune and was then transferred to Chandigarh in 1997, the Petitioner was then in 1999 was transferred to Siliguri Bengal till 2001. Then, the Petitioner from 2002 to 2005 was posted in Jammu & Kashmir. The Petitioner from 2006 to 2009 was posted in Assam. The Petitioner had taken a voluntary retirement in 2009 and Assam was the last sector in which Petitioner has served. The Petitioner all through since 1995 has worked in Military Intelligence. The Petitioner on the eve of his retirement was given a meritorious and exemplary service certificate.

10.05.2014   The Petitioner on 10.05.2014 got an information from his informer i.e. Jiten Kalita (with whom he has worked in past when he was serving the army in Guwahati) that there is unaccounted money to the tune of Rs. 300 crores in cash, 300 Kg Gold and 2 AK47 Rifles in a Kali temple below the main statue of Kali Mata in a cellar (Tahkhana) which is situated in Rani Tea Garden, Near Dispur Airport, District-Guwahati, Assam.

The owner of Rani Tea Garden was one Mridul Bhattacharya who was President of Tea Garden Association of Assam. The said Mridul Bhattacharya used to collect money from owners of Tea Gardens and used to give it to ULFA. The said Mridul Bhattacharya was also involved in smuggling of Gold from Burma. The said Mridul Bhattacharya and his wife were murdered under suspicious circumstances in year 2012.

The army personnel informed Jiten Kalita and others who went along with Jiten Kalita that they will take out the treasurer from the cellar on 1st June 2014.

31.05.2014   The Respondent No. 5 to 17 were having knowledge that army will take the treasure on 1st June, 2014. The said Respondents hatched the conspiracy and took the treasure out from the cellar on 31.05.2014 in the night by digging a cave from outside the temple which is clearly depicted in the photographs (Annexure P-3).

10.06.2014   The Petitioner after seeing the news and information from Jiten Kalita that treasure has been taken out by Respondents No. 5 to 17, reached Guwahati, Assam on 10.06.2014 and stayed there for 20 days and was able to gather several proofs which clearly indicated that the treasure has been taken away by Respondent Nos. 5 to 17 in conspiracy with higher officials of the Police.

30.07.2014   The Petitioner after trying his level best, returned to his native place at Himachal Pradesh and met Mr. Anurag Singh Thakur, Member of Parliament from his constituency and explained him all in relation to treasure. The said Mr. Anurag Singh Thakur wrote a letter on 30.07.2014 to Hon'ble Home Minister mentioning the seriousness of the matter and requesting him to have a high level enquiry into the matter.

When the Petitioner showed the gravity of the issue and with the help of Mr. Anurag Singh Thakur, M.P., the Ministry of Home Affairs ordered Intelligence Bureau Enquiry and further Petitioner on 8th August 2014 got a call from one Rajendra Das Mahapatra and he explained the process of enquiry and accordingly, the Petitioner on 11.08.2014 went to Guwahati and thereafter Mr. Mahapatra never met the Petitioner and started behaving in a very casual manner. It was evident that Mr. Mahapatra was influenced by someone as he was clearly avoiding the Petitioner. The Petitioner again stayed in Guwahati for 15 days and through his sources was able to trace out the whereabouts of the money trail from Respondents No. 5 to 17. The Petitioner left with no option again came back to Delhi and met Mr. Anurag Singh Thakur, M.P. and then private secretary of Home Minister Mr. B.K. Singh made him meet one Manoj Yadav from Intelligence Bureau. That with the help of Manoj Yadav, the Petitioner met Shri Shambhu Singh, the Joint Secretary of North East, Shri Shambhu Singh had a word with Shri S.N. Singh, IGP Law & Order and gave us an envelope and told the Petitioner to meet him (Shri S.N. Singh).

Thereafter the Petitioner once again went to Guwahati in order to meet Shri S.N. Singh. It is submitted that initially Shri S.N. Singh heard and assured the Petitioner that he will take action and when next day the Petitioner went and met him, his attitude towards the Petitioner was changed and he told the Petitioner that he is not interested in any enquiry on the aforesaid issue and further conveyed the Petitioner that he should go and tell this to Shri Shambhu Singh that he (Shri S.N. Singh) is not interested in this issue.

17.09.2014   The Petitioner leaving no stone unturned, wrote a letter on 17.09.2014 to the Hon'ble Prime Minister and the Hon'ble Home Minister stating all the facts and requesting that a CBI team be constituted in order to cull out the truth and to save the exchequer and further to stop the misuse of money, as the same could be used by anti social elements, thereby causing harm to our country.

22.09.2014   The Ministry of Home Affairs through its Principal Secretary wrote a letter on 22nd September, 2014 stating that they cannot initiate a CBI enquiry suo motu and moreover Ministry of Home Affairs have no administrative jurisdiction over CBI.

29.09.2014   The Petitioner again wrote a letter on 29.09.2014 to Hon'ble Prime Minister requesting therein that an F.I.R. be registered and the matter be given to some honest and upright officer of CBI so that the treasure can be recovered. The Petitioner also informed the Hon'ble Prime Minister that he has in his possession call details of the Respondents which clearly shows that all the Respondents are in touch with one another and they are diverting the money through bank accounts.

25.10.2014   On 25th October 2014, the Petitioner received a letter from Mr. Anurag Singh Thakur, M.P. with the letter dated 05.08.2014 enclosed therewith, which was written by the Hon'ble Home Minister to Mr. Anurag Singh Thakur, M.P. ensuring that action in relation to the treasure would be taken.

Hence the present writ petition.

IN THE SUPREME COURT OF INDIA

(Civil Writ Jurisdiction)

WRIT PETITION (CIVIL) NO. ……….. OF 2015

IN THE MATTER OF:

Mr. Manoj Kumar Kaushal,

S/o Sh. Vidya Sagar

R/o VPO Lower Kotla,

Near Baba Balji Gate,

Takka Road, Una,

Himachal Pradesh – 174 303

Petitioner Versus

1.   Union of India
     Through its Secretary
     Ministry of Home Affairs,
     Govt. of India, North Block,
     New Delhi-110001

2.   Department of Personnel & Training,
     Through Joint Secretary
     Ministry of Personnel, Public Grievances & Pensions,
     Govt. of India, North Block,
     New Delhi-110001

3. State of Assam
   Through its Secretary,

4. State of Assam
   Through Director General of Police,
   Govt. of India,
   Uluvar, City-Guwahati,
   Assam-781007

5. Hitesh Kalita (Vill. Kaniha Ischadagaria Rangia Assam Pin Code-781380)

6. Budikhura Mukhtiyar (Oc Rani Police Check Post Guwahti Assam)

7. Dipak Das (C/o Rajat Dass Vill & P.O. Balisatra Rangia (Assam))

8. Balen Kalita (Vill. Athiaboi, P.O. Pubborka P.S. Kamalpur Changsari Kamrup Assam 781101)

9. Abhijit Deka (Narengi, Patharquary oil India Ltd. Otr. No. Bx-14 Guwahati Assam)

10. Jitu Mani Das (C/o Taruun Dass Rinky ladies Corner Near Azara Godhuli Bazar Guwahati Assam 781017)

11. Manju Urang (Murari Basti Raja Pani Chanda, P.O. Rani, Guwahati Assam)

12. Dinesh Das@Bhaskar Das (C/o Aditya Das V.P.O. Rampur Mirza Assam 781132)

13. Giasudin Ahmed (Vill. Hablakha P.O. Khatikuchi Near Nilpur Chowk Nalbari Assam)

14. Mrinal Das (Vill. Baushi P.O. Tetelia Ps Hajo Distt. Kamrup Guwahti Assam 781171)

15. Binod Kalita (Agchia Barjhar Agchia Kamrup Assam 781128)

16. Pravin Musahari (C/o 175 CRPF Bn. Guwahati Assam)

17. Niranjan Kalita (Vill. Bamungaon P.O. Puthimari Rangia Assam 781380)

A WRIT PETITION IN PUBLIC INTEREST UNDER ARTICLE 32 OF THE CONSTITUTION OF INDIA BRINGING THE ISSUE TO FORE OF LOSS TO EXCHEQUER OF 300 CRORES IN CASH, 300 KG GOLD AND 2 AK47 RIFLES WHICH WERE ILLEGALLY TAKEN AWAY BY RESPONDENTS NOS. 5 TO 17 DESPITE THERE BEING FULL INFORMATION TO THE STATE POLICE (RESPONDENT NO. 4)

TO

HON'BLE THE CHIEF JUSTICE OF INDIA AND HIS LORDSHIPS COMPANION JUSTICES OF HON'BLE SUPREME COURT OF INDIA.

THE HUMBLE PETITION OF THE PETITIONER ABOVE-NAMED.

MOST RESPECTFULLY SHOWETH

1. That the Respondents No. 5 to 17 are the private parties. Remaining Respondents No. 1 to 4 herein are State within the meaning of Article 12 of the Constitution, hence, amenable to the Writ Jurisdiction of this Hon'ble Court under Article 32 of the Constitution of India.

2. That the Petitioner is filing the instant writ petition in public interest. The petitioner has no personal interest in the litigation and the petition is not guided by self-gain or for gain of any other person/institution/body and that there is no motive other than that of public interest in filing the writ petition. The present petition, if allowed, would save the government exchequer, which can be utilized for the upliftment of the citizens of India.

3. That the brief facts of the present case leading to the presentation of the aforesaid writ petition is as follows:

4. That the Petitioner joined army in August 1992 as a soldier and in 1995 joined Military Intelligence.

5. The Petitioner has served in several sectors i.e. from 1995 to 1997 the Petitioner was in Pune and was then transferred to Chandigarh in 1997, the Petitioner was then in 1999 was transferred to Siliguri

Bengal till 2001. Then, the Petitioner from 2002 to 2005 was posted in Jammu & Kashmir. The Petitioner from 2006 to 2009 was posted in Assam. The Petitioner had taken a voluntary retirement in 2009 and Assam was the last sector in which Petitioner has served. The Petitioner all through since 1995 has worked in Military Intelligence. The Petitioner on the eve of his retirement was given a meritorious and exemplary service certificate. The certificates dated 28th September 2009 showing the proficiency and merit are annexed as **Annexure P-1** and **Annexure P-2** respectively.

6. The Petitioner on 10.05.2014 got an information from his informer i.e. Jiten Kalita (with whom he has worked in past when he was serving the army in Guwahati) that there is unaccounted money to the tune of Rs. 300 crores in cash, 300 Kg Gold and 2 AK47 Rifles in a Kali temple below the main statue of Kali Mata in a cellar (Tahkhana) which is situated in Rani Tea Garden, Near Dispur Airport, District-Guwahati, Assam.

7. The owner of Rani Tea Garden was one Mridul Bhattacharya who was President of Tea Garden Association of Assam. The said Mridul Bhattacharya used to collect money from owners of Tea Gardens and used to give it to ULFA. The said Mridul Bhattacharya was also involved in smuggling of Gold from Burma. The said Mridul Bhattacharya and his wife were murdered under suspicious circumstances in year 2012.

8. The Petitioner advised Jiten Kalita to get in touch with army in relation to the aforesaid treasure and accordingly Petitioner met army officials and army officials agreed to take the treasure from the cellar which is situated below the statue of Kali.

9. The army personnel informed Jiten Kalita and others who went along with Jiten Kalita that they will take out the treasurer from the cellar on 1st June 2014.

10. That Respondent No. 5 to 17 were having knowledge that army will take the treasure on 1st June, 2014. The said Respondents hatched the conspiracy and took the treasure out from the cellar on 31.05.2014 in the night by digging a cave from outside the temple which is clearly depicted in the photographs annexed herewith as **Annexure P-3.**

11. That the Petitioner after seeing the news and information from Jiten Kalita that treasure has been taken out by Respondents No. 5 to 17, reached Guwahati, Assam on 10.06.2014 and stayed there for 20 days and was able to gather several proofs which clearly indicated that the treasure has been taken away by Respondent Nos. 5 to 17 in conspiracy with higher officials of the Police. Copy of tickets and the copy of the proofs showing that Petitioner stayed at Guwahati Assam for 20 days starting from 10.06.2014 are annexed herewith and marked as **Annexure P-4** and **Annexure P-5** respectively.

12. The Petitioner after trying his level best, returned to his native place at Himachal Pradesh and met Mr. Anurag Singh Thakur, Member of Parliament from his constituency and explained him all in relation to treasure. The said Mr. Anurag Singh Thakur wrote a letter on 30.07.2014 to Hon'ble Home Minister mentioning the seriousness of the matter and requesting him to have a high level enquiry into the matter. Copy of letter dated 30.07.2014 is annexed as **Annexure P-6**.

13. That when the Petitioner showed the gravity of the issue and with the help of Mr. Anurag Singh Thakur, M.P., the Ministry of Home Affairs ordered Intelligence Bureau Enquiry and further Petitioner on 8th August 2014 got a call from one Rajendra Das Mahapatra and he explained the process of enquiry and accordingly, the Petitioner on 11.08.2014 went to Guwahati and thereafter Mr. Mahapatra never met the Petitioner and started behaving in a very casual manner. It was evident that Mr. Mahapatra was influenced by someone as he was clearly avoiding the Petitioner. The Petitioner again stayed in Guwahati for 15 days and through his sources was able to trace out the whereabouts of the money trail from Respondents No. 5 to 17. The Petitioner left with no option again came back to Delhi and met Mr. Anurag Singh Thakur, M.P. and then his private secretary Mr. B.K. Singh made him meet one Manoj Yadav from Intelligence Bureau. That with the help of Manoj Yadav, the Petitioner met Shri Shambhu Singh, the Joint Secretary, then Shri Shambhu Singh had a word with Shri S.N. Singh, IGP Law & Order and gave us an envelope and told the Petitioner to meet him (Shri S.N. Singh).

14. Thereafter the Petitioner once again went to Guwahati in order to meet Shri S.N. Singh. It is submitted that initially Shri S.N. Singh heard and assured the Petitioner that he will take action and when next day the Petitioner went and met him, his attitude towards the Petitioner was changed and he told the Petitioner that he is not interested in any enquiry on the aforesaid issue and further conveyed the Petitioner that he should go and tell this to Shri Shambhu Singh that he (Shri S.N. Singh) is not interested in this issue.

15. The Petitioner leaving no stone unturned, wrote a letter on 17.09.2014 to the Hon'ble Prime Minister and the Hon'ble Home Minister stating all the facts and requesting that a CBI team be constituted in order to cull out the truth and to save the exchequer and further to stop the misuse of money, as the same could be used by anti social elements, thereby causing harm to our country. Copies of the letters dated 17.09.2014 are annexed as **Annexure P-7 (Colly)**.

16. The Ministry of Home Affairs through its Principal Secretary wrote a letter on 22nd September, 2014 stating that they cannot initiate a CBI enquiry suo motu and moreover Ministry of Home Affairs have no administrative jurisdiction over CBI. Copy of the letter dated 22.09.2014 is annexed as **Annexure P-8**.

17. The Petitioner again wrote a letter on 29.09.2014 to Hon'ble Prime Minister requesting therein that an F.I.R. be registered and the matter be given to some honest and upright officer of CBI so that the treasure can be recovered. The Petitioner also informed the Hon'ble Prime Minister that he has in his possession call details of the Respondents which clearly shows that all the Respondents are in touch with one another and they are diverting the money through bank accounts.

18. That on 25th October 2014, the Petitioner received a letter from Mr. Anurag Singh Thakur, M.P. with the letter dated 05.08.2014 enclosed therewith, which was written by the Hon'ble Home Minister to Mr. Anurag Singh Thakur, M.P. ensuring that action in relation to the treasure would be taken. Copies of the letter dated 05.08.2014 and the letter dated 25.10.2014 are annexed as **Annexure P-10** and **Annexure P-11** respectively.

19.   That the Petitioner has consulted several persons in order to initiate proceedings in Guwahati, Assam, but after hearing the Petitioner, nobody shows any interest in the issue.

20.   That the Petitioner who has stayed in Guwahati for several days, with fair amount of certainty can infer that people involved in diverting the exchequer are very influential and having complete collusion with local administration.

21.   That the Petitioner is very worried that the money which Respondents No. 5 to 17 have procured could be used for illegal purposes and can cause threat to the sovereignty of our country, as Assam being a Border State which has seen many turbulences in last decades. The issue raised by the Petitioner relates to the safety of the people of the country, as deadly weapons like AK-47 are also involved which clearly shows that nexus is fairly deep which can only be unearthed if a special team of CBI is constituted to look into the matter and the Petitioner having experience of 18 years in secret military service is ready to lend his services to any team so constituted.

22.   That the matter has broadcasted in several news channels for several days, despite that, no action has been taken by the Police so far, thereby putting the citizens of this country at peril.

23.   That the petitioner states that the petitioner has not filed any other Writ Petition/Appeal, either in this Hon'ble or in any other Court regarding the subject matter of this petition.

24.   That the petitioner further submits that all the annexures appended hereinabove are the true copies of their respective originals and their true typed copies, have been made with due diligence and great care and any deviation therein is purely unintentional and coincidental.

PRAYERS

It is, therefore, most respectfully prayed that this Hon'ble Court may graciously be pleased to:

1.   Issue any writ/order directing Respondent No. 2 to constitute a special team of CBI to register an FIR so as to investigate the aforesaid incident;

2. Pass any other order/s, which your lordships may deem fit and proper in the facts and circumstances of the present case as well as in the interest of justice.

AND FOR THIS ACT OF KINDNESS, THE PETITIONER AS IN DUTY BOUND SHALL FOR EVER PRAY.

PETITIONER THROUGH

NEW DELHI

Dated : April 29, 2015

JASPREET S. RAI

Advocate

Counsel for the Petitioner

B-244, Greater Kailash Part-I,

New Delhi – 110 048

Phones: 4064 8883-4

On 13th April 2016, our case was filed and registered. My case number was 13 and was to be presented to the bench that included the Chief Justice T.S. Thakur, Justice Uday Umesh Lalit, and Justice R. Bhanumati. My lawyer, Mr. Jaspreet Singh Rai, came fully prepared and even I was confident that the bench will lend its ears to our situation. I was also conscious of the bizarre coincidence of numbers that this case was immersed in – The case had 13 culprits to be tried on 13th of April and the case number was also 13. All the three judges carefully listened to the appeal made by my lawyer and concluded that this is very serious issue. The judicial bench also took note of my struggles and were surprised that a soldier had reached such high echelons of governance but was unable to make his case heard. The bench also issued a notice against the central government. It was a glorious day for us and I was personally extremely happy to have made such a huge progress in this case. My faith in the Indian Judicial system was not only restored but became even more reinforced. It was great to see that there is a place in my country where a man can hope to have his voice heard. In the notice, sent by the Supreme Court the date to send the response was 6th May 2016 (given below is the photocopy of the notice). Following this development, the crime and its following incidents reached the Assam media and soon, the national channels also started covering this matter. A few days later when this story picked up pace on state and national media, I started receiving calls from different media channels. I gave them details of the bounty, the heist and the also what transpired after the revelation. I also informed them about the 13 people who were identified as the primary suspects in the case and also their economic status.

PHOTOCOPY OF NOTICE

ITEM NO.13   COURT NO.1   SECTION PIL(W)

S U P R E M E   C O U R T   O F   I N D I A
RECORD OF PROCEEDINGS

Writ Petition(s)(Criminal) No(s). 55/2016

MANOJ KUMAR KAUSHAL   Petitioner(s)

VERSUS

UNION OF INDIA AND ORS.   Respondent(s)

(with appln. (s) for exemption from filing O.T.)

Date : 13/04/2016 This petition was called on for hearing today.

CORAM :
        HON'BLE THE CHIEF JUSTICE
        HON'BLE MRS. JUSTICE R. BANUMATHI
        HON'BLE MR. JUSTICE UDAY UMESH LALIT

For Petitioner(s)   Mr. Jaspreet Singh Rai, Adv.
                       Mr. Harpunit Singh, Adv.
                       Mr. Amrendra Choubey, Adv.
                       Mr. Shyamal Kumar,Adv.

For Respondent(s)   Mr. Maninder Singh, ASG,
                       Mr. R.Balasubramanian, Adv.
                       Mr. Prabhas Bajaj, Adv.
                       Mr. Santosh Kumar, Adv.

          UPON hearing the counsel the Court made the following
                          O R D E R

          Post again on Friday i.e. 06.05.2016.

          A copy of the petition be handed over to Mr. Maninder

Singh, learned ASG who is requested to assist us after taking

instructions in the matter.

                                                     (Veena Khera)
(Shashi Sareen)   Court Master
AR-cum-PS

As the media gained more and more information, it started running an investigation on its own by going to the houses of those 13 named suspects. Through media we came to know that all of those 13 people involved in the heist had built/rebuilt their homes and fashioned them into new and modern structures. Each of those who had rebuilt their houses also made sure that their new homes had a temple. The state of Assam was now aware the heist and all of their riches and their successful escape from the law was impossible with police involvement and co-operation in the case. This is because when I had given the names of 13 people, I had also included the name of Local Inspector in the list. His call details were also with me and it was established that the Gold was in his custody. However, he had continued changing the location of the gold and his son had also bought an Audi car, estimated to be priced at 80 lakhs, within a matter of days. I nudged the media to ask him how was he able to buy a car worth 80 lakhs? He circumvented this question and gave an ambiguous answer which I would like to quote, "Only God knows where I got this car from."

PHOTOS OF THE MEDIA COVERAGE

The Assam Tribune

Ex-Armyman names persons involved

Spl Correspondent

NEW DELHI, April 20 - Surrendered ULFA cadres, cops, a tea baron, a local journalist are all allegedly part of what is emerging as a crime-thriller-like conspiracy that saw them decamping with Rs 300 crore in cash stashed away in a tea garden in Rani near Guwahati.

The case, which is already in the Supreme Court, today took a fresh turn when the main petitioner, Manoj Kumar Kaushal, who was a part of military intelligence, revealed before the media the names of those involved in the siphoning off the loot. He alleged before newsmen today that the main conspirator was one Hitesh Kalita. He identified the others as Dinesh, Manju Orang, Mrinal Das, Subash Kalita alias Bolin Kalita and Binoy Kalita, among others, besides a few Assam Police officials.

The Supreme Court last Wednesday asked the Centre to look into the retired Army officer's petition to hold an inquiry into the alleged disappearance of unaccountable cash to the tune of Rs 300 crore, 300 kg gold and some other articles from a temple in Rani. Kaushal said the wealth was allegedly stolen by some locals in 2014 and the police have refused to inquire into the incident.

A bench, headed by Chief Justice TS Thakur, directed Additional Solicitor General Maninder Singh to look into Kaushal's petition though it did not issue a formal notice for a response. The matter is coming up for further hearing on May 6, when the Centre is likely to file its response.

According to Kaushal, the unaccounted money, gold and two AK 47 rifles were stashed in a cellar in the Kali temple in Rani Tea Garden. Kaushal told the Bench that the petitioner received information about the wealth from one of his informers who worked with him when he was posted with the intelligence unit in Assam.

The money was hidden by the then president of the Tea Garden Association in Assam, who allegedly collected money from owners of tea gardens on behalf of ULFA. Kaushal said the president and his wife were murdered under mysterious circumstances in 2012.

Kaushal informed the Indian Army and as it was about to recover the treasure, some locals stole it.

The officer said he approached officials in Guwahati with his complaint against the robbery but there was no action. He also wrote letters to the Prime Minister's Office and the Ministry of Home Affairs.

He claimed that an informer told him two years ago about the treasure hidden in a vault below the idol. An inquiry revealed that it was lying unclaimed after the mysterious deaths of owner of the garden Mridul Bhattacharya and his wife.

After being informed about it, the Army decided to recover it on June 1, 2014. But when soldiers reached the spot, they were shocked to find a gaping hole and the treasure missing.

Kaushal reported that he visited the spot later, took photographs and gathered intelligence on possible suspects.

Kaushal has named 13 people, whose call records showed they were in touch with each other since the time the theft likely took place, and were diverting huge amounts of money through their bank accounts.

"It is clear that these people hatched the conspiracy and took the treasure out by digging a hole from outside the temple, which is clearly depicted in the photographs," Kaushal alleged.

The Telegraph
India

Sunday , April 24 , 2016

Front Page > North East > Story

Like 0   Tweet   G+

IN TODAY'S PAPER
Front Page
Nation
Calcutta
Bengal
Foreign
Business
Sports
Horse Racing
t2
T2 Online
Opinion
TT Hand In Hand

EPAPER
Calcutta
North Bengal
South Bengal
Jamshedpur
Ranchi
Patna
Guwahati
Bhubaneswar

CITIES & REGIONS
Metro
Northeast
Jharkhand
Bihar
Odisha

WEEKLY FEATURES
Knowhow Mon
Jobs Tue
You Mon
Salt Lake Fri
7days Sun
Graphiti Sun

LEISURE
Sudoku
Sudoku New
Crossword
Jumble
Gallery

ARCHIVES
Since 1 March, 1999

PRESS RELEASES
Businesswire India
NewsVoir
PR Newswire

EXTRAS
Travel

THE TELEGRAPH
About Us
Advertise
Feedback
Contact Us

Accused ready for treasure probe

Avishek Sengupta

Guwahati, April 23: The general secretary of Sangrami Krishak-Shramik Sangha, Dinesh Das, named in a PIL seeking a CBI probe into alleged disappearance of "Rs 300 crore in cash, 300kg of gold and AK-47 rifles" allegedly belonging to Ulfa and stashed away under a temple inside Rani tea garden in Kamrup district in 2014, today claimed innocence and welcomed any inquiry into the case.

A former military intelligence man, Manoj Kumar Kaushal, had on April 13 filed the petition in the Supreme Court, alleging that the treasure was smuggled out of the shrine by 13 individuals, including Das, in connivance with police a day before the army was to recover the cache and found its way back to Ulfa.

A bench headed by the Supreme Court Chief Justice T.S. Thakur had asked additional solicitor-general Maninder Singh to examine the petition and come out with the government's view on Kaushal's plea for a CBI probe.

The Centre was given six weeks to respond to the court's notice.

Personnel of Rani police station, 20km from Guwahati, had in June 2014 found a hole dug under the Kali temple after Das lodged an FIR about secret treasure missing from the temple. His FIR was based on reports doing the rounds about some treasure being stashed away under the temple.

The director-general of Assam police, Mukesh Sahay, when asked about the case, said here today that investigations were on into the allegations. "We have not received any order regarding the PIL in the Supreme Court so far, but we are probing into it on our own. We will move ahead as per law." The district's superintendent of police is investigating the allegations.

Sources said the police had visited the temple and questioned some of the persons named in the PIL, based on media reports.

Das said at the news conference that Kaushal's allegation is "baseless".

The others named in the PIL, Binod Kalita, Jitumani Das, Manju Orang, Prabin Mushahary and Hitesh Kalita (the mastermind in stashing the cache according to the PIL), were also present at the news conference.

"We welcome any inquiry in connection with the missing treasure but the allegations levelled against us are baseless. We were the ones who informed the police about the heist in the first place and not the other way around," Das said.

He said he was informed on May 2, 2014 regarding the cash, gold and arms being dug out from under the temple.

"I did not give importance suspecting it to be a rumour. The rumour grew stronger and when on June 3 we saw that the Kali Mandir was dug, I filed an FIR at Rani police station. What was the point of filing a PIL against me by the person who was the first to lodge the complaint in the first place?" Das asked.

Regarding Kaushal, Kalita said: "He came here in 2014 and introduced himself as Manoj *tantrik* and wanted to know about the temple. He introduced himself as a priest and wanted details about the cache. After almost two years, he is filing the petition and that too against us who had no whiff of the money."

The 376-hectare private Rani tea garden belonged to one Mridul Bhattacharya, who was alleged named in the PIL for allegedly collecting money from owners of other tea gardens for funding Ulfa.

The garden was closed after a protest by the Sangha following the death of a six-year-old boy who was allegedly shot by Bhattacharya in 2010. Bhattacharya and his wife were murdered in 2012. The garden reopened in 2015.

The Sangha was set up in 2011 as a platform to espouse the cause of farmers and common people.

Additional reporting by Kishore Talukdar and Sumir Karmakar

Like 0   Tweet   G+

The media was after those 13 culprits most of whom were either in hiding or absconding. The police were no help in carrying out the investigations or the arrests because they knew that after catching the small fish, they would have go for the bigger fish which also meant trouble for them. Out of the 13, the primary culprits of this case were Dinesh Das and Hitesh Kalita and Bolen Kalita. These three played clever and along with some of their friends conducted a press conference. In this press conference, Dinesh Das clearly confessed that he was among the first ones to phone the SP and told him about the bounty that had been hidden in the basement of the Kali Mata temple. He claimed that he was the one who had first filed the F.I.R whereas there was no reported incident or an F.I.R registered with the local police. Moreover, till now they had not been able to do a foolproof job of stashing and dividing away the money. They were careless and committed many whimsical errors along the way. One of the most prominent ones was the transfer of money. Dinesh Das claimed that when he informed the SP, the money and the goods had already been stolen. The second strategy gone wrong was after they had stolen the money, they called the reporters from Day 365 channel, Vinay Kalita and Girendhar Kalita and blamed ULFA for running away with the bounty. When all this came to fore, our findings were proving to be right and our accusations stood strong. I was documenting everything that these culprits were presenting to me. From the media recordings to the press conference details, other coverages, I kept all of them safe and sound in my custody. I was going to use them in the court against them.

The next court date was 6th May 2016. On this date as well, the case was scheduled to appear at number 13. The solicitor representing the central government was Mohinder Singh. When the Chief Justice, T.S. Thakur and the two other judges on the bench, asked for their response, their solicitor replied, "We do not know anything about such an incident." Chief Justice, T.S. Thakur then issued notices against the Central Government and the D.G.P. He gave them 6 weeks to respond and then the court was closed for the summer break and was to reopen after the holidays.

In that days Joint Director Intelligence Burue Manoj Yadav (who was met me in Home Ministry) was also posted in Guwahati but he did not contact me.

During this time, the media kept in touch with me and asked a lot of questions. I provided them with many details of this crime and appealed to them to bring this matter into the notice of Modi's government. In this endeavor, it was ABVP, News, Zee News, and Aaj Tak that supported and cooperated immensely. They not only gave this issue enough air time but also showed the entire news story.

Nonetheless, I was eagerly waiting for the stipulated 6 weeks to end soon. During this waiting period, fortunately, my wife underwent a successful kidney transplant. The transplant took place on 25th June 2016. I considered my family and myself very lucky to not have to undergo another tragedy lest the transplant was not successful. I attributed this good fortune to my involvement in this uphill quest for truth and to the blessings of Goddess Kali who, perhaps, was also ensuring that my suffering ends soon.

PHOTOCOPY OF THE NOTICE 6TH MAY 2016

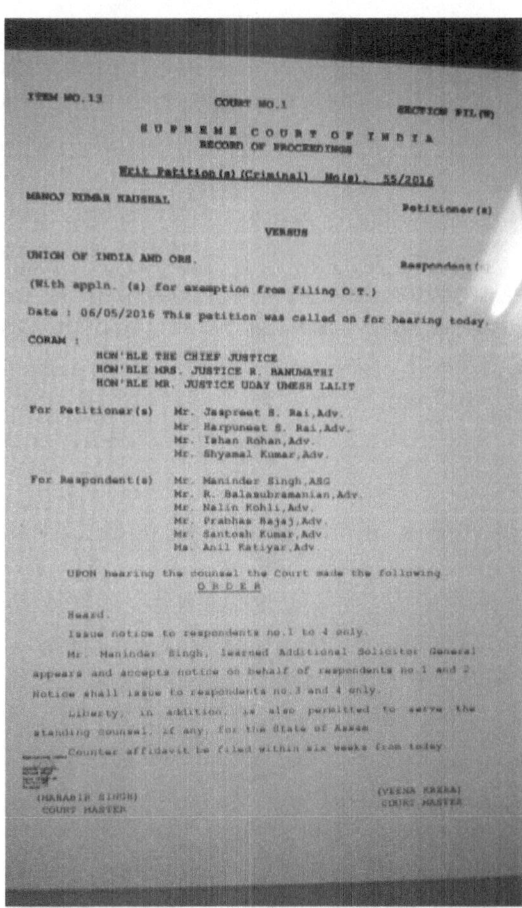

ITEM NO. 13   COURT NO.1   SECTION PIL (W)

SUPREME COURT OF INDIA
RECORD OF PROCEEDINGS

Writ Petition(s) (Criminal) No(s). 55/2016

MANOJ KUMAR KAUSHAL.
                                                        Petitioner(s)

VERSUS

UNION OF INDIA AND ORS.
                                                        Respondent(s)

(With appln. (s) for exemption from filing O.T.)

Date : 06/05/2016 This petition was called on for hearing today.

CORAM :
          HON'BLE THE CHIEF JUSTICE
          HON'BLE MRS. JUSTICE R. BANUMATHI
          HON'BLE MR. JUSTICE UDAY UMESH LALIT

For Petitioner(s)   Mr. Jaspreet S. Rai,Adv.
                     Mr. Harpuneet S. Rai,Adv.
                     Mr. Ishan Rohan,Adv.
                     Mr. Shyamal Kumar,Adv.

For Respondent(s)   Mr. Maninder Singh,ASG
                     Mr. R. Balasubramanian,Adv.
                     Mr. Nalin Kohli,Adv.
                     Mr. Prabhas Bajaj,Adv.
                     Mr. Santosh Kumar,Adv.
                     Ms. Anil Katiyar,Adv.

          UPON hearing the counsel the Court made the following
                    O R D E R

          Heard.
          Issue notice to respondents no.1 to 4 only.
          Mr. Maninder Singh, learned Additional Solicitor General
appears and accepts notice on behalf of respondents no.1 and 2.
Notice shall issue to respondents no.3 and 4 only.
          Liberty, in addition, is also permitted to serve the
standing counsel, if any, for the State of Assam.
          Counter affidavit be filed within six weeks from today.

(NARASIM SINGH)   (VEENA KHERA)
COURT MASTER   COURT MASTER

Chapter 8

Much to my surprise, my destiny kept throwing more and more shocks at me. During the stipulated 6 week period, my lawyer became distant and began to avoid me. I would call him and he would not pick my call. The 6 week period also got over but no response was received. Neither the central government, the state and nor the DGP responded to the notice sent by the Supreme Court. Meanwhile, I kept calling and attempted to meet my lawyer but he growing more and more distant and aloof. I could not put a finger on as to why was he behaving like this but I suspected some foul play.

I could not understand what was happening and was perplexed about the nonchalant and casual attitude of my lawyer. He never demanded any response from the prosecuted parties and neither kept in the loop for any development even when I had already paid him a sum of Rs. 25000/- once and 35000/- another time. Even when he would take my call, he would tell me to instead speak to his assistant, Mr. Munish. His assistant too was no different. Munish kept saying that the necessary will be done and would not answer anything beyond that. It seemed that Munish was either buying time or fooling me. Assessing the happenings of the recent past and the change in the attitude of my lawyer, I understood that those in power after having influenced the executive and the political bodies had now started to exercise their power and influence in the judiciary as well. They were now attempting to influence the workings of the judiciary.

The month of August also went by and it seemed as if I was lost at sea with nothing to bring me back to the shore. No new date was being announced. My lawyer gave me now answers or updates regarding the case. My faith in the judiciary was also dwindling with each passing day. Not knowing how to break this wall of indifference, I decided to write a letter to the Chief Justice T.S. Thakur. On 19th September 2016, I wrote a letter to T.S. Thakur and along with it sent a copy of the call details. This entire mail, letter plus the call details weighed 5.5 kg. I sent it through On Dot courier company on 20th September 2016 to the Chief Justice T.S. Thakur. In this letter I also explained him the series of events and the all that happened since the heist in 2014.

PHOTOCOPY OF THE LETTER TO CHIEF JUSTICE OF INDIA

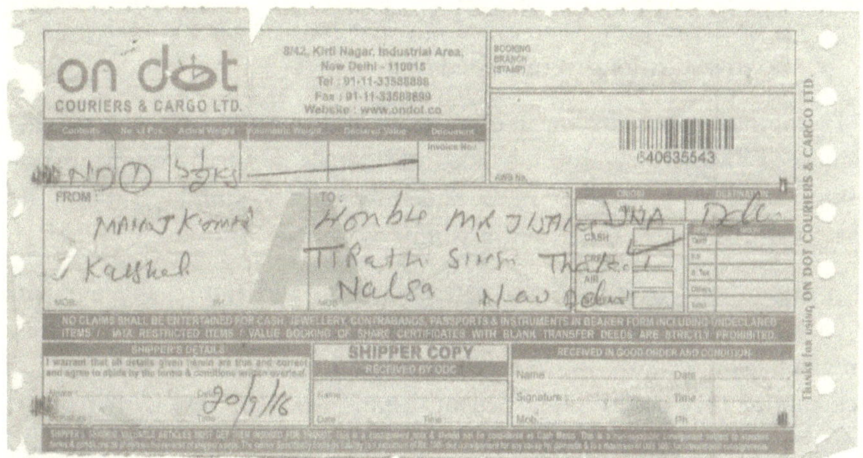

To the

Chief Justice

Supreme Court

New Delhi,

Respected Sir,

This is to request you to consider my plea in a serious matter that concerns our nation. I am Manoj Kumar Kaushal and I belong to Lower Kotla, Zila, Una (Himachal Pradesh). I have served in the intelligence bureau of the Indian Army for almost 18 years. I had taken premature retirement in the month of August 2009 from Assam, where I was posted then. In May 2014, my secret resources stationed in Assam informed me of a secret treasure which consisted of Rupees 300 Crores, 300 Kg Gold biscuits and 2 AK47 rifles. We diligently informed the Army officials in Assam however, before the army could dig out the treasure and the rifles, on 1st June 2014, a group of men orchestrated a heist and stole all of the bounty. These group worked in association with the police. The local media covers this heist but no other channel. I travel to Guwahati and stay there for a period of 20 days. During the duration of my stay I find the names and the call details of all the boys and the police personnel involved.

Once laden with proofs, I contact the home ministry through Mr. Anurag Thakur, who is a member of the parliament and a representative from my area so that investigations can be initiated in the case. We even received a response from Rajnath Singh that he will get the matter looked into but no investigations were carried out.

In the last two years the money from the treasure has been carelessly squandered. Moreover, through the call details we have found banking messages and that these boys by making use of mobile banking have transferred this money to Jammu Kashmir as well.

A bigger concern is that even after so many valid and reliable evidences, the Government of India has not initiated or carried out any investigations. Time and again we have heard that Government of India will retrieve all the black money that has been stashed offshore. However, how is that possible when the government is not even ready to look at the evidence we have been providing them.

On 13th April 2016, the Supreme Court accepted my appeal to file this case and also sent a notice to the Central and the State Government along with the D.G.P. of Assam demanding an answer. The time given by the Supreme Court to was till 6th May 2016 however no response was received from any of the mentioned parties. Another 6 weeks were given to the parties to prepare and answer the notices.

Respected Sir, since 6th May 2014 till date 19th September 2016, the court has not received any answer from the mentioned parties whether the State or the Central Government. Even my lawyer is not responding to my questions. When I call him, he circumvents and avoids sharing any update. I am not able to understand why is there so much delay in this matter. Only the highest court that is the Supreme Court has heard my plea and no other executive or law unit. I have full faith in the judicial system of my country and also in the fact that it will be able to recover the stolen treasure worth Rupees 300 Crore, 300 Kg Gold, and 2 AK47 rifles. I am a retired soldier and I am not even able to pay the expenses of the lawyers I have hired for this case.

In order to prove the worth of my claim, I am attaching the call details of the boys involved in the heist with this letter.

I am also listing my requests:

1. Kindly employ an SIT unit under the supervision of Supreme Court for this case.

2. I request the hearing of these trials is conducted as fast as possible so that the mentioned sum of Rs. 300 Crore, 300 Kg Gold, and 2 AK47s are recovered at the earliest.

3. I request that the CBI is directed to co-operated with me. I am fully willing to offer my services to help resolve this matter.

4. C.B.I must be requested to adopt a fast action attitude and employ quick operations to solve this matter and also submit timely reports to the Supreme Court stating their progress and developments.

5. It must also be investigated that when the army was informed about the treasure twenty days before, why did not they dig out the secret treasure immediately.

I will be highly obliged if you do the needful.

Yours Thankfully,

(Manoj Kumar Kaushal)

Lower Kotla,

Takka Road

Una

Himachal Pradesh

Pin: 174303

Phone: 7807158270, 9816169403

On 29 November 2016, I received another shocking blow. The bank, while I was engaged in the legalities of the case, was preparing the auction of my house since my monthly installments were not being deposited. I found that they had already printed the pamphlets of the auction and announced the auction of my home. I did not lose heart and still prioritized the case over this unfortunate life event.

PHOTOCOPY OF MY HOUSE AUCRION PAMPLATE

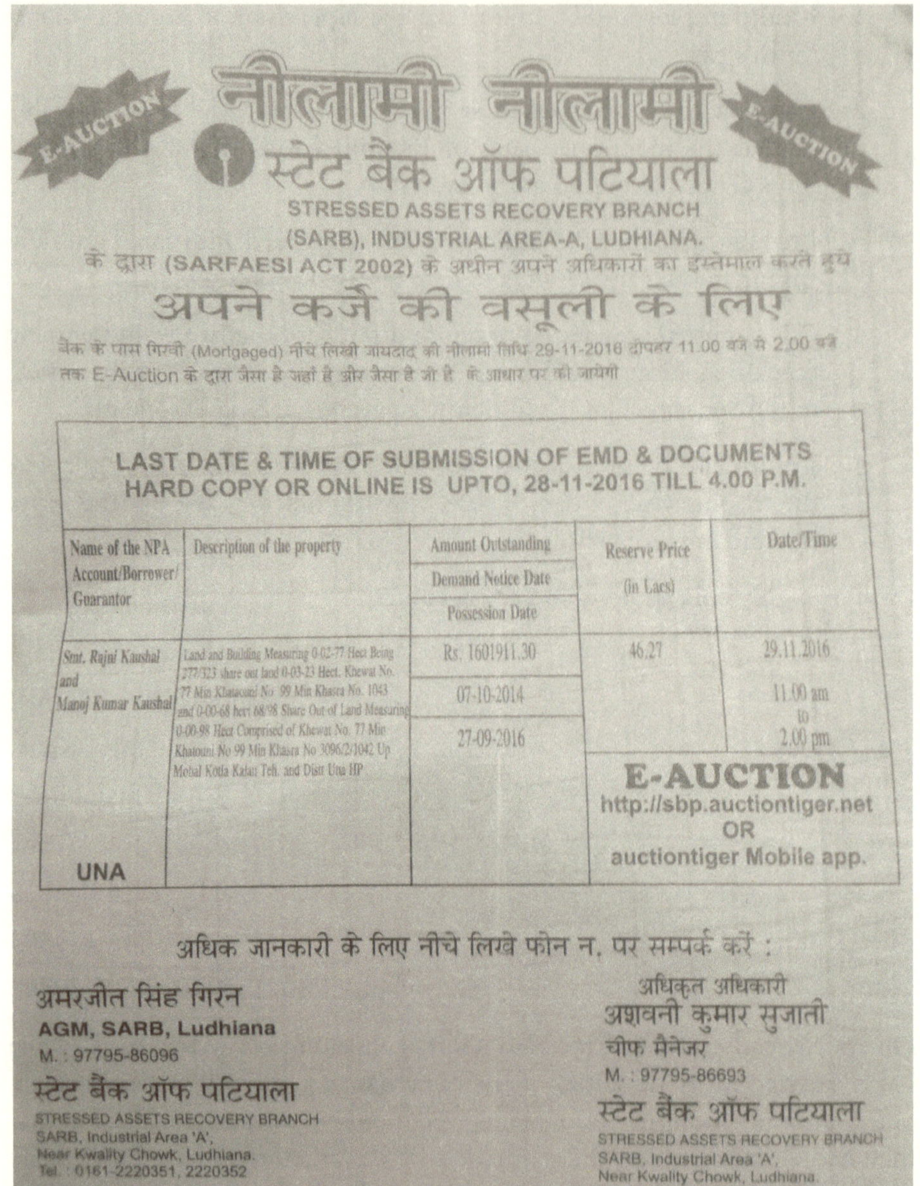

LAST DATE & TIME OF SUBMISSION OF EMD & DOCUMENTS HARD COPY OR ONLINE IS UPTO, 28-11-2016 TILL 4.00 P.M.				
Name of the NPA Account/Borrower/ Guarantor	Description of the property	Amount Outstanding / Demand Notice Date / Possession Date	Reserve Price (in Lacs)	Date/Time
Smt. Rajni Kaushal and Manoj Kumar Kaushal	Land and Building Measuring 0-02-77 Hect Being 272/323 share out land 0-03-23 Hect. Khewat No. 77 Min Khatauni No. 99 Min Khasra No. 1043 and 0-00-68 hect 68/98 Share Out of Land Measuring 0-00-98 Hect Comprised of Khewat No. 77 Min Khatouni No 99 Min Khasra No 3096/2/1042 Up Mohal Kotla Kalan Teh. and Distt Una HP	Rs. 1601911.30 / 07-10-2014 / 27-09-2016	46.27	29.11.2016 11.00 am to 2.00 pm
UNA			E-AUCTION http://sbp.auctiontiger.net OR auctiontiger Mobile app.	

My letter had also reached the CJI by now and he had sent it to my lawyer. He advised me to speak to my lawyer about this. In the letter I had sent to him, I had also requested him to hasten the trial as it had been informed that the Chief Justice T.S. Thakur will be retiring on 3rd January 2017 and I had also already anticipated the verdict that the Chief Justice who will succeed him will announce. Caught up in this complex web of indifference and no-action, I kept waiting for some progress to occur. However, I was not even an inch closer to the conclusion I was hoping for. And just like that even 2016 ended.

Chapter 9

Finally, a date was announced and it was 2nd January 2017. My happiness lasted a few moments because it was changed to 30 January 2017, the day when T.S. Thakur was to retire. Earlier I used to think that our judiciary is an epitome of justice and equality but now I doubted my belief and understood that even our judiciary is not bereft of corruption. I was now convinced that power and influence have penetrated the walls of court room and I already knew what verdict will be announced on the stipulated date. However, hoping that I am proved wrong, I waited for the verdict even though in all actuality it was a mere formality to be undertaken for those involved. That day was 30th Jan 2017.

In the meantime, I met Deepak Vajpayee from the Aam Aadmi Party (AAP) but it was of no use. I went to my previous lawyer, Mr. Jaspreet Singh Rai and took all the documents I had given to him. I searched for a new lawyer. I found Mr. Ajay Marwah who belong to Kullu, Himachal.

30th January 2017 arrived and I had a strong intuition that the court will try to dismiss the case. Mine was the first case on the morning of 30th January 2017. Usually, mentioning cases precede routine cases in trials thus before my case was to be taken up, it was the bail of Bapu Asha Ram which was being heard. In about half an hour's time Bapu Asha Ram's bail was cancelled and it was my turn to go on trial. The bench had a new Chief Justice Mr. Jagdish Singh Khehar and another justice. These two justices constituted the bench which was hearing all the trials.

The moment Chief Justice, J.S. Khehar saw my case, he turned angry and aggressive. He told my lawyer that you are building castles in the air and all your claims are pointless. He also said, "You're wasting the court's time and I will put a fine of one lakh on you." My lawyer responded by informing him that the previous Chief Justice had considered it a matter of great concern and had also sent notices to the Central, State Government and the DGP. However, Justice J.S. Khehar refused to listen to anything. When my lawyer pointed out that we have all the evidence in the form of photographs and call details, Justice Khehar replied, "All those photographs are bogus." Those photographs were not bogus as I had obtained them from actual channel recordings and through the culprit themselves.

I was not expecting anything different to happen in court that day and I had already prepared myself for this scenario. I had already gauged that all this was preplanned and nothing was out of script for the bench. Justice Khehar then gave us time until 2 p.m. and told us to bring more proofs. My lawyer who was new was scared of Justice Khehar's threat of the fine of rupees 1 Lakh. I assured him that these are just means of having the case dismissed and no fine will be levied on us and handed him more proofs. I gave my lawyer more call details and also the record of the money that was invest in Akhnoor in Jammu. However, I was sure that no matter how many proofs we show the court, the Justice will dismiss this case without hesitation. Justice Khehar should have been asking for the response of the notices sent by the previous justice but he was only concerned about dismissing the case. The bench which had sent the notices to the Central and State government in 2016 consisted of three judges but this bench of two judges was hellbent on declaring the evidences fake and unsolicited.

It was 2 in the afternoon when we presented all the proofs and evidences to the bench of Justice J.S. Khehar and another Justice. The bench completely ignored all the evidences and dismissed the case without reason. The case which had demanded answers from the Central and the State government now stood dismissed and nullified. Instead of demanding answers from the government this bench without any explanations given dismissed my case. Moreover, all the call details I had presented to the court disappeared. Nothing happened in the court that day that shocked me. I was fully prepared for exactly this having already gone through a similar fate for the past three years.

I got out of the court and sit on the lawns for sometime. I contemplated about the idea of Supreme Court and its identity as an epitome of justice, equality, and fairness. I wondered if the court could still be hailed the temple of justice where the perpetrators are punished and the truth triumphs. The highest court of the country dismissed such a straightforward case. I was on the verge of crying and cried my heart out at this is deep injustice that had been imposed on my fate.

As I was also lost in my own thoughts and hopelessness, I noticed a few cameramen standing next to me. First I thought, I should go to the media and spill out everything that happened in the court that day but I stopped.

It was now time to focus on my home and family which was threatened by a danger of being auctioned off. While I was caught in this political and legal mess, the bank was readying itself to sell my home. I had requested some time from the bank to sort this matter which was also over now. So I had to completely let go off the case and now had to save my home.

Moreover, in those days, there was another high-profile case which was creating a lot of sensation. The case was of Justice Karan who had been put in jail for six months. So I thought to myself, that in this futile battle for justice, I had lost almost all of my wealth and if I did not leave this case right then, I would also lose my home. So instead of extending my suffering and stretching the case further by going to the media, I returned home.

PHOTOCOPY OF THE DISMISSAL FROM SUPREME COURT

IN THE SUPREME COURT OF INDIA

CRIMINAL ORIGINAL JURISDICTION

WRIT PETITION(CRL.)NO.55 of 2016

MANOJ KUMAR KAUSHAL   ....PETITIONER

VERSUS

                                                       ....RESPONDENTS

UNION OF INDIA AND ORS.

O R D E R

Heard learned counsel for the petitioner.

We find no ground to entertain the instant petition under Article 32 of the Constitution of India on the basis of the material placed on the record of this case.

The writ petition is accordingly dismissed.

..............................CJI.
(JAGDISH SINGH KHEHAR)

...............................J.
(N..V.RAMANA)

NEW DELHI;
JANUARY 30, 2017.

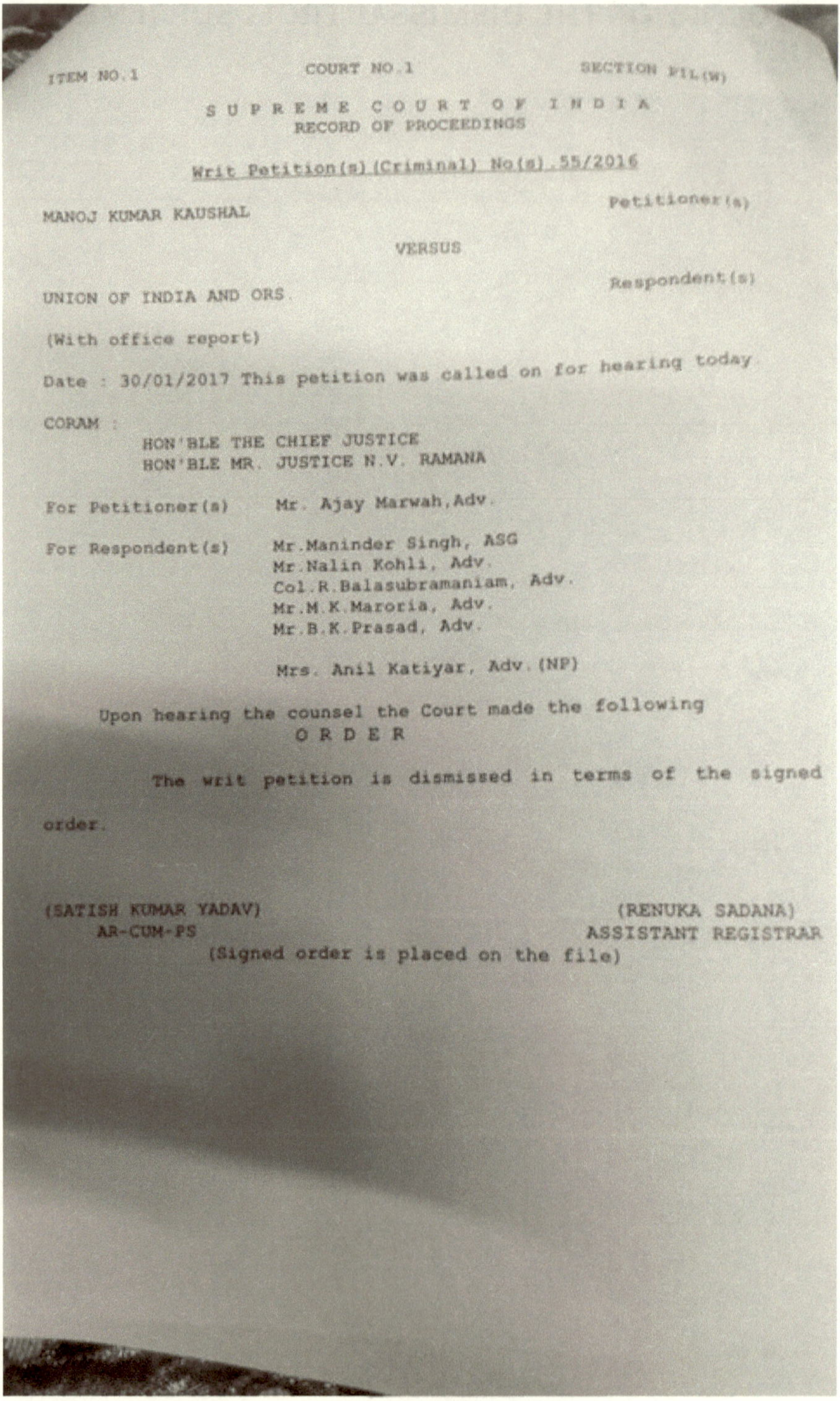

ITEM NO.1   COURT NO.1   SECTION PIL(W)

S U P R E M E   C O U R T   O F   I N D I A
RECORD OF PROCEEDINGS

Writ Petition(s)(Criminal) No(s).55/2016

MANOJ KUMAR KAUSHAL   Petitioner(s)

VERSUS

                                                        Respondent(s)
UNION OF INDIA AND ORS.

(With office report)

Date : 30/01/2017 This petition was called on for hearing today.

CORAM :
        HON'BLE THE CHIEF JUSTICE
        HON'BLE MR. JUSTICE N.V. RAMANA

For Petitioner(s)   Mr. Ajay Marwah,Adv.

For Respondent(s)   Mr.Maninder Singh, ASG
                       Mr.Nalin Kohli, Adv.
                       Col.R.Balasubramaniam, Adv.
                       Mr.M.K.Maroria, Adv.
                       Mr.B.K.Prasad, Adv.

                       Mrs. Anil Katiyar, Adv.(NP)

        Upon hearing the counsel the Court made the following
                    O R D E R

            The writ petition is dismissed in terms of the signed

order.

(SATISH KUMAR YADAV)   (RENUKA SADANA)
   AR-CUM-PS   ASSISTANT REGISTRAR
            (Signed order is placed on the file)

Follow Us:

* India
* Supreme Court dismisses plea for probe into disappearance of treasure

Supreme Court dismisses plea for probe into disappearance of treasure

Supreme Court on Monday dismissed a plea seeking CBI probe into the alleged disappearance of unaccountable cash to the tune of Rs 300 crore, 300 kgs gold and some other articles from a temple in Guwahati in 2014, citing lack of evidence to substantiate the allegations. "You are taking us for a ride. This is [...]

By PTI | New Delhi | Published: January 30, 2017 8:06:25 pm

The Supreme Court of India. (File)

Supreme Court on Monday dismissed a plea seeking CBI probe into the alleged disappearance of unaccountable cash to the tune of Rs 300 crore, 300 kgs gold and some other articles from a temple in Guwahati in 2014, citing lack of evidence to substantiate the allegations. "You are taking us for a ride. This is bogus litigation. Nobody can just come and make allegations about Rs 300 crore, gold and AK-47 without any substance. You show us some material," a bench comprising Chief Justice J S Khehar and Justice N V Ramana said.

It further told the petitioner "You have not placed any substantial material before us. You give us any material on which there can be an investigation…You have come to the court without any material."

The bench told the petitioner's counsel that people have now made a habit of invoking the jurisidiction of apex court. When the counsel tried to show some photographs, the bench said these were all bogus and were no material to be considered.

"This is total misuse of the jurisdiction of this court. Show us one sentence which points directly to the allegations. This is not done," the bench said, which initially told the petitioner that it will dismiss his plea with an exemplary cost of Rs one lakh.

The court had on May 6 last year issued notices to the Centre and Assam government on a petition filed by a former army personnel Manoj Kumar Kaushal.

The complainant had claimed he had received information in May 2014 that there was unaccounted money to the tune of Rs 300 crore in cash, 300 kg of gold and two AK-47 rifles in a Kali temple in a tea garden near Dispur Airport of Guwahati.

He had also claimed that one Mridul Bhattacharya, the owner of that tea garden, used to collect money from owners of tea gardens and give it to ULFA and alleged that this man was also involved in smuggling of gold from Burma.

However, Bhattacharya and his wife were murdered under suspicious circumstances in 2012, Kaushal had said. The petitioner had alleged that 13 persons had hatched a conspiracy and taken away the treasure on May 31, 2014, a day before the army was to recover it.

For all the latest India News, download Indian Express App

Chapter 10

I tried to give rupees 2000/- to my new lawyer as he had worked hard and it was no fault of his but he refused. Upon returning home, I found myself crestfallen and defeated. I had lost all faith in the government, the judiciary, and the State of this country. Even my lawyer was dejected at the thought that a man who has undergone so much trouble to get justice served has been completely rubbished by the court and law and order units. I tried to forget all that happened and wanted to focus completely on my family, especially my children. I wanted to spend all the time I had with them. I requested and appealed to the bank to not sell off my home and borrowed money on interest and a took a loan against my pension to pay off the bank loan. Slowly, I regularized the monthly installment going to the bank and was able to save my house from being taken away from us.

All this while I had also not been able to pay my children's school fee. It had been a year since the last fee was paid. I also cleared off that debt. This battle for justice had cost me nearly the future of my entire family but I still stuck to it. I had put up a factory of cane furniture which had also shut down due to this case yet I still had to pay off its loan. My family which had always been more than supportive was also astonished at the level of corruption and injustice that prevailed in our society. Everything is sellable and it is only money that runs and operates the government from an officer to the judiciary.

Even though I was fully caught up in sorting my domestic affairs, one part of my mind was always occupied with bringing this case to its rightful conclusion. I thought that if these 13 people attack me, I will go to the judge and ask him to set an enquiry on their bank accounts and other documents to know the truth. Trying to solve this puzzle, I contacted my lawyer and asked him if they (13 men I had named) can file a case of harassment against me. He told me the criminal petition takes 6 months and non-criminal takes one year to get processed. I had openly taken their names in TV channels and newspapers out of the 13, 3 were government servants. I was anticipated that they may file a case against me. I started waiting for their notices. One of them was a police officer and two were from CRPF. However, I did not receive notices from anyone. If these culprits were innocent then they would have definitely filed a case of defamation or harassment against me and yet they did not. This is because they were all liars and criminals. Back in 2014, they were all from weak economic backgrounds but today they all had become rich and owners of big assets.

In June 2016, a Muslim man named Ramzan Ali, the brother of Kasem Ali, from the district of Lakhimpur, came on a news channel (Prag News) and said that his brother Kasem Ali had dug out the treasure from the Kali Temple and had buried it in his (Kasem Ali's house) in the presence of Ramjan Ali who had later tipped-off the police regarding Kasem Ali. Ramjan Ali informed the police that Kasem Ali today had 16 cars but they did not do anything regarding it. Even this tip-off did not stir the government or the police for the fact bigger people would have to be arrested. Yadav who posted out to Guwahati in 2015 and Return to back posting in home ministry in January 2017.

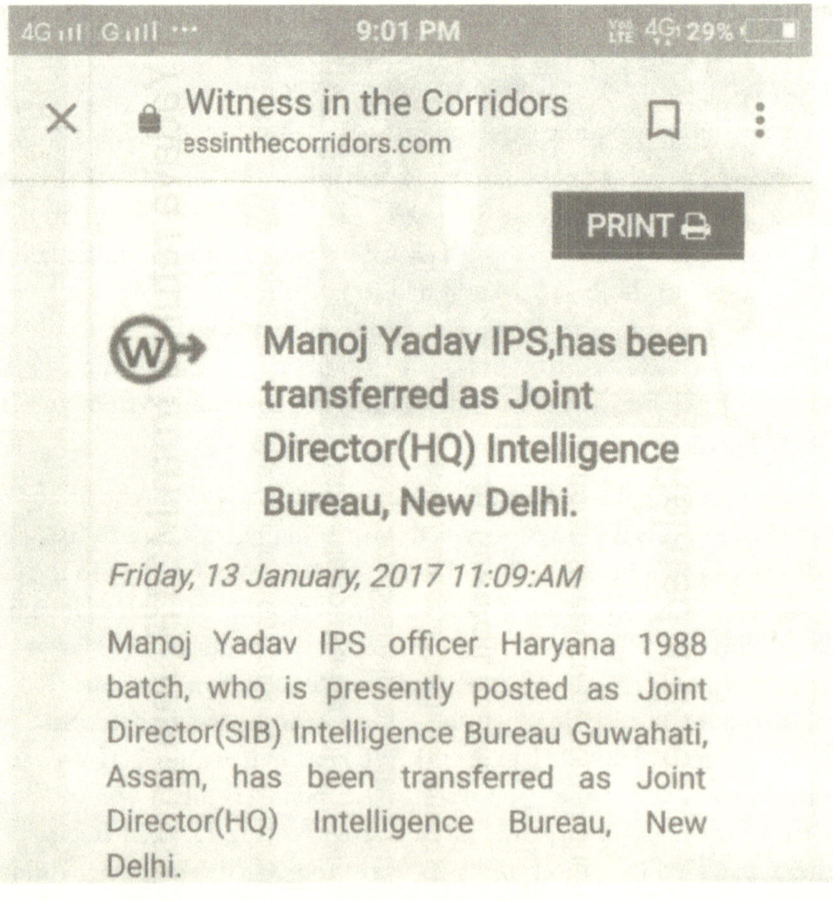

Then four judges from the Supreme Court bench also conducted a press conference. I was once again hopeful and saw a light at the end of a dark tunnel. I thought now that the judges themselves have come on record to acknowledge this incidence then may be the treasure can be recovered and justice can finally achieved. I immediately contacted a new lawyer named, Alok Srivastav and gave him Rs. 20,000/- to file the case again. I was now as concerned with retrieving the treasure as much as I wanted to tell the country that we were right and truthful all along. Also, if the case had been solved, the country would have received a sum of Rs. 300 crore, 300 Kg gold and 2 AK47s which would have been a huge turnaround for the entire nation but destiny had something else in mind.

On 07 August 2018 I asked about action taken by CBI on my grievances application through RTI. Ministry of personal and training sent me copy of letter issued to CBI Director. CBI Replied that that the said application has not been received in this office. And CBI return my RTI.

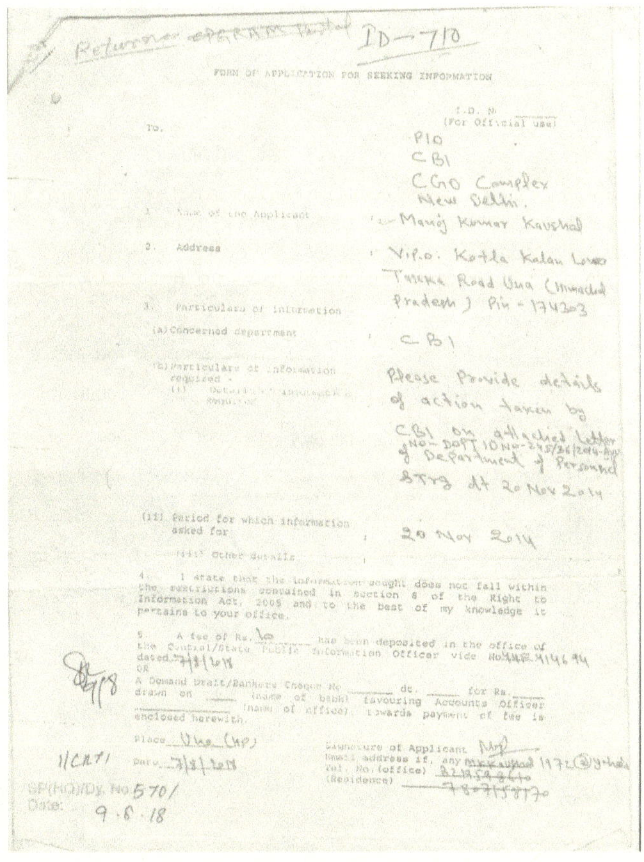

COPY OF CBI REPLY

<u>Speed Post</u>
<u>RTI Act Matter</u>
<u>MOST IMMEDIATE</u>

CENTRAL BUREAU OF INVESTIGATION
(ADMINISTRATION DIVISION)
5 B, 7th Floor, 'A' Wing, CBI H.Q.
Lodhi Road, New Delhi-110003

<u>SUB</u>: RTI application under RTI Act, 2005 dated 07.08.2018 of Shri Manoj Kumar Kaushal R/o V.P.O. Kotla Kalan Takka Road Una (Himachal Pradesh) Pin: 174303, reg.

With reference to your application dated 07.08.2018, you have sought information from CBI on the points as per your grievances application, but the said application has not been received in this office, hence we could not process your application. Therefore, your RTI application is returned herewith.

As per Section 19 of RTI Act, 2005, appeal against this reply can be made to   Shri Anish Prasad, Dy. Director   (Admin.), CBI, Head Office, 7th Floor, B Wing, 5 B, Lodhi Road, New Delhi-110003, as he is the First Appellate Authority for the matter of Appeal, if required within 30 days from the receipt of this letter.

(Manoj Verma)
SP/(HQ) – cum - CPIO
CBI/Head Office/New Delhi

Encl: As above

CBI IDNo. SPHQ/ 2018/___/Misc.Vol-IX/18/ RTI Act /2005-SPH. **Dated .09.2018.**

Shri **Manoj Kumar Kaushal** R/o V.P.O. Kotla Kalan Takka Road Una (Himachal Pradesh) Pin: 174303, reg.

On 18 September 2018 I sent request to Ministry of personal and training about action taken by them on their letter.

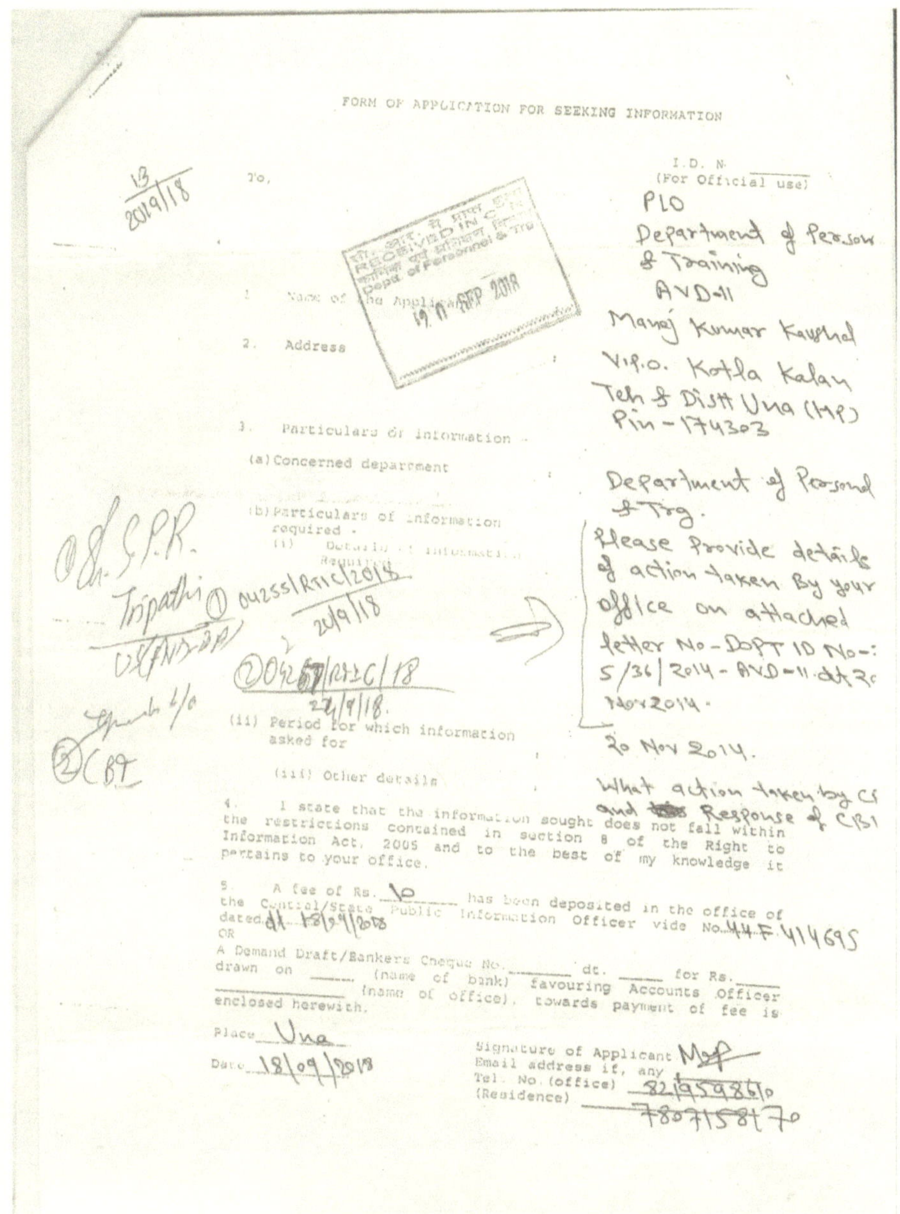

On 25 September 2018 Ministry of personal and training transfer my application to CBI for Reply. And sent me a copy for information.

COPY OF MINISTRY OF PERSONNAL AND TRAINING REPLY

IMMEDIATE/RTI MATTER

No. 2/2/2018 – RTIC/04267
Government of India
Ministry of Personnel, Public Grievances and Pensions
Department of Personnel and Training

North Block, New Delhi-110001
25th September, 2018

OFFICE MEMORANDUM

Subject: Transfer of RTI application under RTI Act, 2005

An RTI application of Shri Manoj Kumar Kaushal, dated 18.09.2018 (reg. No. DOP&T/R/2018/04267), is being transferred to Central Bureau of Investigation under Section 6(3) of the RTI Act, 2005, as the subject matter of information pertains to the aforementioned public authority. The RTI Application has also been forwarded to the CPIO concerned of this Department to whom the information sought closely pertains.

2. Application fee of Rs. 10/- has been received in this Department by IPO No. 44F 414695 vide receipt No. 39204 dated 20.09.2018.

Encl.: as above.

(Brij Mohan)
Under Secretary to the Govt. of India
Tel: 011 2309 3214

To

(1) The CPIO, RTI Cell,
Central Bureau of Investigation (CBI),
CBI Headquarters,
Plot no. 5-B, CGO Complex, Lodhi Road,
New Delhi – 110003.

(ii) Shri S.P.R Tripathi, US(AVD-II A), DOPT

Copy for information to:-

Shri Manoj Kumar Kaushal, V.P.O. Kolla Kalan, Tehsil & Distt- Una, Himachal Pradesh- 174303.	This is not a reply to your RTI application. Your RTI application is being transferred herewith by the RTI cell of DOPT to the CPIOs/Authorities/Ministries who/which are felt dealing with the subject and hence the appropriate CPIO/Authorities to give reply to your application. You are requested to follow up with the aforementioned public authority with reference to information sought by you. 1st appeal against reply of the above Public Authorities may be filed with above Public Authorities directly. 1st Appeal against the above transfer of your RTI Application, may be filed with Shri Juglal Singh, Deputy Secretary (Admn.), DOP&T, North Block, New Delhi-110001 - Telefax - 23092338, within 30 days.

On 6 November 2018 CBI replied me that my grievance petition is not readily treacable in this office.

COPY OF CBI LETTER

RTI MATTER
SPEED POST

No. 21/1 (255)/2018-PD/ *3114*
CENTRAL BUREAU OF INVESTIGATION
POLICY DIVISION, NORTH BLOCK
NEW DELHI-110 001

Dated: *06/11/2018*

To

Shri Manoj Kumar Kaushal,
VPO Kotla Kalan,
Teh & Distt. Una
Himachal Pradesh-174303.

Sub: RTI Application Registration No. DoPT/R/2018/05255 dated 20.09.2018.

Please refer to your RTI request Registration No.DoPT/R/2018/05255 dated 20.09.2018 received in this office on being transferred from Department of Personnel & Training, AVD-II vide letter No.258/05/2018-AVD-II dated 16.10.2018 seeking information about action taken on your Grievance dated 16.10.2014 lodged in CPGRAMS.

2.   Since your Grievance Petition is not readily treacable in this office, it is requested that a copy of Grievance Petition may please be sent to this office for providing a suitable reply in this regard.

(S.Balasubramony)
Asstt.Inspr.Genl. of Police (P)& CPIO/CBI

CBI Lost My Application. In rural area I received letter from ministry of personal and training,but CBI not because of ————————————

IB Joint Director Posted out to Guwahati Because of ————————————

My advocate not taken response of two notices issued by Chief Justice T.S. Thakur because of ————————————

New Chief Justice Jagdish Singh Khehar dismiss my case without replying of two notices issued by previous Chief Justice because of ————————————

Now, I am again ready to fight the battle for truth and striving to file this case in its best potential because two AK47 Riffle were also with 300 crore cash and 300 kg gold. That is very harmful for my country. I would like to appeal to the reader of this strange tale to pray for the victory and prevalence of truth.

I will keep everyone informed regarding the direction that the case took in another narrative very soon.

EPILOGUE

You must be wondering who had stashed away the treasure in the first place at the Kali Temple. Let me tell you.

The treasure referred to in this narration belonged to the owner of the Rani Tea Garden estate, Mridul Bhattacharya. Mridul Bhattacharya was the chairman of the Tea Association of Assam. When the state of Assam was riling under the pressure and power of ULFA (United Liberation Front of Assam), the tea estate owners had to pay the ULFA members security money in order to sustain the operations of their tea estate. This sum amounted to Rupees 100 Crore per year. Mridul, being a chairman would collect all this money from other tea owners and pay them.

However, in 2006–07 when ULFA's hold and influence weakened and a ceasefire was declared, ULFA could not sustain the force as it did over tea estate owners. ULFA stopped demanding money from the tea estate owners but Mridul Bhattacharya continued. He kept extracting money from tea estate owners but instead of giving it to ULFA, he kept everything for himself. In his Rani Tea estate, he constructed a 12 by 12 foot cellar underneath the kali temple and started stashing all the collected wealth in this cellar. He continued to collect the money from 2007 to 2011. He was able to gather Rupees 300 Crore and 300 Kg gold which was brought in from Myanmar. The treasure also included 2 AK47s. Mridul Bhattacharya was maintaining a diary and recording everything he was collecting. The men who had stolen all this money and treasure themselves admitted that all this was stashed away in this cellar. People living near the Rani Tea estate also informed that Mridul Bhattacharya never let anyone go near the temple. But fate had another ending for Mr. Mridul.

In 2012, Mridul Bhattacharya and his wife were burned alive by the workers of the Tea Estate as Mridul had open fired at a male child from the area. Angry and traumatized, the workers set fire to the Mridul Bhattacharya's house which resulted in the demise of Mridul and his wife. The tea garden which had the temple and cellar was also destroyed by the workers. However, no one was able to find out about the money, the gold, and the AK47s stashed away in the cellar. The treasure would have remained a mystery for the entire world if these men had not found Mridul's diary and eventually had not looted the cellar.

This entire story sounds stranger than truth and reality however this is not a lost Bollywood script or a fictional novel but actual happenings which have since their revealing affected many lives, especially mine which continues to find it difficult to cast the shadow of this crime, against the nation, away.

(Rani Tea Garden Heist – The Planning)

PLANNING

In the beginning, one of the boys, Bolen Kalita stole the eyes and the tongue both made from gold from the Kali goddess statue in order to provide for his expenses and routine life. These jewels had been embedded onto the statue by Mridul Bhattacharya, himself. The money obtained from the sale of the eyes and tongue of gold was also used in arranging the cars to and from to the Rani Tea Garden estate. Later on, when the boys had taken out all the bounty they had the eyes and tongue of gold made again and got it embedded on the statue.

Today, the SDPO is suffering from cancer. Almost all the cars of Qasim Ali have been sold. It seems that all those involved in the heist are paying a price for their crime in one or the other way. However, we cannot leave justice to destiny or God. If only, all these investigations were carried out by the government the money retrieved would have been put to some good use. In our own pursuit for justice, we reached the Home Ministry and the Supreme Court yet we could not achieve any success in getting the investigations started on any of the boys. None of the police departments or any crime prevention agencies came forward to help us or were even brave enough to take this case.

I challenge all the private as well as government agencies of India to take the call details from me and begin investigations and tell me if I was shooting in the dark or grossly mistaken. I want them to prove me wrong and tell me that the justice of the Supreme Court is right because of whom Rs. 390 Crore could not be recovered. I did not have enough money that I could have appealed the case to a bench of 5 judges. However, what about the Chief Justice who dismissed the case in a single hearing itself and that too a case in which two notices to the center and the state government were already sent and whose answers were awaited (and are awaited even today).

In my opinion, this is a complete let down. I feel that it is extremely unfortunate that in our nation, such chief justices are appointed to the apex justice body. Today, that chief justice has retired. I am also a retired personnel but I can safely say that I have never in my service have worked against the progress or development of the nation. I can challenge the entire law and crime enforcement units to take the call details from me and begin investigation. My Pettion was not a normal PIL because Two AK47 were also stolen by these boys with the money and gold.

The two groups* which had perpetrated the heist are as follows:

(*I have divided the groups in two for easy identification and the role each played at different stages of the heist):

Group 1

Bolen Kalita

Inspector Budhiram Mukhtiyar

S.D.P.O

Mrinal Nath

Manju Aurang

Satyajit Nath

Dipen Nath

Group 2

Hitesh Kalita

Dinesh Das

Praveen Musahari

N.C. Rai

Vinod Kalita

Girendhar Kalita

Vinay Kalita

Deepak Das

Giyasudin Ahmed

Jitumani Das

Abhijit Dena

Niranjan Kalita A.K.A. Din Bandhu Kalita

Hitesh Kalita from Group 2 gets in touch with Dinesh Das who knows about the Rani Tea Garden. Hitesh Kalita informs Dinesh Das about the entire bounty – the money as well as the gold. Hitesh thinks that if the army gets to know about this bounty, they will lose everything. Instead Hitesh along with Dinesh Das gets in touch with a local channel whose reporter is Girendhar Kalita to stage a fake reporting of the heist. Later along with the rest of the group Vinod Kalita, Jitumani Das, Hitesh contacts Praveen Musahari and N.C. Rai (both from CRPF) and informs them about the buried treasure at the Rani Tea Garden estate. All this takes place between 28th May 2014 to 30th May 2014.

On 29th May 2014, Dinesh Das phones calls the channel reporter Girendhar Kalita and the area Inspector of the Rani Tea Garden estate, Budhiram Mukhtiyar. Later Girendhar also calls the I.C. Budhiram Mukhtiyar. The group is also ready by this time to dig out the treasure and run away with it. Hitesh Kalita along with his friends Deepak Das, Abhijit Dena, Giyasudin Ahmed, Vinod Kalita, and the partner of Girendhar Kalita, a reporter himself prepare themselves to dig out all the buried treasure.

The other culprits Bolen Kalita, Mrinal Nath who was in touch with a SDPO get Budhiram Mukhtiyar's contact and phone him. Manju Aurang, Dipen Nath, and Satyajit Nath join them and the groups begin to prepare to strike when the time would be right. Both the groups gather on the night of 30th May 2014. Both Dinesh Das and Hitesh Kalita switch off their mobiles at 9:28:57 p.m. From the call details of Budhiram Mukhtiyar we get to know that the heist lasts until 1:31:10 a.m. It seems that Hitesh Kalita gets his share on the very next day through Money transactions via phone as he gets his share on 31st May 2014. We get all this information from Budhiram Mukhthiyar's phone details. On 1st June 2014, Bolen Kalita speaks with the I.C. Budhiram Mukhtiyar at 9:36:05 a.m. and in half an hour 10:00:31 asks for an affirmation through a text message, that says "ok." Same night that is one 1st June 2014, Volen Kalita speaks with the I.C. Budhiram Mukhtiyar at 20:20:14 p.m. He also phones the SDPO at 21:37:22 and tells him to change the location of the money and the gold the next day.

Next day on 2nd June 2014, the I.C. Budhiram Mukhtiyar calls the SDPO at 21:27:44 and on his advice changes the location of the stolen money and the gold. All this is clearly visible through the call details and this communication takes place till 00:59:11 a.m. It is also found that during all this communication, it so happens that the I.C. decides to keep the gold to himself at a house in By Lane 3 in Ajra.

When on 11th August 2014 we, along with the IB officers, go to this house to arrest him, he changes the location of the gold and the stolen goods. All this is clearly evident through the call details. This entire investigation lasts till 1:30:07 a.m.

After receiving the money, some of them started buying new houses. Manju Aurang put some of her money in Canara Bank and some of it she invested in Akhnoor in Jammu & Kashmir. She invested her money their through a retired Army Honorary Captain. Today all of them who had no or very little money until May 2014, have loads and loads of money, big houses, and big cars whereas on the other side, we have been staking our lives, our homes, and the future of our kids in order to get them behind bars. Such is the irony of this life, and most uncannily, this bizarre case.

PROOFS

Now I Present Some Proof of This Case:

CDR OF HITESH KALITA

Calling No.	Name	Called No.	Name	Date	Time	Dur(s)
9707762514	NIRANJANKALITA	9707474658	HITESH KALITA	28-May-14	21:12:51	262
9707474658	HITESH KALITA	9085341993	DIPAK DAS	28-May-14	21:42:44	0
9854239285	ABHIJIT DEKA	9707474658	HITESH KALITA	28-May-14	21:50:58	23
9707474658	HITESH KALITA	9854239285	ABHIJIT DEKA	28-May-14	21:51:48	92
8751866423	JITEN KALITA	9707474658	HITESH KALITA	29-May-14	8:00:19	0
9085341993	DIPAK DAS	9707474658	HITESH KALITA	29-May-14	8:00:24	0
9707474658	HITESH KALITA	8751866423	JITEN KALITA	29-May-14	8:01:10	48
9707474658	HITESH KALITA	9854239285	ABHIJIT DEKA	29-May-14	8:47:11	97
9707474658	HITESH KALITA	8751866423	JITEN KALITA	29-May-14	8:58:58	17
9707474658	HITESH KALITA	9854239285	ABHIJIT DEKA	29-May-14	16:18:50	41
9707474658	HITESH KALITA	9085341993	DIPAK DAS	29-May-14	16:20:41	30
9707474658	HITESH KALITA	9085341993	DIPAK DAS	29-May-14	16:48:23	58
9707474658	HITESH KALITA	9085341993	DIPAK DAS	29-May-14	17:11:15	49
8751866423	JITEN KALITA	9707474658	HITESH KALITA	30-May-14	8:18:22	17
9707474658	HITESH KALITA	8751866423	JITEN KALITA	30-May-14	9:35:24	56
8751866423	JITEN KALITA	9707474658	HITESH KALITA	30-May-14	10:18:38	19
9707474658	HITESH KALITA	9707762514	NIRANJANKALITA	30-May-14	17:24:33	53

Calling No.	Name	Called No.	Name	Date	Time	Dur(s)
9707474658	HITESH KALITA	9707762514	NIRANJANKALITA	30-May-14	17:31:52	10
9707762514	NIRANJANKALITA	9707474658	HITESH KALITA	30-May-14	17:40:11	15
9707474658	HITESH KALITA	9707913022	BHASKARDAS	30-May-14	18:58:47	876
9707474658	HITESH KALITA	8751866423	JITEN KALITA	30-May-14	19:38:51	185
9707474658	HITESH KALITA	9707762514	NIRANJANKALITA	30-May-14	20:07:12	70
9707474658	HITESH KALITA	9707762514	NIRANJANKALITA	30-May-14	20:08:42	635
9707474658	HITESH KALITA	8751866423	JITEN KALITA	30-May-14	20:31:59	54
9707474658	HITESH KALITA	8751866423	JITEN KALITA	30-May-14	20:33:06	19
9707474658	HITESH KALITA	8751866423	JITEN KALITA	30-May-14	20:33:45	735
9707474658	HITESH KALITA	9707913022	BHASKARDAS	30-May-14	21:28:57	1091
8751866423	JITEN KALITA	9707474658	HITESH KALITA	31-May-14	6:54:42	106
9707474658	HITESH KALITA	9085341993	DIPAK DAS	31-May-14	7:55:51	51
1C96BC94D0A4F945	BANK MESSAGE	9707474658	HITESH KALITA	31-May-14	8:00:13	0
9707474658	HITESH KALITA	9707762514	NIRANJANKALITA	31-May-14	8:42:24	126
9707474658	HITESH KALITA	8751866423	JITEN KALITA	31-May-14	8:45:49	663
1C96BC94D0A4F945	BANK MESSAGE	9707474658	HITESH KALITA	31-May-14	9:34:41	0
9707474658	HITESH KALITA	8751866423	JITEN KALITA	31-May-14	10:04:49	84
9707474658	HITESH KALITA	8751866423	JITEN KALITA	31-May-14	10:06:33	9
8751866423	JITEN KALITA	9707474658	HITESH KALITA	31-May-14	10:11:01	62
9707474658	HITESH KALITA	9854239285	ABHIJIT DEKA	31-May-14	10:23:08	294
8751866423	JITEN KALITA	9707474658	HITESH KALITA	31-May-14	11:36:21	10

Calling No.	Name	Called No.	Name	Date	Time	Dur(s)
8751866423	JITEN KALITA	9707474658	HITESH KALITA	31-May-14	12:07:54	21
9707474658	HITESH KALITA	9707762514	NIRANJANKALITA	31-May-14	12:10:18	68
1C96BC94D0A4F945	BANK MESSAGE	9707474658	HITESH KALITA	31-May-14	13:27:37	0
9707474658	HITESH KALITA	9707913022	BHASKARDAS	31-May-14	13:56:43	27
9707913022	BHASKARDAS	9707474658	HITESH KALITA	31-May-14	15:36:18	79
9707474658	HITESH KALITA	9854239285	ABHIJIT DEKA	31-May-14	19:37:10	81
9707474658	HITESH KALITA	9707762514	NIRANJANKALITA	31-May-14	19:40:06	122
9707474658	HITESH KALITA	9085341993	DIPAK DAS	31-May-14	19:44:05	0
9707474658	HITESH KALITA	9085341993	DIPAK DAS	31-May-14	19:46:39	0
9707474658	HITESH KALITA	9085341993	DIPAK DAS	31-May-14	19:50:53	0
9707474658	HITESH KALITA	9085341993	DIPAK DAS	31-May-14	20:12:17	0
9707474658	HITESH KALITA	9085341993	DIPAK DAS	31-May-14	21:52:55	0
9707474658	HITESH KALITA	9085341993	DIPAK DAS	31-May-14	23:34:43	0
8751866423	JITEN KALITA	9707474658	HITESH KALITA	1-Jun-14	6:15:38	41
8751866423	JITEN KALITA	9707474658	HITESH KALITA	1-Jun-14	7:08:45	7
8751866423	JITEN KALITA	9707474658	HITESH KALITA	1-Jun-14	7:10:56	12
9707474658	HITESH KALITA	9707762514	NIRANJANKALITA	1-Jun-14	7:18:15	43
9707474658	HITESH KALITA	9707762514	NIRANJANKALITA	1-Jun-14	8:03:06	55
9707762514	NIRANJANKALITA	9707474658	HITESH KALITA	1-Jun-14	8:06:50	21
9707474658	HITESH KALITA	9707762514	NIRANJANKALITA	1-Jun-14	9:34:57	73
9707474658	HITESH KALITA	9085341993	DIPAK DAS	1-Jun-14	10:03:36	10

Calling No.	Name	Called No.	Name	Date	Time	Dur(s)
9707474658	HITESH KALITA	9085341993	DIPAK DAS	1-Jun-14	10:04:06	52
9707474658	HITESH KALITA	9854239285	ABHIJIT DEKA	1-Jun-14	10:12:52	105
9707474658	HITESH KALITA	9707762514	NIRANJANKALITA	1-Jun-14	10:39:58	19
9707762514	NIRANJANKALITA	9707474658	HITESH KALITA	1-Jun-14	10:44:27	159
1C96BC65381CA623	BANK MESSAGE	9707474658	HITESH KALITA	1-Jun-14	12:40:09	0
9707474658	HITESH KALITA	9707762514	NIRANJANKALITA	1-Jun-14	14:03:00	701
1C96B28949255A64	BANK MESSAGE	9707474658	HITESH KALITA	1-Jun-14	14:21:40	0
549697C8E0BCFC56	BANK MESSAGE	9707474658	HITESH KALITA	1-Jun-14	14:22:37	0
549697C8E0BCFC56	BANK MESSAGE	9707474658	HITESH KALITA	1-Jun-14	14:22:39	0
9707474658	HITESH KALITA	9707913022	BHASKARDAS	1-Jun-14	15:00:56	58
9707474658	HITESH KALITA	8751866423	JITEN KALITA	1-Jun-14	15:02:47	144
1C96BC94D0A4F945	BANK MESSAGE	9707474658	HITESH KALITA	1-Jun-14	15:09:36	0
1C96BC94D0A4F945	BANK MESSAGE	9707474658	HITESH KALITA	1-Jun-14	15:11:46	0
9707474658	HITESH KALITA	9085341993	DIPAK DAS	1-Jun-14	16:51:26	0
9707474658	HITESH KALITA	9085341993	DIPAK DAS	1-Jun-14	17:26:52	0
9854239285	ABHIJIT DEKA	9707474658	HITESH KALITA	1-Jun-14	20:20:13	11
9707474658	HITESH KALITA	9854239285	ABHIJIT DEKA	1-Jun-14	20:20:44	187
9707474658	HITESH KALITA	9085341993	DIPAK DAS	1-Jun-14	20:38:15	0
9707474658	HITESH KALITA	9707762514	NIRANJANKALITA	1-Jun-14	20:46:27	204
9707474658	HITESH KALITA	9085341993	DIPAK DAS	1-Jun-14	20:51:02	0
9707762514	NIRANJANKALITA	9707474658	HITESH KALITA	1-Jun-14	20:59:25	66

Calling No.	Name	Called No.	Name	Date	Time	Dur(s)
9707474658	HITESH KALITA	9707762514	NIRANJANKALITA	2-Jun-14	7:16:40	18
9707762514	NIRANJANKALITA	9707474658	HITESH KALITA	2-Jun-14	7:29:32	121
9707474658	HITESH KALITA	8751866423	JITEN KALITA	2-Jun-14	8:10:52	322
9707474658	HITESH KALITA	9707762514	NIRANJANKALITA	2-Jun-14	8:16:55	128
9707474658	HITESH KALITA	8751866423	JITEN KALITA	2-Jun-14	8:36:31	66
9707474658	HITESH KALITA	8751866423	JITEN KALITA	2-Jun-14	9:04:44	29
9707474658	HITESH KALITA	8751866423	JITEN KALITA	2-Jun-14	9:57:31	26
9707474658	HITESH KALITA	8751866423	JITEN KALITA	2-Jun-14	10:31:20	12
44D6B0663B1C0723	BANK MESSAGE	9707474658	HITESH KALITA	2-Jun-14	14:13:14	0
9707474658	HITESH KALITA	9085341993	DIPAK DAS	2-Jun-14	17:49:47	28
9707474658	HITESH KALITA	9854239285	ABHIJIT DEKA	2-Jun-14	18:58:38	99
9707474658	HITESH KALITA	9085341993	DIPAK DAS	2-Jun-14	19:09:09	32
9707474658	HITESH KALITA	9864136262	BINAYKALITA	2-Jun-14	19:15:10	65
9864136262	BINAYKALITA	9707474658	HITESH KALITA	2-Jun-14	19:16:48	351
9864136262	BINAYKALITA	9707474658	HITESH KALITA	2-Jun-14	19:24:08	178
9864136262	BINAYKALITA	9707474658	HITESH KALITA	2-Jun-14	19:27:19	75
9707474658	HITESH KALITA	9085341993	DIPAK DAS	2-Jun-14	20:01:52	30
9707474658	HITESH KALITA	9707762514	NIRANJANKALITA	2-Jun-14	20:59:47	353
9864136262	BINAYKALITA	9707474658	HITESH KALITA	2-Jun-14	21:41:27	41
9864136262	BINAYKALITA	9707474658	HITESH KALITA	2-Jun-14	21:42:56	358
9707913022	BHASKARDAS	9707474658	HITESH KALITA	2-Jun-14	22:24:49	52

Calling No.	Name	Called No.	Name	Date	Time	Dur(s)
9707474658	HITESH KALITA	9707913022	BHASKARDAS	3-Jun-14	6:09:06	499
9707913022	BHASKARDAS	9707474658	HITESH KALITA	3-Jun-14	7:39:25	40
1C96BC94D0A4F945	BANK MESSAGE	9707474658	HITESH KALITA	3-Jun-14	8:05:17	0
9707762514	NIRANJANKALITA	9707474658	HITESH KALITA	3-Jun-14	8:06:05	57
9707474658	HITESH KALITA	9085341993	DIPAK DAS	3-Jun-14	8:08:21	0
9707474658	HITESH KALITA	9864136262	BINAYKALITA	3-Jun-14	8:17:36	24
1C96BC94D0A4F945	BANK MESSAGE	9707474658	HITESH KALITA	3-Jun-14	9:29:05	0
8751866423	JITEN KALITA	9707474658	HITESH KALITA	3-Jun-14	9:57:59	183
9707474658	HITESH KALITA	8751866423	JITEN KALITA	3-Jun-14	11:27:42	192
8751866423	JITEN KALITA	9707474658	HITESH KALITA	3-Jun-14	12:27:23	206
1C96BC94D0A4F945	BANK MESSAGE	9707474658	HITESH KALITA	3-Jun-14	13:26:41	0
9707474658	HITESH KALITA	9085341993	DIPAK DAS	3-Jun-14	14:49:36	26
2D66B889E93A9A65	BANK MESSAGE	9707474658	HITESH KALITA	3-Jun-14	15:05:23	0
8751866423	JITEN KALITA	9707474658	HITESH KALITA	3-Jun-14	15:16:43	70
9707474658	HITESH KALITA	9854239285	ABHIJIT DEKA	3-Jun-14	15:54:02	50
9707474658	HITESH KALITA	9085341993	DIPAK DAS	3-Jun-14	16:33:07	0
9707474658	HITESH KALITA	9085341993	DIPAK DAS	3-Jun-14	17:04:08	24
8751866423	JITEN KALITA	9707474658	HITESH KALITA	3-Jun-14	17:32:02	12
9707474658	HITESH KALITA	9864136262	BINAYKALITA	3-Jun-14	17:35:19	0
9864136262	BINAYKALITA	9707474658	HITESH KALITA	3-Jun-14	17:40:49	43
8751866423	JITEN KALITA	9707474658	HITESH KALITA	3-Jun-14	17:52:00	76

Calling No.	Name	Called No.	Name	Date	Time	Dur(s)
9707474658	HITESH KALITA	9864136262	BINAYKALITA	3-Jun-14	17:56:19	55
9707762514	NIRANJANKALITA	9707474658	HITESH KALITA	3-Jun-14	17:59:54	166
9707474658	HITESH KALITA	8751866423	JITEN KALITA	3-Jun-14	18:14:51	50
9707762514	NIRANJANKALITA	9707474658	HITESH KALITA	3-Jun-14	18:19:19	123
9707913022	BHASKARDAS	9707474658	HITESH KALITA	3-Jun-14	18:46:02	684
9707121577	DEBENCHKALITA	9707474658	HITESH KALITA	3-Jun-14	19:19:10	458
9707474658	HITESH KALITA	9085341993	DIPAK DAS	3-Jun-14	19:46:41	66
9707913022	BHASKARDAS	9707474658	HITESH KALITA	3-Jun-14	19:48:29	162
9707474658	HITESH KALITA	9854239285	ABHIJIT DEKA	3-Jun-14	20:16:31	109
14B6BA643C1E07	BANK MESSAGE	9707474658	HITESH KALITA	3-Jun-14	21:19:54	0
8751866423	JITEN KALITA	9707474658	HITESH KALITA	4-Jun-14	7:10:07	105
9707474658	HITESH KALITA	8751866423	JITEN KALITA	4-Jun-14	8:45:57	51
9707474658	HITESH KALITA	9864136262	BINAYKALITA	4-Jun-14	8:48:31	0
9864136262	BINAYKALITA	9707474658	HITESH KALITA	4-Jun-14	8:49:25	149
1C96BC94D0A4F945	BANK MESSAGE	9707474658	HITESH KALITA	4-Jun-14	8:52:11	0
1C96BC94D0A4F945	BANK MESSAGE	9707474658	HITESH KALITA	4-Jun-14	9:27:08	0
9707474658	HITESH KALITA	9707913022	BHASKARDAS	4-Jun-14	9:49:49	92
9707474658	HITESH KALITA	9707913022	BHASKARDAS	4-Jun-14	9:52:46	550
1C96BC94D0A4F945	BANK MESSAGE	9707474658	HITESH KALITA	4-Jun-14	13:27:06	0
9707474658	HITESH KALITA	8751866423	JITEN KALITA	4-Jun-14	14:06:34	11
9707474658	HITESH KALITA	8751866423	JITEN KALITA	4-Jun-14	14:07:44	106

Calling No.	Name	Called No.	Name	Date	Time	Dur(s)
8751866423	JITEN KALITA	9707474658	HITESH KALITA	4-Jun-14	17:13:54	34
9707913022	BHASKARDAS	9707474658	HITESH KALITA	4-Jun-14	17:53:14	106
9707474658	HITESH KALITA	9707913022	BHASKARDAS	4-Jun-14	17:58:27	653
9707474658	HITESH KALITA	9707913022	BHASKARDAS	5-Jun-14	8:02:53	683
4C66B292D9637A14	BANK MESSAGE	9707474658	HITESH KALITA	5-Jun-14	8:16:40	0
9707474658	HITESH KALITA	8751866423	JITEN KALITA	5-Jun-14	8:19:50	417
9707762514	NIRANJANKALITA	9707474658	HITESH KALITA	5-Jun-14	9:06:24	274
8751866423	JITEN KALITA	9707474658	HITESH KALITA	5-Jun-14	9:16:44	46
1C96BC94D0A4F945	BANK MESSAGE	9707474658	HITESH KALITA	5-Jun-14	10:05:29	0
1C96BC94D0A4F945	BANK MESSAGE	9707474658	HITESH KALITA	5-Jun-14	10:10:54	0
9707474658	HITESH KALITA	8751866423	JITEN KALITA	5-Jun-14	10:21:07	12
9707762514	NIRANJANKALITA	9707474658	HITESH KALITA	5-Jun-14	10:33:10	12
9707474658	HITESH KALITA	9864136262	BINAYKALITA	5-Jun-14	10:56:35	120
9707474658	HITESH KALITA	9864136262	BINAYKALITA	5-Jun-14	10:59:06	0
9707474658	HITESH KALITA	9864136262	BINAYKALITA	5-Jun-14	11:00:35	19
9707474658	HITESH KALITA	9707913022	BHASKARDAS	5-Jun-14	11:02:22	945
9707474658	HITESH KALITA	9707913022	BHASKARDAS	5-Jun-14	11:19:25	0
9707474658	HITESH KALITA	9707913022	BHASKARDAS	5-Jun-14	11:19:53	8
9707474658	HITESH KALITA	9864136262	BINAYKALITA	5-Jun-14	11:27:08	0
9864136262	BINAYKALITA	9707474658	HITESH KALITA	5-Jun-14	11:28:57	59
9707474658	HITESH KALITA	9707913022	BHASKARDAS	5-Jun-14	11:35:07	191

Calling No.	Name	Called No.	Name	Date	Time	Dur(s)
9707474658	HITESH KALITA	9864136262	BINAYKALITA	5-Jun-14	11:56:17	104
9707913022	BHASKARDAS	9707474658	HITESH KALITA	5-Jun-14	12:30:06	91
9707474658	HITESH KALITA	9864136262	BINAYKALITA	5-Jun-14	12:36:04	0
9864136262	BINAYKALITA	9707474658	HITESH KALITA	5-Jun-14	12:43:16	25
1C96BC94D0A4F945	BANK MESSAGE	9707474658	HITESH KALITA	5-Jun-14	13:26:26	0
9707913022	BHASKARDAS	9707474658	HITESH KALITA	5-Jun-14	14:41:50	203
9707474658	HITESH KALITA	9707762514	NIRANJANKALITA	5-Jun-14	15:01:48	12
1C96BC65381CA623	BANK MESSAGE	9707474658	HITESH KALITA	5-Jun-14	15:10:04	0
9707474658	HITESH KALITA	9085341993	DIPAK DAS	5-Jun-14	18:23:14	35
9707474658	HITESH KALITA	9854239285	ABHIJIT DEKA	5-Jun-14	18:24:44	40
9707474658	HITESH KALITA	9707913022	BHASKARDAS	5-Jun-14	18:40:12	42
9707474658	HITESH KALITA	9707068042	CHINMAYBAYAN	5-Jun-14	19:04:38	12
2D66B889E93A1E97	BANK MESSAGE	9707474658	HITESH KALITA	5-Jun-14	19:05:23	0
2D66B889E93A1E97	BANK MESSAGE	9707474658	HITESH KALITA	5-Jun-14	19:06:07	0
2D66B889E93A1E97	BANK MESSAGE	9707474658	HITESH KALITA	5-Jun-14	19:07:36	0
14B6BA643C1E07	BANK MESSAGE	9707474658	HITESH KALITA	6-Jun-14	0:00:45	0
8751866423	JITEN KALITA	9707474658	HITESH KALITA	6-Jun-14	0:00:52	0
9707762514	NIRANJANKALITA	9707474658	HITESH KALITA	6-Jun-14	0:00:54	0
2D66B889E93A1E97	BANK MESSAGE	9707474658	HITESH KALITA	6-Jun-14	5:01:27	0
9707474658	HITESH KALITA	9085341993	DIPAK DAS	6-Jun-14	6:47:35	75
4C66B292D9637A14	BANK MESSAGE	9707474658	HITESH KALITA	6-Jun-14	8:15:02	0

Calling No.	Name	Called No.	Name	Date	Time	Dur(s)
9707474658	HITESH KALITA	9707762514	NIRANJANKALITA	6-Jun-14	8:41:43	247
9707913022	BHASKARDAS	9707474658	HITESH KALITA	6-Jun-14	9:35:49	154
9707474658	HITESH KALITA	9707913022	BHASKARDAS	6-Jun-14	9:38:50	193
9508494530	JINTIKALITA	9707474658	HITESH KALITA	6-Jun-14	12:56:01	86
8751866423	JITEN KALITA	9707474658	HITESH KALITA	6-Jun-14	13:42:11	1077
8751866423	JITEN KALITA	9707474658	HITESH KALITA	7-Jun-14	10:47:13	47
9707474658	HITESH KALITA	9707913022	BHASKARDAS	8-Jun-14	11:03:56	1522
9707474658	HITESH KALITA	9707762514	NIRANJANKALITA	8-Jun-14	11:29:55	198
9707474658	HITESH KALITA	9707762514	NIRANJANKALITA	8-Jun-14	11:33:40	28
9707474658	HITESH KALITA	9707762514	NIRANJANKALITA	8-Jun-14	13:48:46	21
14B6BA643C1E07	BANK MESSAGE	9707474658	HITESH KALITA	9-Jun-14	8:11:41	0
1C96BC65381CA623	BANK MESSAGE	9707474658	HITESH KALITA	10-Jun-14	11:55:54	0
2D66B889E93A9A65	BANK MESSAGE	9707474658	HITESH KALITA	10-Jun-14	17:03:17	0
4C66B292D9637A14	BANK MESSAGE	9707474658	HITESH KALITA	11-Jun-14	9:46:32	0
1C96BC94D0A4F945	BANK MESSAGE	9707474658	HITESH KALITA	11-Jun-14	14:43:37	0
9707474658	HITESH KALITA	9085341993	DIPAK DAS	11-Jun-14	14:45:36	0
1C96BC94D0A4F945	BANK MESSAGE	9707474658	HITESH KALITA	11-Jun-14	14:51:50	0
9707474658	HITESH KALITA	9085341993	DIPAK DAS	11-Jun-14	15:58:17	0
9085341993	DIPAK DAS	9707474658	HITESH KALITA	11-Jun-14	16:00:45	0
9707474658	HITESH KALITA	9085341993	DIPAK DAS	11-Jun-14	16:02:52	0
9707474658	HITESH KALITA	9085341993	DIPAK DAS	11-Jun-14	17:16:29	0

Calling No.	Name	Called No.	Name	Date	Time	Dur(s)
9707474658	HITESH KALITA	9085341993	DIPAK DAS	11-Jun-14	17:56:37	0
9707474658	HITESH KALITA	41562D3534383838	BANK MESSAGE	12-Jun-14	8:42:35	0
9707474658	HITESH KALITA	41562D3534383838	BANK MESSAGE	12-Jun-14	8:42:37	0
9707474658	HITESH KALITA	9707762514	NIRANJANKALITA	12-Jun-14	8:42:39	0
9707474658	HITESH KALITA	9707762514	NIRANJANKALITA	12-Jun-14	8:44:22	45
9707474658	HITESH KALITA	9085341993	DIPAK DAS	12-Jun-14	8:44:22	0
9707474658	HITESH KALITA	9085341993	DIPAK DAS	12-Jun-14	8:44:33	0
9707474658	HITESH KALITA	9085341993	DIPAK DAS	12-Jun-14	8:46:50	71
9707474658	HITESH KALITA	41532D3635303035	BANK MESSAGE	12-Jun-14	12:16:10	0
8751866423	JITEN KALITA	9707474658	HITESH KALITA	12-Jun-14	13:27:16	93
9707474658	HITESH KALITA	564D2D4469736854	BANK MESSAGE	13-Jun-14	11:22:05	0
9707474658	HITESH KALITA	41562D3534383838	BANK MESSAGE	13-Jun-14	11:22:09	0
9707474658	HITESH KALITA	41532D4E5441524F	BANK MESSAGE	13-Jun-14	11:26:25	0
9707474658	HITESH KALITA	41532D4E5441524F	BANK MESSAGE	13-Jun-14	11:30:35	0
8751866423	JITEN KALITA	9707474658	HITESH KALITA	13-Jun-14	11:48:19	138
9707474658	HITESH KALITA	41532D3635303035	BANK MESSAGE	13-Jun-14	12:24:09	0
9707474658	HITESH KALITA	9085341993	DIPAK DAS	13-Jun-14	13:41:16	40
9707474658	HITESH KALITA	9085341993	DIPAK DAS	13-Jun-14	16:02:18	215
9707474658	HITESH KALITA	9085341993	DIPAK DAS	13-Jun-14	16:09:35	55
9707474658	HITESH KALITA	9085341993	DIPAK DAS	13-Jun-14	17:06:31	171
9707474658	HITESH KALITA	41532D4E5441524F	BANK MESSAGE	14-Jun-14	8:48:13	0

Calling No.	Name	Called No.	Name	Date	Time	Dur(s)
9707474658	HITESH KALITA	41422D4149525452	BANK MESSAGE	14-Jun-14	10:48:10	0
9707474658	HITESH KALITA	4.5526E+15		14-Jun-14	10:49:33	0
9707474658	HITESH KALITA	41532D4E5441524F	BANK MESSAGE	14-Jun-14	11:25:51	0
9707474658	HITESH KALITA	41532D4E5441524F	BANK MESSAGE	14-Jun-14	11:30:35	0
9707474658	HITESH KALITA	42542D3532303236	BANK MESSAGE	14-Jun-14	11:49:01	0
9707762514	NIRANJANKALITA	9707474658	HITESH KALITA	14-Jun-14	13:07:05	154
9707474658	HITESH KALITA	9085341993	DIPAK DAS	14-Jun-14	13:24:21	246
9707474658	HITESH KALITA	9085341993	DIPAK DAS	14-Jun-14	14:25:35	76
9707474658	HITESH KALITA	9085341993	DIPAK DAS	14-Jun-14	14:27:20	220
9707474658	HITESH KALITA	9085341993	DIPAK DAS	14-Jun-14	16:25:18	282
9707474658	HITESH KALITA	41422D4149524F41	BANK MESSAGE	14-Jun-14	17:20:16	0
9707474658	HITESH KALITA	9085341993	DIPAK DAS	14-Jun-14	20:29:22	47
9707474658	HITESH KALITA	9854239285	ABHIJIT DEKA	14-Jun-14	21:23:29	566
9707474658	HITESH KALITA	9085341993	DIPAK DAS	14-Jun-14	23:15:52	98
9707474658	HITESH KALITA	41532D4E5441524F	BANK MESSAGE	15-Jun-14	8:49:33	0
9707474658	HITESH KALITA	41532D4E5441524F	BANK MESSAGE	15-Jun-14	9:10:02	0
9707474658	HITESH KALITA	9085341993	DIPAK DAS	15-Jun-14	9:10:51	249
9707474658	HITESH KALITA	41532D3635303033	BANK MESSAGE	15-Jun-14	9:47:27	0
9707474658	HITESH KALITA	41532D4E5441524F	BANK MESSAGE	15-Jun-14	9:56:58	0
9707474658	HITESH KALITA	9085341993	DIPAK DAS	15-Jun-14	12:12:49	87
9707474658	HITESH KALITA	9854239285	ABHIJIT DEKA	15-Jun-14	13:06:49	1688

Calling No.	Name	Called No.	Name	Date	Time	Dur(s)
9707474658	HITESH KALITA	9085341993	DIPAK DAS	15-Jun-14	15:25:40	104
8751866423	JITEN KALITA	9707474658	HITESH KALITA	15-Jun-14	18:11:58	167
9707474658	HITESH KALITA	9085341993	DIPAK DAS	15-Jun-14	20:04:59	241
9707762514	NIRANJANKALITA	9707474658	HITESH KALITA	15-Jun-14	20:26:35	698
9707474658	HITESH KALITA	41532D4E5441524F	BANK MESSAGE	16-Jun-14	8:29:20	0
9707474658	HITESH KALITA	41532D4E5441524F	BANK MESSAGE	16-Jun-14	8:49:05	0
9707474658	HITESH KALITA	41532D4E5441524F	BANK MESSAGE	16-Jun-14	9:28:31	0
9707474658	HITESH KALITA	9085341993	DIPAK DAS	16-Jun-14	13:52:46	155
9707474658	HITESH KALITA	41562D3534383838	BANK MESSAGE	16-Jun-14	18:32:59	0
9707474658	HITESH KALITA	9085341993	DIPAK DAS	16-Jun-14	20:36:13	109
9707474658	HITESH KALITA	9085341993	DIPAK DAS	16-Jun-14	20:36:13	109
9707474658	HITESH KALITA	41562D4149524F41	BANK MESSAGE	16-Jun-14	20:54:38	0
9707474658	HITESH KALITA	9085341993	DIPAK DAS	16-Jun-14	21:36:54	114
9707474658	HITESH KALITA	9085341993	DIPAK DAS	16-Jun-14	21:39:39	14
1C96BC94D0A4F945	BANK MESSAGE	9707474658	HITESH KALITA	17-Jun-14	8:50:17	0
1C96BC94D0A4F945	BANK MESSAGE	9707474658	HITESH KALITA	17-Jun-14	15:48:45	0
9707474658	HITESH KALITA	9085341993	DIPAK DAS	17-Jun-14	15:53:52	0
9707474658	HITESH KALITA	9854375564	DIPAK KALITA	17-Jun-14	16:49:57	204
9707474658	HITESH KALITA	9085341993	DIPAK DAS	17-Jun-14	16:54:39	0
1C96BC94D0A4F945	BANK MESSAGE	9707474658	HITESH KALITA	17-Jun-14	17:01:37	0
9707474658	HITESH KALITA	9085341993	DIPAK DAS	17-Jun-14	21:27:39	0

Calling No.	Name	Called No.	Name	Date	Time	Dur(s)
9707474658	HITESH KALITA	9085341993	DIPAK DAS	17-Jun-14	22:19:03	0
9707474658	HITESH KALITA	9085341993	DIPAK DAS	17-Jun-14	22:23:12	0
9085341993	DIPAK DAS	9707474658	HITESH KALITA	17-Jun-14	22:27:43	0
9707474658	HITESH KALITA	9085341993	DIPAK DAS	17-Jun-14	22:34:23	0
1C96BC94D0A4F945	BANK MESSAGE	9707474658	HITESH KALITA	18-Jun-14	8:24:15	0
9707474658	HITESH KALITA	9085341993	DIPAK DAS	18-Jun-14	8:29:29	0
9707474658	HITESH KALITA	9707762514	NIRANJANKALITA	18-Jun-14	8:54:43	258
1C96BC94D0A4F945	BANK MESSAGE	9707474658	HITESH KALITA	18-Jun-14	9:26:22	0
8751866423	JITEN KALITA	9707474658	HITESH KALITA	18-Jun-14	12:08:25	77
1C96BC94D0A4F945	BANK MESSAGE	9707474658	HITESH KALITA	18-Jun-14	13:26:41	0
9707474658	HITESH KALITA	9085341993	DIPAK DAS	18-Jun-14	14:49:05	0
9707474658	HITESH KALITA	9085341993	DIPAK DAS	18-Jun-14	15:21:05	0
9707474658	HITESH KALITA	9085341993	DIPAK DAS	18-Jun-14	15:59:31	0
9707474658	HITESH KALITA	8751866423	JITEN KALITA	18-Jun-14	16:35:13	789
9707474658	HITESH KALITA	8751866423	JITEN KALITA	18-Jun-14	16:49:31	24
9707474658	HITESH KALITA	9707913022	BHASKARDAS	18-Jun-14	16:56:31	955
1C96B28949255A64	BANK MESSAGE	9707474658	HITESH KALITA	18-Jun-14	18:57:07	0
549697C8E0BCFC56	BANK MESSAGE	9707474658	HITESH KALITA	18-Jun-14	18:57:51	0
9707474658	HITESH KALITA	9085341993	DIPAK DAS	18-Jun-14	22:45:57	0
9707474658	HITESH KALITA	9085341993	DIPAK DAS	18-Jun-14	22:51:43	0
9707474658	HITESH KALITA	9085341993	DIPAK DAS	18-Jun-14	23:06:35	0

Calling No.	Name	Called No.	Name	Date	Time	Dur(s)
1C96BC65381CA613	BANK MESSAGE	9707474658	HITESH KALITA	19-Jun-14	14:41:59	0
9707474658	HITESH KALITA	9085341993	DIPAK DAS	19-Jun-14	18:56:08	13
1C96BC94D0A4F945	BANK MESSAGE	9707474658	HITESH KALITA	20-Jun-14	5:36:53	0
1C96BC94D0A4F945	BANK MESSAGE	9707474658	HITESH KALITA	20-Jun-14	5:38:41	0
9707474658	HITESH KALITA	9085341993	DIPAK DAS	20-Jun-14	5:40:41	0
9707474658	HITESH KALITA	9085341993	DIPAK DAS	20-Jun-14	5:43:31	0
9707474658	HITESH KALITA	9085341993	DIPAK DAS	20-Jun-14	6:50:16	0
1C96BC94D0A4F945	BANK MESSAGE	9707474658	HITESH KALITA	20-Jun-14	9:12:03	0
1C96BC94D0A4F945	BANK MESSAGE	9707474658	HITESH KALITA	20-Jun-14	9:12:13	0
9707474658	HITESH KALITA	9085341993	DIPAK DAS	20-Jun-14	9:24:04	0
1C96BC94D0A4F945	BANK MESSAGE	9707474658	HITESH KALITA	20-Jun-14	13:26:20	0
2D66B889E93A9A65	BANK MESSAGE	9707474658	HITESH KALITA	20-Jun-14	13:46:53	0
9707474658	HITESH KALITA	9085341993	DIPAK DAS	20-Jun-14	15:30:52	0
9707474658	HITESH KALITA	9085341993	DIPAK DAS	20-Jun-14	16:00:03	0
1C96BC65381CA613	BANK MESSAGE	9707474658	HITESH KALITA	20-Jun-14	16:18:45	0
9707474658	HITESH KALITA	9085341993	DIPAK DAS	20-Jun-14	19:19:57	0
9707474658	HITESH KALITA	9085341993	DIPAK DAS	20-Jun-14	20:55:01	0
9707474658	HITESH KALITA	9085341993	DIPAK DAS	20-Jun-14	22:35:45	0
9085341993	DIPAK DAS	9707474658	HITESH KALITA	21-Jun-14	7:02:18	15
1C96BC94D0A4F945	BANK MESSAGE	9707474658	HITESH KALITA	21-Jun-14	7:50:16	0
9707474658	HITESH KALITA	9085341993	DIPAK DAS	21-Jun-14	7:51:09	0

Calling No.	Name	Called No.	Name	Date	Time	Dur(s)
9707474658	HITESH KALITA	9085341993	DIPAK DAS	21-Jun-14	8:33:59	0
1C96BC94D0A4F945	BANK MESSAGE	9707474658	HITESH KALITA	21-Jun-14	9:59:20	0
1C96BC94D0A4F945	BANK MESSAGE	9707474658	HITESH KALITA	21-Jun-14	13:26:43	0
9707474658	HITESH KALITA	9085341993	DIPAK DAS	21-Jun-14	20:33:38	0
9707474658	HITESH KALITA	9085341993	DIPAK DAS	21-Jun-14	20:35:44	0
9707474658	HITESH KALITA	9085341993	DIPAK DAS	21-Jun-14	21:15:40	0
9707474658	HITESH KALITA	9085341993	DIPAK DAS	21-Jun-14	22:41:34	0
1C96BC94D0A4F945	BANK MESSAGE	9707474658	HITESH KALITA	22-Jun-14	7:26:29	0
9707474658	HITESH KALITA	9085341993	DIPAK DAS	22-Jun-14	7:32:39	0
9707474658	HITESH KALITA	9085341993	DIPAK DAS	22-Jun-14	8:23:48	0
1C96BC94D0A4F945	BANK MESSAGE	9707474658	HITESH KALITA	22-Jun-14	9:31:07	0
1C96BC65381C6673	BANK MESSAGE	9707474658	HITESH KALITA	22-Jun-14	9:44:32	0
1C96BC94D0A4F945	BANK MESSAGE	9707474658	HITESH KALITA	22-Jun-14	14:04:31	0
9085341993	DIPAK DAS	9707474658	HITESH KALITA	22-Jun-14	22:24:42	0
9707474658	HITESH KALITA	9085341993	DIPAK DAS	22-Jun-14	23:50:42	0
14B6BA643C1E07	BANK MESSAGE	9707474658	HITESH KALITA	23-Jun-14	16:17:02	0
1C96BC94D0A4F945	BANK MESSAGE	9707474658	HITESH KALITA	23-Jun-14	16:26:29	0
9707474658	HITESH KALITA	9085341993	DIPAK DAS	23-Jun-14	16:27:02	0
1C96BC94D0A4F945	BANK MESSAGE	9707474658	HITESH KALITA	23-Jun-14	16:30:24	0
9707474658	HITESH KALITA	9085341993	DIPAK DAS	23-Jun-14	17:41:41	0
9707474658	HITESH KALITA	9707913022	BHASKARDAS	23-Jun-14	19:17:26	201

Calling No.	Name	Called No.	Name	Date	Time	Dur(s)
9085341993	DIPAK DAS	9707474658	HITESH KALITA	23-Jun-14	19:37:15	0
9085341993	DIPAK DAS	9707474658	HITESH KALITA	23-Jun-14	19:54:02	0
2D66B889E93A9A65	BANK MESSAGE	9707474658	HITESH KALITA	23-Jun-14	20:54:49	0
9707474658	HITESH KALITA	9085341993	DIPAK DAS	23-Jun-14	21:31:45	0
9085341993	DIPAK DAS	9707474658	HITESH KALITA	23-Jun-14	21:59:18	0
9707474658	HITESH KALITA	9085341993	DIPAK DAS	23-Jun-14	22:00:21	0
9085341993	DIPAK DAS	9707474658	HITESH KALITA	23-Jun-14	22:03:54	0
9707474658	HITESH KALITA	9085341993	DIPAK DAS	23-Jun-14	22:34:51	0
9085341993	DIPAK DAS	9707474658	HITESH KALITA	23-Jun-14	22:35:20	0
1C96BC65381C2613	BANK MESSAGE	9707474658	HITESH KALITA	24-Jun-14	11:14:51	0
9085341993	DIPAK DAS	9707474658	HITESH KALITA	24-Jun-14	19:24:02	0
14A6B2894962D964	BANK MESSAGE	9707474658	HITESH KALITA	24-Jun-14	19:28:07	0
9085341993	DIPAK DAS	9707474658	HITESH KALITA	25-Jun-14	15:08:47	0
9707474658	HITESH KALITA	9707913022	BHASKARDAS	25-Jun-14	17:21:22	893
4C66BC653A5E0603	BANK MESSAGE	9707474658	HITESH KALITA	25-Jun-14	18:20:54	0
1C96BC65381C2613	BANK MESSAGE	9707474658	HITESH KALITA	26-Jun-14	11:36:02	0
1C96BC94D0A4F945	BANK MESSAGE	9707474658	HITESH KALITA	26-Jun-14	16:18:37	0
1C96BC94D0A4F945	BANK MESSAGE	9707474658	HITESH KALITA	26-Jun-14	16:20:50	0
9707474658	HITESH KALITA	9085341993	DIPAK DAS	26-Jun-14	16:22:11	0
14B6BA643C1E07	BANK MESSAGE	9707474658	HITESH KALITA	26-Jun-14	17:56:42	0
9707913022	BHASKARDAS	9707474658	HITESH KALITA	26-Jun-14	17:56:48	0

Calling No.	Name	Called No.	Name	Date	Time	Dur(s)
9707474658	HITESH KALITA	9707913022	BHASKARDAS	26-Jun-14	17:57:28	447
9707474658	HITESH KALITA	9707762514	NIRANJANKALITA	26-Jun-14	18:05:30	721
9707474658	HITESH KALITA	9707913022	BHASKARDAS	26-Jun-14	20:30:40	196
9085341993	DIPAK DAS	9707474658	HITESH KALITA	27-Jun-14	16:14:14	0
1C96BC65381CA613	BANK MESSAGE	9707474658	HITESH KALITA	27-Jun-14	16:24:55	0
2D66B889E93A9A65	BANK MESSAGE	9707474658	HITESH KALITA	27-Jun-14	19:08:04	0
9707913022	BHASKARDAS	9707474658	HITESH KALITA	28-Jun-14	12:53:04	340
9707474658	HITESH KALITA	9707913022	BHASKARDAS	28-Jun-14	13:19:17	9
1C96BC94D0A4F945	BANK MESSAGE	9707474658	HITESH KALITA	28-Jun-14	13:20:12	0
9707474658	HITESH KALITA	9707913022	BHASKARDAS	28-Jun-14	13:21:45	0
1C96BC94D0A4F945	BANK MESSAGE	9707474658	HITESH KALITA	28-Jun-14	13:38:04	0
14B6BA643C1E07	BANK MESSAGE	9707474658	HITESH KALITA	28-Jun-14	18:57:51	0
9707474658	HITESH KALITA	9707762514	NIRANJANKALITA	28-Jun-14	19:03:07	244
9707474658	HITESH KALITA	9707762514	NIRANJANKALITA	28-Jun-14	19:11:05	57
9707474658	HITESH KALITA	9707762514	NIRANJANKALITA	28-Jun-14	19:12:24	152
9085341993	DIPAK DAS	9707474658	HITESH KALITA	28-Jun-14	19:52:25	0
9085341993	DIPAK DAS	9707474658	HITESH KALITA	28-Jun-14	20:46:57	0
9707474658	HITESH KALITA	9085341993	DIPAK DAS	28-Jun-14	21:23:15	0
9085341993	DIPAK DAS	9707474658	HITESH KALITA	28-Jun-14	21:25:11	0
9707474658	HITESH KALITA	9085341993	DIPAK DAS	28-Jun-14	21:26:19	0
9085341993	DIPAK DAS	9707474658	HITESH KALITA	28-Jun-14	21:30:28	0

Calling No.	Name	Called No.	Name	Date	Time	Dur(s)
9707474658	HITESH KALITA	9085341993	DIPAK DAS	28-Jun-14	22:15:47	0
9707474658	HITESH KALITA	9085341993	DIPAK DAS	28-Jun-14	22:21:45	0
9707474658	HITESH KALITA	9085341993	DIPAK DAS	28-Jun-14	22:27:04	0
6D66B889E93A9A65	BANK MESSAGE	9707474658	HITESH KALITA	29-Jun-14	12:54:52	0
1C96BC65381C0633	BANK MESSAGE	9707474658	HITESH KALITA	29-Jun-14	13:59:18	0
1C4BC9E56630	BANK MESSAGE	9707474658	HITESH KALITA	29-Jun-14	20:19:48	0
1C4BC9E56630	BANK MESSAGE	9707474658	HITESH KALITA	29-Jun-14	20:19:51	0
1C4BC9E56630	BANK MESSAGE	9707474658	HITESH KALITA	29-Jun-14	20:19:53	0
1C4BC9E56630	BANK MESSAGE	9707474658	HITESH KALITA	29-Jun-14	20:19:56	0
1C4BC9E56630	BANK MESSAGE	9707474658	HITESH KALITA	29-Jun-14	20:19:59	0
1C4BC9E56630	BANK MESSAGE	9707474658	HITESH KALITA	29-Jun-14	20:20:02	0
1C4BC9E56630	BANK MESSAGE	9707474658	HITESH KALITA	29-Jun-14	20:20:04	0
1C4BC9E56630	BANK MESSAGE	9707474658	HITESH KALITA	29-Jun-14	20:20:07	0
1C4BC9E56630	BANK MESSAGE	9707474658	HITESH KALITA	29-Jun-14	20:20:09	0
1C4BC9E56630	BANK MESSAGE	9707474658	HITESH KALITA	29-Jun-14	20:20:12	0
1C4BC9E56630	BANK MESSAGE	9707474658	HITESH KALITA	29-Jun-14	20:20:13	0
9707474658	HITESH KALITA	9707762514	NIRANJANKALITA	29-Jun-14	20:24:16	30
14B6BA643C1E07	BANK MESSAGE	9707474658	HITESH KALITA	29-Jun-14	20:25:13	0
9707474658	HITESH KALITA	9707913022	BHASKARDAS	29-Jun-14	20:44:44	649
9707474658	HITESH KALITA	9707913022	BHASKARDAS	30-Jun-14	12:52:34	13
9707474658	HITESH KALITA	9707913022	BHASKARDAS	30-Jun-14	13:44:41	12

Calling No.	Name	Called No.	Name	Date	Time	Dur(s)
9707474658	HITESH KALITA	9707913022	BHASKARDAS	30-Jun-14	15:45:42	15
1C96BC94D0A4F945	BANK MESSAGE	9707474658	HITESH KALITA	30-Jun-14	16:51:57	0
1C96BC94D0A4F945	BANK MESSAGE	9707474658	HITESH KALITA	30-Jun-14	16:55:01	0
9707474658	HITESH KALITA	9085341993	DIPAK DAS	30-Jun-14	19:34:06	0
2D66B889E93A9A65	BANK MESSAGE	9707474658	HITESH KALITA	30-Jun-14	19:48:50	0
9707474658	HITESH KALITA	9085341993	DIPAK DAS	30-Jun-14	19:58:29	0
9085341993	DIPAK DAS	9707474658	HITESH KALITA	30-Jun-14	19:59:22	0
9085341993	DIPAK DAS	9707474658	HITESH KALITA	30-Jun-14	20:06:19	0
9707474658	HITESH KALITA	9085341993	DIPAK DAS	30-Jun-14	20:07:07	0
9085341993	DIPAK DAS	9707474658	HITESH KALITA	30-Jun-14	20:08:31	0
9707474658	HITESH KALITA	9085341993	DIPAK DAS	30-Jun-14	20:13:43	0
9085341993	DIPAK DAS	9707474658	HITESH KALITA	30-Jun-14	20:15:49	0
9707474658	HITESH KALITA	9085341993	DIPAK DAS	30-Jun-14	20:18:19	0
9707474658	HITESH KALITA	9085341993	DIPAK DAS	30-Jun-14	23:05:06	0
9707474658	HITESH KALITA	9085341993	DIPAK DAS	30-Jun-14	23:05:10	0
9707474658	HITESH KALITA	9085341993	DIPAK DAS	30-Jun-14	23:09:55	0
1C96BC65381C2613	BANK MESSAGE	9707474658	HITESH KALITA	1-Jul-14	10:49:38	0
1C96BC94D0A4F945	BANK MESSAGE	9707474658	HITESH KALITA	1-Jul-14	20:22:59	0
2D66B889E93A9A65	BANK MESSAGE	9707474658	HITESH KALITA	2-Jul-14	20:56:53	0
9085341993	DIPAK DAS	9707474658	HITESH KALITA	2-Jul-14	22:21:20	5
9085341993	DIPAK DAS	9707474658	HITESH KALITA	2-Jul-14	22:33:24	0

Calling No.	Name	Called No.	Name	Date	Time	Dur(s)
9707474658	HITESH KALITA	9085341993	DIPAK DAS	2-Jul-14	22:36:47	0
1C96BC65381C2613	BANK MESSAGE	9707474658	HITESH KALITA	3-Jul-14	10:56:20	0
1C96BC94D0A4F945	BANK MESSAGE	9707474658	HITESH KALITA	3-Jul-14	19:34:01	0
1C96BC94D0A4F945	BANK MESSAGE	9707474658	HITESH KALITA	3-Jul-14	19:36:00	0
9707474658		9085341993	DIPAK DAS	3-Jul-14	19:36:10	0
2D66B889E93A1E97	BANK MESSAGE	9707474658	HITESH KALITA	3-Jul-14	19:37:05	0
2D66B889E93A1E97	BANK MESSAGE	9707474658	HITESH KALITA	3-Jul-14	19:41:16	0
9707474658		9085341993	DIPAK DAS	3-Jul-14	19:43:17	0
9707474658		9085341993	DIPAK DAS	3-Jul-14	23:25:12	0
2D66B889E93A1E97	BANK MESSAGE	9707474658	HITESH KALITA	4-Jul-14	6:55:01	0
1C96BC94D0A4F945	BANK MESSAGE	9707474658	HITESH KALITA	4-Jul-14	9:00:01	0
9707474658	HITESH KALITA	9085341993	DIPAK DAS	4-Jul-14	9:00:44	0
1C96BC94D0A4F945	BANK MESSAGE	9707474658	HITESH KALITA	4-Jul-14	10:20:03	0
9707474658	HITESH KALITA	9085341993	DIPAK DAS	4-Jul-14	13:15:58	0
1C96BC94D0A4F945	BANK MESSAGE	9707474658	HITESH KALITA	4-Jul-14	13:28:28	0
9707474658	HITESH KALITA	9085341993	DIPAK DAS	4-Jul-14	16:20:17	0
9707474658	HITESH KALITA	9085341993	DIPAK DAS	4-Jul-14	21:37:04	0
1C96BC94D0A4F945	BANK MESSAGE	9707474658	HITESH KALITA	5-Jul-14	17:36:06	0
9707474658	HITESH KALITA	8822058995	DHIRAJKALITA	5-Jul-14	17:37:32	0
1C96BC94D0A4F945	BANK MESSAGE	9707474658	HITESH KALITA	5-Jul-14	17:40:21	0
9707474658	HITESH KALITA	9085341993	DIPAK DAS	5-Jul-14	21:12:34	0

Calling No.	Name	Called No.	Name	Date	Time	Dur(s)
9707474658	HITESH KALITA	9085341993	DIPAK DAS	5-Jul-14	21:27:31	0
9707474658	HITESH KALITA	9085341993	DIPAK DAS	5-Jul-14	22:11:16	0
2D66B889E93A9A65	BANK MESSAGE	9707474658	HITESH KALITA	6-Jul-14	12:20:02	0
1C96BC65381C0633	BANK MESSAGE	9707474658	HITESH KALITA	6-Jul-14	13:54:25	0
1C96BC94D0A4F945	BANK MESSAGE	9707474658	HITESH KALITA	6-Jul-14	14:27:26	0
9707474658	HITESH KALITA	9085341993	DIPAK DAS	6-Jul-14	14:29:05	0
1C96BC94D0A4F945	BANK MESSAGE	9707474658	HITESH KALITA	6-Jul-14	14:30:31	0
9707474658	HITESH KALITA	9085341993	DIPAK DAS	6-Jul-14	15:03:34	0
9707474658	HITESH KALITA	9707913022	BHASKARDAS	6-Jul-14	19:26:48	133
9707474658	HITESH KALITA	9085341993	DIPAK DAS	6-Jul-14	21:58:20	0
9707474658	HITESH KALITA	9085341993	DIPAK DAS	6-Jul-14	22:03:45	0
9707474658	HITESH KALITA	9085341993	DIPAK DAS	7-Jul-14	7:30:36	18
14B6BA643C1E07	BANK MESSAGE	9707474658	HITESH KALITA	7-Jul-14	9:28:29	0
9085341993	DIPAK DAS	9707474658	HITESH KALITA	7-Jul-14	9:28:35	0
9707474658	HITESH KALITA	9085341993	DIPAK DAS	7-Jul-14	9:29:50	117
9707474658	HITESH KALITA	9085341993	DIPAK DAS	7-Jul-14	11:20:24	19
9707913022	BHASKARDAS	9707474658	HITESH KALITA	7-Jul-14	12:36:55	0
9707474658	HITESH KALITA	9707913022	BHASKARDAS	7-Jul-14	12:38:06	38
9707474658	HITESH KALITA	9085341993	DIPAK DAS	7-Jul-14	12:46:08	56
1C96B28949255A64	BANK MESSAGE	9707474658	HITESH KALITA	7-Jul-14	13:12:51	0
1C96B28949255A64	BANK MESSAGE	9707474658	HITESH KALITA	7-Jul-14	13:12:55	0

Calling No.	Name	Called No.	Name	Date	Time	Dur(s)
2D66B889E93A9A65	BANK MESSAGE	9707474658	HITESH KALITA	7-Jul-14	15:37:34	0
1C96BC65381C2613	BANK MESSAGE	9707474658	HITESH KALITA	8-Jul-14	10:53:45	0
6D66B889E93A9A65	BANK MESSAGE	9707474658	HITESH KALITA	8-Jul-14	11:27:46	0
9707474658	HITESH KALITA	9085341993	DIPAK DAS	8-Jul-14	12:46:37	29
CC66BC62395D2673	BANK MESSAGE	9707474658	HITESH KALITA	8-Jul-14	13:57:28	0
9085341993	DIPAK DAS	9707474658	HITESH KALITA	8-Jul-14	19:24:54	0
HITESH KALITA	HITESH KALITA	HITESH KALITA	HITESH KALITA	HITESH KALITA	HITESH KALITA	HITESH KALITA
9707474658	HITESH KALITA	9085341993	DIPAK DAS	8-Jul-14	22:23:46	0
9085341993	DIPAK DAS	9707474658	HITESH KALITA	8-Jul-14	22:24:46	0
1C96BC94D0A4F945	BANK MESSAGE	9707474658	HITESH KALITA	8-Jul-14	22:26:08	0
9707474658	HITESH KALITA	9085341993	DIPAK DAS	8-Jul-14	22:27:13	0
9085341993	DIPAK DAS	9707474658	HITESH KALITA	8-Jul-14	22:28:15	0
9707474658	HITESH KALITA	9085341993	DIPAK DAS	8-Jul-14	22:34:13	0
9085341993	DIPAK DAS	9707474658	HITESH KALITA	8-Jul-14	22:35:45	0
9707474658	HITESH KALITA	9085341993	DIPAK DAS	8-Jul-14	22:37:05	0
9085341993	DIPAK DAS	9707474658	HITESH KALITA	8-Jul-14	22:38:57	0
9085341993	DIPAK DAS	9707474658	HITESH KALITA	8-Jul-14	23:27:40	0
9085341993	DIPAK DAS	9707474658	HITESH KALITA	8-Jul-14	23:27:45	0
9707474658	HITESH KALITA	9085341993	DIPAK DAS	8-Jul-14	23:29:41	0
9085341993	DIPAK DAS	9707474658	HITESH KALITA	8-Jul-14	23:34:55	0

Calling No.	Name	Called No.	Name	Date	Time	Dur(s)
9085341993	DIPAK DAS	9707474658	HITESH KALITA	8-Jul-14	23:35:01	0
9707474658	HITESH KALITA	9085341993	DIPAK DAS	8-Jul-14	23:50:06	0
1C96BC94D0A4F945	BANK MESSAGE	9707474658	HITESH KALITA	9-Jul-14	7:29:50	0
9707474658	HITESH KALITA	9085341993	DIPAK DAS	9-Jul-14	7:32:26	0
9707474658	HITESH KALITA	9854239285	ABHIJIT DEKA	9-Jul-14	8:56:32	94
1C96BC94D0A4F945	BANK MESSAGE	9707474658	HITESH KALITA	9-Jul-14	9:21:48	0
9707474658	HITESH KALITA	9854239285	ABHIJIT DEKA	9-Jul-14	10:52:06	76
9085341993	DIPAK DAS	9707474658	HITESH KALITA	9-Jul-14	11:20:21	0
14A6B2894962D964	BANK MESSAGE	9707474658	HITESH KALITA	9-Jul-14	11:35:34	0
9707474658	HITESH KALITA	9085341993	DIPAK DAS	9-Jul-14	11:52:13	0
6D66B889E93A9A65	BANK MESSAGE	9707474658	HITESH KALITA	9-Jul-14	11:54:28	0
1C96B28949255A64	BANK MESSAGE	9707474658	HITESH KALITA	9-Jul-14	12:15:57	0
1C96B28949255A64	BANK MESSAGE	9707474658	HITESH KALITA	9-Jul-14	12:16:01	0
549697C8E0BCFC56	BANK MESSAGE	9707474658	HITESH KALITA	9-Jul-14	12:17:45	0
9707474658	HITESH KALITA	9085341993	DIPAK DAS	9-Jul-14	13:02:28	0
1476B282DB62D964	BANK MESSAGE	9707474658	HITESH KALITA	9-Jul-14	13:07:58	0
9085341993	DIPAK DAS	9707474658	HITESH KALITA	9-Jul-14	13:10:02	0
1C96BC94D0A4F945	BANK MESSAGE	9707474658	HITESH KALITA	9-Jul-14	13:23:53	0
9707474658		9085341993	DIPAK DAS	9-Jul-14	16:04:44	0
9085341993	DIPAK DAS	9707474658	HITESH KALITA	9-Jul-14	16:05:19	0
9085341993	DIPAK DAS	9707474658	HITESH KALITA	9-Jul-14	16:06:05	0

Calling No.	Name	Called No.	Name	Date	Time	Dur(s)
9707474658	HITESH KALITA	9085341993	DIPAK DAS	9-Jul-14	16:10:08	0
9085341993	DIPAK DAS	9707474658	HITESH KALITA	9-Jul-14	16:25:45	0
9085341993	DIPAK DAS	9707474658	HITESH KALITA	9-Jul-14	16:25:48	0
9707474658	HITESH KALITA	9707913022	BHASKARDAS	9-Jul-14	16:27:08	0
9707474658	HITESH KALITA	41562D4149524F41	BANK MESSAGE	9-Jul-14	17:35:59	0
9707474658	HITESH KALITA	41532D4E5441524F	BANK MESSAGE	9-Jul-14	17:48:50	0
9707474658	HITESH KALITA	41532D4E5441524F	BANK MESSAGE	9-Jul-14	17:49:43	0
9707474658	HITESH KALITA	9085341993	DIPAK DAS	9-Jul-14	21:46:04	0
9707474658	HITESH KALITA	9085341993	DIPAK DAS	9-Jul-14	21:48:10	0
9707474658	HITESH KALITA	9085341993	DIPAK DAS	9-Jul-14	21:49:30	0
9707474658	HITESH KALITA	9085341993	DIPAK DAS	9-Jul-14	21:50:14	0
9707474658	HITESH KALITA	9085341993	DIPAK DAS	9-Jul-14	21:51:13	0
9707474658	HITESH KALITA	9085341993	DIPAK DAS	9-Jul-14	21:53:19	0
9707474658	HITESH KALITA	9085341993	DIPAK DAS	9-Jul-14	21:55:58	0
9707474658	HITESH KALITA	9085341993	DIPAK DAS	9-Jul-14	21:59:55	0
9707474658	HITESH KALITA	9085341993	DIPAK DAS	9-Jul-14	22:03:57	0
9707474658	HITESH KALITA	9085341993	DIPAK DAS	9-Jul-14	22:06:46	0
9707474658	HITESH KALITA	9085341993	DIPAK DAS	9-Jul-14	22:08:19	0
9707474658	HITESH KALITA	9085341993	DIPAK DAS	9-Jul-14	22:18:37	0
9707474658	HITESH KALITA	9085341993	DIPAK DAS	9-Jul-14	22:18:55	0
9707474658	HITESH KALITA	9085341993	DIPAK DAS	9-Jul-14	22:20:55	0

Calling No.	Name	Called No.	Name	Date	Time	Dur(s)
9707474658	HITESH KALITA	9085341993	DIPAK DAS	9-Jul-14	22:21:30	0
9707474658	HITESH KALITA	41422D4149524F41	BANK MESSAGE	10-Jul-14	0:22:18	0
9707474658	HITESH KALITA	41532D4E5441524F	BANK MESSAGE	10-Jul-14	5:41:07	0
9707474658	HITESH KALITA	41532D4E5441524F	BANK MESSAGE	10-Jul-14	8:47:54	0
9707474658	HITESH KALITA	41532D4E5441524F	BANK MESSAGE	10-Jul-14	9:01:47	0
9707474658	HITESH KALITA	41532D3635303132	BANK MESSAGE	10-Jul-14	9:14:39	0
9707474658	HITESH KALITA	41532D3635303132	BANK MESSAGE	10-Jul-14	9:14:44	0
9707474658	HITESH KALITA	9085341993	DIPAK DAS	10-Jul-14	9:33:26	36
9707474658	HITESH KALITA	9854239285	ABHIJIT DEKA	10-Jul-14	9:34:53	26
9707474658	HITESH KALITA	524D2D4469736854	BANK MESSAGE	10-Jul-14	17:35:55	0
9707474658	HITESH KALITA	41562D3534383838	BANK MESSAGE	10-Jul-14	17:38:00	0
9707474658	HITESH KALITA	9085341993	DIPAK DAS	10-Jul-14	19:19:08	69
9707474658	HITESH KALITA	9854239285	ABHIJIT DEKA	10-Jul-14	19:21:52	126
9707474658	HITESH KALITA	9707913022	BHASKARDAS	10-Jul-14	20:01:28	0
9707474658	HITESH KALITA	9085341993	DIPAK DAS	10-Jul-14	22:03:42	0
9707474658	HITESH KALITA	9085341993	DIPAK DAS	10-Jul-14	22:18:44	0
9707474658	HITESH KALITA	9085341993	DIPAK DAS	10-Jul-14	22:21:45	0
9707474658	HITESH KALITA	41532D4E5441524F	BANK MESSAGE	11-Jul-14	8:47:57	0
9707474658	HITESH KALITA	41532D4E5441524F	BANK MESSAGE	11-Jul-14	9:54:59	0
9707474658	HITESH KALITA	41532D4E5441524F	BANK MESSAGE	11-Jul-14	9:59:39	0
9707474658	HITESH KALITA	9085341993	DIPAK DAS	11-Jul-14	13:07:16	62

Calling No.	Name	Called No.	Name	Date	Time	Dur(s)
9707474658	HITESH KALITA	9854239285	ABHIJIT DEKA	11-Jul-14	13:09:05	160
9707474658	HITESH KALITA	41422D4149524F41	BANK MESSAGE	11-Jul-14	17:16:14	0
9707474658	HITESH KALITA	9085341993	DIPAK DAS	11-Jul-14	19:11:20	0
9707474658	HITESH KALITA	41562D3534383838	BANK MESSAGE	11-Jul-14	20:39:07	0
9707474658	HITESH KALITA	9085341993	DIPAK DAS	11-Jul-14	20:46:49	0
9707474658	HITESH KALITA	9085341993	DIPAK DAS	11-Jul-14	20:50:02	0
9707474658	HITESH KALITA	9085341993	DIPAK DAS	11-Jul-14	20:55:19	73
9707474658	HITESH KALITA	9085341993	DIPAK DAS	11-Jul-14	20:59:21	0
9707474658	HITESH KALITA	9085341993	DIPAK DAS	11-Jul-14	21:06:44	0
9707474658	HITESH KALITA	41532D4E5441524F	BANK MESSAGE	12-Jul-14	8:49:40	0
9707474658	HITESH KALITA	41532D4E5441524F	BANK MESSAGE	12-Jul-14	10:10:35	0
9707474658	HITESH KALITA	41532D4E5441524F	BANK MESSAGE	12-Jul-14	10:14:52	0
9707474658	HITESH KALITA	9085341993	DIPAK DAS	12-Jul-14	10:51:34	64
9707474658	HITESH KALITA	41562D3534383838	BANK MESSAGE	12-Jul-14	16:27:57	0
9707474658	HITESH KALITA	9085341993	DIPAK DAS	13-Jul-14	0:01:46	0
9707474658	HITESH KALITA	9085341993	DIPAK DAS	13-Jul-14	0:08:44	0
9707474658	HITESH KALITA	9085341993	DIPAK DAS	13-Jul-14	0:08:49	0
9707474658	HITESH KALITA	9085341993	DIPAK DAS	13-Jul-14	2:57:31	0
9707474658	HITESH KALITA	41562D3534383838	BANK MESSAGE	13-Jul-14	2:59:30	0
9707474658	HITESH KALITA	9085341993	DIPAK DAS	13-Jul-14	2:59:34	0
9707474658	HITESH KALITA	9085341993	DIPAK DAS	13-Jul-14	3:01:16	0

Calling No.	Name	Called No.	Name	Date	Time	Dur(s)
9707474658	HITESH KALITA	41532D4E5441524F	BANK MESSAGE	13-Jul-14	3:36:56	0
9707474658	HITESH KALITA	9085341993	DIPAK DAS	13-Jul-14	7:16:20	44
9707474658	HITESH KALITA	41532D4E5441524F	BANK MESSAGE	13-Jul-14	8:48:15	0
9707474658	HITESH KALITA	41532D4E5441524F	BANK MESSAGE	13-Jul-14	9:00:54	0
9707474658	HITESH KALITA	9085341993	DIPAK DAS	13-Jul-14	10:26:45	54
9707474658	HITESH KALITA	9085341993	DIPAK DAS	13-Jul-14	10:27:58	38
9707474658	HITESH KALITA	9854239285	ABHIJIT DEKA	13-Jul-14	10:29:53	52
9707474658	HITESH KALITA	9085341993	DIPAK DAS	13-Jul-14	14:52:50	236
9707474658	HITESH KALITA	9085341993	DIPAK DAS	13-Jul-14	14:58:09	0
9707474658	HITESH KALITA	9085341993	DIPAK DAS	13-Jul-14	15:02:19	0
9707474658	HITESH KALITA	9085341993	DIPAK DAS	13-Jul-14	15:05:00	0
9707474658	HITESH KALITA	9085341993	DIPAK DAS	13-Jul-14	20:02:51	57
9707474658	HITESH KALITA	9085341993	DIPAK DAS	13-Jul-14	20:07:43	70
9707474658	HITESH KALITA	9085341993	DIPAK DAS	13-Jul-14	22:29:09	0
9707474658	HITESH KALITA	9085341993	DIPAK DAS	13-Jul-14	22:34:15	0
9707474658	HITESH KALITA	41532D4E5441524F	BANK MESSAGE	14-Jul-14	8:48:14	0
9707474658	HITESH KALITA	41532D4E5441524F	BANK MESSAGE	14-Jul-14	8:53:52	0
9707474658	HITESH KALITA	41532D4E5441524F	BANK MESSAGE	14-Jul-14	9:54:36	0
9707474658	HITESH KALITA	9085341993	DIPAK DAS	14-Jul-14	16:39:51	35
9707474658	HITESH KALITA	41562D4149524F41	BANK MESSAGE	14-Jul-14	19:51:39	0
9707474658	HITESH KALITA	9854239285	ABHIJIT DEKA	14-Jul-14	21:57:11	104

Calling No.	Name	Called No.	Name	Date	Time	Dur(s)
9707474658	HITESH KALITA	9085341993	DIPAK DAS	14-Jul-14	22:01:18	129
9707474658	HITESH KALITA	9085341993	DIPAK DAS	14-Jul-14	22:22:34	0
9707474658	HITESH KALITA	9085341993	DIPAK DAS	14-Jul-14	22:31:08	0
9707474658	HITESH KALITA	9085341993	DIPAK DAS	14-Jul-14	22:31:14	0
9707474658	HITESH KALITA	9085341993	DIPAK DAS	14-Jul-14	22:31:19	0
9707474658	HITESH KALITA	9085341993	DIPAK DAS	14-Jul-14	22:34:46	0
9707474658	HITESH KALITA	9085341993	DIPAK DAS	14-Jul-14	22:41:13	0
9707474658	HITESH KALITA	9085341993	DIPAK DAS	14-Jul-14	22:41:19	0
9707474658	HITESH KALITA	9085341993	DIPAK DAS	14-Jul-14	22:48:48	0
9707474658	HITESH KALITA	9085341993	DIPAK DAS	14-Jul-14	22:48:53	0
9707474658	HITESH KALITA	9085341993	DIPAK DAS	14-Jul-14	22:50:39	0
9707474658	HITESH KALITA	9085341993	DIPAK DAS	14-Jul-14	22:55:26	0
9707474658	HITESH KALITA	9085341993	DIPAK DAS	14-Jul-14	23:00:57	0
9707474658	HITESH KALITA	9085341993	DIPAK DAS	14-Jul-14	23:01:03	0
9707474658	HITESH KALITA	9085341993	DIPAK DAS	14-Jul-14	23:13:55	0
9707474658	HITESH KALITA	9085341993	DIPAK DAS	14-Jul-14	23:14:00	0
9707474658	HITESH KALITA	9085341993	DIPAK DAS	14-Jul-14	23:35:43	0
9707474658	HITESH KALITA	41532D4E5441524F	BANK MESSAGE	15-Jul-14	7:49:35	0
9707474658	HITESH KALITA	9085341993	DIPAK DAS	15-Jul-14	7:51:18	0
9707474658	HITESH KALITA	9085341993	DIPAK DAS	15-Jul-14	8:02:13	0
9707474658	HITESH KALITA	9085341993	DIPAK DAS	15-Jul-14	8:03:38	0

Calling No.	Name	Called No.	Name	Date	Time	Dur(s)
9707474658	HITESH KALITA	41532D4E5441524F	BANK MESSAGE	15-Jul-14	8:48:19	0
9707474658	HITESH KALITA	41532D4E5441524F	BANK MESSAGE	15-Jul-14	9:24:40	0
9707474658	HITESH KALITA	9854239285	ABHIJIT DEKA	15-Jul-14	12:11:15	119
9707474658	HITESH KALITA	9085341993	DIPAK DAS	15-Jul-14	13:20:19	0
9707474658	HITESH KALITA	9085341993	DIPAK DAS	15-Jul-14	13:52:32	0
9707474658	HITESH KALITA	41542D414952494E	BANK MESSAGE	15-Jul-14	19:01:05	0
9707474658	HITESH KALITA	9085341993	DIPAK DAS	15-Jul-14	19:41:39	0
9707474658	HITESH KALITA	9085341993	DIPAK DAS	15-Jul-14	19:46:32	0
9707474658	HITESH KALITA	9085341993	DIPAK DAS	15-Jul-14	19:50:43	0
9707474658	HITESH KALITA	9085341993	DIPAK DAS	15-Jul-14	20:03:06	0
9707474658	HITESH KALITA	9085341993	DIPAK DAS	15-Jul-14	20:14:26	0
9707474658	HITESH KALITA	9085341993	DIPAK DAS	15-Jul-14	20:17:01	0
9707474658	HITESH KALITA	9085341993	DIPAK DAS	15-Jul-14	20:17:07	0
9707474658	HITESH KALITA	9085341993	DIPAK DAS	15-Jul-14	20:17:12	0
9707474658	HITESH KALITA	9085341993	DIPAK DAS	15-Jul-14	20:31:00	0
9707474658	HITESH KALITA	9085341993	DIPAK DAS	15-Jul-14	20:36:37	0
9707474658	HITESH KALITA	9085341993	DIPAK DAS	15-Jul-14	20:36:41	0
9707474658	HITESH KALITA	9085341993	DIPAK DAS	15-Jul-14	20:38:25	0
9707474658	HITESH KALITA	9085341993	DIPAK DAS	15-Jul-14	20:40:39	0
9707474658	HITESH KALITA	9085341993	DIPAK DAS	15-Jul-14	20:48:06	0
9707474658	HITESH KALITA	9085341993	DIPAK DAS	15-Jul-14	20:51:14	0

Calling No.	Name	Called No.	Name	Date	Time	Dur(s)
9707474658	HITESH KALITA	9085341993	DIPAK DAS	15-Jul-14	20:53:16	0
9707474658	HITESH KALITA	9085341993	DIPAK DAS	15-Jul-14	20:57:00	0
9707474658	HITESH KALITA	9085341993	DIPAK DAS	15-Jul-14	21:50:44	0
9707474658	HITESH KALITA	9085341993	DIPAK DAS	15-Jul-14	21:57:05	0
9707474658	HITESH KALITA	9085341993	DIPAK DAS	15-Jul-14	22:02:12	0
9707474658	HITESH KALITA	9085341993	DIPAK DAS	15-Jul-14	22:12:56	0
9707474658	HITESH KALITA	9085341993	DIPAK DAS	15-Jul-14	22:18:41	0
9707474658	HITESH KALITA	9085341993	DIPAK DAS	15-Jul-14	22:22:34	0
9707474658	HITESH KALITA	9085341993	DIPAK DAS	15-Jul-14	22:24:51	0
9707474658	HITESH KALITA	9085341993	DIPAK DAS	15-Jul-14	22:27:24	0
9707474658	HITESH KALITA	9085341993	DIPAK DAS	15-Jul-14	22:35:31	0
9707474658	HITESH KALITA	41422D4149524F41	BANK MESSAGE	16-Jul-14	0:36:10	0
14B6BA643C1E07	BANK MESSAGE	9707474658	HITESH KALITA	16-Jul-14	6:25:14	0
1C96BC94D0A4F945	BANK MESSAGE	9707474658	HITESH KALITA	16-Jul-14	6:49:42	0
9707474658	HITESH KALITA	9085341993	DIPAK DAS	16-Jul-14	6:51:09	0
1C96BC94D0A4F945	BANK MESSAGE	9707474658	HITESH KALITA	16-Jul-14	8:48:47	0
1C96BC94D0A4F945	BANK MESSAGE	9707474658	HITESH KALITA	16-Jul-14	9:07:42	0
9707474658	HITESH KALITA	9085341993	DIPAK DAS	16-Jul-14	13:03:59	31
1C96BC94D0A4F945	BANK MESSAGE	9707474658	HITESH KALITA	16-Jul-14	13:24:26	0
9707474658	HITESH KALITA	9085341993	DIPAK DAS	16-Jul-14	19:16:57	0
14B6BA643C1E07	BANK MESSAGE	9707474658	HITESH KALITA	16-Jul-14	21:36:30	0

Calling No.	Name	Called No.	Name	Date	Time	Dur(s)
9854239285	ABHIJIT DEKA	9707474658	HITESH KALITA	16-Jul-14	21:36:37	0
9707474658	HITESH KALITA	9085341993	DIPAK DAS	16-Jul-14	21:42:26	0
9707474658	HITESH KALITA	9085341993	DIPAK DAS	16-Jul-14	21:42:30	0
9707474658	HITESH KALITA	9854239285	ABHIJIT DEKA	16-Jul-14	21:47:20	293
9707474658	HITESH KALITA	9085341993	DIPAK DAS	16-Jul-14	21:54:31	0
9707474658	HITESH KALITA	9085341993	DIPAK DAS	16-Jul-14	22:06:21	2
9707474658	HITESH KALITA	9085341993	DIPAK DAS	16-Jul-14	22:07:24	108
9707474658	HITESH KALITA	9085341993	DIPAK DAS	16-Jul-14	22:43:18	0
9707474658	HITESH KALITA	9854239285	ABHIJIT DEKA	17-Jul-14	8:29:20	41
CC66BC81C16158B4	BANK MESSAGE	9707474658	HITESH KALITA	17-Jul-14	9:44:48	0
9707474658	HITESH KALITA	9085341993	DIPAK DAS	17-Jul-14	10:51:01	14
1C96BC65381C2613	BANK MESSAGE	9707474658	HITESH KALITA	17-Jul-14	10:58:34	0
9707474658	HITESH KALITA	9085341993	DIPAK DAS	17-Jul-14	11:18:19	47
9707474658	HITESH KALITA	9854239285	ABHIJIT DEKA	17-Jul-14	12:42:38	527
9707474658	HITESH KALITA	9085341993	DIPAK DAS	17-Jul-14	21:09:39	22
9707474658	HITESH KALITA	9085341993	DIPAK DAS	17-Jul-14	21:31:02	21
9707474658	HITESH KALITA	9854239285	ABHIJIT DEKA	18-Jul-14	7:44:58	223
1C96BC94D0A4F945	BANK MESSAGE	9707474658	HITESH KALITA	18-Jul-14	7:57:50	0
9707474658	HITESH KALITA	9085341993	DIPAK DAS	18-Jul-14	7:59:00	0
1C96BC94D0A4F945	BANK MESSAGE	9707474658	HITESH KALITA	18-Jul-14	9:30:30	0
9707474658	HITESH KALITA	9085341993	DIPAK DAS	18-Jul-14	10:11:08	0

Calling No.	Name	Called No.	Name	Date	Time	Dur(s)
9707474658	HITESH KALITA	9085341993	DIPAK DAS	18-Jul-14	13:25:05	0
1C96BC65381CA623	BANK MESSAGE	9707474658	HITESH KALITA	18-Jul-14	14:39:02	0
9085341993	DIPAK DAS	9707474658	HITESH KALITA	18-Jul-14	19:11:58	8
9707474658	HITESH KALITA	9085341993	DIPAK DAS	18-Jul-14	19:57:53	0
1C96BC94D0A4F945	BANK MESSAGE	9707474658	HITESH KALITA	19-Jul-14	7:46:42	0
9707474658	HITESH KALITA	9085341993	DIPAK DAS	19-Jul-14	7:48:29	0
9707474658	HITESH KALITA	9854239285	ABHIJIT DEKA	19-Jul-14	9:06:33	778
9707474658	HITESH KALITA	9085341993	DIPAK DAS	19-Jul-14	9:20:27	0
1C96BC94D0A4F945	BANK MESSAGE	9707474658	HITESH KALITA	19-Jul-14	9:47:02	0
1C96BC94D0A4F945	BANK MESSAGE	9707474658	HITESH KALITA	19-Jul-14	13:22:38	0
9707474658	HITESH KALITA	9085341993	DIPAK DAS	19-Jul-14	14:33:43	0
9707474658	HITESH KALITA	9085341993	DIPAK DAS	19-Jul-14	21:02:41	0
1C96BC65381C6673	BANK MESSAGE	9707474658	HITESH KALITA	20-Jul-14	9:38:50	0
9707474658	HITESH KALITA	9854239285	ABHIJIT DEKA	20-Jul-14	11:48:38	306
1C96BC65385C6673	BANK MESSAGE	9707474658	HITESH KALITA	20-Jul-14	14:15:59	0
1C96BC94D0A4F945	BANK MESSAGE	9707474658	HITESH KALITA	20-Jul-14	14:59:43	0
9707474658	HITESH KALITA	9085341993	DIPAK DAS	20-Jul-14	15:00:15	0
1C96BC94D0A4F945	BANK MESSAGE	9707474658	HITESH KALITA	20-Jul-14	15:04:50	0
9707474658	HITESH KALITA	9854239285	ABHIJIT DEKA	20-Jul-14	16:24:19	61
9707474658	HITESH KALITA	9854239285	ABHIJIT DEKA	20-Jul-14	16:36:43	25
9707474658	HITESH KALITA	9854239285	ABHIJIT DEKA	20-Jul-14	20:30:52	96

Calling No.	Name	Called No.	Name	Date	Time	Dur(s)
9707474658	HITESH KALITA	9085341993	DIPAK DAS	20-Jul-14	21:02:04	37
9707474658	HITESH KALITA	9085341993	DIPAK DAS	20-Jul-14	22:45:34	79
9707474658	HITESH KALITA	9085341993	DIPAK DAS	21-Jul-14	8:33:35	50
9707474658	HITESH KALITA	9854239285	ABHIJIT DEKA	21-Jul-14	8:38:58	37
1C96BC94D0A4F945	BANK MESSAGE	9707474658	HITESH KALITA	21-Jul-14	11:57:42	0
1C96BC94D0A4F945	BANK MESSAGE	9707474658	HITESH KALITA	21-Jul-14	11:59:42	0
9707474658	HITESH KALITA	9085341993	DIPAK DAS	21-Jul-14	13:06:35	0
9707474658	HITESH KALITA	9085341993	DIPAK DAS	21-Jul-14	13:15:23	198
1C96BC94D0A4F945	BANK MESSAGE	9707474658	HITESH KALITA	21-Jul-14	13:23:14	0
DC66BA62395D2603	BANK MESSAGE	9707474658	HITESH KALITA	21-Jul-14	14:00:58	0
9707474658	HITESH KALITA	9854239285	ABHIJIT DEKA	21-Jul-14	16:23:09	15
9707474658	HITESH KALITA	9085341993	DIPAK DAS	21-Jul-14	18:55:03	0
9707474658	HITESH KALITA	9085341993	DIPAK DAS	21-Jul-14	19:15:56	0
9854239285	ABHIJIT DEKA	9707474658	HITESH KALITA	21-Jul-14	21:30:08	26
1C96BC94D0A4F945	BANK MESSAGE	9707474658	HITESH KALITA	22-Jul-14	9:49:35	0
9707474658	HITESH KALITA	9085341993	DIPAK DAS	22-Jul-14	9:50:28	0
1C96BC94D0A4F945	BANK MESSAGE	9707474658	HITESH KALITA	22-Jul-14	9:54:39	0
9854239285	ABHIJIT DEKA	9707474658	HITESH KALITA	22-Jul-14	10:27:53	4
9707474658	HITESH KALITA	9854239285	ABHIJIT DEKA	22-Jul-14	10:28:22	84
1C96BC94D0A4F945	BANK MESSAGE	9707474658	HITESH KALITA	22-Jul-14	13:22:27	0
2D66B889E93A9A65	BANK MESSAGE	9707474658	HITESH KALITA	22-Jul-14	14:04:40	0

Calling No.	Name	Called No.	Name	Date	Time	Dur(s)
9707474658	HITESH KALITA	9854239285	ABHIJIT DEKA	22-Jul-14	17:06:35	221
9707474658	HITESH KALITA	9854239285	ABHIJIT DEKA	22-Jul-14	17:10:30	89
1C96BC65381CA623	BANK MESSAGE	9707474658	HITESH KALITA	22-Jul-14	17:30:36	0
9707474658	HITESH KALITA	9854239285	ABHIJIT DEKA	23-Jul-14	14:28:23	165
9707474658	HITESH KALITA	9854239285	ABHIJIT DEKA	23-Jul-14	18:44:13	27
9854239285	ABHIJIT DEKA	9707474658	HITESH KALITA	23-Jul-14	19:07:39	56
9707474658	HITESH KALITA	9854239285	ABHIJIT DEKA	23-Jul-14	19:12:18	95
14B6BA643C1E07	BANK MESSAGE	9707474658	HITESH KALITA	24-Jul-14	6:18:16	0
9707474658	HITESH KALITA	9854239285	ABHIJIT DEKA	24-Jul-14	9:22:50	73
1C96BC65381CA623	BANK MESSAGE	9707474658	HITESH KALITA	24-Jul-14	14:08:04	0
9707474658	HITESH KALITA	9854239285	ABHIJIT DEKA	24-Jul-14	17:14:59	113
1C96BC94D0A4F945	BANK MESSAGE	9707474658	HITESH KALITA	25-Jul-14	10:44:06	0
1C96BC94D0A4F945	BANK MESSAGE	9707474658	HITESH KALITA	25-Jul-14	10:45:29	0
1C96BC94D0A4F945	BANK MESSAGE	9707474658	HITESH KALITA	25-Jul-14	13:24:49	0
9707474658	HITESH KALITA	9854239285	ABHIJIT DEKA	25-Jul-14	15:42:46	202
2D66B889E93A9A65	BANK MESSAGE	9707474658	HITESH KALITA	25-Jul-14	16:01:28	0
9707474658	HITESH KALITA	9085341993	DIPAK DAS	25-Jul-14	16:29:18	0
1C96BC65381CA623	BANK MESSAGE	9707474658	HITESH KALITA	26-Jul-14	13:02:36	0
9707474658	HITESH KALITA	9854239285	ABHIJIT DEKA	26-Jul-14	19:25:30	282
9707474658	HITESH KALITA	9854239285	ABHIJIT DEKA	26-Jul-14	19:31:00	219
1C96BC65381C6673	BANK MESSAGE	9707474658	HITESH KALITA	27-Jul-14	9:46:37	0

Calling No.	Name	Called No.	Name	Date	Time	Dur(s)
2D66B889E93A9A65	BANK MESSAGE	9707474658	HITESH KALITA	27-Jul-14	12:41:06	0
9707474658	HITESH KALITA	9854239285	ABHIJIT DEKA	28-Jul-14	10:41:29	338
9707474658	HITESH KALITA	9854239285	ABHIJIT DEKA	28-Jul-14	14:40:32	656
9707474658	HITESH KALITA	9859473420	BIBHA DEKA	28-Jul-14	16:08:12	133
9707474658	HITESH KALITA	9859473420	BIBHA DEKA	28-Jul-14	16:10:44	14
9707474658	HITESH KALITA	9085341993	DIPAK DAS	29-Jul-14	10:00:37	18
1C96BC65381CA623	BANK MESSAGE	9707474658	HITESH KALITA	29-Jul-14	13:31:31	0
2D66B889E93A1E97	BANK MESSAGE	9707474658	HITESH KALITA	29-Jul-14	14:17:59	0
2D66B889E93A1E97	BANK MESSAGE	9707474658	HITESH KALITA	29-Jul-14	14:18:46	0
9707474658	HITESH KALITA	9085341993	DIPAK DAS	29-Jul-14	15:45:51	21
9707474658	HITESH KALITA	9854239285	ABHIJIT DEKA	29-Jul-14	19:03:02	232
6D66B889E93A9A65	BANK MESSAGE	9707474658	HITESH KALITA	29-Jul-14	19:24:13	0
2D66B889E93A9A65	BANK MESSAGE	9707474658	HITESH KALITA	29-Jul-14	19:34:44	0
2D66B889E93A9A65	BANK MESSAGE	9707474658	HITESH KALITA	29-Jul-14	19:34:45	0
2D66B889E93A1E97	BANK MESSAGE	9707474658	HITESH KALITA	30-Jul-14	4:08:54	0
9707474658	HITESH KALITA	9085341993	DIPAK DAS	30-Jul-14	18:54:36	40
9707474658	HITESH KALITA	9854239285	ABHIJIT DEKA	30-Jul-14	19:34:00	402
1C96BC94D0A4F945	BANK MESSAGE	9707474658	HITESH KALITA	30-Jul-14	20:17:06	0
9085341993	DIPAK DAS	9707474658	HITESH KALITA	31-Jul-14	0:16:10	0
9085341993	DIPAK DAS	9707474658	HITESH KALITA	31-Jul-14	0:16:15	0
9707474658	HITESH KALITA	9085341993	DIPAK DAS	31-Jul-14	0:24:58	0

Calling No.	Name	Called No.	Name	Date	Time	Dur(s)
14B6BA643C1E07	BANK MESSAGE	9707474658	HITESH KALITA	31-Jul-14	9:06:20	0
9707474658	HITESH KALITA	9085341993	DIPAK DAS	31-Jul-14	9:19:05	16
6D66B889E93A9A65	BANK MESSAGE	9707474658	HITESH KALITA	31-Jul-14	12:40:41	0
4526B29452E01A34	BANK MESSAGE	9707474658	HITESH KALITA	31-Jul-14	17:32:08	0
9707474658	HITESH KALITA	9854239285	ABHIJIT DEKA	31-Jul-14	19:56:12	336
1C96BC94D0A4F945	BANK MESSAGE	9707474658	HITESH KALITA	31-Jul-14	21:22:05	0
9707474658	HITESH KALITA	9085341993	DIPAK DAS	31-Jul-14	21:28:53	0
9707474658	HITESH KALITA	9085341993	DIPAK DAS	31-Jul-14	21:28:57	0
9707474658	HITESH KALITA	9085341993	DIPAK DAS	31-Jul-14	22:47:20	30
9707474658	HITESH KALITA	9085341993	DIPAK DAS	31-Jul-14	22:49:54	230
9707474658	HITESH KALITA	9085341993	DIPAK DAS	31-Jul-14	22:54:11	2
9707474658	HITESH KALITA	9085341993	DIPAK DAS	31-Jul-14	22:55:18	240

Calling No.	Name	Called No.	Name	Date	Time	Dur(s)
9085341993	DIPAK DAS	9707474658	HITESH KALITA	1-Aug-14	0:02:59	0
14B6BA643C1E07	BANK MESSAGE	9707474658	HITESH KALITA	1-Aug-14	0:06:17	0
9085341993	DIPAK DAS	9707474658	HITESH KALITA	1-Aug-14	0:06:22	0
9707474658	HITESH KALITA	9854239285	ABHIJIT DEKA	1-Aug-14	10:17:08	44
9854239285	ABHIJIT DEKA	9707474658	HITESH KALITA	1-Aug-14	12:53:48	27
9085341993	DIPAK DAS	9707474658	HITESH KALITA	1-Aug-14	13:46:51	17
1C96BC65381CA623	BANK MESSAGE	9707474658	HITESH KALITA	1-Aug-14	14:53:46	0
9707474658	HITESH KALITA	9854239285	ABHIJIT DEKA	1-Aug-14	18:16:52	289
9707474658	HITESH KALITA	9854239285	ABHIJIT DEKA	1-Aug-14	18:22:09	212
9707474658	HITESH KALITA	9854239285	ABHIJIT DEKA	2-Aug-14	11:28:32	130
6D66B889E93A9A65	BANK MESSAGE	9707474658	HITESH KALITA	2-Aug-14	15:26:46	0
1C96BC65381C6643	BANK MESSAGE	9707474658	HITESH KALITA	2-Aug-14	15:52:03	0
9854239285	ABHIJIT DEKA	9707474658	HITESH KALITA	2-Aug-14	17:37:02	7
9707474658	HITESH KALITA	9854239285	ABHIJIT DEKA	2-Aug-14	20:05:32	1
9707474658	HITESH KALITA	9854239285	ABHIJIT DEKA	2-Aug-14	20:06:50	115
8822455206	RUPALIDAS	9707474658	HITESH KALITA	3-Aug-14	8:57:44	0
1C96BC65381C6643	BANK MESSAGE	9707474658	HITESH KALITA	3-Aug-14	15:07:22	0
1C96BC65381C0633	BANK MESSAGE	9707474658	HITESH KALITA	3-Aug-14	17:04:26	0
9707474658	HITESH KALITA	9854239285	ABHIJIT DEKA	4-Aug-14	11:50:46	62
9707474658	HITESH KALITA	8822058995	DHIRAJKALITA	4-Aug-14	12:09:08	11
1C96BC65381C6643	BANK MESSAGE	9707474658	HITESH KALITA	4-Aug-14	14:41:16	0

Calling No.	Name	Called No.	Name	Date	Time	Dur(s)
9854239285	ABHIJIT DEKA	9707474658	HITESH KALITA	4-Aug-14	16:49:19	11
9707474658	HITESH KALITA	9854239285	ABHIJIT DEKA	5-Aug-14	8:28:39	306
1C96BC65381C6643	BANK MESSAGE	9707474658	HITESH KALITA	5-Aug-14	10:48:36	0
1C96BC94D0A4F945	BANK MESSAGE	9707474658	HITESH KALITA	5-Aug-14	12:02:18	0
9707474658	HITESH KALITA	9085341993	DIPAK DAS	5-Aug-14	12:04:21	0
1C96BC94D0A4F945	BANK MESSAGE	9707474658	HITESH KALITA	5-Aug-14	12:04:55	0
1C96BC94D0A4F945	BANK MESSAGE	9707474658	HITESH KALITA	5-Aug-14	13:47:15	0
9707474658	HITESH KALITA	9085341993	DIPAK DAS	5-Aug-14	15:30:17	103
1C96BC65381C2613	BANK MESSAGE	9707474658	HITESH KALITA	5-Aug-14	16:38:37	0
9707474658	HITESH KALITA	9085341993	DIPAK DAS	5-Aug-14	19:50:19	85
9707474658	HITESH KALITA	9085341993	DIPAK DAS	6-Aug-14	10:02:24	32
14B6BA643C1E07	BANK MESSAGE	9707474658	HITESH KALITA	6-Aug-14	10:08:07	0
9707474658	HITESH KALITA	9085341993	DIPAK DAS	6-Aug-14	12:41:36	80
9707474658	HITESH KALITA	9085341993	DIPAK DAS	7-Aug-14	14:33:51	26
1C96BC65381C2613	BANK MESSAGE	9707474658	HITESH KALITA	7-Aug-14	14:44:57	0
549697C8E0BCFC56	BANK MESSAGE	9707474658	HITESH KALITA	7-Aug-14	18:25:25	0
14B6BA643C1E07	BANK MESSAGE	9707474658	HITESH KALITA	8-Aug-14	13:04:24	0
9707474658	HITESH KALITA	9854239285	ABHIJIT DEKA	8-Aug-14	13:32:30	118
1C96BC65381CA623	BANK MESSAGE	9707474658	HITESH KALITA	8-Aug-14	15:02:08	0
9707474658	HITESH KALITA	9085341993	DIPAK DAS	8-Aug-14	20:47:25	26
9707474658	HITESH KALITA	9085341993	DIPAK DAS	8-Aug-14	21:36:34	14

Calling No.	Name	Called No.	Name	Date	Time	Dur(s)
9707474658	HITESH KALITA	9085341993	DIPAK DAS	8-Aug-14	22:21:19	133
9707474658	HITESH KALITA	9085341993	DIPAK DAS	8-Aug-14	22:24:10	33
1C96BC65381C2623	BANK MESSAGE	9707474658	HITESH KALITA	9-Aug-14	15:07:48	0
9707474658	HITESH KALITA	9854239285	ABHIJIT DEKA	9-Aug-14	20:34:31	279
1C96BC65381C0633	BANK MESSAGE	9707474658	HITESH KALITA	10-Aug-14	13:19:53	0
1C96BC94D0A4F945	BANK MESSAGE	9707474658	HITESH KALITA	10-Aug-14	14:58:11	0
9707474658	HITESH KALITA	9085341993	DIPAK DAS	10-Aug-14	14:59:14	0
1C96BC94D0A4F945	BANK MESSAGE	9707474658	HITESH KALITA	10-Aug-14	14:59:30	0
9707474658	HITESH KALITA	9085341993	DIPAK DAS	10-Aug-14	15:24:29	71
14B6BA643C1E07	BANK MESSAGE	9707474658	HITESH KALITA	10-Aug-14	15:24:30	0
9085341993	DIPAK DAS	9707474658	HITESH KALITA	10-Aug-14	15:24:39	0
1476B282DB62D964	BANK MESSAGE	9707474658	HITESH KALITA	10-Aug-14	15:40:07	0
1476B282DB62D964	BANK MESSAGE	9707474658	HITESH KALITA	10-Aug-14	15:40:13	0
9707474658	HITESH KALITA	9085341993	DIPAK DAS	10-Aug-14	21:26:41	0
14B6BA643C1E07	BANK MESSAGE	9707474658	HITESH KALITA	10-Aug-14	22:53:13	0
9707474658	HITESH KALITA	9085341993	DIPAK DAS	11-Aug-14	7:42:25	32
14B6BA643C1E07	BANK MESSAGE	9707474658	HITESH KALITA	11-Aug-14	9:24:03	0
9085341993	DIPAK DAS	9707474658	HITESH KALITA	11-Aug-14	9:24:10	0
1C96BC94D0A4F945	BANK MESSAGE	9707474658	HITESH KALITA	11-Aug-14	16:35:02	0
9707474658	HITESH KALITA	9085341993	DIPAK DAS	11-Aug-14	16:36:12	0
1C96BC94D0A4F945	BANK MESSAGE	9707474658	HITESH KALITA	11-Aug-14	16:39:19	0

Calling No.	Name	Called No.	Name	Date	Time	Dur(s)
9707474658	HITESH KALITA	9085341993	DIPAK DAS	11-Aug-14	18:46:09	16
9707474658	HITESH KALITA	9854409154	KUSHAL KALITA	11-Aug-14	19:33:37	17
9707474658	HITESH KALITA	9854239285	ABHIJIT DEKA	12-Aug-14	6:36:16	44
1C96BC94D0A4F945	BANK MESSAGE	9707474658	HITESH KALITA	12-Aug-14	7:11:01	0
9707474658	HITESH KALITA	9085341993	DIPAK DAS	12-Aug-14	7:14:22	0
1C96BC94D0A4F945	BANK MESSAGE	9707474658	HITESH KALITA	12-Aug-14	9:44:55	0
1C96BC65381C2613	BANK MESSAGE	9707474658	HITESH KALITA	12-Aug-14	11:15:25	0
1C96BC94D0A4F945	BANK MESSAGE	9707474658	HITESH KALITA	12-Aug-14	13:36:20	0
9707474658	HITESH KALITA	9085341993	DIPAK DAS	12-Aug-14	13:46:45	0
549697C8E0BCFC56	BANK MESSAGE	9707474658	HITESH KALITA	12-Aug-14	18:20:26	0
9707474658	HITESH KALITA	9854239285	ABHIJIT DEKA	12-Aug-14	19:56:38	760
9707474658	HITESH KALITA	9854239285	ABHIJIT DEKA	12-Aug-14	20:54:05	540
9707474658	HITESH KALITA	9085341993	DIPAK DAS	12-Aug-14	21:39:04	0
9707474658	HITESH KALITA	9085341993	DIPAK DAS	12-Aug-14	22:21:41	0
1C96BC94D0A4F945	BANK MESSAGE	9707474658	HITESH KALITA	14-Aug-14	10:46:30	0
1C96BC94D0A4F945	BANK MESSAGE	9707474658	HITESH KALITA	14-Aug-14	11:03:04	0
1C96BC94D0A4F945	BANK MESSAGE	9707474658	HITESH KALITA	14-Aug-14	13:38:41	0
4C66B29F42A09AC4	BANK MESSAGE	9707474658	HITESH KALITA	14-Aug-14	15:21:24	0
1C96BC94D0A4F945	BANK MESSAGE	9707474658	HITESH KALITA	15-Aug-14	6:42:05	0
1C96BC94D0A4F945	BANK MESSAGE	9707474658	HITESH KALITA	15-Aug-14	9:56:29	0
1C96BC94D0A4F945	BANK MESSAGE	9707474658	HITESH KALITA	15-Aug-14	13:38:46	0

Calling No.	Name	Called No.	Name	Date	Time	Dur(s)
9707474658	HITESH KALITA	9854239285	ABHIJIT DEKA	15-Aug-14	19:31:22	217
9707474658	HITESH KALITA	9854239285	ABHIJIT DEKA	15-Aug-14	19:35:35	314
9085341993	DIPAK DAS	9707474658	HITESH KALITA	15-Aug-14	20:19:22	0
9085341993	DIPAK DAS	9707474658	HITESH KALITA	15-Aug-14	20:19:28	0
9707474658	HITESH KALITA	9085341993	DIPAK DAS	15-Aug-14	23:10:55	0
2D66B889E93A9A65	BANK MESSAGE	9707474658	HITESH KALITA	16-Aug-14	10:07:54	0
14B6BA643C1E07	BANK MESSAGE	9707474658	HITESH KALITA	16-Aug-14	13:36:03	0
9854239285	ABHIJIT DEKA	9707474658	HITESH KALITA	17-Aug-14	7:42:57	81
1C96BC65381C0633	BANK MESSAGE	9707474658	HITESH KALITA	17-Aug-14	11:29:00	0

CDR OF BUDIRAM MUKHTYAR

Callg Party No.	Name 1 Name 2 Name 3	Calld Party No.	Name 1 Name 2 Name 3	Start Date	Call Time	Bill Duration	Call Direction
9954724388	Nur Hussain	9864056457	BUDHIRAMUKTAIR	28-May-14	12:34:25	14	IN___CALL
9707913022	BHASKARDAS	9864056457	BUDHIRAMUKTAIR	29-May-14	11:25:4	135	IN___CALL
9954030931	REPORTER	9864056457	BUDHIRAMUKTAIR	29-May-14	12:11:1	34	IN___CALL
9954724388	Nur Hussain	9864056457	BUDHIRAMUKTAIR	29-May-14	19:7:3	41	IN___CALL
9864056457	BUDHIRAMUKTAIR	9954724388	Nur Hussain	29-May-14	20:58:5	27	OUT_CALL
9954724388	Nur Hussain	9864056457	BUDHIRAMUKTAIR	30-May-14	10:51:6	16	IN___CALL
9864056457	BUDHIRAMUKTAIR	9954724388	Nur Hussain	30-May-14	11:47:11	30	OUT_CALL
9864056457	BUDHIRAMUKTAIR	9954724388	Nur Hussain	30-May-14	18:45:51	20	OUT_CALL
9864056457	BUDHIRAMUKTAIR	9401311321	RANJIT MUKTIAR	30-May-14	22:2:59	170	OUT_CALL
9864056457	BUDHIRAMUKTAIR	9508756457	AMARENDRACHOUDHURY	30-May-14	23:0:33	184	OUT_CALL
9435156924	HITESH GOYARI	9864056457	BUDHIRAMUKTAIR	31-May-14	1:31:10	31	IN___CALL
9864056457	BUDHIRAMUKTAIR	9954724388	Nur Hussain	31-May-14	8:39:16	29	OUT_CALL
9707243173	BALENNAKALITA	9864056457	BUDHIRAMUKTAIR	01-Jun-14	20:20:14	73	IN___CALL
9707243173	BALENNAKALITA	9864056457	BUDHIRAMUKTAIR	01-Jun-14	21:2:27	35	IN___CALL
9707243173	BALENNAKALITA	9864056457	BUDHIRAMUKTAIR	01-Jun-14	21:37:22	29	IN___CALL
9707243173	BALENNAKALITA	9864056457	BUDHIRAMUKTAIR	02-Jun-14	9:9:34	23	IN___CALL
9864056457	BUDHIRAMUKTAIR	9435110176	KANTESWAR GOGOI	02-Jun-14	18:38:54	104	OUT_CALL
9707243173	BALENNAKALITA	9864056457	BUDHIRAMUKTAIR	02-Jun-14	18:53:30	11	IN___CALL
9864056457	BUDHIRAMUKTAIR	9707243173	BALENNAKALITA	02-Jun-14	19:27:44	13	OUT_CALL

Callg Party No.	Name 1 Name 2 Name 3	Calld Party No.	Name 1 Name 2 Name 3	Start Date	Call Time	Bill Duration	Call Direction
9707243173	BALENNAKALITA	9864056457	BUDHIRAMUKTAIR	02-Jun-14	21:48:23	29	IN___CALL
9707243173	BALENNAKALITA	9864056457	BUDHIRAMUKTAIR	02-Jun-14	22:23:34	21	IN___CALL
9707243173	BALENNAKALITA	9864056457	BUDHIRAMUKTAIR	02-Jun-14	22:41:21	32	IN___CALL
9435110176	KANTESWAR GOGOI	9864056457	BUDHIRAMUKTAIR	02-Jun-14	23:9:21	38	IN___CALL
9864056457	BUDHIRAMUKTAIR	9707243173	BALENNAKALITA	02-Jun-14	23:24:17	23	OUT_CALL
9707243173	BALENNAKALITA	9864056457	BUDHIRAMUKTAIR	02-Jun-14	23:38:41	61	IN___CALL
9864056457	BUDHIRAMUKTAIR	9707243173	BALENNAKALITA	03-Jun-14	0:29:3	28	OUT_CALL
9864056457	BUDHIRAMUKTAIR	9707243173	BALENNAKALITA	03-Jun-14	0:33:47	69	OUT_CALL
9707243173	BALENNAKALITA	9864056457	BUDHIRAMUKTAIR	03-Jun-14	0:38:16	24	IN___CALL
9707243173	BALENNAKALITA	9864056457	BUDHIRAMUKTAIR	03-Jun-14	0:43:2	17	IN___CALL
9707243173	BALENNAKALITA	9864056457	BUDHIRAMUKTAIR	03-Jun-14	0:49:32	31	IN___CALL
9435110176	KANTESWAR GOGOI	9864056457	BUDHIRAMUKTAIR	03-Jun-14	0:59:11	86	IN___CALL
9954030931	REPORTER	9864056457	BUDHIRAMUKTAIR	03-Jun-14	18:17:13	104	IN___CALL
9707913022	BHASKARDAS	9864056457	BUDHIRAMUKTAIR	03-Jun-14	19:21:36	23	IN___CALL
9577488227	DIPAK SARMA	9864056457	BUDHIRAMUKTAIR	04-Jun-14	8:19:6	2	IN___CALL
9864056457	BUDHIRAMUKTAIR	9577488227	DIPAK SARMA	04-Jun-14	8:21:30	32	OUT_CALL
9954030931	REPORTER	9864056457	BUDHIRAMUKTAIR	04-Jun-14	8:54:38	163	IN___CALL
9954724388	Nur Hussain	9864056457	BUDHIRAMUKTAIR	04-Jun-14	11:57:35	24	IN___CALL
9954724388	Nur Hussain	9864056457	BUDHIRAMUKTAIR	04-Jun-14	18:13:37	36	IN___CALL

Callg Party No.	Name 1 Name 2 Name 3	Calld Party No.	Name 1 Name 2 Name 3	Start Date	Call Time	Bill Duration	Call Direction
9954724388	Nur Hussain	9864056457	BUDHIRAMUKTAIR	04-Jun-14	18:19:17	11	IN___CALL
9954724388	Nur Hussain	9864056457	BUDHIRAMUKTAIR	04-Jun-14	18:49:24	18	IN___CALL
9864056457	BUDHIRAMUKTAIR	9707913022	BHASKARDAS	04-Jun-14	19:18:15	21	OUT_CALL
9707913022	BHASKARDAS	9864056457	BUDHIRAMUKTAIR	04-Jun-14	19:29:44	10	IN___CALL
9954724388	Nur Hussain	9864056457	BUDHIRAMUKTAIR	04-Jun-14	20:22:12	14	IN___CALL
9954030931	REPORTER	9864056457	BUDHIRAMUKTAIR	05-Jun-14	13:6:25	45	IN___CALL
9435110176	KANTESWAR GOGOI	9864056457	BUDHIRAMUKTAIR	05-Jun-14	23:12:22	248	IN___CALL
9954724388	Nur Hussain	9864056457	BUDHIRAMUKTAIR	08-Jun-14	9:40:0	69	IN___CALL
9954724388	Nur Hussain	9864056457	BUDHIRAMUKTAIR	08-Jun-14	14:42:13	87	IN___CALL
9954724388	Nur Hussain	9864056457	BUDHIRAMUKTAIR	08-Jun-14	18:30:58	17	IN___CALL
9435110176	KANTESWAR GOGOI	9864056457	BUDHIRAMUKTAIR	09-Jun-14	10:13:29	136	IN___CALL
9864056457	BUDHIRAMUKTAIR	9435110176	KANTESWAR GOGOI	09-Jun-14	14:43:46	39	OUT_CALL
9954724388	Nur Hussain	9864056457	BUDHIRAMUKTAIR	09-Jun-14	21:19:34	213	IN___CALL
9864056457	BUDHIRAMUKTAIR	9435110176	KANTESWAR GOGOI	10-Jun-14	8:47:9	15	OUT_CALL
9864056457	BUDHIRAMUKTAIR	9954724388	Nur Hussain	10-Jun-14	17:41:18	20	OUT_CALL
9864056457	BUDHIRAMUKTAIR	9954724388	Nur Hussain	11-Jun-14	9:12:45	39	OUT_CALL
9954724388	Nur Hussain	9864056457	BUDHIRAMUKTAIR	12-Jun-14	21:36:18	10	IN___CALL
9954724388	Nur Hussain	9864056457	BUDHIRAMUKTAIR	13-Jun-14	14:9:14	23	IN___CALL
9954724388	Nur Hussain	9864056457	BUDHIRAMUKTAIR	13-Jun-14	16:28:26	31	IN___CALL

Callg Party No.	Name 1 Name 2 Name 3	Calld Party No.	Name 1 Name 2 Name 3	Start Date	Call Time	Bill Duration	Call Direction
9577488227	DIPAK SARMA	9864056457	BUDHIRAMUKTAIR	14-Jun-14	13:43:26	33	IN___CALL
9864056457	BUDHIRAMUKTAIR	9954724388	Nur Hussain	14-Jun-14	14:52:53	30	OUT_CALL
9864056457	BUDHIRAMUKTAIR	9435110176	KANTESWAR GOGOI	14-Jun-14	17:25:26	64	OUT_CALL
9435110176	KANTESWAR GOGOI	9864056457	BUDHIRAMUKTAIR	14-Jun-14	17:38:24	372	IN___CALL
9577488227	DIPAK SARMA	9864056457	BUDHIRAMUKTAIR	15-Jun-14	13:12:25	23	IN___CALL
9954724388	NOOR HUSSAIN	9864056457	BUDHIRAMUKTAIR	16-Jun-14	12:48:12	76	IN___CALL
9954030931	REPORTER	9864056457	BUDHIRAMUKTAIR	16-Jun-14	13:51:45	27	IN___CALL
9954724388	NOOR HUSSAIN	9864056457	BUDHIRAMUKTAIR	16-Jun-14	18:0:57	10	IN___CALL
9864056457	BUDHIRAMUKTAIR	9954724388	NOOR HUSSAIN	17-Jun-14	8:37:24	33	OUT_CALL
9954724388	NOOR HUSSAIN	9864056457	BUDHIRAMUKTAIR	17-Jun-14	8:40:8	38	IN___CALL
9954724388	NOOR HUSSAIN	9864056457	BUDHIRAMUKTAIR	17-Jun-14	8:48:5	56	IN___CALL
9864056457	BUDHIRAMUKTAIR	9954724388	NOOR HUSSAIN	17-Jun-14	13:16:7	32	OUT_CALL
9954724388	NOOR HUSSAIN	9864056457	BUDHIRAMUKTAIR	17-Jun-14	13:19:54	30	IN___CALL
9954724388	NOOR HUSSAIN	9864056457	BUDHIRAMUKTAIR	18-Jun-14	9:21:4	23	IN___CALL
9954030931	REPORTER	9864056457	BUDHIRAMUKTAIR	21-Jun-14	14:6:19	47	IN___CALL
9864056457	BUDHIRAMUKTAIR	9954724388	NOOR HUSSAIN	21-Jun-14	14:7:45	36	OUT_CALL
9954724388	NOOR HUSSAIN	9864056457	BUDHIRAMUKTAIR	21-Jun-14	14:9:19	53	IN___CALL
9864056457	BUDHIRAMUKTAIR	9954724388	NOOR HUSSAIN	21-Jun-14	14:12:13	20	OUT_CALL
9954724388	NOOR HUSSAIN	9864056457	BUDHIRAMUKTAIR	25-Jun-14	20:37:44	51	IN___CALL
9401564532		9864056457	BUDHIRAMUKTAIR	25-Jun-14	21:48:49	106	IN___CALL

Callg Party No.	Name 1 Name 2 Name 3	Calld Party No.	Name 1 Name 2 Name 3	Start Date	Call Time	Bill Duration	Call Direction
9864056457	BUDHIRAMUKTAIR	9954724388	NOOR HUSSAIN	25-Jun-14	22:50:44	35	OUT_CALL
9864056457	BUDHIRAMUKTAIR	9954724388	NOOR HUSSAIN	26-Jun-14	11:53:53	100	OUT_CALL
9954724388	NOOR HUSSAIN	9864056457	BUDHIRAMUKTAIR	26-Jun-14	12:12:5	8	IN___CALL
9864056457	BUDHIRAMUKTAIR	9954724388	NOOR HUSSAIN	27-Jun-14	18:42:3	36	OUT_CALL
9864056457	BUDHIRAMUKTAIR	9954724388	NOOR HUSSAIN	29-Jun-14	10:2:6	21	OUT_CALL
9954724388	NOOR HUSSAIN	9864056457	BUDHIRAMUKTAIR	29-Jun-14	21:3:58	189	IN___CALL
9954724388	NOOR HUSSAIN	9864056457	BUDHIRAMUKTAIR	04-Jul-14	10:31:45	25	IN___CALL
9954724388	NOOR HUSSAIN	9864056457	BUDHIRAMUKTAIR	04-Jul-14	13:12:30	56	IN___CALL
9954724388	NOOR HUSSAIN	9864056457	BUDHIRAMUKTAIR	05-Jul-14	11:27:58	41	IN___CALL
9864056457	BUDHIRAMUKTAIR	9954724388	NOOR HUSSAIN	05-Jul-14	14:43:34	9	OUT_CALL
9954724388	NOOR HUSSAIN	9864056457	BUDHIRAMUKTAIR	05-Jul-14	15:1:1	24	IN___CALL
9864056457	BUDHIRAMUKTAIR	9954724388	NOOR HUSSAIN	05-Jul-14	22:18:36	54	OUT_CALL
9954724388	NOOR HUSSAIN	9864056457	BUDHIRAMUKTAIR	09-Jul-14	12:20:50	13	IN___CALL
9954724388	NOOR HUSSAIN	9864056457	BUDHIRAMUKTAIR	11-Jul-14	8:40:45	28	IN___CALL
9954724388	NOOR HUSSAIN	9864056457	BUDHIRAMUKTAIR	11-Jul-14	11:15:24	35	IN___CALL
9954724388	NOOR HUSSAIN	9864056457	BUDHIRAMUKTAIR	11-Jul-14	21:47:22	29	IN___CALL
9954724388	NOOR HUSSAIN	9864056457	BUDHIRAMUKTAIR	12-Jul-14	7:49:10	118	IN___CALL
9954724388	NOOR HUSSAIN	9864056457	BUDHIRAMUKTAIR	12-Jul-14	8:26:22	16	IN___CALL
9954724388	NOOR HUSSAIN	9864056457	BUDHIRAMUKTAIR	12-Jul-14	22:51:32	72	IN___CALL
9954724388	NOOR HUSSAIN	9864056457	BUDHIRAMUKTAIR	13-Jul-14	9:56:5	58	IN___CALL
9954724388	NOOR HUSSAIN	9864056457	BUDHIRAMUKTAIR	13-Jul-14	22:22:16	88	IN___CALL

Callg Party No.	Name 1 Name 2 Name 3	Calld Party No.	Name 1 Name 2 Name 3	Start Date	Call Time	Bill Duration	Call Direction
9864056457	BUDHIRAMUKTAIR	9954724388	NOOR HUSSAIN	13-Jul-14	22:24:12	328	OUT_CALL
9954724388	NOOR HUSSAIN	9864056457	BUDHIRAMUKTAIR	15-Jul-14	9:47:58	20	IN__CALL
9954724388	NOOR HUSSAIN	9864056457	BUDHIRAMUKTAIR	19-Jul-14	13:59:29	45	IN__CALL
9954724388	NOOR HUSSAIN	9864056457	BUDHIRAMUKTAIR	19-Jul-14	14:23:31	49	IN__CALL
9954724388	NOOR HUSSAIN	9864056457	BUDHIRAMUKTAIR	19-Jul-14	14:33:32	38	IN__CALL
9954724388	NOOR HUSSAIN	9864056457	BUDHIRAMUKTAIR	19-Jul-14	16:41:15	30	IN__CALL
9954724388	NOOR HUSSAIN	9864056457	BUDHIRAMUKTAIR	20-Jul-14	7:11:37	30	IN__CALL
9954724388	NOOR HUSSAIN	9864056457	BUDHIRAMUKTAIR	20-Jul-14	18:33:49	57	IN__CALL
9954724388	NOOR HUSSAIN	9864056457	BUDHIRAMUKTAIR	20-Jul-14	19:16:43	23	IN__CALL
9954724388	NOOR HUSSAIN	9864056457	BUDHIRAMUKTAIR	21-Jul-14	21:12:39	110	IN__CALL
9954724388	NOOR HUSSAIN	9864056457	BUDHIRAMUKTAIR	23-Jul-14	8:32:23	13	IN__CALL
9954724388	NOOR HUSSAIN	9864056457	BUDHIRAMUKTAIR	26-Jul-14	10:36:7	23	IN__CALL
9954724388	NOOR HUSSAIN	9864056457	BUDHIRAMUKTAIR	26-Jul-14	20:39:29	50	IN__CALL
9954724388	NOOR HUSSAIN	9864056457	BUDHIRAMUKTAIR	26-Jul-14	22:33:20	17	IN__CALL
9954724388	NOOR HUSSAIN	9864056457	BUDHIRAMUKTAIR	27-Jul-14	7:54:49	74	IN__CALL
9954724388	NOOR HUSSAIN	9864056457	BUDHIRAMUKTAIR	27-Jul-14	9:8:26	29	IN__CALL
9954724388	NOOR HUSSAIN	9864056457	BUDHIRAMUKTAIR	30-Jul-14	10:53:43	8	IN__CALL
9954724388	NOOR HUSSAIN	9864056457	BUDHIRAMUKTAIR	30-Jul-14	11:5:35	28	IN__CALL
9954724388	NOOR HUSSAIN	9864056457	BUDHIRAMUKTAIR	30-Jul-14	12:4:41	13	IN__CALL
9954724388	NOOR HUSSAIN	9864056457	BUDHIRAMUKTAIR	30-Jul-14	13:26:30	57	IN__CALL

Callg Party No.	Name 1 Name 2 Name 3	Calld Party No.	Name 1 Name 2 Name 3	Start Date	Call Time	Bill Duration	Call Direction
9954724388	NOOR HUSSAIN	9864056457	BUDHIRAMUKTAIR	30-Jul-14	16:6:14	91	IN___CALL
9954724388	NOOR HUSSAIN	9864056457	BUDHIRAMUKTAIR	31-Jul-14	6:54:10	29	IN___CALL
9954724388	NOOR HUSSAIN	9864056457	BUDHIRAMUKTAIR	31-Jul-14	12:17:57	13	IN___CALL
9954724388	NOOR HUSSAIN	9864056457	BUDHIRAMUKTAIR	01-Aug-14	18:3:23	5	IN___CALL
9954724388	NOOR HUSSAIN	9864056457	BUDHIRAMUKTAIR	01-Aug-14	19:9:39	7	IN___CALL
9864056457	BUDHIRAMUKTAIR	9954724388	NOOR HUSSAIN	03-Aug-14	21:37:11	85	OUT_CALL
9954724388	NOOR HUSSAIN	9864056457	BUDHIRAMUKTAIR	03-Aug-14	21:40:31	38	IN___CALL
9954724388	NOOR HUSSAIN	9864056457	BUDHIRAMUKTAIR	05-Aug-14	12:50:21	183	IN___CALL
9954724388	NOOR HUSSAIN	9864056457	BUDHIRAMUKTAIR	05-Aug-14	19:27:28	30	IN___CALL
9954724388	NOOR HUSSAIN	9864056457	BUDHIRAMUKTAIR	06-Aug-14	12:14:51	72	IN___CALL
9954724388	NOOR HUSSAIN	9864056457	BUDHIRAMUKTAIR	07-Aug-14	7:2:26	9	IN___CALL
9954724388	NOOR HUSSAIN	9864056457	BUDHIRAMUKTAIR	08-Aug-14	12:2:52	29	IN___CALL
9864056457	BUDHIRAMUKTAIR	9954724388	NOOR HUSSAIN	09-Aug-14	21:8:27	9	OUT_CALL
9954724388	NOOR HUSSAIN	9864056457	BUDHIRAMUKTAIR	09-Aug-14	21:8:57	81	IN___CALL
9954724388	NOOR HUSSAIN	9864056457	BUDHIRAMUKTAIR	10-Aug-14	9:2:21	26	IN___CALL
9864056457		9954724388	NOOR HUSSAIN	10-Aug-14	10:16:54	1	OUT_CALL
9954724388	NOOR HUSSAIN	9864056457	BUDHIRAMUKTAIR	10-Aug-14	10:17:11	16	IN___CALL
9954724388	NOOR HUSSAIN	9864056457	BUDHIRAMUKTAIR	11-Aug-14	10:29:12	14	IN___CALL
9954724388	NOOR HUSSAIN	9864056457	BUDHIRAMUKTAIR	11-Aug-14	22:20:58	147	IN___CALL
9954724388	NOOR HUSSAIN	9864056457	BUDHIRAMUKTAIR	11-Aug-14	22:31:13	62	IN___CALL

Callg Party No.	Name 1 Name 2 Name 3	Calld Party No.	Name 1 Name 2 Name 3	Start Date	Call Time	Bill Duration	Call Direction
9954724388	NOOR HUSSAIN	9864056457	BUDHIRAMUKTAIR	11-Aug-14	22:37:40	261	IN___CALL
9954724388	NOOR HUSSAIN	9864056457	BUDHIRAMUKTAIR	11-Aug-14	23:4:45	33	IN___CALL
9954724388	NOOR HUSSAIN	9864056457	BUDHIRAMUKTAIR	12-Aug-14	0:52:40	37	IN___CALL
9954724388	NOOR HUSSAIN	9864056457	BUDHIRAMUKTAIR	12-Aug-14	0:54:46	30	IN___CALL
9954724388	NOOR HUSSAIN	9864056457	BUDHIRAMUKTAIR	12-Aug-14	0:57:9	11	IN___CALL
9954724388	NOOR HUSSAIN	9864056457	BUDHIRAMUKTAIR	12-Aug-14	0:59:50		IN___SMS
9954724388	NOOR HUSSAIN	9864056457	BUDHIRAMUKTAIR	12-Aug-14	1:0:32		IN___SMS
9954724388	NOOR HUSSAIN	9864056457	BUDHIRAMUKTAIR	12-Aug-14	1:0:43	9	IN___CALL
9954724388	NOOR HUSSAIN	9864056457	BUDHIRAMUKTAIR	12-Aug-14	1:19:47	57	IN___CALL
9954724388	NOOR HUSSAIN	9864056457	BUDHIRAMUKTAIR	12-Aug-14	1:30:7	46	IN___CALL
9954724388	NOOR HUSSAIN	9864056457	BUDHIRAMUKTAIR	12-Aug-14	6:44:0	21	IN___CALL
9954724388	NOOR HUSSAIN	9864056457	BUDHIRAMUKTAIR	12-Aug-14	10:26:58	58	IN___CALL

CDR OF MANJU ORANG

Calling No.	Name 1 Name 2 Name 3	Called No.	Name 1 Name 2 Name 3	Date	Time	Dur(s)
9796666409	Akhnoor (J&K)	9954454011	MRS MANJU URANG	28-May-14	20:42:16	20
9796666409	Akhnoor (J&K)	9954454011	MRS MANJU URANG	28-May-14	20:48:43	257
9954454011	MRS MANJU URANG	9796666409	Akhnoor (J&K)	29-May-14	17:06:04	300
9707243173	BALENNAKALITA	9954454011	MRS MANJU URANG	30-May-14	11:11:25	21
9401165464	HITESWAR KALITA	9954454011	MRS MANJU URANG	30-May-14	14:56:23	58
9707243173	BALENNAKALITA	9954454011	MRS MANJU URANG	1-Jun-14	20:22:10	64
9707243173	BALENNAKALITA	9954454011	MRS MANJU URANG	1-Jun-14	20:26:49	48
9707243173	BALENNAKALITA	9954454011	MRS MANJU URANG	1-Jun-14	20:32:20	64
059697C8E0BCFC56	Bank Message	9954454011	MRS MANJU URANG	2-Jun-14	19:02:36	0
9401794760	MR MIRNAL DAS	9954454011	MRS MANJU URANG	3-Jun-14	12:25:24	73
9796666409	Akhnoor (J&K)	9954454011	MRS MANJU URANG	3-Jun-14	20:36:17	1197
9577658674	NAYAN MURARI	9954454011	MRS MANJU URANG	3-Jun-14	22:15:13	96
9577657408	SAYTAJIT DAS	9954454011	MRS MANJU URANG	4-Jun-14	10:38:26	33
9577657408	SAYTAJIT DAS	9954454011	MRS MANJU URANG	4-Jun-14	10:43:19	31
14B6BA643C1E07	Bank Message	9954454011	MRS MANJU URANG	6-Jun-14	15:47:08	0
9596726858	Akhnoor (J&K)	9954454011	MRS MANJU URANG	6-Jun-14	15:49:08	41
9796666409	Akhnoor (J&K)	9954454011	MRS MANJU URANG	7-Jun-14	12:22:07	700
4C66BCA942219A84	Bank Message	9954454011	MRS MANJU URANG	8-Jun-14	9:41:04	0
14B6BA643C1E07	Bank Message	9954454011	MRS MANJU URANG	9-Jun-14	11:51:15	0

Calling No.	Name 1 Name 2 Name 3	Called No.	Name 1 Name 2 Name 3	Date	Time	Dur(s)
1426BCA942219A84	Bank Message	9954454011	MRS MANJU URANG	9-Jun-14	11:55:36	0
44D6BCA942219A84	Bank Message	9954454011	MRS MANJU URANG	11-Jun-14	16:09:42	0
1426BCA942219A84	Bank Message	9954454011	MRS MANJU URANG	12-Jun-14	15:28:31	0
9469897501	Akhnoor (J&K)	9954454011	MRS MANJU URANG	13-Jun-14	21:40:54	58
9469897501	Akhnoor (J&K)	9954454011	MRS MANJU URANG	14-Jun-14	7:03:55	40
9469897501	Akhnoor (J&K)	9954454011	MRS MANJU URANG	14-Jun-14	7:05:11	37
9469897501	Akhnoor (J&K)	9954454011	MRS MANJU URANG	14-Jun-14	7:06:40	20
9469897501	Akhnoor (J&K)	9954454011	MRS MANJU URANG	14-Jun-14	7:07:30	128
1426BCA942219A84	Bank Message	9954454011	MRS MANJU URANG	14-Jun-14	14:17:47	0
1426BCA942219A84	Bank Message	9954454011	MRS MANJU URANG	14-Jun-14	17:56:39	0
9469897501	Akhnoor (J&K)	9954454011	MRS MANJU URANG	16-Jun-14	10:04:42	63
9469897501	Akhnoor (J&K)	9954454011	MRS MANJU URANG	16-Jun-14	15:02:46	906
9469897501	Akhnoor (J&K)	9954454011	MRS MANJU URANG	16-Jun-14	15:18:50	221
9469897501	Akhnoor (J&K)	9954454011	MRS MANJU URANG	17-Jun-14	19:49:11	293
9469897501	Akhnoor (J&K)	9954454011	MRS MANJU URANG	17-Jun-14	19:54:42	405
9954454011	MRS MANJU URANG	9796665001	Akhnoor (J&K)	18-Jun-14	13:54:53	137
9796665001	Akhnoor (J&K)	9954454011	MRS MANJU URANG	18-Jun-14	14:01:02	325
9954454011	MRS MANJU URANG	9906006851	Akhnoor (J&K)	21-Jun-14	7:42:56	38
9906006851	Akhnoor (J&K)	9954454011	MRS MANJU URANG	21-Jun-14	10:20:41	520
9906006851	Akhnoor (J&K)	9954454011	MRS MANJU URANG	21-Jun-14	13:35:01	24

Calling No.	Name 1 Name 2 Name 3	Called No.	Name 1 Name 2 Name 3	Date	Time	Dur(s)
9906006851	Akhnoor (J&K)	9954454011	MRS MANJU URANG	23-Jun-14	8:01:45	67
9906006851	Akhnoor (J&K)	9954454011	MRS MANJU URANG	23-Jun-14	18:06:19	138
9954454011	MRS MANJU URANG	9906006851	Akhnoor (J&K)	24-Jun-14	19:13:18	300
9906006851	Akhnoor (J&K)	9954454011	MRS MANJU URANG	25-Jun-14	7:28:59	88
9906006851	Akhnoor (J&K)	9954454011	MRS MANJU URANG	25-Jun-14	7:31:10	63
14B6BA643C1E07	Bank Message	9954454011	MRS MANJU URANG	25-Jun-14	16:11:32	0
9906006851	Akhnoor (J&K)	9954454011	MRS MANJU URANG	25-Jun-14	19:56:59	809
9906006851	Akhnoor (J&K)	9954454011	MRS MANJU URANG	27-Jun-14	10:52:16	94
9906006851	Akhnoor (J&K)	9954454011	MRS MANJU URANG	27-Jun-14	11:32:23	22
1426BCA942219A84	Bank Message	9954454011	MRS MANJU URANG	27-Jun-14	15:29:47	0
9906006851	Akhnoor (J&K)	9954454011	MRS MANJU URANG	27-Jun-14	19:02:36	241
1426BCA942219A84	Bank Message	9954454011	MRS MANJU URANG	29-Jun-14	14:05:49	0
9906006851	Akhnoor (J&K)	9954454011	MRS MANJU URANG	30-Jun-14	9:40:44	579
1426BCA942219A84	Bank Message	9954454011	MRS MANJU URANG	30-Jun-14	17:42:44	0
4C66BCA942219A84	Bank Message	9954454011	MRS MANJU URANG	1-Jul-14	13:08:41	0
9906006851	Akhnoor (J&K)	9954454011	MRS MANJU URANG	1-Jul-14	13:57:10	391
9906006851	Akhnoor (J&K)	9954454011	MRS MANJU URANG	3-Jul-14	19:59:33	72
9906006851	Akhnoor (J&K)	9954454011	MRS MANJU URANG	3-Jul-14	20:30:52	63
9906006851	Akhnoor (J&K)	9954454011	MRS MANJU URANG	4-Jul-14	6:00:19	385
4C66BCA942219A84	Bank Message	9954454011	MRS MANJU URANG	4-Jul-14	13:03:06	0

Calling No.	Name 1 Name 2 Name 3	Called No.	Name 1 Name 2 Name 3	Date	Time	Dur(s)
9954454011	MRS MANJU URANG	9906006851	Akhnoor (J&K)	4-Jul-14	19:13:36	240
9906006851	Akhnoor (J&K)	9954454011	MRS MANJU URANG	4-Jul-14	19:18:16	297
4C66BCA942219A84	Bank Message	9954454011	MRS MANJU URANG	5-Jul-14	14:21:50	0
9906006851	Akhnoor (J&K)	9954454011	MRS MANJU URANG	6-Jul-14	17:09:43	830
9906006851	Akhnoor (J&K)	9954454011	MRS MANJU URANG	7-Jul-14	15:04:43	31
9906006851	Akhnoor (J&K)	9954454011	MRS MANJU URANG	7-Jul-14	20:16:40	285
9796666409	Akhnoor (J&K)	9954454011	MRS MANJU URANG	9-Jul-14	21:06:52	88
9796666409	Akhnoor (J&K)	9954454011	MRS MANJU URANG	10-Jul-14	13:16:24	432
9796666409	Akhnoor (J&K)	9954454011	MRS MANJU URANG	10-Jul-14	19:41:11	16
9796666409	Akhnoor (J&K)	9954454011	MRS MANJU URANG	10-Jul-14	19:42:25	470
9796666409	Akhnoor (J&K)	9954454011	MRS MANJU URANG	11-Jul-14	17:53:51	2
9796666409	Akhnoor (J&K)	9954454011	MRS MANJU URANG	11-Jul-14	17:55:26	291
9678243858	Pankaj Rabha	9954454011	MRS MANJU URANG	14-Jul-14	12:11:55	5
059697C8E0BCFC56	Bank Message	9954454011	MRS MANJU URANG	14-Jul-14	13:44:07	0
9954454011	MRS MANJU URANG	9796666409	Akhnoor (J&K)	14-Jul-14	14:01:03	45
24D6BCA942219A84	Bank Message	9954454011	MRS MANJU URANG	16-Jul-14	10:32:30	0
24D6BCA942219A84	Bank Message	9954454011	MRS MANJU URANG	17-Jul-14	12:04:02	0
2CB6BCA942219A84	Bank Message	9954454011	MRS MANJU URANG	18-Jul-14	14:08:49	0
14B6BA643C1E07	Bank Message	9954454011	MRS MANJU URANG	19-Jul-14	6:07:31	0
2CB6BCA942219A84	Bank Message	9954454011	MRS MANJU URANG	20-Jul-14	16:55:39	0

Calling No.	Name 1 Name 2 Name 3	Called No.	Name 1 Name 2 Name 3	Date	Time	Dur(s)
2CB6BCA942219A84	Bank Message	9954454011	MRS MANJU URANG	21-Jul-14	17:08:51	0
14B6BA643C1E07	Bank Message	9954454011	MRS MANJU URANG	22-Jul-14	17:31:00	0
2CB6BCA942219A84	Bank Message	9954454011	MRS MANJU URANG	22-Jul-14	17:33:17	0
6D66BCA942219A84	Bank Message	9954454011	MRS MANJU URANG	22-Jul-14	19:15:57	0
6D66BCA942219A84	Bank Message	9954454011	MRS MANJU URANG	22-Jul-14	19:16:13	0
2CB6BCA942219A84	Bank Message	9954454011	MRS MANJU URANG	23-Jul-14	16:59:50	0
2486BCA942219A84	Bank Message	9954454011	MRS MANJU URANG	30-Jul-14	16:03:19	0
14B6BA643C1E07	Bank Message	9954454011	MRS MANJU URANG	2-Aug-14	19:22:39	0
14B6BA643C1E07	Bank Message	9954454011	MRS MANJU URANG	2-Aug-14	19:23:05	0
2486BCA942219A84	Bank Message	9954454011	MRS MANJU URANG	2-Aug-14	19:25:58	0
2486BCA942219A84	Bank Message	9954454011	MRS MANJU URANG	3-Aug-14	12:30:52	0
14B6BA643C1E07	Bank Message	9954454011	MRS MANJU URANG	4-Aug-14	8:51:58	0
CC66BCA942219A84	Bank Message	9954454011	MRS MANJU URANG	4-Aug-14	18:13:06	0
CC66BCA942219A84	Bank Message	9954454011	MRS MANJU URANG	5-Aug-14	13:52:30	0
1C66BCA942219A84	Bank Message	9954454011	MRS MANJU URANG	6-Aug-14	18:42:13	0
1C66BCA942219A84	Bank Message	9954454011	MRS MANJU URANG	6-Aug-14	18:42:18	0
1C66BCA942219A84	Bank Message	9954454011	MRS MANJU URANG	7-Aug-14	12:41:12	0

CDR OF DIPAK DAS

Calling (A) Party Telephone Number/ MSISDN	Name	Called (B) Party Telephone Number/ Access Point Name	Name	Date	Time	Duration In Secs.
9085341993	DIPAK DAS	9707783876	GIASUDDINAHMED	3/8/2014	7:05:32	0
9085341993	DIPAK DAS	9707783876	GIASUDDINAHMED	3/8/2014	6:39:09	0
9085341993	DIPAK DAS	9707783876	GIASUDDINAHMED	3/8/2014	0:33:39	0
9085341993	DIPAK DAS	9707783876	GIASUDDINAHMED	3/8/2014	0:29:45	0
9085341993	DIPAK DAS	9707783876	GIASUDDINAHMED	3/8/2014	0:25:58	0
9085341993	DIPAK DAS	9707783876	GIASUDDINAHMED	3/8/2014	0:20:32	0
9085341993	DIPAK DAS	9707783876	GIASUDDINAHMED	3/8/2014	0:17:53	0
9085341993	DIPAK DAS	9707783876	GIASUDDINAHMED	3/8/2014	0:17:25	0
9085341993	DIPAK DAS	9707783876	GIASUDDINAHMED	3/8/2014	0:14:32	0
9085341993	DIPAK DAS	9707783876	GIASUDDINAHMED	3/8/2014	0:12:55	0
9085341993	DIPAK DAS	9707783876	GIASUDDINAHMED	3/8/2014	0:10:37	0
9085341993	DIPAK DAS	9707783876	GIASUDDINAHMED	3/8/2014	0:07:58	0
9085341993	DIPAK DAS	9707783876	GIASUDDINAHMED	3/8/2014	0:05:25	0
9085341993	DIPAK DAS	9707783876	GIASUDDINAHMED	3/8/2014	0:04:04	0
9085341993	DIPAK DAS	9707783876	GIASUDDINAHMED	3/8/2014	0:02:14	0
9085341993	DIPAK DAS	9707783876	GIASUDDINAHMED	2/8/2014	23:59:28	0
9085341993	DIPAK DAS	9707783876	GIASUDDINAHMED	2/8/2014	23:59:02	0

Calling (A) Party Telephone Number/ MSISDN	Name	Called (B) Party Telephone Number/ Access Point Name	Name	Date	Time	Duration In Secs.
9085341993	DIPAK DAS	9707783876	GIASUDDINAHMED	2/8/2014	23:56:30	0
9085341993	DIPAK DAS	9707783876	GIASUDDINAHMED	2/8/2014	23:55:21	0
9085341993	DIPAK DAS	9707783876	GIASUDDINAHMED	2/8/2014	23:53:13	0
9085341993	DIPAK DAS	9707783876	GIASUDDINAHMED	2/8/2014	23:36:55	899
9085341993	DIPAK DAS	9707783876	GIASUDDINAHMED	2/8/2014	23:34:49	0
9085341993	DIPAK DAS	9707783876	GIASUDDINAHMED	2/8/2014	23:32:53	0
9085341993	DIPAK DAS	9707783876	GIASUDDINAHMED	2/8/2014	23:32:19	0
9085341993	DIPAK DAS	9707783876	GIASUDDINAHMED	2/8/2014	23:28:10	121
9085341993	DIPAK DAS	9707783876	GIASUDDINAHMED	2/8/2014	23:26:45	0
9085341993	DIPAK DAS	9707783876	GIASUDDINAHMED	2/8/2014	23:24:40	0
9085341993	DIPAK DAS	9707783876	GIASUDDINAHMED	2/8/2014	23:21:54	0
9085341993	DIPAK DAS	9707783876	GIASUDDINAHMED	2/8/2014	23:20:10	0
9085341993	DIPAK DAS	9707783876	GIASUDDINAHMED	2/8/2014	23:19:31	0
9085341993	DIPAK DAS	9707783876	GIASUDDINAHMED	2/8/2014	23:16:24	0
9085341993	DIPAK DAS	9707783876	GIASUDDINAHMED	2/8/2014	23:14:34	0
9085341993	DIPAK DAS	9707783876	GIASUDDINAHMED	2/8/2014	23:10:00	125
9085341993	DIPAK DAS	9707783876	GIASUDDINAHMED	2/8/2014	23:06:14	0
9085341993	DIPAK DAS	9707783876	GIASUDDINAHMED	2/8/2014	23:04:14	0

Calling (A) Party Telephone Number/ MSISDN	Name	Called (B) Party Telephone Number/ Access Point Name	Name	Date	Time	Duration In Secs.
9085341993	DIPAK DAS	'51985		2/8/2014	23:02:31	0
9085341993	DIPAK DAS	'51985		2/8/2014	23:02:28	0
9085341993	DIPAK DAS	9707783876	GIASUDDINAHMED	2/8/2014	23:02:23	0
9085341993	DIPAK DAS	9707783876	GIASUDDINAHMED	2/8/2014	22:59:03	0
9085341993	DIPAK DAS	9707783876	GIASUDDINAHMED	2/8/2014	22:50:17	109
9085341993	DIPAK DAS	9085835737	RAMANDRA BARMAN	2/8/2014	22:46:08	0
9085341993	DIPAK DAS	9707783876	GIASUDDINAHMED	2/8/2014	22:42:03	0
9085341993	DIPAK DAS	9707783876	GIASUDDINAHMED	2/8/2014	22:42:01	0
9085341993	DIPAK DAS	9707783876	GIASUDDINAHMED	2/8/2014	22:38:55	0
9085341993	DIPAK DAS	9707783876	GIASUDDINAHMED	2/8/2014	22:35:01	0
9085341993	DIPAK DAS	'IK-Idea		2/8/2014	22:30:22	0
9085341993	DIPAK DAS	'IK-Idea		2/8/2014	22:29:48	0
9085341993	DIPAK DAS	'IK-Idea		2/8/2014	22:29:35	0
9085341993	DIPAK DAS	'58595		2/8/2014	22:29:12	0
9085341993	DIPAK DAS	9707783876	GIASUDDINAHMED	2/8/2014	22:28:47	107
9085341993	DIPAK DAS	'IK-Idea		2/8/2014	22:28:28	0
9085341993	DIPAK DAS	9707783876	GIASUDDINAHMED	2/8/2014	22:28:09	0

CDR OF NIRANJAN KALITA

Callg Party No.	Name 1 Name 2 Name 3	Calld Party No.	Name 1 Name 2 Name 3	Start Date	Call Time	Bill Duration	Call Direction
9707762514	NIRANJANKALITA	9707474658	HITESH KALITA	28-May-14	8:14:40	441	OUT_CALL
9707762514	NIRANJANKALITA	9707474658	HITESH KALITA	28-May-14	21:12:51	262	OUT_CALL
9707474658	HITESH KALITA	9707762514	NIRANJANKALITA	29-May-14	11:22:31	36	IN___CALL
9707762514	NIRANJANKALITA	9707474658	HITESH KALITA	29-May-14	13:35:52	72	OUT_CALL
9707474658	HITESH KALITA	9707762514	NIRANJANKALITA	29-May-14	15:51:29	8	IN___CALL
9707474658	HITESH KALITA	9707762514	NIRANJANKALITA	30-May-14	7:42:58	157	IN___CALL
9707474658	HITESH KALITA	9707762514	NIRANJANKALITA	30-May-14	17:24:33	53	IN___CALL
9707474658	HITESH KALITA	9707762514	NIRANJANKALITA	30-May-14	17:31:51	11	IN___CALL
9707762514	NIRANJANKALITA	9707474658	HITESH KALITA	30-May-14	17:40:11	15	OUT_CALL
9707474658	HITESH KALITA	9707762514	NIRANJANKALITA	30-May-14	20:7:12	71	IN___CALL
9707474658	HITESH KALITA	9707762514	NIRANJANKALITA	30-May-14	20:8:42	635	IN___CALL
9707474658	HITESH KALITA	9707762514	NIRANJANKALITA	31-May-14	8:42:24	126	IN___CALL
9707474658	HITESH KALITA	9707762514	NIRANJANKALITA	31-May-14	12:10:18	68	IN___CALL
9707474658	HITESH KALITA	9707762514	NIRANJANKALITA	31-May-14	19:40:6	122	IN___CALL
9707474658	HITESH KALITA	9707762514	NIRANJANKALITA	01-Jun-14	7:18:15	43	IN___CALL
9707474658	HITESH KALITA	9707762514	NIRANJANKALITA	01-Jun-14	8:3:6	55	IN___CALL
9707474658	HITESH KALITA	9707762514	NIRANJANKALITA	01-Jun-14	9:34:57	73	IN___CALL
9707474658	HITESH KALITA	9707762514	NIRANJANKALITA	01-Jun-14	10:39:59	20	IN___CALL
9707474658	HITESH KALITA	9707762514	NIRANJANKALITA	01-Jun-14	14:3:0	701	IN___CALL

Callg Party No.	Name 1 Name 2 Name 3	Calld Party No.	Name 1 Name 2 Name 3	Start Date	Call Time	Bill Duration	Call Direction
9707474658	HITESH KALITA	9707762514	NIRANJANKALITA	01-Jun-14	20:46:27	204	IN___CALL
9707474658	HITESH KALITA	9707762514	NIRANJANKALITA	02-Jun-14	7:16:39	18	IN___CALL
9707474658	HITESH KALITA	9707762514	NIRANJANKALITA	02-Jun-14	8:16:54	128	IN___CALL
9707474658	HITESH KALITA	9707762514	NIRANJANKALITA	02-Jun-14	20:59:46	354	IN___CALL
9707762514	NIRANJANKALITA	9707474658	HITESH KALITA	03-Jun-14	8:6:6	57	OUT_CALL
9707762514	NIRANJANKALITA	9707474658	HITESH KALITA	03-Jun-14	17:59:55	166	OUT_CALL
9707762514	NIRANJANKALITA	9707474658	HITESH KALITA	03-Jun-14	18:19:19	123	OUT_CALL
9707762514	NIRANJANKALITA	9707474658	HITESH KALITA	05-Jun-14	9:6:25	274	OUT_CALL
9707762514	NIRANJANKALITA	9707474658	HITESH KALITA	05-Jun-14	10:33:10	12	OUT_CALL
9707474658	HITESH KALITA	9707762514	NIRANJANKALITA	05-Jun-14	15:1:48	12	IN___CALL
9707474658	HITESH KALITA	9707762514	NIRANJANKALITA	06-Jun-14	8:41:43	247	IN___CALL
9707474658	HITESH KALITA	9707762514	NIRANJANKALITA	08-Jun-14	11:29:56	198	IN___CALL
9707474658	HITESH KALITA	9707762514	NIRANJANKALITA	08-Jun-14	11:33:39	28	IN___CALL
9707474658	HITESH KALITA	9707762514	NIRANJANKALITA	08-Jun-14	13:48:45	21	IN___CALL
9707474658	HITESH KALITA	9707762514	NIRANJANKALITA	09-Jun-14	18:52:26	1052	IN___CALL
9707474658	HITESH KALITA	9707762514	NIRANJANKALITA	12-Jun-14	8:44:21	53	IN___CALL
9707474658	HITESH KALITA	9707762514	NIRANJANKALITA	26-Jun-14	18:5:30	721	IN___CALL
9707474658	HITESH KALITA	9707762514	NIRANJANKALITA	28-Jun-14	19:3:6	244	IN___CALL
9707474658	HITESH KALITA	9707762514	NIRANJANKALITA	28-Jun-14	19:11:5	57	IN___CALL
9707474658	HITESH KALITA	9707762514	NIRANJANKALITA	28-Jun-14	19:12:23	153	IN___CALL
9707474658	HITESH KALITA	9707762514	NIRANJANKALITA	29-Jun-14	20:24:16	31	IN___CALL

A Party No.	Name 1 Name 2 Name 3	B Party No.	Name 1 Name 2 Name 3	Call_Date	Call_Time	Duration
9508818870	DWIPENNATH	8876935401	DWIPENNATH	28-MAY-2014	08:29:39	100
8876935401	MRINAL NATH	9401794646	SATYAJIT DAS	28-MAY-2014	20:32:56	1
8876935401	MRINAL NATH	9401794646	SATYAJIT DAS	29-MAY-2014	18:07:52	1
8876935401	MRINAL NATH	9401794646	SATYAJIT DAS	30-MAY-2014	10:23:05	1
9706991838	SATYAJIT DAS	8876935401	MRINAL NATH	30-MAY-2014	10:25:05	1
8751866423	JITEN KALITA	8876935401	MRINAL NATH	30-MAY-2014	16:34:12	62
8751866423	JITEN KALITA	8876935401	MRINAL NATH	30-MAY-2014	18:07:28	97
8876935401	MRINAL NATH	9401794646	SATYAJIT DAS	31-MAY-2014	13:34:27	1
9401794646	SRI SATYAJIT DAS	8876935401	SRI SATYAJIT DAS	01-JUN-2014	14:22:08	133
8876935401	MRINAL NATH	9401794646	SATYAJIT DAS	01-JUN-2014	18:28:29	1
8751866423	JITEN KALITA	8876935401	MRINAL NATH	01-JUN-2014	19:07:26	206
8876935401	MRINAL NATH	9401794646	SATYAJIT DAS	03-JUN-2014	11:39:31	1
8876935401	MRINAL NATH	9401794646	SATYAJIT DAS	03-JUN-2014	11:39:37	1
8876935401	MRINAL NATH	9508818870	DWIPEN NATH	03-JUN-2014	17:27:03	1
8876935401	MRINAL NATH	9401794646	SATYAJIT DAS	03-JUN-2014	17:27:15	1
8876935401	MRINAL NATH	9707243173	BOLEN KALITA	03-JUN-2014	17:27:19	1
9707243173	BALENNAKALITA	8876935401	BALENNAKALITA	03-JUN-2014	18:10:04	149
9707243173	BALENNAKALITA	8876935401	BALENNAKALITA	03-JUN-2014	20:35:18	80
8876935401	MRINAL NATH	9707243173	BOLEN KALITA	04-JUN-2014	16:42:08	1
8876935401	MRINAL NATH	9508818870	DWIPEN NATH	04-JUN-2014	23:12:13	1

A Party No.	Name 1 Name 2 Name 3	B Party No.	Name 1 Name 2 Name 3	Call_Date	Call_Time	Duration
8876935401	MRINAL NATH	9707243173	BOLEN KALITA	05-JUN-2014	09:25:16	1
9707243173	BALENNAKALITA	8876935401	MRINAL NATH	05-JUN-2014	19:09:11	64
8876935401	MRINAL NATH	9401794646	SATYAJIT DAS	06-JUN-2014	19:36:33	1
9706991838	SATYAJIT DAS	8876935401	MRINAL NATH	06-JUN-2014	19:39:20	1
8876935401	MRINAL NATH	9401794646	SATYAJIT DAS	06-JUN-2014	19:41:23	1
8876935401	MRINAL NATH	9707243173	BOLEN KALITA	06-JUN-2014	23:20:23	1
9707243173	BALENNAKALITA	8876935401	MRINAL NATH	07-JUN-2014	10:34:35	49
8876935401	MRINAL NATH	9401794646	SATYAJIT DAS	07-JUN-2014	14:43:59	1
8876935401	MRINAL NATH	9401794646	SATYAJIT DAS	08-JUN-2014	21:46:30	1
9706991838	SATYAJIT DAS	8876935401	SATYAJIT DAS	08-JUN-2014	21:48:00	1
8876935401	MRINAL NATH	9508818870	DWIPEN NATH	08-JUN-2014	22:41:20	1
8876935401	MRINAL NATH	9707243173	BOLEN KALITA	08-JUN-2014	22:41:45	1
8876935401	MRINAL NATH	9401794646	SATYAJIT DAS	08-JUN-2014	23:15:12	1
9707243173	BALENNAKALITA	8876935401	BALENNAKALITA	09-JUN-2014	08:52:31	17
8876935401	MRINAL NATH	9401794646	SATYAJIT DAS	09-JUN-2014	10:32:56	1
8876935401	MRINAL NATH	9401794646	SATYAJIT DAS	10-JUN-2014	11:59:31	1
9706991838	SATYAJIT DAS	8876935401	SATYAJIT DAS	10-JUN-2014	12:04:47	1
8876935401	MRINAL NATH	9401794646	SATYAJIT DAS	10-JUN-2014	12:06:33	1
9706991838	SATYAJIT DAS	8876935401	MRINAL NATH	10-JUN-2014	12:33:48	1
9401794646	SRI SATYAJIT DAS	8876935401	MRINAL NATH	10-JUN-2014	22:24:08	334

A Party No.	Name 1 Name 2 Name 3	B Party No.	Name 1 Name 2 Name 3	Call_Date	Call_Time	Duration
9401794646	SRI SATYAJIT DAS	8876935401	MRINAL NATH	11-JUN-2014	10:08:51	59
8876935401	MRINAL NATH	9401794646	SRI SATYAJIT DAS	12-JUN-2014	09:29:46	1
8876935401	MRINAL NATH	9401794646	SRI SATYAJIT DAS	12-JUN-2014	16:47:32	1
8876935401	MRINAL NATH	9401794646	SRI SATYAJIT DAS	12-JUN-2014	18:05:35	1
9706991838	SATYAJIT DAS	8876935401	MRINAL NATH	12-JUN-2014	18:08:19	1
8876935401	PANESWAR DAS	9401794646	SRI SATYAJIT DAS	12-JUN-2014	18:13:50	1
9508818870	DWIPENNATH	8876935401	MRINAL NATH	13-JUN-2014	15:59:47	77
9508818870	DWIPENNATH	8876935401	MRINAL NATH	13-JUN-2014	16:43:01	27
8876935401	MRINAL NATH	9401794646	SRI SATYAJIT DAS	13-JUN-2014	16:44:09	1
8751866423	JITEN KALITA	8876935401	MRINAL NATH	14-JUN-2014	11:53:03	296
8876935401	MRINAL NATH	9401794646	SRI SATYAJIT DAS	14-JUN-2014	13:12:36	1
8876935401	MRINAL NATH	9401794646	SRI SATYAJIT DAS	14-JUN-2014	17:47:36	1
8876935401	MRINAL NATH	9401794646	SRI SATYAJIT DAS	14-JUN-2014	17:52:28	1
8876935401	MRINAL NATH	9401794646	SRI SATYAJIT DAS	14-JUN-2014	18:27:09	1
8876935401	MRINAL NATH	9401794646	SRI SATYAJIT DAS	14-JUN-2014	18:35:19	1
8876935401	MRINAL NATH	9401794646	SRI SATYAJIT DAS	15-JUN-2014	11:29:29	1
8876935401	MRINAL NATH	9401794646	SRI SATYAJIT DAS	15-JUN-2014	11:33:46	1
8876935401	MRINAL NATH	9401794646	SRI SATYAJIT DAS	15-JUN-2014	19:37:49	1
8876935401	MRINAL NATH	9401794646	SRI SATYAJIT DAS	15-JUN-2014	19:37:55	1
8876935401	MRINAL NATH	9401794646	SRI SATYAJIT DAS	15-JUN-2014	19:41:25	1

A Party No.	Name 1 Name 2 Name 3	B Party No.	Name 1 Name 2 Name 3	Call_Date	Call_Time	Duration
8876935401	MRINAL NATH	9401794646	SRI SATYAJIT DAS	15-JUN-2014	21:02:22	1
8876935401	MRINAL NATH	9401794646	SRI SATYAJIT DAS	16-JUN-2014	13:15:28	1
8876935401	MRINAL NATH	9401794646	SRI SATYAJIT DAS	17-JUN-2014	13:02:47	1
8876935401	MRINAL NATH	9401794646	SRI SATYAJIT DAS	17-JUN-2014	13:02:52	1
8876935401	MRINAL NATH	9401794646	SRI SATYAJIT DAS	17-JUN-2014	13:11:08	1
8876935401	MRINAL NATH	9401794646	SRI SATYAJIT DAS	17-JUN-2014	13:11:13	1
8876935401	MRINAL NATH	9401794646	SRI SATYAJIT DAS	17-JUN-2014	17:55:40	1
8876935401	MRINAL NATH	9401794646	SRI SATYAJIT DAS	18-JUN-2014	15:12:17	1
8876935401	MRINAL NATH	9401794646	SRI SATYAJIT DAS	18-JUN-2014	17:56:17	1
8876935401	MRINAL NATH	9401794646	SRI SATYAJIT DAS	18-JUN-2014	22:04:29	1
8876935401	MRINAL NATH	9401794646	SRI SATYAJIT DAS	19-JUN-2014	20:59:07	1
8876935401	MRINAL NATH	9401794646	SRI SATYAJIT DAS	19-JUN-2014	21:13:37	1
8876935401	MRINAL NATH	9401794646	SRI SATYAJIT DAS	19-JUN-2014	21:15:00	1
8876935401	MRINAL NATH	9401794646	SRI SATYAJIT DAS	19-JUN-2014	21:21:09	1
8876935401	MRINAL NATH	9401794646	SRI SATYAJIT DAS	20-JUN-2014	12:55:22	1
8876935401	MRINAL NATH	9401794646	SRI SATYAJIT DAS	20-JUN-2014	17:39:22	1
8876935401	MRINAL NATH	9401794646	SRI SATYAJIT DAS	20-JUN-2014	18:30:44	1
8876935401	MRINAL NATH	9401794646	SRI SATYAJIT DAS	20-JUN-2014	21:46:25	1
8876935401	MRINAL NATH	9401794646	SRI SATYAJIT DAS	20-JUN-2014	21:47:03	1
8876935401	MRINAL NATH	9401794646	SRI SATYAJIT DAS	21-JUN-2014	12:44:18	1

A Party No.	Name 1 Name 2 Name 3	B Party No.	Name 1 Name 2 Name 3	Call_Date	Call_Time	Duration
8876935401	MRINAL NATH	9401794646	SRI SATYAJIT DAS	21-JUN-2014	12:45:47	1
8876935401	MRINAL NATH	9401794646	SRI SATYAJIT DAS	21-JUN-2014	12:48:44	1
8876935401	MRINAL NATH	9401794646	SRI SATYAJIT DAS	21-JUN-2014	12:52:30	1
8876935401	MRINAL NATH	9401794646	SRI SATYAJIT DAS	21-JUN-2014	12:53:29	1
8876935401	MRINAL NATH	9401794646	SRI SATYAJIT DAS	22-JUN-2014	21:31:48	1
8876935401	MRINAL NATH	9401794646	SRI SATYAJIT DAS	22-JUN-2014	21:32:46	1
8876935401	MRINAL NATH	9401794646	SRI SATYAJIT DAS	23-JUN-2014	20:38:15	1
9508818870	DWIPENNATH	8876935401	MRINAL NATH	24-JUN-2014	08:53:17	152
9508818870	DWIPENNATH	8876935401	MRINAL NATH	24-JUN-2014	14:16:31	123
9508818870	DWIPENNATH	8876935401	MRINAL NATH	24-JUN-2014	18:40:36	109
8876935401	MRINAL NATH	9401794646	PANESWAR DAS	24-JUN-2014	20:19:18	1
9401794646	SRI SATYAJIT DAS	8876935401	MRINAL NATH	24-JUN-2014	22:03:04	269
9508818870	DWIPENNATH	8876935401	MRINAL NATH	25-JUN-2014	07:27:00	88
8876935401	PANESWAR DAS	9401794646	SRI SATYAJIT DAS	25-JUN-2014	20:45:53	1
8876935401	MRINAL NATH	9401794646	SRI SATYAJIT DAS	25-JUN-2014	20:47:38	1
9401794646	SRI SATYAJIT DAS	8876935401	MRINAL NATH	25-JUN-2014	21:10:03	321
8876935401	PANESWAR DAS	9401794646	SRI SATYAJIT DAS	25-JUN-2014	22:01:40	1
8876935401	PANESWAR DAS	9401794646	SRI SATYAJIT DAS	25-JUN-2014	22:19:33	1
8876935401	PANESWAR DAS	9401794646	PANESWAR DAS	26-JUN-2014	09:49:11	1
8751866423	JITEN KALITA	8876935401	MRINAL NATH	26-JUN-2014	09:58:34	180

A Party No.	Name 1 Name 2 Name 3	B Party No.	Name 1 Name 2 Name 3	Call_Date	Call_Time	Duration
9401794646	SRI SATYAJIT DAS	8876935401	MRINAL NATH	26-JUN-2014	10:22:36	487
8876935401	MRINAL NATH	9401794646	SRI SATYAJIT DAS	26-JUN-2014	10:52:10	1
8876935401	MRINAL NATH	9401794646	SRI SATYAJIT DAS	26-JUN-2014	21:26:37	1
9508818870	DWIPENNATH	8876935401	MRINAL NATH	29-JUN-2014	22:16:21	51
9508818870	DWIPENNATH	8876935401	MRINAL NATH	30-JUN-2014	14:22:39	37
9508818870	DWIPENNATH	8876935401	MRINAL NATH	30-JUN-2014	15:14:43	114
9508818870	DWIPENNATH	8876935401	MRINAL NATH	30-JUN-2014	15:37:14	72
9401794646	SRI SATYAJIT DAS	8876935401	MRINAL NATH	02-JUL-2014	19:17:28	93
9401794646	SRI SATYAJIT DAS	8876935401	MRINAL NATH	03-JUL-2014	11:26:02	250

MRINAL CDR 2

Calling (A) Party	Name 1 Name 2 Name 3	Called (B) Party	Name 1 Name 2 Name 3	Call Date	Call Time	Call Duration (in second)
9401794760	MR MIRNAL DAS	9508818870	DWIPENNATH	1/6/2014	06:16:31	25
9401794760	MR MIRNAL DAS	9706089524	MRINAL NATH	1/6/2014	06:38:04	61
9401794760	MR MIRNAL DAS	8751866423	JITEN KALITA	1/6/2014	07:14:43	66
8751866423	JITEN KALITA	9401794760	MR MIRNAL DAS	1/6/2014	07:45:24	10
66b 81 16158b BANK MESSAGE		9401794760	MR MIRNAL DAS	1/6/2014	10:05:42	1
66b 81 16158b BANK MESSAGE		9401794760	MR MIRNAL DAS	1/6/2014	10:05:55	1
66b 81 16158b BANK MESSAGE		9401794760	MR MIRNAL DAS	1/6/2014	10:06:47	1
9508818870	DWIPENNATH	9401794760	MR MIRNAL DAS	1/6/2014	12:09:17	45
9401794760	MR MIRNAL DAS	9508818870	DWIPENNATH	1/6/2014	12:10:31	41
9707243173	BALENNAKALITA	9401794760	MR MIRNAL DAS	1/6/2014	13:39:40	99
9508818870	DWIPENNATH	9401794760	MR MIRNAL DAS	1/6/2014	13:45:34	322
9401794760	MR MIRNAL DAS	9401794646	SRI SATYAJIT DAS	1/6/2014	16:08:21	547
9508818870	DWIPENNATH	9401794760	MR MIRNAL DAS	1/6/2014	19:32:57	207
9707243173	BALENNAKALITA	9401794760	MR MIRNAL DAS	1/6/2014	20:03:35	32
9707243173	BALENNAKALITA	9401794760	MR MIRNAL DAS	1/6/2014	20:53:23	60
66b 81 16158b BANK MESSAGE		9401794760	MR MIRNAL DAS	1/6/2014	23:36:44	1
66b 81 16158b BANK MESSAGE		9401794760	MR MIRNAL DAS	1/6/2014	23:36:57	1
66b 81 16158b BANK MESSAGE		9401794760	MR MIRNAL DAS	1/6/2014	23:37:48	1
9401794760	MR MIRNAL DAS	9401794646	SRI SATYAJIT DAS	2/6/2014	09:30:45	180

Calling (A) Party	Name 1 Name 2 Name 3	Called (B) Party	Name 1 Name 2 Name 3	Call Date	Call Time	Call Duration (in second)
9508818870	DWIPENNATH	9401794760	MR MIRNAL DAS	2/6/2014	09:34:03	56
9401794760	MR MIRNAL DAS	8751866423	JITEN KALITA	2/6/2014	09:35:42	44
9706991838	SATYAJIT DAS	9401794760	MR MIRNAL DAS	2/6/2014	13:41:25	1
9401794760	MR MIRNAL DAS	9401794646	SRI SATYAJIT DAS	2/6/2014	13:42:00	31
9401794646	SRI SATYAJIT DAS	9401794760	MR MIRNAL DAS	2/6/2014	13:44:06	145
9401794760	MR MIRNAL DAS	9706089524	MRINAL NATH	2/6/2014	14:32:37	54
9401794646	SRI SATYAJIT DAS	9401794760	MR MIRNAL DAS	2/6/2014	14:43:34	74
9706089524	MRINAL NATH	9401794760	MR MIRNAL DAS	2/6/2014	14:56:46	23
9401794760	MR MIRNAL DAS	9401794646	SRI SATYAJIT DAS	2/6/2014	15:10:53	15
9401794760	MR MIRNAL DAS	9401794646	SRI SATYAJIT DAS	2/6/2014	15:37:07	20
9401794760	MR MIRNAL DAS	9401794646	SRI SATYAJIT DAS	2/6/2014	19:40:27	351
9401794646	SRI SATYAJIT DAS	9401794760	MR MIRNAL DAS	2/6/2014	21:05:27	330
24b6b 653bd 060 BANK MESSAGE		9401794760	MR MIRNAL DAS	3/6/2014	09:26:49	1
4426b068385 060 BANK MESSAGE		9401794760	MR MIRNAL DAS	3/6/2014	09:27:28	1
8751866423	JITEN KALITA	9401794760	MR MIRNAL DAS	3/6/2014	10:04:15	112
9401794760	MR MIRNAL DAS	9707243173	BALENNAKALITA	3/6/2014	10:07:45	79
9401794760	MR MIRNAL DAS	9707243173	BALENNAKALITA	3/6/2014	10:13:15	34
9706991838	SATYAJIT DAS	9401794760	MR MIRNAL DAS	3/6/2014	11:06:49	1
9401794760	MR MIRNAL DAS	9707243173	BALENNAKALITA	3/6/2014	12:11:47	52
9401794760	MR MIRNAL DAS	9954454011	MRS MANJU URANG	3/6/2014	12:24:58	73

Calling (A) Party	Name 1 Name 2 Name 3	Called (B) Party	Name 1 Name 2 Name 3	Call Date	Call Time	Call Duration (in second)
9401794760	MR MIRNAL DAS	9401794646	SRI SATYAJIT DAS	3/6/2014	12:45:46	38
9401794760	MR MIRNAL DAS	9503818870	DWIPENNATH	3/6/2014	12:55:00	44
9706991838	SATYAJIT DAS	9401794760	MR MIRNAL DAS	3/6/2014	14:21:56	1
24b6b 61399d660	BANK MESSAGE	9401794760	MR MIRNAL DAS	3/6/2014	14:46:19	1
9401794646	SRI SATYAJIT DAS	9401794760	MR MIRNAL DAS	3/6/2014	15:22:22	120
9706991838	SATYAJIT DAS	9401794760	MR MIRNAL DAS	3/6/2014	15:53:44	1
24b6b 6539d 463	BANK MESSAGE	9401794760	MR MIRNAL DAS	3/6/2014	16:05:53	1
9707243173	BALENNAKALITA	9401794760	MR MIRNAL DAS	4/6/2014	21:09:14	205
9707243173	BALENNAKALITA	9401794760	MR MIRNAL DAS	4/6/2014	21:19:12	270
9508818870	DWIPENNATH	9401794760	MR MIRNAL DAS	4/6/2014	21:25:50	762
9707243173	BALENNAKALITA	9401794760	MR MIRNAL DAS	4/6/2014	22:47:08	267
9401794760	MR MIRNAL DAS	9707243173	BALENNAKALITA	4/6/2014	22:52:03	175
9707243173	BALENNAKALITA	9401794760	MR MIRNAL DAS	4/6/2014	22:59:02	128
9707243173	BALENNAKALITA	9401794760	MR MIRNAL DAS	5/6/2014	00:16:04	11
9707243173	BALENNAKALITA	9401794760	MR MIRNAL DAS	5/6/2014	00:16:33	55
9401794760	MR MIRNAL DAS	9707243173	BALENNAKALITA	5/6/2014	09:19:43	14
9401794760	MR MIRNAL DAS	9707243173	BALENNAKALITA	5/6/2014	09:34:08	19
9706991838	SATYAJIT DAS	9401794760	MR MIRNAL DAS	5/6/2014	10:27:11	1
9508818870	DWIPENNATH	9401794760	MR MIRNAL DAS	5/6/2014	10:36:50	257
9401794646	SRI SATYAJIT DAS	9401794760	MR MIRNAL DAS	5/6/2014	12:37:26	501

Calling (A) Party	Name 1 Name 2 Name 3	Called (B) Party	Name 1 Name 2 Name 3	Call Date	Call Time	Call Duration (in second)
9401794760	MR MIRNAL DAS	9508818870	DWIPENNATH	5/6/2014	12:56:09	19
9508818870	DWIPENNATH	9401794760	MR MIRNAL DAS	5/6/2014	13:08:57	17
9508818870	DWIPENNATH	9401794760	MR MIRNAL DAS	5/6/2014	13:13:21	25
9706991838	SATYAJIT DAS	9401794760	MR MIRNAL DAS	5/6/2014	13:14:22	1
9706991838	SATYAJIT DAS	9401794760	MR MIRNAL DAS	5/6/2014	13:15:48	1
9707243173	BALENNAKALITA	9401794760	MR MIRNAL DAS	5/6/2014	13:24:18	59
24b6b 653bd 060 BANK MESSAGE		9401794760	MR MIRNAL DAS	5/6/2014	14:20:14	1
9707243173	BALENNAKALITA	9401794760	MR MIRNAL DAS	5/6/2014	15:23:04	41
9508818870	DWIPENNATH	9401794760	MR MIRNAL DAS	5/6/2014	18:26:02	138
9401794760	MR MIRNAL DAS	9508818870	DWIPENNATH	5/6/2014	19:31:54	13
9706991838	SATYAJIT DAS	9401794760	MR MIRNAL DAS	5/6/2014	20:02:34	341
9706991838	SATYAJIT DAS	9401794760	MR MIRNAL DAS	5/6/2014	20:14:14	1
9706991838	SATYAJIT DAS	9401794760	MR MIRNAL DAS	5/6/2014	20:43:32	1
9401794760	MR MIRNAL DAS	9957684410	BUDHARU DEKA	5/6/2014	20:56:49	162
9508818870	DWIPENNATH	9401794760	MR MIRNAL DAS	5/6/2014	22:05:30	1
24b6b 653bd 060 BANK MESSAGE BANK MESSAGE		9401794760	MR MIRNAL DAS	6/6/2014	09:23:42	1
9401794646	SRI SATYAJIT DAS	9401794760	MR MIRNAL DAS	6/6/2014	11:53:22	80
9508818870	DWIPENNATH	9401794760	MR MIRNAL DAS	6/6/2014	12:00:33	90
9401794646	SRI SATYAJIT DAS	9401794760	MR MIRNAL DAS	6/6/2014	12:48:34	33

Calling (A) Party	Name 1 Name 2 Name 3	Called (B) Party	Name 1 Name 2 Name 3	Call Date	Call Time	Call Duration (in second)
9706991838	SATYAJIT DAS	9401794760	MR MIRNAL DAS	6/6/2014	14:48:20	1
9401794760	MR MIRNAL DAS	9401794646	SRI SATYAJIT DAS	6/6/2014	14:54:11	24
9706991838	SATYAJIT DAS	9401794760	MR MIRNAL DAS	6/6/2014	18:11:31	1
9706991838	SATYAJIT DAS	9401794760	MR MIRNAL DAS	6/6/2014	18:14:10	1
9706991838	SATYAJIT DAS	9401794760	MR MIRNAL DAS	6/6/2014	18:18:16	1
9401794646	SRI SATYAJIT DAS	9401794760	MR MIRNAL DAS	6/6/2014	20:08:49	476
9508818870	DWIPENNATH	9401794760	MR MIRNAL DAS	6/6/2014	21:04:00	177
9508818870	DWIPENNATH	9401794760	MR MIRNAL DAS	7/6/2014	09:34:19	31
9706991838	SATYAJIT DAS	9401794760	MR MIRNAL DAS	7/6/2014	09:48:56	1
9401794646	SRI SATYAJIT DAS	9401794760	MR MIRNAL DAS	7/6/2014	11:17:20	70
9508818870	DWIPENNATH	9401794760	MR MIRNAL DAS	7/6/2014	11:18:43	70
9401794760	MR MIRNAL DAS	9707243173	BALENNAKALITA	7/6/2014	11:52:07	29
24b6b 653bd 060	BANK MESSAGE	9401794760	MR MIRNAL DAS	7/6/2014	12:28:12	1
9401794760	MR MIRNAL DAS	9401794646	SRI SATYAJIT DAS	7/6/2014	14:40:27	66
9401794760	MR MIRNAL DAS	9707243173	BALENNAKALITA	7/6/2014	14:50:37	22
9706991838	SATYAJIT DAS	9401794760	MR MIRNAL DAS	7/6/2014	14:51:12	1
9706991838	SATYAJIT DAS	9401794760	MR MIRNAL DAS	7/6/2014	15:01:05	1
9401794760	MR MIRNAL DAS	9401794646	SRI SATYAJIT DAS	7/6/2014	16:08:17	10
9401794760	MR MIRNAL DAS	9401794646	SRI SATYAJIT DAS	7/6/2014	16:09:09	153
9401794760	MR MIRNAL DAS	9401794646	SRI SATYAJIT DAS	7/6/2014	16:42:07	28

Calling (A) Party	Name 1 Name 2 Name 3	Called (B) Party	Name 1 Name 2 Name 3	Call Date	Call Time	Call Duration (in second)
9706991838	SATYAJIT DAS	9401794760	MR MIRNAL DAS	7/6/2014	17:08:20	1
9401794760	MR MIRNAL DAS	9401794646	SRI SATYAJIT DAS	7/6/2014	17:09:46	174
9706991838	SATYAJIT DAS	9401794760	MR MIRNAL DAS	7/6/2014	17:14:56	1
9854059657	BIPUL GOSWAMI	9401794760	MR MIRNAL DAS	7/6/2014	17:15:25	58
9401794646	SRI SATYAJIT DAS	9401794760	MR MIRNAL DAS	7/6/2014	17:37:51	13
9401794646	SRI SATYAJIT DAS	9401794760	MR MIRNAL DAS	7/6/2014	18:02:37	58
9508818870	DWIPENNATH	9401794760	MR MIRNAL DAS	7/6/2014	20:33:55	28
9401794646	SRI SATYAJIT DAS	9401794760	MR MIRNAL DAS	7/6/2014	20:37:37	36
9401794760	MR MIRNAL DAS	9508818870	DWIPENNATH	7/6/2014	21:48:03	10
9401794646	SRI SATYAJIT DAS	9401794760	MR MIRNAL DAS	7/6/2014	22:16:51	523
9401794760	MR MIRNAL DAS	9508818870	DWIPENNATH	7/6/2014	22:25:57	21
9401794760	MR MIRNAL DAS	9707243173	BALENNAKALITA	8/6/2014	00:13:47	94
4 66b682 9e4589	BANK MESSAGE	9401794760	MR MIRNAL DAS	8/6/2014	07:32:02	1
8751866423	JITEN KALITA	9401794760	MR MIRNAL DAS	8/6/2014	09:07:03	45
9401794760	MR MIRNAL DAS	9707243173	BALENNAKALITA	8/6/2014	09:08:38	72
24b6b 61395da65	BANK MESSAGE	9401794760	MR MIRNAL DAS	8/6/2014	10:14:01	1
9401794646	SRI SATYAJIT DAS	9401794760	MR MIRNAL DAS	8/6/2014	10:19:56	38
9401794760	MR MIRNAL DAS	9508818870	DWIPENNATH	8/6/2014	10:51:56	16
9401794760	MR MIRNAL DAS	9508818870	DWIPENNATH	8/6/2014	11:40:29	167
9401794646	SRI SATYAJIT DAS	9401794760	MR MIRNAL DAS	8/6/2014	11:45:54	27

Calling (A) Party	Name 1 Name 2 Name 3	Called (B) Party	Name 1 Name 2 Name 3	Call Date	Call Time	Call Duration (in second)
9401794760	MR MIRNAL DAS	9401794646	SRI SATYAJIT DAS	8/6/2014	12:17:36	10
9401794760	MR MIRNAL DAS	9707243173	BALENNAKALITA	8/6/2014	12:29:26	35
24b6b 653bd 060 BANK MESSAGE		9401794760	MR MIRNAL DAS	8/6/2014	12:30:34	1
9401794646	SRI SATYAJIT DAS	9401794760	MR MIRNAL DAS	8/6/2014	13:04:00	26
9401794760	MR MIRNAL DAS	9401794646	SRI SATYAJIT DAS	8/6/2014	14:40:19	8
9508818870	DWIPENNATH	9401794760	MR MIRNAL DAS	8/6/2014	14:53:58	19
9508818870	DWIPENNATH	9401794760	MR MIRNAL DAS	8/6/2014	15:34:43	93
9706991838	SATYAJIT DAS	9401794760	MR MIRNAL DAS	8/6/2014	16:11:13	1
9706991838	SATYAJIT DAS	9401794760	MR MIRNAL DAS	8/6/2014	16:26:42	1
9401794760	MR MIRNAL DAS	9401794646	SRI SATYAJIT DAS	8/6/2014	16:29:15	194
9401794646	SRI SATYAJIT DAS	9401794760	MR MIRNAL DAS	8/6/2014	16:38:33	121
9706991838	SATYAJIT DAS	9401794760	MR MIRNAL DAS	8/6/2014	17:31:35	1
9401794646	SRI SATYAJIT DAS	9401794760	MR MIRNAL DAS	8/6/2014	19:44:15	380
9508818870	DWIPENNATH	9401794760	MR MIRNAL DAS	8/6/2014	20:37:58	47
9401794760	MR MIRNAL DAS	9707243173	BALENNAKALITA	8/6/2014	21:18:11	49
9401794760	MR MIRNAL DAS	9707243173	BALENNAKALITA	8/6/2014	21:19:35	146
9401794646	SRI SATYAJIT DAS	9401794760	MR MIRNAL DAS	8/6/2014	22:02:49	24
9706991838	SATYAJIT DAS	9401794760	MR MIRNAL DAS	8/6/2014	22:29:16	1
9706991838	SATYAJIT DAS	9401794760	MR MIRNAL DAS	8/6/2014	22:32:13	1
9706991838	SATYAJIT DAS	9401794760	MR MIRNAL DAS	8/6/2014	22:59:26	1

Calling (A) Party	Name 1 Name 2 Name 3	Called (B) Party	Name 1 Name 2 Name 3	Call Date	Call Time	Call Duration (in second)
9401794760	MR MIRNAL DAS	9707243173	BALENNAKALITA	8/6/2014	23:01:59	35
9401794760	MR MIRNAL DAS	9401794646	SRI SATYAJIT DAS	9/6/2014	08:45:50	102
9706991838	SATYAJIT DAS	9401794760	MR MIRNAL DAS	9/6/2014	09:02:26	1
4426b066381 061 BANK MESSAGE		9401794760	MR MIRNAL DAS	9/6/2014	09:50:51	1
4426b066381 061 BANK MESSAGE		9401794760	MR MIRNAL DAS	9/6/2014	09:53:10	1
9401794646	SRI SATYAJIT DAS	9401794760	MR MIRNAL DAS	9/6/2014	11:34:44	104
9508818870	DWIPENNATH	9401794760	MR MIRNAL DAS	9/6/2014	11:58:50	58
24b6b 653bd 060 BANK MESSAGE		9401794760	MR MIRNAL DAS	9/6/2014	12:26:34	1
9707243173	BALENNAKALITA	9401794760	MR MIRNAL DAS	9/6/2014	12:47:27	43
9401794646	SRI SATYAJIT DAS	9401794760	MR MIRNAL DAS	9/6/2014	13:18:58	32
9401794760	MR MIRNAL DAS	9954898960	PRABHAT NATH	9/6/2014	13:23:40	18
9401794760	MR MIRNAL DAS	9401794646	SRI SATYAJIT DAS	9/6/2014	13:58:09	33
9401794646	SRI SATYAJIT DAS	9401794760	MR MIRNAL DAS	9/6/2014	14:07:48	16
9401794646	SRI SATYAJIT DAS	9401794760	MR MIRNAL DAS	9/6/2014	21:19:33	317
9401794760	MR MIRNAL DAS	9401794646	SRI SATYAJIT DAS	9/6/2014	21:27:53	209
9401794760	MR MIRNAL DAS	9508818870	DWIPENNATH	9/6/2014	21:33:39	6
9508818870	DWIPENNATH	9401794760	MR MIRNAL DAS	9/6/2014	22:29:30	834
9401794760	MR MIRNAL DAS	9508818870	DWIPENNATH	########	08:00:59	25
9706991838	SATYAJIT DAS	9401794760	MR MIRNAL DAS	########	09:02:55	1
9508818870	DWIPENNATH	9401794760	MR MIRNAL DAS	########	10:08:28	37

Calling (A) Party	Name 1 Name 2 Name 3	Called (B) Party	Name 1 Name 2 Name 3	Call Date	Call Time	Call Duration (in second)
9401794760	MR MIRNAL DAS	9508818870	DWIPENNATH	########	10:35:42	7
9401794646	SRI SATYAJIT DAS	9401794760	MR MIRNAL DAS	########	10:41:47	62
9401794760	MR MIRNAL DAS	9401794646	SRI SATYAJIT DAS	########	12:08:00	14
9401794760	MR MIRNAL DAS	9864055963	RANJAN KATAKI	########	12:16:19	15
9401794760	MR MIRNAL DAS	9401794646	SRI SATYAJIT DAS	########	12:17:56	6
9706991838	SATYAJIT DAS	9401794760	MR MIRNAL DAS	########	16:00:37	1
9508818870	DWIPENNATH	9401794760	MR MIRNAL DAS	########	16:01:51	19
9706991838	SATYAJIT DAS	9401794760	MR MIRNAL DAS	########	16:04:03	1
9401794760	MR MIRNAL DAS	9508818870	DWIPENNATH	########	16:27:45	35
24b6b 6539d 463	BANK MESSAGE	9401794760	MR MIRNAL DAS	########	16:29:34	1
9508818870	DWIPENNATH	9401794760	MR MIRNAL DAS	########	16:36:31	22
9401794646	SRI SATYAJIT DAS	9401794760	MR MIRNAL DAS	########	19:50:29	57
9401794760	MR MIRNAL DAS	9401794646	SRI SATYAJIT DAS	########	11:10:56	246
9508818870	DWIPENNATH	9401794760	MR MIRNAL DAS	########	11:44:01	26
9706991838	SATYAJIT DAS	9401794760	MR MIRNAL DAS	########	11:56:27	1
9706991838	SATYAJIT DAS	9401794760	MR MIRNAL DAS	########	12:07:17	1
9401794760	MR MIRNAL DAS	9401794646	SRI SATYAJIT DAS	########	12:45:05	69
9401794760	MR MIRNAL DAS	9401794646	SRI SATYAJIT DAS	########	14:07:00	225
9401794760	MR MIRNAL DAS	9401794646	SRI SATYAJIT DAS	########	14:57:36	3
9401794760	MR MIRNAL DAS	9401794646	SRI SATYAJIT DAS	########	14:58:50	17

Calling (A) Party	Name 1 Name 2 Name 3	Called (B) Party	Name 1 Name 2 Name 3	Call Date	Call Time	Call Duration (in second)
9508818870	DWIPENNATH	9401794760	MR MIRNAL DAS	########	15:26:09	56
9401794760	MR MIRNAL DAS	9859833928	ADHIR DUTTA	########	16:33:42	78
9706991838	SATYAJIT DAS	9401794760	MR MIRNAL DAS	########	17:50:50	1
9706991838	SATYAJIT DAS	9401794760	MR MIRNAL DAS	########	17:53:43	1
9706991838	SATYAJIT DAS	9401794760	MR MIRNAL DAS	########	18:07:04	1
9706991838	SATYAJIT DAS	9401794760	MR MIRNAL DAS	########	18:08:14	1
9508818870	DWIPENNATH	9401794760	MR MIRNAL DAS	########	18:11:36	123
24b6b 653bd 060 BANK MESSAGE		9401794760	MR MIRNAL DAS	########	18:16:40	1
9706991838	SATYAJIT DAS	9401794760	MR MIRNAL DAS	########	19:02:42	1
9706991838	SATYAJIT DAS	9401794760	MR MIRNAL DAS	########	19:10:16	1
9706991838	SATYAJIT DAS	9401794760	MR MIRNAL DAS	########	19:30:02	1
9401794646	SRI SATYAJIT DAS	9401794760	MR MIRNAL DAS	########	20:43:54	554
9401794646	SRI SATYAJIT DAS	9401794760	MR MIRNAL DAS	########	10:05:57	220
24b6b 61399d660 BANK MESSAGE		9401794760	MR MIRNAL DAS	########	10:10:46	1
9401794646	SRI SATYAJIT DAS	9401794760	MR MIRNAL DAS	########	14:31:45	76
9401794760	MR MIRNAL DAS	9401794646	SRI SATYAJIT DAS	########	15:29:30	271
24b6b 65ba9de68 BANK MESSAGE		9401794760	MR MIRNAL DAS	########	16:30:11	1
9401794646	SRI SATYAJIT DAS	9401794760	MR MIRNAL DAS	########	16:38:53	344
2 96b 65b81 060 BANK MESSAGE		9401794760	MR MIRNAL DAS	########	22:50:30	1
9401794646	SRI SATYAJIT DAS	9401794760	MR MIRNAL DAS	13-06-2014	10:38:01	41

Calling (A) Party	Name 1 Name 2 Name 3	Called (B) Party	Name 1 Name 2 Name 3	Call Date	Call Time	Call Duration (in second)
9401794646	SRI SATYAJIT DAS	9401794760	MR MIRNAL DAS	13-06-2014	11:04:44	323
9508818870	DWIPENNATH	9401794760	MR MIRNAL DAS	13-06-2014	11:32:31	74
4526b 85763b 9e BANK MESSAGE		9401794760	MR MIRNAL DAS	13-06-2014	13:31:50	1
24a6b 62389 60 BANK MESSAGE		9401794760	MR MIRNAL DAS	13-06-2014	16:33:44	1
9508818870	DWIPENNATH	9401794760	MR MIRNAL DAS	13-06-2014	17:22:32	29
9401794760	MR MIRNAL DAS	9508818870	DWIPENNATH	13-06-2014	18:07:38	26
9508818870	DWIPENNATH	9401794760	MR MIRNAL DAS	13-06-2014	18:09:00	24
9401794646	SRI SATYAJIT DAS	9401794760	MR MIRNAL DAS	13-06-2014	19:05:35	411
9401794646	SRI SATYAJIT DAS	9401794760	MR MIRNAL DAS	14-06-2014	11:13:38	280
4426b066381 060 BANK MESSAGE		9401794760	MR MIRNAL DAS	14-06-2014	12:04:37	1
4426b066381 060 BANK MESSAGE		9401794760	MR MIRNAL DAS	14-06-2014	12:05:58	1
66b 61ba1ea60 BANK MESSAGE		9401794760	MR MIRNAL DAS	14-06-2014	16:43:09	1
66b 61ba1ea60 BANK MESSAGE		9401794760	MR MIRNAL DAS	14-06-2014	16:44:15	1
9401794646	SRI SATYAJIT DAS	9401794760	MR MIRNAL DAS	14-06-2014	17:46:22	14
4526b 85763b 9e BANK MESSAGE		9401794760	MR MIRNAL DAS	14-06-2014	18:02:02	1
9401794646	SRI SATYAJIT DAS	9401794760	MR MIRNAL DAS	14-06-2014	18:14:26	35
9401794646	SRI SATYAJIT DAS	9401794760	MR MIRNAL DAS	14-06-2014	18:56:42	132
8876351801	CHASIN NATH	9401794760	MR MIRNAL DAS	14-06-2014	19:03:18	137
9401794760	MR MIRNAL DAS	9401794646	SRI SATYAJIT DAS	14-06-2014	19:26:13	34
9401794646	SRI SATYAJIT DAS	9401794760	MR MIRNAL DAS	14-06-2014	21:34:54	72

Calling (A) Party	Name 1 Name 2 Name 3	Called (B) Party	Name 1 Name 2 Name 3	Call Date	Call Time	Call Duration (in second)
4526b 85763b 9e	BANK MESSAGE	9401794760	MR MIRNAL DAS	15-06-2014	11:26:41	1
4526b 85763b 9e	BANK MESSAGE	9401794760	MR MIRNAL DAS	15-06-2014	11:31:57	1
9401794760	MR MIRNAL DAS	9706991838	SATYAJIT DAS	15-06-2014	12:04:57	141
9401794646	SRI SATYAJIT DAS	9401794760	MR MIRNAL DAS	15-06-2014	19:19:21	401
24b6b 61395da65	BANK MESSAGE	9401794760	MR MIRNAL DAS	16-06-2014	10:20:15	1
9508818870	DWIPENNATH	9401794760	MR MIRNAL DAS	16-06-2014	12:29:46	905
24b6b 61b81 461	BANK MESSAGE	9401794760	MR MIRNAL DAS	16-06-2014	14:01:23	1
9401794646	SRI SATYAJIT DAS	9401794760	MR MIRNAL DAS	16-06-2014	15:45:04	475
9401794646	SRI SATYAJIT DAS	9401794760	MR MIRNAL DAS	16-06-2014	18:26:56	214
9401794646	SRI SATYAJIT DAS	9401794760	MR MIRNAL DAS	16-06-2014	20:12:12	18
9401794646	SRI SATYAJIT DAS	9401794760	MR MIRNAL DAS	17-06-2014	12:58:16	185
9401794760	MR MIRNAL DAS	9707243173	BALENNAKALITA	17-06-2014	13:14:29	47
9401794646	SRI SATYAJIT DAS	9401794760	MR MIRNAL DAS	17-06-2014	13:44:06	443
9401794646	SRI SATYAJIT DAS	9401794760	MR MIRNAL DAS	17-06-2014	19:33:01	214
9508818870	DWIPENNATH	9401794760	MR MIRNAL DAS	17-06-2014	20:20:12	117
9508818870	DWIPENNATH	9401794760	MR MIRNAL DAS	18-06-2014	09:23:07	32
9401794646	SRI SATYAJIT DAS	9401794760	MR MIRNAL DAS	18-06-2014	09:49:08	33
9401794646	SRI SATYAJIT DAS	9401794760	MR MIRNAL DAS	18-06-2014	10:06:06	32
9401794646	SRI SATYAJIT DAS	9401794760	MR MIRNAL DAS	18-06-2014	10:08:46	85
9401794646	SRI SATYAJIT DAS	9401794760	MR MIRNAL DAS	18-06-2014		85

Calling (A) Party	Name 1 Name 2 Name 3	Called (B) Party	Name 1 Name 2 Name 3	Call Date	Call Time	Call Duration (in second)
9401794760	MR MIRNAL DAS	9401794646	SRI SATYAJIT DAS	18-06-2014	13:37:36	20
9401794646	SRI SATYAJIT DAS	9401794760	MR MIRNAL DAS	18-06-2014	14:15:55	18
9401794760	MR MIRNAL DAS	9401794646	SRI SATYAJIT DAS	18-06-2014	14:31:21	88
9401794646	SRI SATYAJIT DAS	9401794760	MR MIRNAL DAS	18-06-2014	15:22:47	54
2 96b 65b81 060 BANK MESSAGE		9401794760	MR MIRNAL DAS	18-06-2014	15:25:11	1
9508818870	DWIPENNATH	9401794760	MR MIRNAL DAS	18-06-2014	17:46:29	17
9401794646	SRI SATYAJIT DAS	9401794760	MR MIRNAL DAS	18-06-2014	18:08:43	126
9401794646	SRI SATYAJIT DAS	9401794760	MR MIRNAL DAS	18-06-2014	21:19:27	894
4526b 85763b 9e BANK MESSAGE		9401794760	MR MIRNAL DAS	19-06-2014	12:24:55	1
4526b 85763b 9e BANK MESSAGE		9401794760	MR MIRNAL DAS	19-06-2014	12:25:02	1
9401794760	MR MIRNAL DAS	9401794646	SRI SATYAJIT DAS	19-06-2014	12:34:21	150
2 96b 65b81 060 BANK MESSAGE		9401794760	MR MIRNAL DAS	19-06-2014	13:43:49	1
24b6b 65b 1 060 BANK MESSAGE		9401794760	MR MIRNAL DAS	19-06-2014	15:41:00	1
4526b 85763b 9e BANK MESSAGE		9401794760	MR MIRNAL DAS	19-06-2014	16:31:30	1
4526b 85763b 9e BANK MESSAGE		9401794760	MR MIRNAL DAS	19-06-2014	16:32:54	1
24b6b 653bd 060 BANK MESSAGE		9401794760	MR MIRNAL DAS	19-06-2014	16:57:09	1
9401794760	MR MIRNAL DAS	9401794646	SRI SATYAJIT DAS	19-06-2014	19:02:37	184
24a6ba62389 e60 BANK MESSAGE		9401794760	MR MIRNAL DAS	20-06-2014	09:09:52	1
24b6b 61399d660 BANK MESSAGE		9401794760	MR MIRNAL DAS	20-06-2014	09:13:37	1
24b6b 653b5d 66 BANK MESSAGE		9401794760	MR MIRNAL DAS	20-06-2014	10:55:15	1

Calling (A) Party	Name 1 Name 2 Name 3	Called (B) Party	Name 1 Name 2 Name 3	Call Date	Call Time	Call Duration (in second)
9401794760	MR MIRNAL DAS	9401794646	SRI SATYAJIT DAS	20-06-2014	11:56:58	111
9401794760	MR MIRNAL DAS	9401794646	SRI SATYAJIT DAS	20-06-2014	12:14:32	124
9401794646	SRI SATYAJIT DAS	9401794760	MR MIRNAL DAS	20-06-2014	12:23:15	1
24a6b 85763b 9e BANK MESSAGE		9401794760	MR MIRNAL DAS	20-06-2014	12:49:05	1
24a6b 85763b 9e BANK MESSAGE		9401794760	MR MIRNAL DAS	20-06-2014	12:49:09	1
4 66b 85763b 9e BANK MESSAGE		9401794760	MR MIRNAL DAS	20-06-2014	12:52:35	1
4 66b 85763b 9e BANK MESSAGE		9401794760	MR MIRNAL DAS	20-06-2014	12:52:48	1
9401794760	MR MIRNAL DAS	9401794646	SRI SATYAJIT DAS	20-06-2014	13:33:52	122
9401794760	MR MIRNAL DAS	9707243173	BALENNAKALITA	20-06-2014	17:20:46	65
4 66b 85763b 9e BANK MESSAGE BANK MESSAGE		9401794760	MR MIRNAL DAS	20-06-2014	18:11:20	1
4 66b 85763b 9e BANK MESSAGE		9401794760	MR MIRNAL DAS	20-06-2014	18:26:22	1
9401794760	MR MIRNAL DAS	9508818870	DWIPENNATH	20-06-2014	18:26:28	44
9401794646	SRI SATYAJIT DAS	9401794760	MR MIRNAL DAS	20-06-2014	19:11:18	342
9508818870	DWIPENNATH	9401794760	MR MIRNAL DAS	20-06-2014	19:36:58	11
9401794760	MR MIRNAL DAS	9508818870	DWIPENNATH	20-06-2014	19:38:14	13
9401794760	MR MIRNAL DAS	9508818870	DWIPENNATH	20-06-2014	19:41:11	23
24b6b 653bd 060 BANK MESSAGE		9401794760	MR MIRNAL DAS	21-06-2014	09:11:17	1
9401794760	MR MIRNAL DAS	9954898960	PRABHAT NATH	21-06-2014	11:28:36	165
2 96b 65b81 061 BANK MESSAGE		9401794760	MR MIRNAL DAS	21-06-2014	11:28:52	1

Calling (A) Party	Name 1 Name 2 Name 3	Called (B) Party	Name 1 Name 2 Name 3	Call Date	Call Time	Call Duration (in second)
9401794646	SRI SATYAJIT DAS	9401794760	MR MIRNAL DAS	21-06-2014	11:42:09	354
4526b 85763b 9e BANK MESSAGE		9401794760	MR MIRNAL DAS	21-06-2014	12:46:32	1
4526b 85763b 9e BANK MESSAGE		9401794760	MR MIRNAL DAS	21-06-2014	12:46:35	1
9401794760	MR MIRNAL DAS	9508818870	DWIPENNATH	21-06-2014	18:02:52	118
9401794760	MR MIRNAL DAS	9508818870	DWIPENNATH	21-06-2014	19:04:18	103
24b6b 61395da65 BANK MESSAGE		9401794760	MR MIRNAL DAS	22-06-2014	10:15:05	1
24b6b 653bd 060 BANK MESSAGE		9401794760	MR MIRNAL DAS	22-06-2014	10:19:31	1
24b6b 653b1e 68 BANK MESSAGE		9401794760	MR MIRNAL DAS	22-06-2014	11:20:40	1
9401794760	MR MIRNAL DAS	9707243173	BALENNAKALITA	22-06-2014	11:21:19	62
9401794760	MR MIRNAL DAS	9707243173	BALENNAKALITA	23-06-2014	09:33:37	33
4526b 85763b 9e BANK MESSAGE		9401794760	MR MIRNAL DAS	23-06-2014	10:27:12	1
9401794646	SRI SATYAJIT DAS	9401794760	MR MIRNAL DAS	23-06-2014	11:22:02	85
24b6b 61b81 460 BANK MESSAGE		9401794760	MR MIRNAL DAS	23-06-2014	13:30:52	1
24b6b 653bd 060 BANK MESSAGE		9401794760	MR MIRNAL DAS	23-06-2014	16:15:58	1
9401794646	SRI SATYAJIT DAS	9401794760	MR MIRNAL DAS	23-06-2014	20:29:13	304
2 96b 65b81 060 BANK MESSAGE		9401794760	MR MIRNAL DAS	23-06-2014	20:30:23	1
4526b 85763b 9e BANK MESSAGE		9401794760	MR MIRNAL DAS	24-06-2014	09:23:29	1
9401794760	MR MIRNAL DAS	9401794646	SRI SATYAJIT DAS	24-06-2014	11:09:44	161
9401794760	MR MIRNAL DAS	9508818870	DWIPENNATH	24-06-2014	12:02:30	5
9401794760	MR MIRNAL DAS	9401794645	SRI SATYAJIT DAS	24-06-2014	12:03:52	52

Calling (A) Party	Name 1 Name 2 Name 3	Called (B) Party	Name 1 Name 2 Name 3	Call Date	Call Time	Call Duration (in second)
9401794760	MR MIRNAL DAS	9508818870	DWIPENNATH	24-06-2014	12:05:13	79
9401794760	MR MIRNAL DAS	9401794646	SRI SATYAJIT DAS	24-06-2014	13:05:55	18
9401794646	SRI SATYAJIT DAS	9401794760	MR MIRNAL DAS	24-06-2014	13:55:04	58
9401794760	MR MIRNAL DAS	9508818870	DWIPENNATH	24-06-2014	13:58:23	94
9401794760	MR MIRNAL DAS	9401794646	SRI SATYAJIT DAS	24-06-2014	14:14:14	6
9401794646	SRI SATYAJIT DAS	9401794760	MR MIRNAL DAS	24-06-2014	19:26:08	51
9401794760	MR MIRNAL DAS	9508818870	DWIPENNATH	24-06-2014	20:05:16	6
9401794646	SRI SATYAJIT DAS	9401794760	MR MIRNAL DAS	24-06-2014	21:32:20	11
9401794760	MR MIRNAL DAS	9401794646	SRI SATYAJIT DAS	25-06-2014	11:30:43	10
24b6b 65b9d 061 BANK MESSAGE		9401794760	MR MIRNAL DAS	26-06-2014	12:19:24	1
2 96b 65b81 060 BANK MESSAGE		9401794760	MR MIRNAL DAS	26-06-2014	12:19:40	1
9401794760	MR MIRNAL DAS	9401794646	SRI SATYAJIT DAS	26-06-2014	15:03:01	143
9401794646	SRI SATYAJIT DAS	9401794760	MR MIRNAL DAS	26-06-2014	16:39:48	106
9401794646	SRI SATYAJIT DAS	9401794760	MR MIRNAL DAS	26-06-2014	19:20:27	239
9401794760	MR MIRNAL DAS	9508818870	DWIPENNATH	27-06-2014	10:59:23	1
9401794760	MR MIRNAL DAS	9508818870	DWIPENNATH	27-06-2014	10:59:52	40
2 96b 65b81 060 BANK MESSAGE		9401794760	MR MIRNAL DAS	27-06-2014	13:14:18	1
9401794760	MR MIRNAL DAS	9401794646	SRI SATYAJIT DAS	27-06-2014	13:28:15	63
9401794760	MR MIRNAL DAS	9401794646	SRI SATYAJIT DAS	27-06-2014	13:42:37	146
9401794760	MR MIRNAL DAS	9401794646	SRI SATYAJIT DAS	27-06-2014	14:44:09	27

Calling (A) Party	Name 1 Name 2 Name 3	Called (B) Party	Name 1 Name 2 Name 3	Call Date	Call Time	Call Duration (in second)
2 96b 65b81 060 BANK MESSAGE		9401794760	MR MIRNAL DAS	27-06-2014	15:46:21	1
1 66b 85763b 9e BANK MESSAGE		9401794760	MR MIRNAL DAS	27-06-2014	22:36:42	1
1 66b 85763b 9e BANK MESSAGE BANK MESSAGE		9401794760	MR MIRNAL DAS	27-06-2014	22:38:03	1
9401794760	MR MIRNAL DAS	9401794646	SRI SATYAJIT DAS	27-06-2014	22:40:28	122
24b6b 61399d660 BANK MESSAGE		9401794760	MR MIRNAL DAS	28-06-2014	13:46:30	1
24b6b 653bd 060 BANK MESSAGE		9401794760	MR MIRNAL DAS	29-06-2014	10:31:16	1
24b6b 61399d660 BANK MESSAGE		9401794760	MR MIRNAL DAS	29-06-2014	16:52:48	1
24b6b 653 1e060 BANK MESSAGE		9401794760	MR MIRNAL DAS	30-06-2014	10:13:03	1
24b6b 65ba1e078 BANK MESSAGE		9401794760	MR MIRNAL DAS	30-06-2014	12:51:17	1
4 66b682 9e4589 BANK MESSAGE		9401794760	MR MIRNAL DAS	1/7/2014	08:44:20	1
24b6b 653bd 060 BANK MESSAGE		9401794760	MR MIRNAL DAS	1/7/2014	14:35:26	1
24b6b 6539d 463 BANK MESSAGE		9401794760	MR MIRNAL DAS	1/7/2014	14:53:44	1
24b6b 653bd 060 BANK MESSAGE		9401794760	MR MIRNAL DAS	2/7/2014	17:10:30	1
24b6b 653bd 060 BANK MESSAGE		9401794760	MR MIRNAL DAS	3/7/2014	10:54:16	1
24b6b 61399d660 BANK MESSAGE		9401794760	MR MIRNAL DAS	3/7/2014	16:35:08	1
9707243173	BALENNAKALITA	9401794760	MR MIRNAL DAS	4/7/2014	11:09:29	55
2486b062ba9da61 BANK MESSAGE		9401794760	MR MIRNAL DAS	4/7/2014	11:28:06	1
24b6b 61399d660 BANK MESSAGE		9401794760	MR MIRNAL DAS	5/7/2014	09:21:22	1
24b6b 61399d660 BANK MESSAGE		9401794760	MR MIRNAL DAS	5/7/2014	10:30:09	1

Calling (A) Party	Name 1 Name 2 Name 3	Called (B) Party	Name 1 Name 2 Name 3	Call Date	Call Time	Call Duration (in second)
9707243173	BALENNAKALITA	9401794760	MR MIRNAL DAS	6/7/2014	05:16:09	33
24b6b 61399d660 BANK MESSAGE		9401794760	MR MIRNAL DAS	6/7/2014	15:50:17	1
24b6b 61399d660 BANK MESSAGE		9401794760	MR MIRNAL DAS	6/7/2014	17:35:44	1
24b6be9659e4b81 BANK MESSAGE		9401794760	MR MIRNAL DAS	6/7/2014	19:11:27	1
24b6b 61399d660 BANK MESSAGE		9401794760	MR MIRNAL DAS	7/7/2014	10:39:25	1
66b 85763b 9e BANK MESSAGE		9401794760	MR MIRNAL DAS	7/7/2014	10:59:51	1
66b 85763b 9e BANK MESSAGE		9401794760	MR MIRNAL DAS	7/7/2014	10:59:56	1
24b6b 6539d 463 BANK MESSAGE		9401794760	MR MIRNAL DAS	7/7/2014	15:44:54	1
2 96b 65b81 060 BANK MESSAGE		9401794760	MR MIRNAL DAS	7/7/2014	21:01:37	1
24b6b 61399d660 BANK MESSAGE		9401794760	MR MIRNAL DAS	8/7/2014	09:04:52	1
2 96b 65b81 060 BANK MESSAGE		9401794760	MR MIRNAL DAS	8/7/2014	10:55:58	1
24b6b8a2d4e39ab BANK MESSAGE		9401794760	MR MIRNAL DAS	9/7/2014	09:36:34	1
24b6b 65ba1e078 BANK MESSAGE		9401794760	MR MIRNAL DAS	9/7/2014	10:06:56	1
83add468b d a64 BANK MESSAGE		9401794760	MR MIRNAL DAS	9/7/2014	17:53:56	1
83add468b d a64 BANK MESSAGE		9401794760	MR MIRNAL DAS	9/7/2014	17:55:04	1
83add468b d a64 BANK MESSAGE		9401794760	MR MIRNAL DAS	9/7/2014	17:56:12	1
83add468b d a64 BANK MESSAGE		9401794760	MR MIRNAL DAS	9/7/2014	17:57:19	1
83add468b d a64 BANK MESSAGE		9401794760	MR MIRNAL DAS	9/7/2014	17:58:31	1
83add468b d a64 BANK MESSAGE		9401794760	MR MIRNAL DAS	9/7/2014	17:59:36	1
83add468b d a64 BANK MESSAGE		9401794760	MR MIRNAL DAS	9/7/2014	18:00:44	1

Calling (A) Party	Name 1 Name 2 Name 3	Called (B) Party	Name 1 Name 2 Name 3	Call Date	Call Time	Call Duration (in second)
83add468b d a64 BANK MESSAGE		9401794760	MR MIRNAL DAS	9/7/2014	19:01:45	1
9707243173	BALENNAKALITA	9401794760	MR MIRNAL DAS	########	09:30:47	33
24b6b 653bd 060 BANK MESSAGE		9401794760	MR MIRNAL DAS	########	17:37:47	1
24b6b 61395da65 BANK MESSAGE		9401794760	MR MIRNAL DAS	########	10:26:50	1
9401794646	SRI SATYAJIT DAS	9401794760	MR MIRNAL DAS	########	11:29:46	67
66b0663b1d265 BANK MESSAGE		9401794760	MR MIRNAL DAS	########	14:37:13	1
9401794646	SRI SATYAJIT DAS	9401794760	MR MIRNAL DAS	########	14:59:36	144
24b6b8a2d4e39ab BANK MESSAGE		9401794760	MR MIRNAL DAS	########	09:01:06	1
9401794646	SRI SATYAJIT DAS	9401794760	MR MIRNAL DAS	########	11:39:01	84
9401794646	SRI SATYAJIT DAS	9401794760	MR MIRNAL DAS	########	12:33:51	289
9401794646	SRI SATYAJIT DAS	9401794760	MR MIRNAL DAS	########	14:07:38	44
24b6b 6539d 463 BANK MESSAGE		9401794760	MR MIRNAL DAS	########	14:13:09	1
2 96b 65b81 060 BANK MESSAGE		9401794760	MR MIRNAL DAS	########	14:14:07	1
24b6be9e 6e358 BANK MESSAGE		9401794760	MR MIRNAL DAS	14-07-2014	10:05:55	1
24b6be9e 6e358 BANK MESSAGE		9401794760	MR MIRNAL DAS	14-07-2014	10:05:58	1
24b6b 653bd 060 BANK MESSAGE		9401794760	MR MIRNAL DAS	14-07-2014	10:44:24	1
9401794646	SRI SATYAJIT DAS	9401794760	MR MIRNAL DAS	14-07-2014	19:58:51	269
24b6b8a2d4e39ab BANK MESSAGE		9401794760	MR MIRNAL DAS	15-07-2014	09:01:19	1
24b6b 65ba9de68 BANK MESSAGE		9401794760	MR MIRNAL DAS	15-07-2014	12:11:37	1
2 96b 65b81 060 BANK MESSAGE		9401794760	MR MIRNAL DAS	15-07-2014	14:43:25	1

Calling (A) Party	Name 1 Name 2 Name 3	Called (B) Party	Name 1 Name 2 Name 3	Call Date	Call Time	Call Duration (in second)
24b6b 653bd 060 BANK MESSAGE		9401794760	MR MIRNAL DAS	15-07-2014	18:55:25	1
24b6b 61395da65 BANK MESSAGE		9401794760	MR MIRNAL DAS	16-07-2014	10:14:34	1
24b6b 61399d660 BANK MESSAGE		9401794760	MR MIRNAL DAS	16-07-2014	10:57:03	1
24b6b 61399d660 BANK MESSAGE		9401794760	MR MIRNAL DAS	16-07-2014	10:57:07	1
24b6b 61b81 461 BANK MESSAGE		9401794760	MR MIRNAL DAS	16-07-2014	12:39:59	1
9401794760	MR MIRNAL DAS	9508818870	DWIPENNATH	16-07-2014	13:34:16	17
24b6b 65ba9de68 BANK MESSAGE		9401794760	MR MIRNAL DAS	16-07-2014	13:45:37	1
24b6b8a2d4e39ab BANK MESSAGE		9401794760	MR MIRNAL DAS	17-07-2014	09:05:23	1
24b6b 653 1e060 BANK MESSAGE		9401794760	MR MIRNAL DAS	17-07-2014	10:32:19	1
24b6b 65ba9de68 BANK MESSAGE		9401794760	MR MIRNAL DAS	17-07-2014	11:40:37	1
24b6b8a2d4e39ab BANK MESSAGE		9401794760	MR MIRNAL DAS	18-07-2014	09:01:36	1
24b6b8a2d4e39ab BANK MESSAGE		9401794760	MR MIRNAL DAS	19-07-2014	09:01:41	1
9401794646	SRI SATYAJIT DAS	9401794760	MR MIRNAL DAS	19-07-2014	10:40:19	29
9401794760	MR MIRNAL DAS	9508818870	DWIPENNATH	19-07-2014	11:25:47	44
9508818870	DWIPENNATH	9401794760	MR MIRNAL DAS	19-07-2014	11:32:09	45
24b6b8a2d4e39ab BANK MESSAGE BANK MESSAGE		9401794760	MR MIRNAL DAS	21-07-2014	09:03:05	1
2 96b 65b81 060 BANK MESSAGE		9401794760	MR MIRNAL DAS	21-07-2014	13:09:48	1
24b6b 653bd 060 BANK MESSAGE		9401794760	MR MIRNAL DAS	22-07-2014	15:18:09	1
2 96b 65b81 060 BANK MESSAGE		9401794760	MR MIRNAL DAS	22-07-2014	16:35:37	1

Calling (A) Party	Name 1 Name 2 Name 3	Called (B) Party	Name 1 Name 2 Name 3	Call Date	Call Time	Call Duration (in second)
9401794646	SRI SATYAJIT DAS	9401794760	MR MIRNAL DAS	22-07-2014	19:35:50	55
2 96b 65b81 060 BANK MESSAGE		9401794760	MR MIRNAL DAS	22-07-2014	20:03:51	1
24b6b061381 060 BANK MESSAGE		9401794760	MR MIRNAL DAS	23-07-2014	15:59:32	1
24b6b8a2d4e39ab BANK MESSAGE		9401794760	MR MIRNAL DAS	24-07-2014	09:02:07	1
24b6b 653b1e 68 BANK MESSAGE		9401794760	MR MIRNAL DAS	24-07-2014	16:26:54	1
24b6b 653bd 060 BANK MESSAGE		9401794760	MR MIRNAL DAS	24-07-2014	16:31:11	1
2 96b 65b81 060 BANK MESSAGE		9401794760	MR MIRNAL DAS	24-07-2014	17:40:07	1
9401794760	MR MIRNAL DAS	9401794646	SRI SATYAJIT DAS	24-07-2014	17:46:16	153
2 96b 65b81 060 BANK MESSAGE		9401794760	MR MIRNAL DAS	24-07-2014	17:50:44	1
9401794646	SRI SATYAJIT DAS	9401794760	MR MIRNAL DAS	24-07-2014	19:56:01	34
2 96b 65b81 060 BANK MESSAGE		9401794760	MR MIRNAL DAS	25-07-2014	08:39:04	1
24b6b8a2d4e39ab BANK MESSAGE		9401794760	MR MIRNAL DAS	25-07-2014	09:02:14	1
9707243173	BALENNAKALITA	9401794760	MR MIRNAL DAS	25-07-2014	19:03:42	69
24b6b8a2d4e39ab BANK MESSAGE		9401794760	MR MIRNAL DAS	26-07-2014	09:02:17	1
9401794646	SRI SATYAJIT DAS	9401794760	MR MIRNAL DAS	26-07-2014	11:53:10	274
4 66b682 9e4589 BANK MESSAGE		9401794760	MR MIRNAL DAS	26-07-2014	17:05:57	1
9401794646	SRI SATYAJIT DAS	9401794760	MR MIRNAL DAS	27-07-2014	11:43:41	37
24b6b 6539d 463 BANK MESSAGE		9401794760	MR MIRNAL DAS	27-07-2014	14:00:21	1
24b6b8a2d4e39ab BANK MESSAGE		9401794760	MR MIRNAL DAS	28-07-2014	09:02:09	1
9401794646	SRI SATYAJIT DAS	9401794760	MR MIRNAL DAS	28-07-2014	10:58:05	38

Calling (A) Party	Name 1 Name 2 Name 3	Called (B) Party	Name 1 Name 2 Name 3	Call Date	Call Time	Call Duration (in second)
24b6b 61395da65	BANK MESSAGE	9401794760	MR MIRNAL DAS	28-07-2014	13:13:25	1
4 66b682 9e4589	BANK MESSAGE	9401794760	MR MIRNAL DAS	28-07-2014	13:29:31	1
2 96b 65b81 060	BANK MESSAGE	9401794760	MR MIRNAL DAS	28-07-2014	19:05:32	1
9401794646	SRI SATYAJIT DAS	9401794760	MR MIRNAL DAS	28-07-2014	19:28:18	12
24b6b 653bd 060	BANK MESSAGE	9401794760	MR MIRNAL DAS	28-07-2014	19:30:23	1
24 6b284d6e4589	BANK MESSAGE	9401794760	MR MIRNAL DAS	28-07-2014	20:23:29	1
24 6b284d6e4589	BANK MESSAGE	9401794760	MR MIRNAL DAS	28-07-2014	20:24:43	1
9401794646	SRI SATYAJIT DAS	9401794760	MR MIRNAL DAS	28-07-2014	22:00:10	43
9508818870	DWIPENNATH	9401794760	MR MIRNAL DAS	28-07-2014	22:00:56	40
9508818870	DWIPENNATH	9401794760	MR MIRNAL DAS	28-07-2014	22:02:04	1
9508818870	DWIPENNATH	9401794760	MR MIRNAL DAS	28-07-2014	22:03:06	52
24b6b8a2d4e39ab	BANK MESSAGE	9401794760	MR MIRNAL DAS	29-07-2014	09:02:04	1
24b6b 65ba9de68	BANK MESSAGE	9401794760	MR MIRNAL DAS	29-07-2014	10:52:45	1
24b6b8a2d4e39ab	BANK MESSAGE	9401794760	MR MIRNAL DAS	30-07-2014	09:02:06	1
24b6b 65b9d 061	BANK MESSAGE	9401794760	MR MIRNAL DAS	30-07-2014	13:50:34	1
24b6b 65ba1e078	BANK MESSAGE	9401794760	MR MIRNAL DAS	30-07-2014	18:04:58	1
24b6b8a2d4e39ab	BANK MESSAGE	9401794760	MR MIRNAL DAS	31-07-2014	09:02:12	1
24 6b284d6e4589	BANK MESSAGE	9401794760	MR MIRNAL DAS	31-07-2014	09:13:12	1
24b6b 653bd 060	BANK MESSAGE	9401794760	MR MIRNAL DAS	31-07-2014	09:33:41	1
4 66b682 9e4589	BANK MESSAGE	9401794760	MR MIRNAL DAS	1/8/2014	10:11:47	1

Calling (A) Party	Name 1 Name 2 Name 3	Called (B) Party	Name 1 Name 2 Name 3	Call Date	Call Time	Call Duration (in second)
24b6b 6539d 463 BANK MESSAGE		9401794760	MR MIRNAL DAS	1/8/2014	16:56:57	1
9401794646	SRI SATYAJIT DAS	9401794760	MR MIRNAL DAS	1/8/2014	17:46:56	395
24b6b 61395da65 BANK MESSAGE		9401794760	MR MIRNAL DAS	2/8/2014	15:31:31	1
9401794646	SRI SATYAJIT DAS	9401794760	MR MIRNAL DAS	2/8/2014	17:58:15	251
2 96b 65b81 060 BANK MESSAGE		9401794760	MR MIRNAL DAS	2/8/2014	18:50:04	1
2 96b 65b81 060 BANK MESSAGE		9401794760	MR MIRNAL DAS	3/8/2014	09:32:15	1
9401794646	SRI SATYAJIT DAS	9401794760	MR MIRNAL DAS	3/8/2014	19:15:48	342
24b6b 65ba9de68 BANK MESSAGE		9401794760	MR MIRNAL DAS	4/8/2014	10:51:39	1
9401794760	MR MIRNAL DAS	9401794646	SRI SATYAJIT DAS	4/8/2014	12:28:06	179
2 96b 65b81 060 BANK MESSAGE		9401794760	MR MIRNAL DAS	4/8/2014	15:25:35	1
24b6b 61399d660 BANK MESSAGE		9401794760	MR MIRNAL DAS	5/8/2014	09:18:17	1
24b6b 65ba1d867 BANK MESSAGE		9401794760	MR MIRNAL DAS	5/8/2014	12:58:58	1
24b6b 61395da65 BANK MESSAGE		9401794760	MR MIRNAL DAS	5/8/2014	18:42:11	1
24 6b284d6e4589 BANK MESSAGE		9401794760	MR MIRNAL DAS	5/8/2014	19:07:45	1
2 96b 65b81 060 BANK MESSAGE		9401794760	MR MIRNAL DAS	5/8/2014	20:32:14	1
24b6b8a2d4e39ab BANK MESSAGE		9401794760	MR MIRNAL DAS	6/8/2014	08:30:01	1
24b6b 653 1e060 BANK MESSAGE		9401794760	MR MIRNAL DAS	6/8/2014	10:33:45	1
24b6b 61399d660 BANK MESSAGE		9401794760	MR MIRNAL DAS	6/8/2014	11:08:46	1
9401794646	SRI SATYAJIT DAS	9401794760	MR MIRNAL DAS	7/8/2014	08:53:12	32
9706991838	SATYAJIT DAS	9401794760	MR MIRNAL DAS	7/8/2014	11:09:00	1

Calling (A) Party	Name 1 Name 2 Name 3	Called (B) Party	Name 1 Name 2 Name 3	Call Date	Call Time	Call Duration (in second)
9401794760	MR MIRNAL DAS	9401794646	SRI SATYAJIT DAS	7/8/2014	12:48:41	13
24 6b284d6e4589	BANK MESSAGE	9401794760	MR MIRNAL DAS	7/8/2014	13:47:28	1
24 6b284d6e4589	BANK MESSAGE	9401794760	MR MIRNAL DAS	7/8/2014	13:49:06	1
24b6b 6539d 463	BANK MESSAGE	9401794760	MR MIRNAL DAS	7/8/2014	16:10:08	1
4 66b066381 061	BANK MESSAGE	9401794760	MR MIRNAL DAS	7/8/2014	17:12:12	1
9401794646	SRI SATYAJIT DAS	9401794760	MR MIRNAL DAS	7/8/2014	19:56:52	278
4d06b 81 16158b	BANK MESSAGE	9401794760	MR MIRNAL DAS	7/8/2014	21:26:52	1
4d06b 81 16158b	BANK MESSAGE	9401794760	MR MIRNAL DAS	7/8/2014	21:26:54	1
4d06b 81 16158b	BANK MESSAGE	9401794760	MR MIRNAL DAS	7/8/2014	21:26:57	1
9706991838	SATYAJIT DAS	9401794760	MR MIRNAL DAS	7/8/2014	21:29:42	1
9401794760	MR MIRNAL DAS	9401794646	SRI SATYAJIT DAS	7/8/2014	21:30:46	25
9401794646	SRI SATYAJIT DAS	9401794760	MR MIRNAL DAS	7/8/2014	21:38:23	112
9401794760	MR MIRNAL DAS	9401794646	SRI SATYAJIT DAS	7/8/2014	21:49:04	64
9401794646	SRI SATYAJIT DAS	9401794760	MR MIRNAL DAS	8/8/2014	13:39:33	176
9706991838	SATYAJIT DAS	9401794760	MR MIRNAL DAS	8/8/2014	13:57:02	1
9706991838	SATYAJIT DAS	9401794760	MR MIRNAL DAS	8/8/2014	16:42:03	1
24 6b284d6e4589	BANK MESSAGE	9401794760	MR MIRNAL DAS	8/8/2014	19:18:10	1
2 96b 65b81 060	BANK MESSAGE	9401794760	MR MIRNAL DAS	9/8/2014	20:03:43	1
2 96b 65b81 060	BANK MESSAGE	9401794760	MR MIRNAL DAS	########	11:01:59	1
24b6b 65ba1d867	BANK MESSAGE	9401794760	MR MIRNAL DAS	########	14:25:19	1

Calling (A) Party	Name 1 Name 2 Name 3	Called (B) Party	Name 1 Name 2 Name 3	Call Date	Call Time	Call Duration (in second)
24b6b 653bd 060 BANK MESSAGE		9401794760	MR MIRNAL DAS	########	14:43:07	1
9401794760	MR MIRNAL DAS	9401794646	SRI SATYAJIT DAS	########	14:58:27	61
2 96b 65b81 060 BANK MESSAGE		9401794760	MR MIRNAL DAS	########	17:30:11	1
9401794646	SRI SATYAJIT DAS	9401794760	MR MIRNAL DAS	########	19:13:54	231
9706991838	SATYAJIT DAS	9401794760	MR MIRNAL DAS	########	08:37:18	1
24b6b 65ba1e078 BANK MESSAGE BANK MESSAGE		9401794760	MR MIRNAL DAS	########	09:49:37	1
24b6b 61395da65 BANK MESSAGE		9401794760	MR MIRNAL DAS	########	10:50:22	1
9706991838	SATYAJIT DAS	9401794760	MR MIRNAL DAS	########	11:42:28	1
9401794646	SRI SATYAJIT DAS	9401794760	MR MIRNAL DAS	########	12:32:35	573
9401794646	SRI SATYAJIT DAS	9401794760	MR MIRNAL DAS	########	12:45:51	75
2 96b 65b81 060 BANK MESSAGE		9401794760	MR MIRNAL DAS	########	13:02:04	1
9401794760	MR MIRNAL DAS	9401794646	SRI SATYAJIT DAS	########	14:31:06	26
24b6b 653bd 060 BANK MESSAGE		9401794760	MR MIRNAL DAS	########	16:09:48	1
2 96b 65b81 060 BANK MESSAGE		9401794760	MR MIRNAL DAS	########	16:30:44	1
2 96b 65b81 060 BANK MESSAGE		9401794760	MR MIRNAL DAS	########	11:10:50	1
9401794760	MR MIRNAL DAS	9401794646	SRI SATYAJIT DAS	########	11:26:05	153
9401794646	SRI SATYAJIT DAS	9401794760	MR MIRNAL DAS	########	19:38:30	6
24b6ba914b615ab BANK MESSAGE		9401794760	MR MIRNAL DAS	########	21:36:40	1
24b6ba914b615ab BANK MESSAGE		9401794760	MR MIRNAL DAS	########	21:36:45	1

Calling (A) Party	Name 1 Name 2 Name 3	Called (B) Party	Name 1 Name 2 Name 3	Call Date	Call Time	Call Duration (in second)
24b6b 653bd 060 BANK MESSAGE		9401794760	MR MIRNAL DAS	13-08-2014	11:37:15	1
2 96b 65b81 060 BANK MESSAGE		9401794760	MR MIRNAL DAS	13-08-2014	13:32:58	1
9706991838	SATYAJIT DAS	9401794760	MR MIRNAL DAS	13-08-2014	13:47:53	1
9706991838	SATYAJIT DAS	9401794760	MR MIRNAL DAS	13-08-2014	14:19:53	1
2 96b 65b81 060 BANK MESSAGE		9401794760	MR MIRNAL DAS	13-08-2014	19:25:19	1
9401794646	SRI SATYAJIT DAS	9401794760	MR MIRNAL DAS	13-08-2014	19:29:46	364
2 96b 65b81 060 BANK MESSAGE		9401794760	MR MIRNAL DAS	13-08-2014	19:47:01	1
9401794760	MR MIRNAL DAS	9401794646	SRI SATYAJIT DAS	14-08-2014	11:56:32	177
2 96b 65b81 060 BANK MESSAGE		9401794760	MR MIRNAL DAS	14-08-2014	12:36:28	1
9401794760	MR MIRNAL DAS	9401794646	SRI SATYAJIT DAS	14-08-2014	20:06:21	123
24b6b 653bd 060 BANK MESSAGE		9401794760	MR MIRNAL DAS	15-08-2014	13:11:29	1
24b6b 65ba1d867 BANK MESSAGE		9401794760	MR MIRNAL DAS	15-08-2014	13:42:18	1
2 96b 65b81 060 BANK MESSAGE		9401794760	MR MIRNAL DAS	15-08-2014	14:55:19	1
9401794760	MR MIRNAL DAS	9401794646	SRI SATYAJIT DAS	15-08-2014	19:29:42	32
2 96b 65b81 060 BANK MESSAGE		9401794760	MR MIRNAL DAS	15-08-2014	19:40:58	1
2 96b 65b81 060 BANK MESSAGE		9401794760	MR MIRNAL DAS	16-08-2014	09:30:01	1
24b6b 653bd 060 BANK MESSAGE		9401794760	MR MIRNAL DAS	16-08-2014	09:38:42	1
2 96b 65b81 060 BANK MESSAGE		9401794760	MR MIRNAL DAS	16-08-2014	19:40:08	1

CDR OF DIPAK DAS

Calling (A) Party Telephone Number/MSISDN	Name	Called (B) Party Telephone Number/Access Point Name	Name	Date	Time	Duration In Secs.
9085341993	DIPAK DAS	9707783876	GIASUDDINAHMED	18-08-2014	8:17:22	0
9085341993	DIPAK DAS	9707783876	GIASUDDINAHMED	18-08-2014	8:14:28	0
9085341993	DIPAK DAS	9707783876	GIASUDDINAHMED	16-08-2014	18:17:19	278
9085341993	DIPAK DAS	9707783876	GIASUDDINAHMED	16-08-2014	18:15:38	40
9085341993	DIPAK DAS	9707783876	GIASUDDINAHMED	16-08-2014	18:11:39	153
9085341993	DIPAK DAS	9707783876	GIASUDDINAHMED	16-08-2014	18:06:42	0
9085341993	DIPAK DAS	9707783876	GIASUDDINAHMED	16-08-2014	18:01:46	0
9085341993	DIPAK DAS	9707783876	GIASUDDINAHMED	16-08-2014	18:01:23	0
9085341993	DIPAK DAS	9707783876	GIASUDDINAHMED	16-08-2014	18:00:19	0
9085341993	DIPAK DAS	9707783876	GIASUDDINAHMED	16-08-2014	17:47:56	0
9085341993	DIPAK DAS	9707783876	GIASUDDINAHMED	16-08-2014	17:47:54	0
9085341993	DIPAK DAS	9707783876	GIASUDDINAHMED	16-08-2014	17:47:53	0
9085341993	DIPAK DAS	9707474658	HITESH KALITA	15-08-2014	20:19:23	0
9085341993	DIPAK DAS	9707474658	HITESH KALITA	15-08-2014	20:19:16	0
9085341993	DIPAK DAS	9707783876	GIASUDDINAHMED	15-08-2014	20:13:45	0
9085341993	DIPAK DAS	9707783876	GIASUDDINAHMED	15-08-2014	20:00:38	0
9085341993	DIPAK DAS	9707783876	GIASUDDINAHMED	15-08-2014	19:53:31	0

Calling (A) Party Telephone Number/MSISDN	Name	Called (B) Party Telephone Number/Access Point Name	Name	Date	Time	Duration In Secs.
9085341993	DIPAK DAS	9707783876	GIASUDDINAHMED	15-08-2014	19:51:58	0
9085341993	DIPAK DAS	9707783876	GIASUDDINAHMED	15-08-2014	12:49:40	0
9085341993	DIPAK DAS	9707783876	GIASUDDINAHMED	15-08-2014	11:53:57	0
9085341993	DIPAK DAS	9707783876	GIASUDDINAHMED	15-08-2014	11:49:08	0
9085341993	DIPAK DAS	9707783876	GIASUDDINAHMED	13-08-2014	22:39:36	0
9085341993	DIPAK DAS	9707783876	GIASUDDINAHMED	13-08-2014	22:33:01	0
9085341993	DIPAK DAS	9707783876	GIASUDDINAHMED	13-08-2014	22:19:35	0
9085341993	DIPAK DAS	9707783876	GIASUDDINAHMED	13-08-2014	22:11:02	0
9085341993	DIPAK DAS	9707783876	GIASUDDINAHMED	13-08-2014	21:31:33	0
9085341993	DIPAK DAS	9707783876	GIASUDDINAHMED	13-08-2014	19:31:02	0
9085341993	DIPAK DAS	9707783876	GIASUDDINAHMED	13-08-2014	19:22:51	0
9085341993	DIPAK DAS	9707783876	GIASUDDINAHMED	13-08-2014	19:22:49	0
9085341993	DIPAK DAS	9707783876	GIASUDDINAHMED	13-08-2014	19:22:47	0
9085341993	DIPAK DAS	9707783876	GIASUDDINAHMED	13-08-2014	18:16:02	0
9085341993	DIPAK DAS	9707783876	GIASUDDINAHMED	13-08-2014	18:15:23	0
9085341993	DIPAK DAS	9707783876	GIASUDDINAHMED	13-08-2014	18:11:28	0
9085341993	DIPAK DAS	9707783876	GIASUDDINAHMED	13-08-2014	17:55:57	0
9085341993	DIPAK DAS	9707783876	GIASUDDINAHMED	13-08-2014	17:49:55	0

Calling (A) Party Telephone Number/MSISDN	Name	Called (B) Party Telephone Number/Access Point Name	Name	Date	Time	Duration In Secs.
9085341993	DIPAK DAS	9707783876	GIASUDDINAHMED	13-08-2014	17:48:31	0
9085341993	DIPAK DAS	9707783876	GIASUDDINAHMED	13-08-2014	17:46:43	0
9085341993	DIPAK DAS	9707783876	GIASUDDINAHMED	13-08-2014	17:32:42	0
9085341993	DIPAK DAS	9707783876	GIASUDDINAHMED	13-08-2014	17:27:24	0
9085341993	DIPAK DAS	9707474658	HITESH KALITA	12/8/2014	22:38:18	0
9085341993	DIPAK DAS	9707783876	GIASUDDINAHMED	12/8/2014	22:27:04	0
9085341993	DIPAK DAS	9707783876	GIASUDDINAHMED	12/8/2014	21:54:43	0
9085341993	DIPAK DAS	9707474658	HITESH KALITA	12/8/2014	21:39:05	0
9085341993	DIPAK DAS	9707783876	GIASUDDINAHMED	12/8/2014	21:25:39	0
9085341993	DIPAK DAS	9707783876	GIASUDDINAHMED	12/8/2014	21:22:14	0
9085341993	DIPAK DAS	9707783876	GIASUDDINAHMED	12/8/2014	20:58:43	0
9085341993	DIPAK DAS	9707783876	GIASUDDINAHMED	12/8/2014	20:39:18	0
9085341993	DIPAK DAS	9707474658	HITESH KALITA	12/8/2014	16:48:48	0
9085341993	DIPAK DAS	9707783876	GIASUDDINAHMED	12/8/2014	6:28:02	0
9085341993	DIPAK DAS	9707783876	GIASUDDINAHMED	12/8/2014	6:19:07	0
9085341993	DIPAK DAS	9707783876	GIASUDDINAHMED	11/8/2014	23:20:34	0
9085341993	DIPAK DAS	9707783876	GIASUDDINAHMED	11/8/2014	22:19:44	0
9085341993	DIPAK DAS	9707783876	GIASUDDINAHMED	11/8/2014	22:11:58	0

Calling (A) Party Telephone Number/MSISDN	Name	Called (B) Party Telephone Number/Access Point Name	Name	Date	Time	Duration In Secs.
9085341993	DIPAK DAS	9707783876	GIASUDDINAHMED	11/8/2014	21:59:30	720
9085341993	DIPAK DAS	9707783876	GIASUDDINAHMED	11/8/2014	21:38:52	846
9085341993	DIPAK DAS	9707474658	HITESH KALITA	11/8/2014	18:46:09	16
9085341993	DIPAK DAS	9401165464	HITESWAR KALITA	11/8/2014	7:44:28	39
9085341993	DIPAK DAS	9707474658	HITESH KALITA	11/8/2014	7:42:25	32
9085341993	DIPAK DAS	9707783876	GIASUDDINAHMED	10/8/2014	20:36:38	28
9085341993	DIPAK DAS	9707783876	GIASUDDINAHMED	10/8/2014	20:29:36	148
9085341993	DIPAK DAS	9707783876	GIASUDDINAHMED	10/8/2014	20:06:53	4
9085341993	DIPAK DAS	9707783876	GIASUDDINAHMED	10/8/2014	19:36:38	0
9085341993	DIPAK DAS	9707783876	GIASUDDINAHMED	10/8/2014	19:36:36	0
9085341993	DIPAK DAS	9707783876	GIASUDDINAHMED	10/8/2014	15:56:36	0
9085341993	DIPAK DAS	9707783876	GIASUDDINAHMED	10/8/2014	15:52:39	1
9085341993	DIPAK DAS	9707474658	HITESH KALITA	10/8/2014	15:24:29	71
9085341993	DIPAK DAS	9707474658	HITESH KALITA	10/8/2014	15:22:14	0
9085341993	DIPAK DAS	9707783876	GIASUDDINAHMED	10/8/2014	12:42:28	0
9085341993	DIPAK DAS	9707783876	GIASUDDINAHMED	10/8/2014	10:34:11	0
9085341993	DIPAK DAS	9707783876	GIASUDDINAHMED	9/8/2014	21:41:48	0
9085341993	DIPAK DAS	9707783876	GIASUDDINAHMED	9/8/2014	21:40:00	0

Calling (A) Party Telephone Number/MSISDN	Name	Called (B) Party Telephone Number/Access Point Name	Name	Date	Time	Duration In Secs.
9085341993	DIPAK DAS	9707783876	GIASUDDINAHMED	9/8/2014	20:48:22	448
9085341993	DIPAK DAS	9707783876	GIASUDDINAHMED	9/8/2014	20:01:58	0
9085341993	DIPAK DAS	9707783876	GIASUDDINAHMED	9/8/2014	19:52:03	0
9085341993	DIPAK DAS	9707783876	GIASUDDINAHMED	9/8/2014	19:51:56	0
9085341993	DIPAK DAS	9707783876	GIASUDDINAHMED	9/8/2014	19:49:21	0
9085341993	DIPAK DAS	9707783876	GIASUDDINAHMED	9/8/2014	19:20:22	0
9085341993	DIPAK DAS	9707474658	HITESH KALITA	8/8/2014	22:24:10	34
9085341993	DIPAK DAS	9707474658	HITESH KALITA	8/8/2014	22:21:19	134
9085341993	DIPAK DAS	9707783876	GIASUDDINAHMED	8/8/2014	22:17:12	193
9085341993	DIPAK DAS	9707783876	GIASUDDINAHMED	8/8/2014	21:37:59	313
9085341993	DIPAK DAS	9707474658	HITESH KALITA	8/8/2014	21:36:34	14
9085341993	DIPAK DAS	9707783876	GIASUDDINAHMED	8/8/2014	21:33:34	0
9085341993	DIPAK DAS	9707783876	GIASUDDINAHMED	8/8/2014	21:31:54	20
9085341993	DIPAK DAS	9707783876	GIASUDDINAHMED	8/8/2014	21:29:19	88
9085341993	DIPAK DAS	9707474658	HITESH KALITA	8/8/2014	20:47:25	26
9085341993	DIPAK DAS	9707783876	GIASUDDINAHMED	8/8/2014	20:09:03	0
9085341993	DIPAK DAS	9707783876	GIASUDDINAHMED	8/8/2014	19:18:29	0
9085341993	DIPAK DAS	9707783876	GIASUDDINAHMED	8/8/2014	6:58:24	0

Calling (A) Party Telephone Number/MSISDN	Name	Called (B) Party Telephone Number/Access Point Name	Name	Date	Time	Duration In Secs.
9085341993	DIPAK DAS	9707783876	GIASUDDINAHMED	7/8/2014	21:24:56	448
9085341993	DIPAK DAS	9707783876	GIASUDDINAHMED	7/8/2014	20:02:52	61
9085341993	DIPAK DAS	9707783876	GIASUDDINAHMED	7/8/2014	20:02:20	0
9085341993	DIPAK DAS	9707783876	GIASUDDINAHMED	7/8/2014	19:54:28	0
9085341993	DIPAK DAS	9707783876	GIASUDDINAHMED	7/8/2014	17:08:53	0
9085341993	DIPAK DAS	9707474658	HITESH KALITA	7/8/2014	14:33:51	26
9085341993	DIPAK DAS	9707783876	GIASUDDINAHMED	6/8/2014	20:36:24	0
9085341993	DIPAK DAS	9707783876	GIASUDDINAHMED	6/8/2014	15:17:39	111
9085341993	DIPAK DAS	9707474658	HITESH KALITA	6/8/2014	12:41:36	81
9085341993	DIPAK DAS	9707474658	HITESH KALITA	6/8/2014	10:02:24	32
9085341993	DIPAK DAS	9707783876	GIASUDDINAHMED	5/8/2014	22:28:30	0
9085341993	DIPAK DAS	9707783876	GIASUDDINAHMED	5/8/2014	22:24:03	0
9085341993	DIPAK DAS	9707783876	GIASUDDINAHMED	5/8/2014	22:02:17	961
9085341993	DIPAK DAS	9707783876	GIASUDDINAHMED	5/8/2014	22:00:26	0
9085341993	DIPAK DAS	9707783876	GIASUDDINAHMED	5/8/2014	18:39:36	0
9085341993	DIPAK DAS	9707783876	GIASUDDINAHMED	5/8/2014	18:28:54	0
9085341993	DIPAK DAS	9707783876	GIASUDDINAHMED	5/8/2014	16:08:07	0
9085341993	DIPAK DAS	9707474658	HITESH KALITA	5/8/2014	15:30:17	103

Calling (A) Party Telephone Number/MSISDN	Name	Called (B) Party Telephone Number/Access Point Name	Name	Date	Time	Duration In Secs.
9085341993	DIPAK DAS	9707474658	HITESH KALITA	5/8/2014	15:11:22	0
9085341993	DIPAK DAS	9707783876	GIASUDDINAHMED	4/8/2014	22:38:25	0
9085341993	DIPAK DAS	9707783876	GIASUDDINAHMED	4/8/2014	20:57:54	0
9085341993	DIPAK DAS	9707783876	GIASUDDINAHMED	4/8/2014	20:51:34	263
9085341993	DIPAK DAS	9707783876	GIASUDDINAHMED	4/8/2014	20:26:38	0
9085341993	DIPAK DAS	9707783876	GIASUDDINAHMED	4/8/2014	18:51:43	0
9085341993	DIPAK DAS	9707783876	GIASUDDINAHMED	4/8/2014	18:48:44	31
9085341993	DIPAK DAS	9707783876	GIASUDDINAHMED	3/8/2014	23:27:09	0
9085341993	DIPAK DAS	9707783876	GIASUDDINAHMED	3/8/2014	23:25:04	0
9085341993	DIPAK DAS	9707783876	GIASUDDINAHMED	3/8/2014	23:21:52	0
9085341993	DIPAK DAS	9707783876	GIASUDDINAHMED	3/8/2014	23:18:05	0
9085341993	DIPAK DAS	9707783876	GIASUDDINAHMED	3/8/2014	23:16:24	0
9085341993	DIPAK DAS	9707783876	GIASUDDINAHMED	3/8/2014	23:16:22	0
9085341993	DIPAK DAS	9707783876	GIASUDDINAHMED	3/8/2014	23:16:18	0
9085341993	DIPAK DAS	9707783876	GIASUDDINAHMED	3/8/2014	20:47:49	0
9085341993	DIPAK DAS	9707783876	GIASUDDINAHMED	3/8/2014	20:37:47	0
9085341993	DIPAK DAS	9707783876	GIASUDDINAHMED	3/8/2014	20:16:32	0
9085341993	DIPAK DAS	9707783876	GIASUDDINAHMED	3/8/2014	19:59:29	0

Calling (A) Party Telephone Number/MSISDN	Name	Called (B) Party Telephone Number/Access Point Name	Name	Date	Time	Duration In Secs.
9085341993	DIPAK DAS	9707783876	GIASUDDINAHMED	3/8/2014	19:11:03	0
9085341993	DIPAK DAS	9707783876	GIASUDDINAHMED	3/8/2014	7:05:32	0
9085341993	DIPAK DAS	9707783876	GIASUDDINAHMED	3/8/2014	6:39:09	0
9085341993	DIPAK DAS	9707783876	GIASUDDINAHMED	3/8/2014	0:33:39	0
9085341993	DIPAK DAS	9707783876	GIASUDDINAHMED	3/8/2014	0:29:45	0
9085341993	DIPAK DAS	9707783876	GIASUDDINAHMED	3/8/2014	0:25:58	0
9085341993	DIPAK DAS	9707783876	GIASUDDINAHMED	3/8/2014	0:20:32	0
9085341993	DIPAK DAS	9707783876	GIASUDDINAHMED	3/8/2014	0:17:53	0
9085341993	DIPAK DAS	9707783876	GIASUDDINAHMED	3/8/2014	0:17:25	0
9085341993	DIPAK DAS	9707783876	GIASUDDINAHMED	3/8/2014	0:14:32	0
9085341993	DIPAK DAS	9707783876	GIASUDDINAHMED	3/8/2014	0:12:55	0
9085341993	DIPAK DAS	9707783876	GIASUDDINAHMED	3/8/2014	0:10:37	0
9085341993	DIPAK DAS	9707783876	GIASUDDINAHMED	3/8/2014	0:07:58	0
9085341993	DIPAK DAS	9707783876	GIASUDDINAHMED	3/8/2014	0:05:25	0
9085341993	DIPAK DAS	9707783876	GIASUDDINAHMED	3/8/2014	0:04:04	0
9085341993	DIPAK DAS	9707783876	GIASUDDINAHMED	3/8/2014	0:02:14	0
9085341993	DIPAK DAS	9707783876	GIASUDDINAHMED	2/8/2014	23:59:28	0
9085341993	DIPAK DAS	9707783876	GIASUDDINAHMED	2/8/2014	23:59:02	0

Calling (A) Party Telephone Number/MSISDN	Name	Called (B) Party Telephone Number/Access Point Name	Name	Date	Time	Duration In Secs.
9085341993	DIPAK DAS	9707783876	GIASUDDINAHMED	2/8/2014	23:56:30	0
9085341993	DIPAK DAS	9707783876	GIASUDDINAHMED	2/8/2014	23:55:21	0
9085341993	DIPAK DAS	9707783876	GIASUDDINAHMED	2/8/2014	23:53:13	0
9085341993	DIPAK DAS	9707783876	GIASUDDINAHMED	2/8/2014	23:36:55	899
9085341993	DIPAK DAS	9707783876	GIASUDDINAHMED	2/8/2014	23:34:49	0
9085341993	DIPAK DAS	9707783876	GIASUDDINAHMED	2/8/2014	23:32:53	0
9085341993	DIPAK DAS	9707783876	GIASUDDINAHMED	2/8/2014	23:32:19	0
9085341993	DIPAK DAS	9707783876	GIASUDDINAHMED	2/8/2014	23:28:10	121
9085341993	DIPAK DAS	9707783876	GIASUDDINAHMED	2/8/2014	23:26:45	0
9085341993	DIPAK DAS	9707783876	GIASUDDINAHMED	2/8/2014	23:24:40	0
9085341993	DIPAK DAS	9707783876	GIASUDDINAHMED	2/8/2014	23:21:54	0
9085341993	DIPAK DAS	9707783876	GIASUDDINAHMED	2/8/2014	23:20:10	0
9085341993	DIPAK DAS	9707783876	GIASUDDINAHMED	2/8/2014	23:19:31	0
9085341993	DIPAK DAS	9707783876	GIASUDDINAHMED	2/8/2014	23:16:24	0
9085341993	DIPAK DAS	9707783876	GIASUDDINAHMED	2/8/2014	23:14:34	0
9085341993	DIPAK DAS	9707783876	GIASUDDINAHMED	2/8/2014	23:10:00	125
9085341993	DIPAK DAS	9707783876	GIASUDDINAHMED	2/8/2014	23:06:14	0
9085341993	DIPAK DAS	9707783876	GIASUDDINAHMED	2/8/2014	23:04:14	0

Calling (A) Party Telephone Number/MSISDN	Name	Called (B) Party Telephone Number/Access Point Name	Name	Date	Time	Duration In Secs.
9085341993	DIPAK DAS	9707783876	GIASUDDINAHMED	2/8/2014	23:02:23	0
9085341993	DIPAK DAS	9707783876	GIASUDDINAHMED	2/8/2014	22:59:03	0
9085341993	DIPAK DAS	9707783876	GIASUDDINAHMED	2/8/2014	22:50:17	109
9085341993	DIPAK DAS	9707783876	GIASUDDINAHMED	2/8/2014	22:42:03	0
9085341993	DIPAK DAS	9707783876	GIASUDDINAHMED	2/8/2014	22:42:01	0
9085341993	DIPAK DAS	9707783876	GIASUDDINAHMED	2/8/2014	22:38:55	0
9085341993	DIPAK DAS	9707783876	GIASUDDINAHMED	2/8/2014	22:35:01	0
9085341993	DIPAK DAS	9707783876	GIASUDDINAHMED	2/8/2014	22:28:47	107
9085341993	DIPAK DAS	9707783876	GIASUDDINAHMED	2/8/2014	22:28:09	0
9085341993	DIPAK DAS	9707783876	GIASUDDINAHMED	2/8/2014	22:04:00	100
9085341993	DIPAK DAS	9707783876	GIASUDDINAHMED	2/8/2014	22:03:21	0
9085341993	DIPAK DAS	9707783876	GIASUDDINAHMED	2/8/2014	22:02:41	0
9085341993	DIPAK DAS	9707783876	GIASUDDINAHMED	2/8/2014	22:02:26	0
9085341993	DIPAK DAS	9707783876	GIASUDDINAHMED	2/8/2014	22:02:23	0
9085341993	DIPAK DAS	9707783876	GIASUDDINAHMED	2/8/2014	22:02:13	0
9085341993	DIPAK DAS	9707783876	GIASUDDINAHMED	2/8/2014	22:02:11	0
9085341993	DIPAK DAS	9707783876	GIASUDDINAHMED	2/8/2014	22:01:59	0
9085341993	DIPAK DAS	9707783876	GIASUDDINAHMED	2/8/2014	21:58:16	0

Calling (A) Party Telephone Number/MSISDN	Name	Called (B) Party Telephone Number/Access Point Name	Name	Date	Time	Duration In Secs.
9085341993	DIPAK DAS	9707783876	GIASUDDINAHMED	2/8/2014	21:58:09	0
9085341993	DIPAK DAS	9707783876	GIASUDDINAHMED	2/8/2014	21:57:57	0
9085341993	DIPAK DAS	9707783876	GIASUDDINAHMED	2/8/2014	21:57:49	0
9085341993	DIPAK DAS	9707783876	GIASUDDINAHMED	2/8/2014	21:40:58	0
9085341993	DIPAK DAS	9707783876	GIASUDDINAHMED	2/8/2014	21:33:01	0
9085341993	DIPAK DAS	9707783876	GIASUDDINAHMED	2/8/2014	21:30:25	0
9085341993	DIPAK DAS	9707783876	GIASUDDINAHMED	2/8/2014	21:28:19	0
9085341993	DIPAK DAS	9707783876	GIASUDDINAHMED	2/8/2014	21:22:38	0
9085341993	DIPAK DAS	9707783876	GIASUDDINAHMED	2/8/2014	21:22:36	0
9085341993	DIPAK DAS	9707783876	GIASUDDINAHMED	2/8/2014	21:05:01	0
9085341993	DIPAK DAS	9707783876	GIASUDDINAHMED	2/8/2014	20:59:02	0
9085341993	DIPAK DAS	9707783876	GIASUDDINAHMED	2/8/2014	20:57:03	0
9085341993	DIPAK DAS	9707783876	GIASUDDINAHMED	2/8/2014	20:48:25	0
9085341993	DIPAK DAS	9707783876	GIASUDDINAHMED	2/8/2014	20:37:00	624
9085341993	DIPAK DAS	9707474658	HITESH KALITA	1/8/2014	13:46:51	17
9085341993	DIPAK DAS	9707783876	GIASUDDINAHMED	1/8/2014	9:09:22	411
9085341993	DIPAK DAS	9707783876	GIASUDDINAHMED	1/8/2014	8:57:00	421
9085341993	DIPAK DAS	9707783876	GIASUDDINAHMED	1/8/2014	8:54:30	96

Calling (A) Party Telephone Number/MSISDN	Name	Called (B) Party Telephone Number/Access Point Name	Name	Date	Time	Duration In Secs.
9085341993	DIPAK DAS	9707783876	GIASUDDINAHMED	1/8/2014	8:30:41	1
9085341993	DIPAK DAS	9707783876	GIASUDDINAHMED	1/8/2014	0:58:48	0
9085341993	DIPAK DAS	9707474658	HITESH KALITA	31-07-2014	23:03:48	0
9085341993	DIPAK DAS	9707474658	HITESH KALITA	31-07-2014	23:00:42	0
9085341993	DIPAK DAS	9707474658	HITESH KALITA	31-07-2014	23:00:34	0
9085341993	DIPAK DAS	9707474658	HITESH KALITA	31-07-2014	22:55:18	240
9085341993	DIPAK DAS	9707474658	HITESH KALITA	31-07-2014	22:54:11	2
9085341993	DIPAK DAS	9707474658	HITESH KALITA	31-07-2014	22:49:54	231
9085341993	DIPAK DAS	9707474658	HITESH KALITA	31-07-2014	22:47:20	30
9085341993	DIPAK DAS	9707783876	GIASUDDINAHMED	31-07-2014	22:34:21	0
9085341993	DIPAK DAS	9707783876	GIASUDDINAHMED	31-07-2014	22:34:15	0
9085341993	DIPAK DAS	9401165464	HITESWAR KALITA	31-07-2014	19:52:54	118
9085341993	DIPAK DAS	9707783876	GIASUDDINAHMED	31-07-2014	19:10:45	0
9085341993	DIPAK DAS	9707474658	HITESH KALITA	31-07-2014	9:19:05	16
9085341993	DIPAK DAS	9707474658	HITESH KALITA	31-07-2014	0:16:07	0
9085341993	DIPAK DAS	9707474658	HITESH KALITA	31-07-2014	0:16:03	0
9085341993	DIPAK DAS	9707783876	GIASUDDINAHMED	30-07-2014	23:13:03	0
9085341993	DIPAK DAS	9707783876	GIASUDDINAHMED	30-07-2014	23:10:20	0

Calling (A) Party Telephone Number/MSISDN	Name	Called (B) Party Telephone Number/Access Point Name	Name	Date	Time	Duration In Secs.
9085341993	DIPAK DAS	9707783876	GIASUDDINAHMED	30-07-2014	23:00:33	0
9085341993	DIPAK DAS	9707783876	GIASUDDINAHMED	30-07-2014	22:57:03	0
9085341993	DIPAK DAS	9707783876	GIASUDDINAHMED	30-07-2014	22:52:42	0
9085341993	DIPAK DAS	9707783876	GIASUDDINAHMED	30-07-2014	22:43:20	270
9085341993	DIPAK DAS	9707783876	GIASUDDINAHMED	30-07-2014	22:38:41	0
9085341993	DIPAK DAS	9707783876	GIASUDDINAHMED	30-07-2014	22:36:41	0
9085341993	DIPAK DAS	9707474658	HITESH KALITA	30-07-2014	18:54:36	40
9085341993	DIPAK DAS	9707783876	GIASUDDINAHMED	30-07-2014	18:15:31	0
9085341993	DIPAK DAS	9707783876	GIASUDDINAHMED	30-07-2014	18:11:42	0
9085341993	DIPAK DAS	9707783876	GIASUDDINAHMED	30-07-2014	18:05:09	0
9085341993	DIPAK DAS	9707783876	GIASUDDINAHMED	30-07-2014	17:59:08	0
9085341993	DIPAK DAS	9707783876	GIASUDDINAHMED	30-07-2014	17:59:04	0
9085341993	DIPAK DAS	9707783876	GIASUDDINAHMED	30-07-2014	17:52:13	0
9085341993	DIPAK DAS	9707783876	GIASUDDINAHMED	30-07-2014	17:50:26	0
9085341993	DIPAK DAS	9707783876	GIASUDDINAHMED	30-07-2014	17:50:23	0
9085341993	DIPAK DAS	9707783876	GIASUDDINAHMED	30-07-2014	17:50:21	0
9085341993	DIPAK DAS	9707783876	GIASUDDINAHMED	30-07-2014	17:50:19	0
9085341993	DIPAK DAS	9707783876	GIASUDDINAHMED	30-07-2014	17:50:17	0

Calling (A) Party Telephone Number/MSISDN	Name	Called (B) Party Telephone Number/Access Point Name	Name	Date	Time	Duration In Secs.
9085341993	DIPAK DAS	9707783876	GIASUDDINAHMED	30-07-2014	10:28:40	0
9085341993	DIPAK DAS	9707783876	GIASUDDINAHMED	30-07-2014	10:28:31	0
9085341993	DIPAK DAS	9707783876	GIASUDDINAHMED	30-07-2014	10:28:24	0
9085341993	DIPAK DAS	9707783876	GIASUDDINAHMED	30-07-2014	10:10:55	0
9085341993	DIPAK DAS	9707783876	GIASUDDINAHMED	30-07-2014	10:10:49	0
9085341993	DIPAK DAS	9707783876	GIASUDDINAHMED	30-07-2014	10:10:43	0
9085341993	DIPAK DAS	9707783876	GIASUDDINAHMED	30-07-2014	10:10:37	0
9085341993	DIPAK DAS	9707783876	GIASUDDINAHMED	30-07-2014	9:33:07	0
9085341993	DIPAK DAS	9707783876	GIASUDDINAHMED	30-07-2014	9:29:29	43
9085341993	DIPAK DAS	9707783876	GIASUDDINAHMED	29-07-2014	23:04:06	0
9085341993	DIPAK DAS	9707783876	GIASUDDINAHMED	29-07-2014	22:58:18	0
9085341993	DIPAK DAS	9707783876	GIASUDDINAHMED	29-07-2014	22:56:06	0
9085341993	DIPAK DAS	9707783876	GIASUDDINAHMED	29-07-2014	22:35:40	0
9085341993	DIPAK DAS	9707783876	GIASUDDINAHMED	29-07-2014	22:33:55	0
9085341993	DIPAK DAS	9707783876	GIASUDDINAHMED	29-07-2014	22:32:14	52
9085341993	DIPAK DAS	9707783876	GIASUDDINAHMED	29-07-2014	18:29:39	0
9085341993	DIPAK DAS	9707474658	HITESH KALITA	29-07-2014	15:45:51	21
9085341993	DIPAK DAS	9707474658	HITESH KALITA	29-07-2014	10:00:37	18

Calling (A) Party Telephone Number/MSISDN	Name	Called (B) Party Telephone Number/Access Point Name	Name	Date	Time	Duration In Secs.
9085341993	DIPAK DAS	9707783876	GIASUDDINAHMED	29-07-2014	7:22:13	0
9085341993	DIPAK DAS	9707783876	GIASUDDINAHMED	29-07-2014	7:22:10	0
9085341993	DIPAK DAS	9707783876	GIASUDDINAHMED	28-07-2014	23:13:56	835
9085341993	DIPAK DAS	9707783876	GIASUDDINAHMED	28-07-2014	23:13:36	2
9085341993	DIPAK DAS	9707783876	GIASUDDINAHMED	28-07-2014	23:13:04	0
9085341993	DIPAK DAS	9707783876	GIASUDDINAHMED	28-07-2014	22:16:38	421
9085341993	DIPAK DAS	9707783876	GIASUDDINAHMED	28-07-2014	22:12:47	0
9085341993	DIPAK DAS	9707783876	GIASUDDINAHMED	28-07-2014	22:12:45	0
9085341993	DIPAK DAS	9707783876	GIASUDDINAHMED	27-07-2014	23:13:47	0
9085341993	DIPAK DAS	9707783876	GIASUDDINAHMED	27-07-2014	23:08:22	0
9085341993	DIPAK DAS	9707783876	GIASUDDINAHMED	27-07-2014	22:58:29	0
9085341993	DIPAK DAS	9707783876	GIASUDDINAHMED	27-07-2014	22:38:47	0
9085341993	DIPAK DAS	9707783876	GIASUDDINAHMED	27-07-2014	22:38:36	0
9085341993	DIPAK DAS	9707783876	GIASUDDINAHMED	27-07-2014	18:56:37	0
9085341993	DIPAK DAS	9707783876	GIASUDDINAHMED	27-07-2014	18:55:30	0
9085341993	DIPAK DAS	9707783876	GIASUDDINAHMED	26-07-2014	14:25:30	0
9085341993	DIPAK DAS	9707783876	GIASUDDINAHMED	26-07-2014	14:25:28	0
9085341993	DIPAK DAS	9707783876	GIASUDDINAHMED	26-07-2014	8:29:21	0

Calling (A) Party Telephone Number/MSISDN	Name	Called (B) Party Telephone Number/Access Point Name	Name	Date	Time	Duration In Secs.
9085341993	DIPAK DAS	9707783876	GIASUDDINAHMED	25-07-2014	21:35:37	0
9085341993	DIPAK DAS	9707783876	GIASUDDINAHMED	25-07-2014	21:34:44	0
9085341993	DIPAK DAS	9707783876	GIASUDDINAHMED	25-07-2014	21:33:46	0
9085341993	DIPAK DAS	9707783876	GIASUDDINAHMED	25-07-2014	20:32:49	161
9085341993	DIPAK DAS	9707783876	GIASUDDINAHMED	25-07-2014	19:19:53	0
9085341993	DIPAK DAS	9707474658	HITESH KALITA	25-07-2014	16:29:19	0
9085341993	DIPAK DAS	9707783876	GIASUDDINAHMED	25-07-2014	16:18:24	0
9085341993	DIPAK DAS	9707783876	GIASUDDINAHMED	25-07-2014	16:18:21	0
9085341993	DIPAK DAS	9707783876	GIASUDDINAHMED	25-07-2014	16:04:35	42
9085341993	DIPAK DAS	9707474658	HITESH KALITA	22-07-2014	9:53:16	0
9085341993	DIPAK DAS	9707783876	GIASUDDINAHMED	22-07-2014	9:07:37	251
9085341993	DIPAK DAS	9707783876	GIASUDDINAHMED	22-07-2014	8:58:13	0
9085341993	DIPAK DAS	9707783876	GIASUDDINAHMED	21-07-2014	23:34:09	0
9085341993	DIPAK DAS	9707783876	GIASUDDINAHMED	21-07-2014	22:41:51	0
9085341993	DIPAK DAS	9707783876	GIASUDDINAHMED	21-07-2014	19:29:07	0
9085341993	DIPAK DAS	9707474658	HITESH KALITA	21-07-2014	19:16:01	0
9085341993	DIPAK DAS	9707474658	HITESH KALITA	21-07-2014	18:55:08	0
9085341993	DIPAK DAS	9707783876	GIASUDDINAHMED	21-07-2014	18:02:53	12

Calling (A) Party Telephone Number/MSISDN	Name	Called (B) Party Telephone Number/Access Point Name	Name	Date	Time	Duration In Secs.
9085341993	DIPAK DAS	9707783876	GIASUDDINAHMED	21-07-2014	15:43:52	0
9085341993	DIPAK DAS	9707783876	GIASUDDINAHMED	21-07-2014	15:38:52	0
9085341993	DIPAK DAS	9707783876	GIASUDDINAHMED	21-07-2014	15:13:59	0
9085341993	DIPAK DAS	9707783876	GIASUDDINAHMED	21-07-2014	14:51:03	0
9085341993	DIPAK DAS	9707783876	GIASUDDINAHMED	21-07-2014	14:48:19	0
9085341993	DIPAK DAS	9707783876	GIASUDDINAHMED	21-07-2014	14:39:39	0
9085341993	DIPAK DAS	9707783876	GIASUDDINAHMED	21-07-2014	14:31:29	0
9085341993	DIPAK DAS	9707783876	GIASUDDINAHMED	21-07-2014	14:06:13	0
9085341993	DIPAK DAS	9707783876	GIASUDDINAHMED	21-07-2014	13:37:30	0
9085341993	DIPAK DAS	9707474658	HITESH KALITA	21-07-2014	13:15:23	198
9085341993	DIPAK DAS	9707474658	HITESH KALITA	21-07-2014	13:06:39	0
9085341993	DIPAK DAS	9707783876	GIASUDDINAHMED	21-07-2014	12:28:10	0
9085341993	DIPAK DAS	9707783876	GIASUDDINAHMED	21-07-2014	12:12:35	0
9085341993	DIPAK DAS	9707783876	GIASUDDINAHMED	21-07-2014	11:48:12	0
9085341993	DIPAK DAS	9707783876	GIASUDDINAHMED	21-07-2014	10:03:10	0
9085341993	DIPAK DAS	9707474658	HITESH KALITA	21-07-2014	8:33:35	50
9085341993	DIPAK DAS	9707783876	GIASUDDINAHMED	20-07-2014	23:41:12	0
9085341993	DIPAK DAS	9707783876	GIASUDDINAHMED	20-07-2014	23:38:10	42

Calling (A) Party Telephone Number/MSISDN	Name	Called (B) Party Telephone Number/Access Point Name	Name	Date	Time	Duration In Secs.
9085341993	DIPAK DAS	9707783876	GIASUDDINAHMED	20-07-2014	23:31:40	0
9085341993	DIPAK DAS	9707783876	GIASUDDINAHMED	20-07-2014	23:23:38	179
9085341993	DIPAK DAS	9707783876	GIASUDDINAHMED	20-07-2014	23:20:03	0
9085341993	DIPAK DAS	9707783876	GIASUDDINAHMED	20-07-2014	23:16:11	41
9085341993	DIPAK DAS	9707783876	GIASUDDINAHMED	20-07-2014	23:14:16	0
9085341993	DIPAK DAS	9707783876	GIASUDDINAHMED	20-07-2014	23:12:23	0
9085341993	DIPAK DAS	9707783876	GIASUDDINAHMED	20-07-2014	23:08:59	0
9085341993	DIPAK DAS	9707783876	GIASUDDINAHMED	20-07-2014	23:05:36	0
9085341993	DIPAK DAS	9707783876	GIASUDDINAHMED	20-07-2014	23:00:13	0
9085341993	DIPAK DAS	9707783876	GIASUDDINAHMED	20-07-2014	22:54:24	0
9085341993	DIPAK DAS	9707783876	GIASUDDINAHMED	20-07-2014	22:46:06	0
9085341993	DIPAK DAS	9707474658	HITESH KALITA	20-07-2014	22:45:34	79
9085341993	DIPAK DAS	9707783876	GIASUDDINAHMED	20-07-2014	22:40:24	11
9085341993	DIPAK DAS	9707783876	GIASUDDINAHMED	20-07-2014	22:35:15	0
9085341993	DIPAK DAS	9707783876	GIASUDDINAHMED	20-07-2014	22:28:41	0
9085341993	DIPAK DAS	9707783876	GIASUDDINAHMED	20-07-2014	21:31:35	602
9085341993	DIPAK DAS	9707783876	GIASUDDINAHMED	20-07-2014	21:29:46	95
9085341993	DIPAK DAS	9707783876	GIASUDDINAHMED	20-07-2014	21:27:59	0

Calling (A) Party Telephone Number/MSISDN	Name	Called (B) Party Telephone Number/Access Point Name	Name	Date	Time	Duration In Secs.
9085341993	DIPAK DAS	9707474658	HITESH KALITA	20-07-2014	21:02:03	38
9085341993	DIPAK DAS	9707783876	GIASUDDINAHMED	20-07-2014	19:51:54	0
9085341993	DIPAK DAS	9707783876	GIASUDDINAHMED	20-07-2014	19:38:18	0
9085341993	DIPAK DAS	9707783876	GIASUDDINAHMED	20-07-2014	19:23:13	0
9085341993	DIPAK DAS	9707783876	GIASUDDINAHMED	20-07-2014	19:18:11	60
9085341993	DIPAK DAS	9707474658	HITESH KALITA	20-07-2014	15:00:20	0
9085341993	DIPAK DAS	9707783876	GIASUDDINAHMED	19-07-2014	22:45:22	0
9085341993	DIPAK DAS	9707783876	GIASUDDINAHMED	19-07-2014	22:38:53	22
9085341993	DIPAK DAS	9707783876	GIASUDDINAHMED	19-07-2014	22:38:12	2
9085341993	DIPAK DAS	9707783876	GIASUDDINAHMED	19-07-2014	22:22:33	0
9085341993	DIPAK DAS	9707783876	GIASUDDINAHMED	19-07-2014	22:14:00	0
9085341993	DIPAK DAS	9707783876	GIASUDDINAHMED	19-07-2014	21:52:17	0
9085341993	DIPAK DAS	9707474658	HITESH KALITA	19-07-2014	21:02:45	0
9085341993	DIPAK DAS	9707783876	GIASUDDINAHMED	19-07-2014	20:17:46	0
9085341993	DIPAK DAS	9707783876	GIASUDDINAHMED	19-07-2014	18:25:17	0
9085341993	DIPAK DAS	9707474658	HITESH KALITA	19-07-2014	14:33:46	0
9085341993	DIPAK DAS	9707474658	HITESH KALITA	19-07-2014	9:20:33	0
9085341993	DIPAK DAS	9707783876	GIASUDDINAHMED	19-07-2014	9:08:35	0

Calling (A) Party Telephone Number/MSISDN	Name	Called (B) Party Telephone Number/Access Point Name	Name	Date	Time	Duration In Secs.
9085341993	DIPAK DAS	9707783876	GIASUDDINAHMED	19-07-2014	8:50:10	41
9085341993	DIPAK DAS	9707474658	HITESH KALITA	19-07-2014	7:48:33	0
9085341993	DIPAK DAS	9707783876	GIASUDDINAHMED	18-07-2014	22:59:26	0
9085341993	DIPAK DAS	9707783876	GIASUDDINAHMED	18-07-2014	22:52:45	0
9085341993	DIPAK DAS	9707783876	GIASUDDINAHMED	18-07-2014	22:43:42	496
9085341993	DIPAK DAS	9707783876	GIASUDDINAHMED	18-07-2014	22:06:48	0
9085341993	DIPAK DAS	9707783876	GIASUDDINAHMED	18-07-2014	22:06:45	0
9085341993	DIPAK DAS	9707783876	GIASUDDINAHMED	18-07-2014	22:01:38	273
9085341993	DIPAK DAS	9707474658	HITESH KALITA	18-07-2014	19:58:10	0
9085341993	DIPAK DAS	9707474658	HITESH KALITA	18-07-2014	19:11:58	7
9085341993	DIPAK DAS	9707474658	HITESH KALITA	18-07-2014	13:26:51	0
9085341993	DIPAK DAS	9707474658	HITESH KALITA	18-07-2014	7:59:03	0
9085341993	DIPAK DAS	9707783876	GIASUDDINAHMED	18-07-2014	7:26:10	42
9085341993	DIPAK DAS	9707783876	GIASUDDINAHMED	18-07-2014	7:26:02	0
9085341993	DIPAK DAS	9707783876	GIASUDDINAHMED	18-07-2014	7:24:33	7
9085341993	DIPAK DAS	9707783876	GIASUDDINAHMED	18-07-2014	7:22:06	0
9085341993	DIPAK DAS	9707783876	GIASUDDINAHMED	17-07-2014	23:05:59	0
9085341993	DIPAK DAS	9707783876	GIASUDDINAHMED	17-07-2014	22:33:26	7

Calling (A) Party Telephone Number/MSISDN	Name	Called (B) Party Telephone Number/Access Point Name	Name	Date	Time	Duration In Secs.
9085341993	DIPAK DAS	9707783876	GIASUDDINAHMED	17-07-2014	22:31:52	0
9085341993	DIPAK DAS	9707783876	GIASUDDINAHMED	17-07-2014	22:24:58	0
9085341993	DIPAK DAS	9707783876	GIASUDDINAHMED	17-07-2014	22:14:57	224
9085341993	DIPAK DAS	9707783876	GIASUDDINAHMED	17-07-2014	21:52:45	0
9085341993	DIPAK DAS	9707783876	GIASUDDINAHMED	17-07-2014	21:37:43	133
9085341993	DIPAK DAS	9707474658	HITESH KALITA	17-07-2014	21:31:02	22
9085341993	DIPAK DAS	9707474658	HITESH KALITA	17-07-2014	21:09:39	22
9085341993	DIPAK DAS	9707783876	GIASUDDINAHMED	17-07-2014	20:51:14	0
9085341993	DIPAK DAS	9707783876	GIASUDDINAHMED	17-07-2014	19:51:54	0
9085341993	DIPAK DAS	9707783876	GIASUDDINAHMED	17-07-2014	16:15:59	0
9085341993	DIPAK DAS	9707783876	GIASUDDINAHMED	17-07-2014	14:45:05	0
9085341993	DIPAK DAS	9707783876	GIASUDDINAHMED	17-07-2014	14:45:02	0
9085341993	DIPAK DAS	9707474658	HITESH KALITA	17-07-2014	11:18:19	47
9085341993	DIPAK DAS	9707474658	HITESH KALITA	17-07-2014	10:51:01	14
9085341993	DIPAK DAS	9707783876	GIASUDDINAHMED	17-07-2014	10:48:33	8
9085341993	DIPAK DAS	9707783876	GIASUDDINAHMED	17-07-2014	10:14:57	0
9085341993	DIPAK DAS	9707783876	GIASUDDINAHMED	17-07-2014	10:05:37	0
9085341993	DIPAK DAS	9707783876	GIASUDDINAHMED	17-07-2014	10:02:26	0

Calling (A) Party Telephone Number/MSISDN	Name	Called (B) Party Telephone Number/Access Point Name	Name	Date	Time	Duration In Secs.
9085341993	DIPAK DAS	9707783876	GIASUDDINAHMED	17-07-2014	10:01:03	0
9085341993	DIPAK DAS	9707783876	GIASUDDINAHMED	17-07-2014	9:58:08	0
9085341993	DIPAK DAS	9707783876	GIASUDDINAHMED	17-07-2014	9:27:06	0
9085341993	DIPAK DAS	9707783876	GIASUDDINAHMED	16-07-2014	22:52:08	0
9085341993	DIPAK DAS	9707474658	HITESH KALITA	16-07-2014	22:43:21	0
9085341993	DIPAK DAS	9707783876	GIASUDDINAHMED	16-07-2014	22:25:59	0
9085341993	DIPAK DAS	9707783876	GIASUDDINAHMED	16-07-2014	22:24:02	0
9085341993	DIPAK DAS	9707783876	GIASUDDINAHMED	16-07-2014	22:14:58	0
9085341993	DIPAK DAS	9707783876	GIASUDDINAHMED	16-07-2014	22:11:49	0
9085341993	DIPAK DAS	9707474658	HITESH KALITA	16-07-2014	22:07:24	108
9085341993	DIPAK DAS	9707474658	HITESH KALITA	16-07-2014	22:06:20	3
9085341993	DIPAK DAS	9707474658	HITESH KALITA	16-07-2014	22:04:41	0
9085341993	DIPAK DAS	9707783876	GIASUDDINAHMED	16-07-2014	21:50:15	0
9085341993	DIPAK DAS	9707783876	GIASUDDINAHMED	16-07-2014	21:44:24	0
9085341993	DIPAK DAS	9707474658	HITESH KALITA	16-07-2014	21:42:42	0
9085341993	DIPAK DAS	9707474658	HITESH KALITA	16-07-2014	21:42:33	0
9085341993	DIPAK DAS	9707783876	GIASUDDINAHMED	16-07-2014	21:36:59	0
9085341993	DIPAK DAS	9707783876	GIASUDDINAHMED	16-07-2014	21:28:07	0

Calling (A) Party Telephone Number/MSISDN	Name	Called (B) Party Telephone Number/Access Point Name	Name	Date	Time	Duration In Secs.
9085341993	DIPAK DAS	97077783876	GIASUDDINAHMED	16-07-2014	21:17:07	0
9085341993	DIPAK DAS	97077783876	GIASUDDINAHMED	16-07-2014	21:03:39	0
9085341993	DIPAK DAS	97077783876	GIASUDDINAHMED	16-07-2014	21:03:31	0
9085341993	DIPAK DAS	97077783876	GIASUDDINAHMED	16-07-2014	20:56:51	0
9085341993	DIPAK DAS	97077783876	GIASUDDINAHMED	16-07-2014	20:36:37	0
9085341993	DIPAK DAS	97077783876	GIASUDDINAHMED	16-07-2014	20:16:04	0
9085341993	DIPAK DAS	97074474658	HITESH KALITA	16-07-2014	19:17:02	0
9085341993	DIPAK DAS	97074474658	HITESH KALITA	16-07-2014	13:03:59	32
9085341993	DIPAK DAS	97077783876	GIASUDDINAHMED	16-07-2014	13:01:30	0
9085341993	DIPAK DAS	97077783876	GIASUDDINAHMED	16-07-2014	8:32:23	0
9085341993	DIPAK DAS	97077783876	GIASUDDINAHMED	16-07-2014	8:20:40	0
9085341993	DIPAK DAS	97077783876	GIASUDDINAHMED	16-07-2014	8:20:35	0
9085341993	DIPAK DAS	97077783876	GIASUDDINAHMED	16-07-2014	8:07:24	0
9085341993	DIPAK DAS	97077783876	GIASUDDINAHMED	16-07-2014	8:05:23	0
9085341993	DIPAK DAS	97077783876	GIASUDDINAHMED	16-07-2014	8:01:42	0
9085341993	DIPAK DAS	97077783876	GIASUDDINAHMED	16-07-2014	7:55:47	239
9085341993	DIPAK DAS	97077783876	GIASUDDINAHMED	16-07-2014	7:54:47	0
9085341993	DIPAK DAS	97077783876	GIASUDDINAHMED	16-07-2014	7:42:24	374

Calling (A) Party Telephone Number/MSISDN	Name	Called (B) Party Telephone Number/Access Point Name	Name	Date	Time	Duration In Secs.
9085341993	DIPAK DAS	9707783876	GIASUDDINAHMED	16-07-2014	7:42:02	0
9085341993	DIPAK DAS	9707783876	GIASUDDINAHMED	16-07-2014	7:39:57	0
9085341993	DIPAK DAS	9707783876	GIASUDDINAHMED	16-07-2014	7:38:34	0
9085341993	DIPAK DAS	9707783876	GIASUDDINAHMED	16-07-2014	7:35:15	0
9085341993	DIPAK DAS	9707783876	GIASUDDINAHMED	16-07-2014	7:29:49	0
9085341993	DIPAK DAS	9707783876	GIASUDDINAHMED	16-07-2014	7:27:25	0
9085341993	DIPAK DAS	9707783876	GIASUDDINAHMED	16-07-2014	7:19:37	0
9085341993	DIPAK DAS	9707783876	GIASUDDINAHMED	16-07-2014	7:14:41	0
9085341993	DIPAK DAS	9707783876	GIASUDDINAHMED	16-07-2014	7:12:16	0
9085341993	DIPAK DAS	9707783876	GIASUDDINAHMED	16-07-2014	7:04:39	0
9085341993	DIPAK DAS	9707783876	GIASUDDINAHMED	16-07-2014	7:04:27	0
9085341993	DIPAK DAS	9707783876	GIASUDDINAHMED	16-07-2014	7:04:22	0
9085341993	DIPAK DAS	9707783876	GIASUDDINAHMED	16-07-2014	7:00:13	0
9085341993	DIPAK DAS	9707474658	HITESH KALITA	16-07-2014	6:51:15	0
9085341993	DIPAK DAS	9707783876	GIASUDDINAHMED	15-07-2014	22:58:45	0
9085341993	DIPAK DAS	9707783876	GIASUDDINAHMED	15-07-2014	22:57:08	0
9085341993	DIPAK DAS	9707783876	GIASUDDINAHMED	15-07-2014	22:53:10	0
9085341993	DIPAK DAS	9707783876	GIASUDDINAHMED	15-07-2014	22:44:11	0

Calling (A) Party Telephone Number/MSISDN	Name	Called (B) Party Telephone Number/Access Point Name	Name	Date	Time	Duration In Secs.
9085341993	DIPAK DAS	9707783876	GIASUDDINAHMED	15-07-2014	22:40:31	0
9085341993	DIPAK DAS	9707474658	HITESH KALITA	15-07-2014	22:35:38	0
9085341993	DIPAK DAS	9707474658	HITESH KALITA	15-07-2014	22:27:30	0
9085341993	DIPAK DAS	9707783876	GIASUDDINAHMED	15-07-2014	22:26:54	0
9085341993	DIPAK DAS	9707783876	GIASUDDINAHMED	15-07-2014	22:24:52	0
9085341993	DIPAK DAS	9707474658	HITESH KALITA	15-07-2014	22:23:42	0
9085341993	DIPAK DAS	9707783876	GIASUDDINAHMED	15-07-2014	22:23:16	0
9085341993	DIPAK DAS	9707474658	HITESH KALITA	15-07-2014	22:22:40	0
9085341993	DIPAK DAS	9707474658	HITESH KALITA	15-07-2014	22:13:02	0
9085341993	DIPAK DAS	9707474658	HITESH KALITA	15-07-2014	22:12:36	0
9085341993	DIPAK DAS	9707783876	GIASUDDINAHMED	15-07-2014	22:07:56	0
9085341993	DIPAK DAS	9707474658	HITESH KALITA	15-07-2014	22:02:19	0
9085341993	DIPAK DAS	9707474658	HITESH KALITA	15-07-2014	21:57:04	0
9085341993	DIPAK DAS	9707474658	HITESH KALITA	15-07-2014	21:50:54	0
9085341993	DIPAK DAS	9707783876	GIASUDDINAHMED	15-07-2014	21:40:21	0
9085341993	DIPAK DAS	9707783876	GIASUDDINAHMED	15-07-2014	21:40:13	0
9085341993	DIPAK DAS	9707783876	GIASUDDINAHMED	15-07-2014	21:37:02	0
9085341993	DIPAK DAS	9707783876	GIASUDDINAHMED	15-07-2014	21:35:17	0

Calling (A) Party Telephone Number/MSISDN	Name	Called (B) Party Telephone Number/Access Point Name	Name	Date	Time	Duration In Secs.
9085341993	DIPAK DAS	9707783876	GIASUDDINAHMED	15-07-2014	21:29:17	0
9085341993	DIPAK DAS	9707474658	HITESH KALITA	15-07-2014	20:57:21	0
9085341993	DIPAK DAS	9707474658	HITESH KALITA	15-07-2014	20:52:29	0
9085341993	DIPAK DAS	9707474658	HITESH KALITA	15-07-2014	20:51:21	0
9085341993	DIPAK DAS	9707474658	HITESH KALITA	15-07-2014	20:48:05	0
9085341993	DIPAK DAS	9707474658	HITESH KALITA	15-07-2014	20:40:46	0
9085341993	DIPAK DAS	9707474658	HITESH KALITA	15-07-2014	20:38:24	0
9085341993	DIPAK DAS	9707474658	HITESH KALITA	15-07-2014	20:36:45	0
9085341993	DIPAK DAS	9707474658	HITESH KALITA	15-07-2014	20:34:34	0
9085341993	DIPAK DAS	9707474658	HITESH KALITA	15-07-2014	20:26:18	0
9085341993	DIPAK DAS	9707474658	HITESH KALITA	15-07-2014	20:23:34	0
9085341993	DIPAK DAS	9707474658	HITESH KALITA	15-07-2014	20:23:16	0
9085341993	DIPAK DAS	9707474658	HITESH KALITA	15-07-2014	20:22:55	0
9085341993	DIPAK DAS	9707474658	HITESH KALITA	15-07-2014	20:22:47	0
9085341993	DIPAK DAS	9707474658	HITESH KALITA	15-07-2014	20:03:04	0
9085341993	DIPAK DAS	9707474658	HITESH KALITA	15-07-2014	19:50:50	0
9085341993	DIPAK DAS	9707474658	HITESH KALITA	15-07-2014	19:46:32	0
9085341993	DIPAK DAS	9707474658	HITESH KALITA	15-07-2014	19:43:27	0

Calling (A) Party Telephone Number/MSISDN	Name	Called (B) Party Telephone Number/Access Point Name	Name	Date	Time	Duration In Secs.
9085341993	DIPAK DAS	9707783876	GIASUDDINAHMED	15-07-2014	19:14:14	0
9085341993	DIPAK DAS	9707783876	GIASUDDINAHMED	15-07-2014	19:10:35	0
9085341993	DIPAK DAS	9707783876	GIASUDDINAHMED	15-07-2014	19:10:30	0
9085341993	DIPAK DAS	9707783876	GIASUDDINAHMED	15-07-2014	19:06:54	0
9085341993	DIPAK DAS	9707783876	GIASUDDINAHMED	15-07-2014	18:44:09	0
9085341993	DIPAK DAS	9707783876	GIASUDDINAHMED	15-07-2014	18:44:04	0
9085341993	DIPAK DAS	9707783876	GIASUDDINAHMED	15-07-2014	17:11:54	0
9085341993	DIPAK DAS	9707783876	GIASUDDINAHMED	15-07-2014	16:53:39	0
9085341993	DIPAK DAS	9707474658	HITESH KALITA	15-07-2014	14:08:48	0
9085341993	DIPAK DAS	9707474658	HITESH KALITA	15-07-2014	13:20:25	0
9085341993	DIPAK DAS	9707474658	HITESH KALITA	15-07-2014	8:42:34	0
9085341993	DIPAK DAS	9707474658	HITESH KALITA	15-07-2014	8:02:12	0
9085341993	DIPAK DAS	9707474658	HITESH KALITA	15-07-2014	7:51:24	0
9085341993	DIPAK DAS	9707474658	HITESH KALITA	14-07-2014	23:35:49	0
9085341993	DIPAK DAS	9707474658	HITESH KALITA	14-07-2014	23:14:13	0
9085341993	DIPAK DAS	9707474658	HITESH KALITA	14-07-2014	23:14:04	0
9085341993	DIPAK DAS	9707474658	HITESH KALITA	14-07-2014	23:01:01	0
9085341993	DIPAK DAS	9707474658	HITESH KALITA	14-07-2014	23:00:56	0

Calling (A) Party Telephone Number/MSISDN	Name	Called (B) Party Telephone Number/Access Point Name	Name	Date	Time	Duration In Secs.
9085341993	DIPAK DAS	9707474658	HITESH KALITA	14-07-2014	22:55:32	0
9085341993	DIPAK DAS	9707474658	HITESH KALITA	14-07-2014	22:50:38	0
9085341993	DIPAK DAS	9707474658	HITESH KALITA	14-07-2014	22:49:06	0
9085341993	DIPAK DAS	9707474658	HITESH KALITA	14-07-2014	22:48:56	0
9085341993	DIPAK DAS	9707474658	HITESH KALITA	14-07-2014	22:41:18	0
9085341993	DIPAK DAS	9707474658	HITESH KALITA	14-07-2014	22:41:12	0
9085341993	DIPAK DAS	9707474658	HITESH KALITA	14-07-2014	22:34:51	0
9085341993	DIPAK DAS	9707474658	HITESH KALITA	14-07-2014	22:31:18	0
9085341993	DIPAK DAS	9707474658	HITESH KALITA	14-07-2014	22:31:12	0
9085341993	DIPAK DAS	9707474658	HITESH KALITA	14-07-2014	22:31:06	0
9085341993	DIPAK DAS	9707474658	HITESH KALITA	14-07-2014	22:22:40	0
9085341993	DIPAK DAS	9707474658	HITESH KALITA	14-07-2014	22:01:18	128
9085341993	DIPAK DAS	9707783876	GIASUDDINAHMED	14-07-2014	17:36:41	719
9085341993	DIPAK DAS	9707783876	GIASUDDINAHMED	14-07-2014	17:35:38	40
9085341993	DIPAK DAS	9707474658	HITESH KALITA	14-07-2014	16:39:50	36
9085341993	DIPAK DAS	9707783876	GIASUDDINAHMED	13-07-2014	22:54:59	0
9085341993	DIPAK DAS	9707474658	HITESH KALITA	13-07-2014	22:34:14	0
9085341993	DIPAK DAS	9707474658	HITESH KALITA	13-07-2014	22:29:15	0

Calling (A) Party Telephone Number/MSISDN	Name	Called (B) Party Telephone Number/Access Point Name	Name	Date	Time	Duration In Secs.
9085341993	DIPAK DAS	9706470353	HITESH KALITA	13-07-2014	22:28:08	22
9085341993	DIPAK DAS	97077783876	GIASUDDINAHMED	13-07-2014	22:18:49	0
9085341993	DIPAK DAS	97077783876	GIASUDDINAHMED	13-07-2014	21:45:37	0
9085341993	DIPAK DAS	97077783876	GIASUDDINAHMED	13-07-2014	21:38:27	0
9085341993	DIPAK DAS	97077783876	GIASUDDINAHMED	13-07-2014	21:36:08	0
9085341993	DIPAK DAS	97077783876	GIASUDDINAHMED	13-07-2014	21:30:06	0
9085341993	DIPAK DAS	97077783876	GIASUDDINAHMED	13-07-2014	21:29:05	0
9085341993	DIPAK DAS	97077783876	GIASUDDINAHMED	13-07-2014	21:27:35	0
9085341993	DIPAK DAS	97077783876	GIASUDDINAHMED	13-07-2014	21:27:14	0
9085341993	DIPAK DAS	97077783876	GIASUDDINAHMED	13-07-2014	21:23:48	0
9085341993	DIPAK DAS	97077783876	GIASUDDINAHMED	13-07-2014	21:21:02	0
9085341993	DIPAK DAS	97077783876	GIASUDDINAHMED	13-07-2014	21:16:38	80
9085341993	DIPAK DAS	97074474658	HITESH KALITA	13-07-2014	20:07:42	72
9085341993	DIPAK DAS	97074474658	HITESH KALITA	13-07-2014	20:02:51	58
9085341993	DIPAK DAS	97077783876	GIASUDDINAHMED	13-07-2014	19:50:20	0
9085341993	DIPAK DAS	97077783876	GIASUDDINAHMED	13-07-2014	19:45:47	0
9085341993	DIPAK DAS	97077783876	GIASUDDINAHMED	13-07-2014	19:42:47	0
9085341993	DIPAK DAS	97077783876	GIASUDDINAHMED	13-07-2014	19:23:11	0

Calling (A) Party Telephone Number/MSISDN	Name	Called (B) Party Telephone Number/Access Point Name	Name	Date	Time	Duration In Secs.
9085341993	DIPAK DAS	9707783876	GIASUDDINAHMED	13-07-2014	16:38:35	0
9085341993	DIPAK DAS	9707783876	GIASUDDINAHMED	13-07-2014	16:36:17	0
9085341993	DIPAK DAS	9707783876	GIASUDDINAHMED	13-07-2014	16:35:04	0
9085341993	DIPAK DAS	9707783876	GIASUDDINAHMED	13-07-2014	16:33:37	0
9085341993	DIPAK DAS	9707474658	HITESH KALITA	13-07-2014	15:05:00	0
9085341993	DIPAK DAS	9707474658	HITESH KALITA	13-07-2014	15:02:26	0
9085341993	DIPAK DAS	9707783876	GIASUDDINAHMED	13-07-2014	15:01:36	0
9085341993	DIPAK DAS	9707474658	HITESH KALITA	13-07-2014	14:58:09	0
9085341993	DIPAK DAS	9707474658	HITESH KALITA	13-07-2014	14:52:50	237
9085341993	DIPAK DAS	9707783876	GIASUDDINAHMED	13-07-2014	13:23:59	0
9085341993	DIPAK DAS	9707783876	GIASUDDINAHMED	13-07-2014	12:48:10	0
9085341993	DIPAK DAS	9707783876	GIASUDDINAHMED	13-07-2014	11:05:43	0
9085341993	DIPAK DAS	9707783876	GIASUDDINAHMED	13-07-2014	11:01:22	0
9085341993	DIPAK DAS	9707783876	GIASUDDINAHMED	13-07-2014	10:55:10	0
9085341993	DIPAK DAS	9707783876	GIASUDDINAHMED	13-07-2014	10:34:57	0
9085341993	DIPAK DAS	9707474658	HITESH KALITA	13-07-2014	10:27:58	38
9085341993	DIPAK DAS	9707474658	HITESH KALITA	13-07-2014	10:26:44	55
9085341993	DIPAK DAS	9707783876	GIASUDDINAHMED	13-07-2014	9:51:52	0

Calling (A) Party Telephone Number/MSISDN	Name	Called (B) Party Telephone Number/Access Point Name	Name	Date	Time	Duration In Secs.
9085341993	DIPAK DAS	9707783876	GIASUDDINAHMED	13-07-2014	9:28:08	0
9085341993	DIPAK DAS	9707783876	GIASUDDINAHMED	13-07-2014	9:20:30	0
9085341993	DIPAK DAS	9707783876	GIASUDDINAHMED	13-07-2014	9:19:26	0
9085341993	DIPAK DAS	9707783876	GIASUDDINAHMED	13-07-2014	8:56:14	0
9085341993	DIPAK DAS	9707474658	HITESH KALITA	13-07-2014	7:16:20	46
9085341993	DIPAK DAS	9707474658	HITESH KALITA	13-07-2014	3:01:22	0
9085341993	DIPAK DAS	9707474658	HITESH KALITA	13-07-2014	0:13:51	0
9085341993	DIPAK DAS	9707783876	GIASUDDINAHMED	13-07-2014	0:11:11	0
9085341993	DIPAK DAS	9707783876	GIASUDDINAHMED	13-07-2014	0:11:06	0
9085341993	DIPAK DAS	9707474658	HITESH KALITA	13-07-2014	0:09:13	0
9085341993	DIPAK DAS	9707474658	HITESH KALITA	13-07-2014	0:09:04	0
9085341993	DIPAK DAS	9707783876	GIASUDDINAHMED	13-07-2014	0:07:55	0
9085341993	DIPAK DAS	9707783876	GIASUDDINAHMED	13-07-2014	0:07:55	0
9085341993	DIPAK DAS	9707783876	GIASUDDINAHMED	13-07-2014	0:03:55	0
9085341993	DIPAK DAS	9707783876	GIASUDDINAHMED	13-07-2014	0:03:38	0
9085341993	DIPAK DAS	9707783876	GIASUDDINAHMED	13-07-2014	0:02:03	0
9085341993	DIPAK DAS	9707783876	GIASUDDINAHMED	13-07-2014	0:02:03	0
9085341993	DIPAK DAS	9707783876	GIASUDDINAHMED	12/7/2014	23:59:35	0

Calling (A) Party Telephone Number/MSISDN	Name	Called (B) Party Telephone Number/Access Point Name	Name	Date	Time	Duration In Secs.
9085341993	DIPAK DAS	97077783876	GIASUDDINAHMED	12/7/2014	23:57:24	0
9085341993	DIPAK DAS	97077783876	GIASUDDINAHMED	12/7/2014	23:52:54	0
9085341993	DIPAK DAS	97077783876	GIASUDDINAHMED	12/7/2014	23:47:39	501
9085341993	DIPAK DAS	97077783876	GIASUDDINAHMED	12/7/2014	23:45:56	0
9085341993	DIPAK DAS	97077783876	GIASUDDINAHMED	12/7/2014	23:43:59	0
9085341993	DIPAK DAS	97077783876	GIASUDDINAHMED	12/7/2014	23:43:56	0
9085341993	DIPAK DAS	97077783876	GIASUDDINAHMED	12/7/2014	23:41:00	0
9085341993	DIPAK DAS	97077783876	GIASUDDINAHMED	12/7/2014	23:37:53	0
9085341993	DIPAK DAS	97077783876	GIASUDDINAHMED	12/7/2014	23:37:41	0
9085341993	DIPAK DAS	97077783876	GIASUDDINAHMED	12/7/2014	23:34:35	0
9085341993	DIPAK DAS	97077783876	GIASUDDINAHMED	12/7/2014	23:34:29	0
9085341993	DIPAK DAS	97077783876	GIASUDDINAHMED	12/7/2014	23:32:34	0
9085341993	DIPAK DAS	97077783876	GIASUDDINAHMED	12/7/2014	23:32:31	0
9085341993	DIPAK DAS	97077783876	GIASUDDINAHMED	12/7/2014	23:31:53	0
9085341993	DIPAK DAS	97077783876	GIASUDDINAHMED	12/7/2014	23:28:36	0
9085341993	DIPAK DAS	97077783876	GIASUDDINAHMED	12/7/2014	23:25:51	149
9085341993	DIPAK DAS	97077783876	GIASUDDINAHMED	12/7/2014	23:23:24	0
9085341993	DIPAK DAS	97077783876	GIASUDDINAHMED	12/7/2014	23:21:49	0

Calling (A) Party Telephone Number/MSISDN	Name	Called (B) Party Telephone Number/Access Point Name	Name	Date	Time	Duration In Secs.
9085341993	DIPAK DAS	9707783876	GIASUDDINAHMED	12/7/2014	23:19:31	0
9085341993	DIPAK DAS	9707783876	GIASUDDINAHMED	12/7/2014	23:11:34	0
9085341993	DIPAK DAS	9707783876	GIASUDDINAHMED	12/7/2014	23:08:18	0
9085341993	DIPAK DAS	9707783876	GIASUDDINAHMED	12/7/2014	23:03:25	0
9085341993	DIPAK DAS	9707783876	GIASUDDINAHMED	12/7/2014	23:02:37	0
9085341993	DIPAK DAS	9707783876	GIASUDDINAHMED	12/7/2014	23:00:42	0
9085341993	DIPAK DAS	9707783876	GIASUDDINAHMED	12/7/2014	22:58:20	0
9085341993	DIPAK DAS	9707783876	GIASUDDINAHMED	12/7/2014	22:58:15	0
9085341993	DIPAK DAS	9707783876	GIASUDDINAHMED	12/7/2014	22:55:44	0
9085341993	DIPAK DAS	9707783876	GIASUDDINAHMED	12/7/2014	22:53:45	0
9085341993	DIPAK DAS	9707783876	GIASUDDINAHMED	12/7/2014	22:51:57	0
9085341993	DIPAK DAS	9707783876	GIASUDDINAHMED	12/7/2014	22:45:37	0
9085341993	DIPAK DAS	9707783876	GIASUDDINAHMED	12/7/2014	22:42:58	0
9085341993	DIPAK DAS	9707783876	GIASUDDINAHMED	12/7/2014	22:39:56	0
9085341993	DIPAK DAS	9707783876	GIASUDDINAHMED	12/7/2014	22:39:39	0
9085341993	DIPAK DAS	9707783876	GIASUDDINAHMED	12/7/2014	22:36:17	0
9085341993	DIPAK DAS	9707783876	GIASUDDINAHMED	12/7/2014	22:26:06	0
9085341993	DIPAK DAS	9707783876	GIASUDDINAHMED	12/7/2014	22:21:12	0

Calling (A) Party Telephone Number/MSISDN	Name	Called (B) Party Telephone Number/Access Point Name	Name	Date	Time	Duration In Secs.
9085341993	DIPAK DAS	9707783876	GIASUDDINAHMED	12/7/2014	22:18:56	0
9085341993	DIPAK DAS	9707783876	GIASUDDINAHMED	12/7/2014	22:17:15	0
9085341993	DIPAK DAS	9707783876	GIASUDDINAHMED	12/7/2014	22:15:47	41
9085341993	DIPAK DAS	9707783876	GIASUDDINAHMED	12/7/2014	22:05:51	0
9085341993	DIPAK DAS	9707783876	GIASUDDINAHMED	12/7/2014	22:04:24	0
9085341993	DIPAK DAS	9707783876	GIASUDDINAHMED	12/7/2014	21:42:52	0
9085341993	DIPAK DAS	9707783876	GIASUDDINAHMED	12/7/2014	21:13:08	0
9085341993	DIPAK DAS	9707783876	GIASUDDINAHMED	12/7/2014	21:08:36	0
9085341993	DIPAK DAS	9707783876	GIASUDDINAHMED	12/7/2014	21:08:03	0
9085341993	DIPAK DAS	9707783876	GIASUDDINAHMED	12/7/2014	21:07:20	20
9085341993	DIPAK DAS	9707783876	GIASUDDINAHMED	12/7/2014	21:05:37	58
9085341993	DIPAK DAS	9707783876	GIASUDDINAHMED	12/7/2014	20:22:06	0
9085341993	DIPAK DAS	9707783876	GIASUDDINAHMED	12/7/2014	20:19:40	0
9085341993	DIPAK DAS	9707474658	HITESH KALITA	12/7/2014	19:27:03	0
9085341993	DIPAK DAS	9707783876	GIASUDDINAHMED	12/7/2014	19:18:05	0
9085341993	DIPAK DAS	9707783876	GIASUDDINAHMED	12/7/2014	19:13:59	120
9085341993	DIPAK DAS	9707783876	GIASUDDINAHMED	12/7/2014	19:10:20	0
9085341993	DIPAK DAS	9707783876	GIASUDDINAHMED	12/7/2014	19:09:41	0

Calling (A) Party Telephone Number/MSISDN	Name	Called (B) Party Telephone Number/Access Point Name	Name	Date	Time	Duration In Secs.
9085341993	DIPAK DAS	9707783876	GIASUDDINAHMED	12/7/2014	19:04:01	0
9085341993	DIPAK DAS	9707783876	GIASUDDINAHMED	12/7/2014	19:02:50	0
9085341993	DIPAK DAS	9707783876	GIASUDDINAHMED	12/7/2014	18:59:38	0
9085341993	DIPAK DAS	9707474658	HITESH KALITA	12/7/2014	10:51:33	63
9085341993	DIPAK DAS	9707783876	GIASUDDINAHMED	12/7/2014	9:30:52	0
9085341993	DIPAK DAS	9707783876	GIASUDDINAHMED	12/7/2014	8:47:58	0
9085341993	DIPAK DAS	9707783876	GIASUDDINAHMED	12/7/2014	8:26:15	0
9085341993	DIPAK DAS	9707783876	GIASUDDINAHMED	12/7/2014	8:21:47	0
9085341993	DIPAK DAS	9707783876	GIASUDDINAHMED	12/7/2014	8:15:27	0
9085341993	DIPAK DAS	9707783876	GIASUDDINAHMED	12/7/2014	8:12:31	0
9085341993	DIPAK DAS	9707783876	GIASUDDINAHMED	12/7/2014	8:09:55	0
9085341993	DIPAK DAS	9707783876	GIASUDDINAHMED	12/7/2014	8:08:42	0
9085341993	DIPAK DAS	9707783876	GIASUDDINAHMED	12/7/2014	8:04:47	0
9085341993	DIPAK DAS	9707783876	GIASUDDINAHMED	12/7/2014	8:02:21	0
9085341993	DIPAK DAS	9707783876	GIASUDDINAHMED	12/7/2014	7:59:37	0
9085341993	DIPAK DAS	9707783876	GIASUDDINAHMED	12/7/2014	7:57:28	0
9085341993	DIPAK DAS	9707783876	GIASUDDINAHMED	12/7/2014	7:56:07	0
9085341993	DIPAK DAS	9707783876	GIASUDDINAHMED	12/7/2014	7:55:02	0

Calling (A) Party Telephone Number/MSISDN	Name	Called (B) Party Telephone Number/Access Point Name	Name	Date	Time	Duration In Secs.
9085341993	DIPAK DAS	9707783876	GIASUDDINAHMED	12/7/2014	7:52:24	0
9085341993	DIPAK DAS	9707783876	GIASUDDINAHMED	11/7/2014	23:09:36	0
9085341993	DIPAK DAS	9707783876	GIASUDDINAHMED	11/7/2014	23:05:41	0
9085341993	DIPAK DAS	9707783876	GIASUDDINAHMED	11/7/2014	22:58:46	0
9085341993	DIPAK DAS	9707783876	GIASUDDINAHMED	11/7/2014	22:49:19	0
9085341993	DIPAK DAS	9707783876	GIASUDDINAHMED	11/7/2014	22:47:52	0
9085341993	DIPAK DAS	9707783876	GIASUDDINAHMED	11/7/2014	22:47:27	0
9085341993	DIPAK DAS	9707783876	GIASUDDINAHMED	11/7/2014	22:44:23	145
9085341993	DIPAK DAS	9707783876	GIASUDDINAHMED	11/7/2014	22:33:39	0
9085341993	DIPAK DAS	9707783876	GIASUDDINAHMED	11/7/2014	22:32:25	0
9085341993	DIPAK DAS	9707783876	GIASUDDINAHMED	11/7/2014	22:27:33	0
9085341993	DIPAK DAS	9707783876	GIASUDDINAHMED	11/7/2014	21:25:42	0
9085341993	DIPAK DAS	9707474658	HITESH KALITA	11/7/2014	21:07:17	0
9085341993	DIPAK DAS	9707474658	HITESH KALITA	11/7/2014	20:59:21	0
9085341993	DIPAK DAS	9707474658	HITESH KALITA	11/7/2014	20:55:19	73
9085341993	DIPAK DAS	9707783876	GIASUDDINAHMED	11/7/2014	20:45:31	0
9085341993	DIPAK DAS	9707783876	GIASUDDINAHMED	11/7/2014	20:43:32	0
9085341993	DIPAK DAS	9707783876	GIASUDDINAHMED	11/7/2014	20:39:55	0

Calling (A) Party Telephone Number/MSISDN	Name	Called (B) Party Telephone Number/Access Point Name	Name	Date	Time	Duration In Secs.
9085341993	DIPAK DAS	9707783876	GIASUDDINAHMED	11/7/2014	20:38:02	0
9085341993	DIPAK DAS	9707474658	HITESH KALITA	11/7/2014	20:25:49	0
9085341993	DIPAK DAS	9401165464	HITESWAR KALITA	11/7/2014	20:24:01	0
9085341993	DIPAK DAS	9707474658	HITESH KALITA	11/7/2014	19:11:20	0
9085341993	DIPAK DAS	9707783876	GIASUDDINAHMED	11/7/2014	19:10:38	0
9085341993	DIPAK DAS	9707783876	GIASUDDINAHMED	11/7/2014	18:31:06	0
9085341993	DIPAK DAS	9707783876	GIASUDDINAHMED	11/7/2014	16:46:40	0
9085341993	DIPAK DAS	9707783876	GIASUDDINAHMED	11/7/2014	15:23:59	0
9085341993	DIPAK DAS	9707783876	GIASUDDINAHMED	11/7/2014	15:17:18	0
9085341993	DIPAK DAS	9707783876	GIASUDDINAHMED	11/7/2014	14:54:32	0
9085341993	DIPAK DAS	9707783876	GIASUDDINAHMED	11/7/2014	14:38:43	0
9085341993	DIPAK DAS	9707783876	GIASUDDINAHMED	11/7/2014	14:32:23	0
9085341993	DIPAK DAS	9707783876	GIASUDDINAHMED	11/7/2014	14:31:42	0
9085341993	DIPAK DAS	9707783876	GIASUDDINAHMED	11/7/2014	14:28:35	0
9085341993	DIPAK DAS	9707783876	GIASUDDINAHMED	11/7/2014	14:21:04	0
9085341993	DIPAK DAS	9707783876	GIASUDDINAHMED	11/7/2014	14:20:28	0
9085341993	DIPAK DAS	9707783876	GIASUDDINAHMED	11/7/2014	14:16:31	0
9085341993	DIPAK DAS	9707783876	GIASUDDINAHMED	11/7/2014	14:11:52	0

Calling (A) Party Telephone Number/MSISDN	Name	Called (B) Party Telephone Number/Access Point Name	Name	Date	Time	Duration In Secs.
9085341993	DIPAK DAS	9707783876	GIASUDDINAHMED	11/7/2014	13:56:41	0
9085341993	DIPAK DAS	9707783876	GIASUDDINAHMED	11/7/2014	13:51:10	0
9085341993	DIPAK DAS	9707783876	GIASUDDINAHMED	11/7/2014	13:33:02	0
9085341993	DIPAK DAS	9707783876	GIASUDDINAHMED	11/7/2014	13:32:08	0
9085341993	DIPAK DAS	9707783876	GIASUDDINAHMED	11/7/2014	13:08:47	0
9085341993	DIPAK DAS	9707474658	HITESH KALITA	11/7/2014	13:07:16	62
9085341993	DIPAK DAS	9707783876	GIASUDDINAHMED	11/7/2014	12:57:53	0
9085341993	DIPAK DAS	9707783876	GIASUDDINAHMED	11/7/2014	10:35:40	0
9085341993	DIPAK DAS	9707783876	GIASUDDINAHMED	11/7/2014	10:15:48	0
9085341993	DIPAK DAS	9707783876	GIASUDDINAHMED	11/7/2014	10:05:25	0
9085341993	DIPAK DAS	9707783876	GIASUDDINAHMED	11/7/2014	9:57:34	0
9085341993	DIPAK DAS	9707783876	GIASUDDINAHMED	11/7/2014	9:48:08	0
9085341993	DIPAK DAS	9707783876	GIASUDDINAHMED	11/7/2014	9:43:44	0
9085341993	DIPAK DAS	9707783876	GIASUDDINAHMED	11/7/2014	9:43:09	0
9085341993	DIPAK DAS	9707783876	GIASUDDINAHMED	11/7/2014	9:42:49	0
9085341993	DIPAK DAS	9707783876	GIASUDDINAHMED	11/7/2014	9:41:16	0
9085341993	DIPAK DAS	9707783876	GIASUDDINAHMED	11/7/2014	9:10:23	0
9085341993	DIPAK DAS	9707783876	GIASUDDINAHMED	11/7/2014	9:05:52	0

Calling (A) Party Telephone Number/MSISDN	Name	Called (B) Party Telephone Number/Access Point Name	Name	Date	Time	Duration In Secs.
9085341993	DIPAK DAS	9707783876	GIASUDDINAHMED	11/7/2014	9:01:08	0
9085341993	DIPAK DAS	9707783876	GIASUDDINAHMED	11/7/2014	9:00:38	0
9085341993	DIPAK DAS	9707783876	GIASUDDINAHMED	11/7/2014	8:59:46	0
9085341993	DIPAK DAS	9707783876	GIASUDDINAHMED	11/7/2014	8:29:58	0
9085341993	DIPAK DAS	9707783876	GIASUDDINAHMED	11/7/2014	8:27:39	0
9085341993	DIPAK DAS	9707783876	GIASUDDINAHMED	11/7/2014	8:19:35	0
9085341993	DIPAK DAS	9707783876	GIASUDDINAHMED	11/7/2014	8:18:30	0
9085341993	DIPAK DAS	9707783876	GIASUDDINAHMED	11/7/2014	8:12:21	0
9085341993	DIPAK DAS	9707783876	GIASUDDINAHMED	11/7/2014	8:03:53	38
9085341993	DIPAK DAS	9707783876	GIASUDDINAHMED	11/7/2014	8:03:05	0
9085341993	DIPAK DAS	9707783876	GIASUDDINAHMED	11/7/2014	7:59:16	0
9085341993	DIPAK DAS	9707783876	GIASUDDINAHMED	11/7/2014	7:45:50	0
9085341993	DIPAK DAS	9707783876	GIASUDDINAHMED	11/7/2014	7:37:44	0
9085341993	DIPAK DAS	9707783876	GIASUDDINAHMED	11/7/2014	1:18:31	0
9085341993	DIPAK DAS	9707783876	GIASUDDINAHMED	10/7/2014	23:00:01	0
9085341993	DIPAK DAS	9707783876	GIASUDDINAHMED	10/7/2014	22:57:34	0
9085341993	DIPAK DAS	9707783876	GIASUDDINAHMED	10/7/2014	22:48:20	0
9085341993	DIPAK DAS	9707783876	GIASUDDINAHMED	10/7/2014	22:40:24	0

Calling (A) Party Telephone Number/MSISDN	Name	Called (B) Party Telephone Number/Access Point Name	Name	Date	Time	Duration In Secs.
9085341993	DIPAK DAS	9707474658	HITESH KALITA	10/7/2014	22:21:44	0
9085341993	DIPAK DAS	9707474658	HITESH KALITA	10/7/2014	22:18:51	0
9085341993	DIPAK DAS	9707474658	HITESH KALITA	10/7/2014	22:03:41	0
9085341993	DIPAK DAS	9707783876	GIASUDDINAHMED	10/7/2014	22:01:50	0
9085341993	DIPAK DAS	9707783876	GIASUDDINAHMED	10/7/2014	22:00:22	0
9085341993	DIPAK DAS	9707474658	HITESH KALITA	10/7/2014	19:19:07	70
9085341993	DIPAK DAS	9707783876	GIASUDDINAHMED	10/7/2014	18:54:48	0
9085341993	DIPAK DAS	9707783876	GIASUDDINAHMED	10/7/2014	15:10:17	0
9085341993	DIPAK DAS	9707783876	GIASUDDINAHMED	10/7/2014	15:03:51	0
9085341993	DIPAK DAS	9707783876	GIASUDDINAHMED	10/7/2014	14:46:15	0
9085341993	DIPAK DAS	9707783876	GIASUDDINAHMED	10/7/2014	11:27:29	0
9085341993	DIPAK DAS	9707783876	GIASUDDINAHMED	10/7/2014	11:21:32	0
9085341993	DIPAK DAS	9707783876	GIASUDDINAHMED	10/7/2014	11:17:19	0
9085341993	DIPAK DAS	9707783876	GIASUDDINAHMED	10/7/2014	10:52:24	0
9085341993	DIPAK DAS	9707474658	HITESH KALITA	10/7/2014	9:33:26	37
9085341993	DIPAK DAS	9707783876	GIASUDDINAHMED	10/7/2014	8:26:20	0
9085341993	DIPAK DAS	9707783876	GIASUDDINAHMED	10/7/2014	8:21:47	0
9085341993	DIPAK DAS	9707783876	GIASUDDINAHMED	10/7/2014	8:19:18	0

Calling (A) Party Telephone Number/MSISDN	Name	Called (B) Party Telephone Number/Access Point Name	Name	Date	Time	Duration In Secs.
9085341993	DIPAK DAS	9707783876	GIASUDDINAHMED	10/7/2014	8:12:44	0
9085341993	DIPAK DAS	9707783876	GIASUDDINAHMED	10/7/2014	8:11:12	0
9085341993	DIPAK DAS	9707783876	GIASUDDINAHMED	10/7/2014	8:03:45	0
9085341993	DIPAK DAS	9707783876	GIASUDDINAHMED	10/7/2014	6:52:45	0
9085341993	DIPAK DAS	9707783876	GIASUDDINAHMED	10/7/2014	5:31:40	0
9085341993	DIPAK DAS	9707783876	GIASUDDINAHMED	9/7/2014	22:52:34	0
9085341993	DIPAK DAS	9707783876	GIASUDDINAHMED	9/7/2014	22:46:34	337
9085341993	DIPAK DAS	9854051825	K.D. CEMENTS	9/7/2014	22:46:12	56
9085341993	DIPAK DAS	9707783876	GIASUDDINAHMED	9/7/2014	22:38:15	0
9085341993	DIPAK DAS	9707783876	GIASUDDINAHMED	9/7/2014	22:31:41	0
9085341993	DIPAK DAS	9707474658	HITESH KALITA	9/7/2014	22:21:36	0
9085341993	DIPAK DAS	9707474658	HITESH KALITA	9/7/2014	22:20:54	0
9085341993	DIPAK DAS	9707474658	HITESH KALITA	9/7/2014	22:18:45	0
9085341993	DIPAK DAS	9707474658	HITESH KALITA	9/7/2014	22:14:31	0
9085341993	DIPAK DAS	9707474658	HITESH KALITA	9/7/2014	22:08:18	0
9085341993	DIPAK DAS	9707474658	HITESH KALITA	9/7/2014	22:06:52	0
9085341993	DIPAK DAS	9707474658	HITESH KALITA	9/7/2014	22:03:57	0
9085341993	DIPAK DAS	9707474658	HITESH KALITA	9/7/2014	22:00:12	0

Calling (A) Party Telephone Number/MSISDN	Name	Called (B) Party Telephone Number/Access Point Name	Name	Date	Time	Duration In Secs.
9085341993	DIPAK DAS	9707474658	HITESH KALITA	9/7/2014	21:55:57	0
9085341993	DIPAK DAS	9707783876	GIASUDDINAHMED	9/7/2014	21:54:12	0
9085341993	DIPAK DAS	9707474658	HITESH KALITA	9/7/2014	21:53:26	0
9085341993	DIPAK DAS	9707783876	GIASUDDINAHMED	9/7/2014	21:53:09	0
9085341993	DIPAK DAS	9707474658	HITESH KALITA	9/7/2014	21:51:12	0
9085341993	DIPAK DAS	9707474658	HITESH KALITA	9/7/2014	21:50:20	0
9085341993	DIPAK DAS	9707474658	HITESH KALITA	9/7/2014	21:49:29	0
9085341993	DIPAK DAS	9707474658	HITESH KALITA	9/7/2014	21:48:48	0
9085341993	DIPAK DAS	9707474658	HITESH KALITA	9/7/2014	21:46:03	0
9085341993	DIPAK DAS	9707783876	GIASUDDINAHMED	9/7/2014	21:37:16	0
9085341993	DIPAK DAS	9707783876	GIASUDDINAHMED	9/7/2014	20:29:53	0
9085341993	DIPAK DAS	9707783876	GIASUDDINAHMED	9/7/2014	19:23:42	0
9085341993	DIPAK DAS	9707783876	GIASUDDINAHMED	9/7/2014	19:15:44	0
9085341993	DIPAK DAS	9707783876	GIASUDDINAHMED	9/7/2014	19:05:01	0
9085341993	DIPAK DAS	9707783876	GIASUDDINAHMED	9/7/2014	19:03:34	0
9085341993	DIPAK DAS	9707783876	GIASUDDINAHMED	9/7/2014	19:02:06	0
9085341993	DIPAK DAS	9707783876	GIASUDDINAHMED	9/7/2014	19:02:03	0
9085341993	DIPAK DAS	9707783876	GIASUDDINAHMED	9/7/2014	18:57:52	0

Calling (A) Party Telephone Number/MSISDN	Name	Called (B) Party Telephone Number/Access Point Name	Name	Date	Time	Duration In Secs.
9085341993	DIPAK DAS	9707783876	GIASUDDINAHMED	9/7/2014	18:52:06	0
9085341993	DIPAK DAS	9707783876	GIASUDDINAHMED	9/7/2014	18:52:00	0
9085341993	DIPAK DAS	9707783876	GIASUDDINAHMED	9/7/2014	18:31:27	0
9085341993	DIPAK DAS	9707783876	GIASUDDINAHMED	9/7/2014	18:06:57	0
9085341993	DIPAK DAS	9707783876	GIASUDDINAHMED	9/7/2014	17:39:00	0
9085341993	DIPAK DAS	9707783876	GIASUDDINAHMED	9/7/2014	17:17:28	0
9085341993	DIPAK DAS	9707474658	HITESH KALITA	9/7/2014	16:23:40	0
9085341993	DIPAK DAS	9707474658	HITESH KALITA	9/7/2014	16:15:12	0
9085341993	DIPAK DAS	9707783876	GIASUDDINAHMED	9/7/2014	16:10:50	0
9085341993	DIPAK DAS	9707474658	HITESH KALITA	9/7/2014	16:10:43	0
9085341993	DIPAK DAS	9707474658	HITESH KALITA	9/7/2014	16:06:01	0
9085341993	DIPAK DAS	9707474658	HITESH KALITA	9/7/2014	16:05:15	0
9085341993	DIPAK DAS	9707474658	HITESH KALITA	9/7/2014	16:04:50	0
9085341993	DIPAK DAS	9707783876	GIASUDDINAHMED	9/7/2014	14:03:37	0
9085341993	DIPAK DAS	9707783876	GIASUDDINAHMED	9/7/2014	13:58:56	0
9085341993	DIPAK DAS	9707783876	GIASUDDINAHMED	9/7/2014	13:56:20	0
9085341993	DIPAK DAS	9707783876	GIASUDDINAHMED	9/7/2014	13:52:02	0
9085341993	DIPAK DAS	9707783876	GIASUDDINAHMED	9/7/2014	13:34:37	0

Calling (A) Party Telephone Number/MSISDN	Name	Called (B) Party Telephone Number/Access Point Name	Name	Date	Time	Duration In Secs.
9085341993	DIPAK DAS	97077783876	GIASUDDINAHMED	9/7/2014	13:21:38	0
9085341993	DIPAK DAS	97077783876	GIASUDDINAHMED	9/7/2014	13:15:17	0
9085341993	DIPAK DAS	97074474658	HITESH KALITA	9/7/2014	13:09:57	0
9085341993	DIPAK DAS	97074474658	HITESH KALITA	9/7/2014	13:02:33	0
9085341993	DIPAK DAS	97074474658	HITESH KALITA	9/7/2014	11:52:17	0
9085341993	DIPAK DAS	97077783876	GIASUDDINAHMED	9/7/2014	11:29:43	0
9085341993	DIPAK DAS	97074474658	HITESH KALITA	9/7/2014	11:20:17	0
9085341993	DIPAK DAS	97077783876	GIASUDDINAHMED	9/7/2014	9:09:40	0
9085341993	DIPAK DAS	97077783876	GIASUDDINAHMED	9/7/2014	9:08:48	0
9085341993	DIPAK DAS	97074474658	HITESH KALITA	9/7/2014	7:32:34	0
9085341993	DIPAK DAS	97077783876	GIASUDDINAHMED	9/7/2014	7:20:02	0
9085341993	DIPAK DAS	97077783876	GIASUDDINAHMED	9/7/2014	6:18:27	0
9085341993	DIPAK DAS	97074474658	HITESH KALITA	8/7/2014	23:50:08	0
9085341993	DIPAK DAS	97074474658	HITESH KALITA	8/7/2014	23:34:54	0
9085341993	DIPAK DAS	97074474658	HITESH KALITA	8/7/2014	23:34:48	0
9085341993	DIPAK DAS	97074474658	HITESH KALITA	8/7/2014	23:29:43	0
9085341993	DIPAK DAS	97074474658	HITESH KALITA	8/7/2014	23:27:38	0
9085341993	DIPAK DAS	97074474658	HITESH KALITA	8/7/2014	23:27:33	0

Calling (A) Party Telephone Number/MSISDN	Name	Called (B) Party Telephone Number/Access Point Name	Name	Date	Time	Duration In Secs.
9085341993	DIPAK DAS	9707783876	GIASUDDINAHMED	8/7/2014	22:51:47	0
9085341993	DIPAK DAS	9707474658	HITESH KALITA	8/7/2014	22:38:52	0
9085341993	DIPAK DAS	9707474658	HITESH KALITA	8/7/2014	22:37:11	0
9085341993	DIPAK DAS	9707474658	HITESH KALITA	8/7/2014	22:35:41	0
9085341993	DIPAK DAS	9707474658	HITESH KALITA	8/7/2014	22:34:47	0
9085341993	DIPAK DAS	9707783876	GIASUDDINAHMED	8/7/2014	22:31:41	0
9085341993	DIPAK DAS	9707474658	HITESH KALITA	8/7/2014	22:28:10	0
9085341993	DIPAK DAS	9707474658	HITESH KALITA	8/7/2014	22:27:18	0
9085341993	DIPAK DAS	9707474658	HITESH KALITA	8/7/2014	22:24:41	0
9085341993	DIPAK DAS	9707474658	HITESH KALITA	8/7/2014	22:23:51	0
9085341993	DIPAK DAS	9707783876	GIASUDDINAHMED	8/7/2014	22:18:32	0
9085341993	DIPAK DAS	9707783876	GIASUDDINAHMED	8/7/2014	22:18:27	0
9085341993	DIPAK DAS	9707783876	GIASUDDINAHMED	8/7/2014	22:12:11	0
9085341993	DIPAK DAS	9707783876	GIASUDDINAHMED	8/7/2014	21:54:28	0
9085341993	DIPAK DAS	9707783876	GIASUDDINAHMED	8/7/2014	21:43:50	360
9085341993	DIPAK DAS	9707783876	GIASUDDINAHMED	8/7/2014	21:37:07	0
9085341993	DIPAK DAS	9707783876	GIASUDDINAHMED	8/7/2014	21:35:40	37
9085341993	DIPAK DAS	9707783876	GIASUDDINAHMED	8/7/2014	20:56:33	0

Calling (A) Party Telephone Number/MSISDN	Name	Called (B) Party Telephone Number/Access Point Name	Name	Date	Time	Duration In Secs.
9085341993	DIPAK DAS	9707474658	HITESH KALITA	8/7/2014	19:24:49	0
9085341993	DIPAK DAS	9707783876	GIASUDDINAHMED	8/7/2014	18:58:33	0
9085341993	DIPAK DAS	9707783876	GIASUDDINAHMED	8/7/2014	18:57:44	0
9085341993	DIPAK DAS	9707783876	GIASUDDINAHMED	8/7/2014	18:21:15	0
9085341993	DIPAK DAS	9707474658	HITESH KALITA	8/7/2014	12:46:37	29
9085341993	DIPAK DAS	9707783876	GIASUDDINAHMED	7/7/2014	23:24:06	95
9085341993	DIPAK DAS	9707783876	GIASUDDINAHMED	7/7/2014	23:03:52	123
9085341993	DIPAK DAS	9707783876	GIASUDDINAHMED	7/7/2014	22:57:28	0
9085341993	DIPAK DAS	9707783876	GIASUDDINAHMED	7/7/2014	22:54:25	0
9085341993	DIPAK DAS	9707783876	GIASUDDINAHMED	7/7/2014	22:51:08	0
9085341993	DIPAK DAS	9707783876	GIASUDDINAHMED	7/7/2014	22:48:39	62
9085341993	DIPAK DAS	9707783876	GIASUDDINAHMED	7/7/2014	22:44:30	0
9085341993	DIPAK DAS	9707783876	GIASUDDINAHMED	7/7/2014	22:40:10	0
9085341993	DIPAK DAS	9707783876	GIASUDDINAHMED	7/7/2014	22:39:14	4
9085341993	DIPAK DAS	9707783876	GIASUDDINAHMED	7/7/2014	22:38:07	0
9085341993	DIPAK DAS	9707783876	GIASUDDINAHMED	7/7/2014	22:07:15	0
9085341993	DIPAK DAS	9707783876	GIASUDDINAHMED	7/7/2014	17:21:41	0
9085341993	DIPAK DAS	9707783876	GIASUDDINAHMED	7/7/2014	17:03:49	569

Calling (A) Party Telephone Number/MSISDN	Name	Called (B) Party Telephone Number/Access Point Name	Name	Date	Time	Duration In Secs.
9085341993	DIPAK DAS	9707783876	GIASUDDINAHMED	7/7/2014	16:36:39	0
9085341993	DIPAK DAS	9707474658	HITESH KALITA	7/7/2014	12:46:08	56
9085341993	DIPAK DAS	9707474658	HITESH KALITA	7/7/2014	11:20:24	20
9085341993	DIPAK DAS	9707783876	GIASUDDINAHMED	7/7/2014	9:53:05	0
9085341993	DIPAK DAS	9707783876	GIASUDDINAHMED	7/7/2014	9:47:56	179
9085341993	DIPAK DAS	9707474658	HITESH KALITA	7/7/2014	9:29:50	117
9085341993	DIPAK DAS	9707474658	HITESH KALITA	7/7/2014	7:30:36	18
9085341993	DIPAK DAS	9707474658	HITESH KALITA	6/7/2014	22:03:48	0
9085341993	DIPAK DAS	9707783876	GIASUDDINAHMED	6/7/2014	21:59:00	0
9085341993	DIPAK DAS	9707474658	HITESH KALITA	6/7/2014	21:58:23	0
9085341993	DIPAK DAS	9707783876	GIASUDDINAHMED	6/7/2014	21:44:49	70
9085341993	DIPAK DAS	9707783876	GIASUDDINAHMED	6/7/2014	19:53:07	0
9085341993	DIPAK DAS	9707783876	GIASUDDINAHMED	6/7/2014	15:26:00	0
9085341993	DIPAK DAS	9707474658	HITESH KALITA	6/7/2014	15:03:39	0
9085341993	DIPAK DAS	9401165464	HITESWAR KALITA	6/7/2014	14:41:57	35
9085341993	DIPAK DAS	9707474658	HITESH KALITA	6/7/2014	14:29:11	0
9085341993	DIPAK DAS	9707783876	GIASUDDINAHMED	6/7/2014	12:55:15	0
9085341993	DIPAK DAS	9707783876	GIASUDDINAHMED	6/7/2014	11:14:37	161

Calling (A) Party Telephone Number/MSISDN	Name	Called (B) Party Telephone Number/Access Point Name	Name	Date	Time	Duration In Secs.
9085341993	DIPAK DAS	9707783876	GIASUDDINAHMED	6/7/2014	10:57:49	117
9085341993	DIPAK DAS	9707783876	GIASUDDINAHMED	6/7/2014	10:32:01	0
9085341993	DIPAK DAS	9707783876	GIASUDDINAHMED	5/7/2014	23:37:51	0
9085341993	DIPAK DAS	9707783876	GIASUDDINAHMED	5/7/2014	23:36:02	0
9085341993	DIPAK DAS	9707783876	GIASUDDINAHMED	5/7/2014	23:35:28	4
9085341993	DIPAK DAS	9707783876	GIASUDDINAHMED	5/7/2014	23:29:51	0
9085341993	DIPAK DAS	9707783876	GIASUDDINAHMED	5/7/2014	23:27:49	86
9085341993	DIPAK DAS	9707783876	GIASUDDINAHMED	5/7/2014	23:09:04	0
9085341993	DIPAK DAS	9707783876	GIASUDDINAHMED	5/7/2014	22:50:29	0
9085341993	DIPAK DAS	9707783876	GIASUDDINAHMED	5/7/2014	22:41:52	15
9085341993	DIPAK DAS	9707783876	GIASUDDINAHMED	5/7/2014	22:38:21	3
9085341993	DIPAK DAS	9707783876	GIASUDDINAHMED	5/7/2014	22:37:37	0
9085341993	DIPAK DAS	9707783876	GIASUDDINAHMED	5/7/2014	22:35:24	0
9085341993	DIPAK DAS	9707783876	GIASUDDINAHMED	5/7/2014	22:29:40	91
9085341993	DIPAK DAS	9707783876	GIASUDDINAHMED	5/7/2014	22:25:10	103
9085341993	DIPAK DAS	9707783876	GIASUDDINAHMED	5/7/2014	22:24:55	0
9085341993	DIPAK DAS	9707783876	GIASUDDINAHMED	5/7/2014	22:19:10	0
9085341993	DIPAK DAS	9707474658	HITESH KALITA	5/7/2014	22:11:21	0

Calling (A) Party Telephone Number/MSISDN	Name	Called (B) Party Telephone Number/Access Point Name	Name	Date	Time	Duration In Secs.
9085341993	DIPAK DAS	9707783876	GIASUDDINAHMED	5/7/2014	21:50:04	0
9085341993	DIPAK DAS	9707474658	HITESH KALITA	5/7/2014	21:27:35	0
9085341993	DIPAK DAS	9707474658	HITESH KALITA	5/7/2014	21:12:39	0
9085341993	DIPAK DAS	9707783876	GIASUDDINAHMED	5/7/2014	19:53:51	0
9085341993	DIPAK DAS	9707783876	GIASUDDINAHMED	5/7/2014	19:47:47	181
9085341993	DIPAK DAS	9707783876	GIASUDDINAHMED	5/7/2014	19:44:15	89
9085341993	DIPAK DAS	9707783876	GIASUDDINAHMED	5/7/2014	19:40:15	73
9085341993	DIPAK DAS	9707783876	GIASUDDINAHMED	5/7/2014	17:33:33	65
9085341993	DIPAK DAS	9707783876	GIASUDDINAHMED	5/7/2014	17:28:49	0
9085341993	DIPAK DAS	9401165464	HITESWAR KALITA	5/7/2014	17:27:21	30
9085341993	DIPAK DAS	9707783876	GIASUDDINAHMED	5/7/2014	14:46:09	54
9085341993	DIPAK DAS	9401165464	HITESWAR KALITA	5/7/2014	14:20:28	52
9085341993	DIPAK DAS	9401165464	HITESWAR KALITA	5/7/2014	12:00:38	27
9085341993	DIPAK DAS	9707783876	GIASUDDINAHMED	4/7/2014	21:43:59	455
9085341993	DIPAK DAS	9707474658	HITESH KALITA	4/7/2014	21:37:08	0
9085341993	DIPAK DAS	9707783876	GIASUDDINAHMED	4/7/2014	21:02:31	17
9085341993	DIPAK DAS	9707783876	GIASUDDINAHMED	4/7/2014	20:24:55	0
9085341993	DIPAK DAS	9707783876	GIASUDDINAHMED	4/7/2014	19:29:06	0

Calling (A) Party Telephone Number/MSISDN	Name	Called (B) Party Telephone Number/Access Point Name	Name	Date	Time	Duration In Secs.
9085341993	DIPAK DAS	9401165464	HITESWAR KALITA	4/7/2014	19:08:39	7
9085341993	DIPAK DAS	9401165464	HITESWAR KALITA	4/7/2014	19:07:44	2
9085341993	DIPAK DAS	9707474658	HITESH KALITA	4/7/2014	16:36:11	0
9085341993	DIPAK DAS	9707783876	GIASUDDINAHMED	4/7/2014	15:51:31	0
9085341993	DIPAK DAS	9707783876	GIASUDDINAHMED	4/7/2014	15:49:56	64
9085341993	DIPAK DAS	9707783876	GIASUDDINAHMED	4/7/2014	15:42:49	1
9085341993	DIPAK DAS	9707474658	HITESH KALITA	4/7/2014	13:16:02	0
9085341993	DIPAK DAS	9401165464	HITESWAR KALITA	4/7/2014	9:24:18	25
9085341993	DIPAK DAS	9707474658	HITESH KALITA	4/7/2014	9:00:48	0
9085341993	DIPAK DAS	9707783876	GIASUDDINAHMED	4/7/2014	8:54:37	0
9085341993	DIPAK DAS	9707474658	HITESH KALITA	3/7/2014	23:25:18	0
9085341993	DIPAK DAS	9707783876	GIASUDDINAHMED	3/7/2014	22:31:24	0
9085341993	DIPAK DAS	9707783876	GIASUDDINAHMED	3/7/2014	21:45:34	84
9085341993	DIPAK DAS	9707783876	GIASUDDINAHMED	3/7/2014	21:43:20	0
9085341993	DIPAK DAS	9707474658	HITESH KALITA	3/7/2014	19:45:09	0
9085341993	DIPAK DAS	9707474658	HITESH KALITA	3/7/2014	19:36:15	0
9085341993	DIPAK DAS	9401165464	HITESWAR KALITA	3/7/2014	10:13:23	16
9085341993	DIPAK DAS	9707783876	GIASUDDINAHMED	3/7/2014	8:22:44	0

Calling (A) Party Telephone Number/MSISDN	Name	Called (B) Party Telephone Number/Access Point Name	Name	Date	Time	Duration In Secs.
9085341993	DIPAK DAS	9707783876	GIASUDDINAHMED	3/7/2014	8:16:16	303
9085341993	DIPAK DAS	9707783876	GIASUDDINAHMED	3/7/2014	8:13:47	0
9085341993	DIPAK DAS	9707783876	GIASUDDINAHMED	2/7/2014	23:36:01	0
9085341993	DIPAK DAS	9707783876	GIASUDDINAHMED	2/7/2014	23:32:18	0
9085341993	DIPAK DAS	9707783876	GIASUDDINAHMED	2/7/2014	23:32:01	0
9085341993	DIPAK DAS	9707783876	GIASUDDINAHMED	2/7/2014	23:25:52	0
9085341993	DIPAK DAS	9707783876	GIASUDDINAHMED	2/7/2014	23:21:30	0
9085341993	DIPAK DAS	9707783876	GIASUDDINAHMED	2/7/2014	23:17:46	0
9085341993	DIPAK DAS	9707783876	GIASUDDINAHMED	2/7/2014	23:15:32	0
9085341993	DIPAK DAS	9707783876	GIASUDDINAHMED	2/7/2014	23:14:17	0
9085341993	DIPAK DAS	9707783876	GIASUDDINAHMED	2/7/2014	23:11:57	0
9085341993	DIPAK DAS	9707783876	GIASUDDINAHMED	2/7/2014	23:08:12	0
9085341993	DIPAK DAS	9707783876	GIASUDDINAHMED	2/7/2014	23:05:46	0
9085341993	DIPAK DAS	9707783876	GIASUDDINAHMED	2/7/2014	23:05:40	0
9085341993	DIPAK DAS	9707783876	GIASUDDINAHMED	2/7/2014	22:59:11	0
9085341993	DIPAK DAS	9707783876	GIASUDDINAHMED	2/7/2014	22:55:07	0
9085341993	DIPAK DAS	9707783876	GIASUDDINAHMED	2/7/2014	22:55:01	0
9085341993	DIPAK DAS	9707783876	GIASUDDINAHMED	2/7/2014	22:44:25	0

Calling (A) Party Telephone Number/MSISDN	Name	Called (B) Party Telephone Number/Access Point Name	Name	Date	Time	Duration In Secs.
9085341993	DIPAK DAS	9707783876	GIASUDDINAHMED	2/7/2014	22:41:38	0
9085341993	DIPAK DAS	9707783876	GIASUDDINAHMED	2/7/2014	22:38:21	0
9085341993	DIPAK DAS	9707474658	HITESH KALITA	2/7/2014	22:36:53	0
9085341993	DIPAK DAS	9707474658	HITESH KALITA	2/7/2014	22:33:19	0
9085341993	DIPAK DAS	9401165464	HITESWAR KALITA	2/7/2014	22:22:09	7
9085341993	DIPAK DAS	9707474658		2/7/2014	22:21:21	5
9085341993	DIPAK DAS	9707783876	GIASUDDINAHMED	2/7/2014	22:12:56	0
9085341993	DIPAK DAS	9707783876	GIASUDDINAHMED	2/7/2014	22:11:14	0
9085341993	DIPAK DAS	9707783876	GIASUDDINAHMED	2/7/2014	22:02:56	0
9085341993	DIPAK DAS	9707783876	GIASUDDINAHMED	2/7/2014	20:29:12	0
9085341993	DIPAK DAS	9707783876	GIASUDDINAHMED	2/7/2014	20:29:09	0
9085341993	DIPAK DAS	9707783876	GIASUDDINAHMED	2/7/2014	20:26:08	0
9085341993	DIPAK DAS	9707783876	GIASUDDINAHMED	2/7/2014	15:25:33	0
9085341993	DIPAK DAS	9707783876	GIASUDDINAHMED	2/7/2014	14:11:48	0
9085341993	DIPAK DAS	9707783876	GIASUDDINAHMED	2/7/2014	8:15:23	0
9085341993	DIPAK DAS	9707783876	GIASUDDINAHMED	2/7/2014	8:13:03	0
9085341993	DIPAK DAS	9707783876	GIASUDDINAHMED	2/7/2014	8:09:17	0
9085341993	DIPAK DAS	9707783876	GIASUDDINAHMED	2/7/2014	8:08:32	0

Calling (A) Party Telephone Number/MSISDN	Name	Called (B) Party Telephone Number/Access Point Name	Name	Date	Time	Duration In Secs.
9085341993	DIPAK DAS	9707783876	GIASUDDINAHMED	2/7/2014	8:05:03	0
9085341993	DIPAK DAS	9707783876	GIASUDDINAHMED	2/7/2014	8:02:45	0
9085341993	DIPAK DAS	9707783876	GIASUDDINAHMED	2/7/2014	8:01:13	0
9085341993	DIPAK DAS	9707783876	GIASUDDINAHMED	2/7/2014	7:59:36	0
9085341993	DIPAK DAS	9707783876	GIASUDDINAHMED	2/7/2014	7:55:27	0
9085341993	DIPAK DAS	9707783876	GIASUDDINAHMED	2/7/2014	7:52:39	0
9085341993	DIPAK DAS	9707783876	GIASUDDINAHMED	2/7/2014	7:51:17	0
9085341993	DIPAK DAS	9707783876	GIASUDDINAHMED	2/7/2014	7:49:50	0
9085341993	DIPAK DAS	9707783876	GIASUDDINAHMED	2/7/2014	7:47:49	0
9085341993	DIPAK DAS	9707783876	GIASUDDINAHMED	2/7/2014	7:45:42	0
9085341993	DIPAK DAS	9707783876	GIASUDDINAHMED	2/7/2014	7:41:28	0
9085341993	DIPAK DAS	9707783876	GIASUDDINAHMED	1/7/2014	21:28:38	0
9085341993	DIPAK DAS	9707783876	GIASUDDINAHMED	1/7/2014	21:27:06	0
9085341993	DIPAK DAS	9707783876	GIASUDDINAHMED	1/7/2014	21:25:13	0
9085341993	DIPAK DAS	9707783876	GIASUDDINAHMED	1/7/2014	21:23:42	0
9085341993	DIPAK DAS	9707783876	GIASUDDINAHMED	1/7/2014	21:23:15	0
9085341993	DIPAK DAS	9707783876	GIASUDDINAHMED	1/7/2014	21:23:10	0
9085341993	DIPAK DAS	9707783876	GIASUDDINAHMED	1/7/2014	21:06:25	0

Calling (A) Party Telephone Number/MSISDN	Name	Called (B) Party Telephone Number/Access Point Name	Name	Date	Time	Duration In Secs.
9085341993	DIPAK DAS	9707783876	GIASUDDINAHMED	1/7/2014	20:50:05	0
9085341993	DIPAK DAS	9707783876	GIASUDDINAHMED	1/7/2014	20:47:54	0
9085341993	DIPAK DAS	9707783876	GIASUDDINAHMED	1/7/2014	20:46:05	0
9085341993	DIPAK DAS	9707783876	GIASUDDINAHMED	1/7/2014	20:40:18	0
9085341993	DIPAK DAS	9707783876	GIASUDDINAHMED	1/7/2014	19:34:52	0
9085341993	DIPAK DAS	9707783876	GIASUDDINAHMED	1/7/2014	16:01:31	0
9085341993	DIPAK DAS	9707783876	GIASUDDINAHMED	1/7/2014	15:59:27	0
9085341993	DIPAK DAS	9707783876	GIASUDDINAHMED	1/7/2014	15:56:32	0
9085341993	DIPAK DAS	9707783876	GIASUDDINAHMED	1/7/2014	15:37:54	0
9085341993	DIPAK DAS	9707783876	GIASUDDINAHMED	1/7/2014	15:26:18	0
9085341993	DIPAK DAS	9707783876	GIASUDDINAHMED	1/7/2014	15:24:50	0
9085341993	DIPAK DAS	9707783876	GIASUDDINAHMED	1/7/2014	15:24:18	0
9085341993	DIPAK DAS	9707783876	GIASUDDINAHMED	1/7/2014	15:23:37	2
9085341993	DIPAK DAS	9401165464	HITESWAR KALITA	1/7/2014	15:00:48	39
9085341993	DIPAK DAS	9401165464	HITESWAR KALITA	1/7/2014	14:04:53	44
9085341993	DIPAK DAS	9707783876	GIASUDDINAHMED	1/7/2014	13:18:26	0
9085341993	DIPAK DAS	9707783876	GIASUDDINAHMED	1/7/2014	11:24:10	0
9085341993	DIPAK DAS	9707783876	GIASUDDINAHMED	1/7/2014	11:20:53	0

Calling (A) Party Telephone Number/MSISDN	Name	Called (B) Party Telephone Number/Access Point Name	Name	Date	Time	Duration In Secs.
9085341993	DIPAK DAS	97077783876	GIASUDDINAHMED	1/7/2014	9:29:25	0
9085341993	DIPAK DAS	97077783876	GIASUDDINAHMED	1/7/2014	9:28:17	0
9085341993	DIPAK DAS	97077783876	GIASUDDINAHMED	1/7/2014	9:22:14	0
9085341993	DIPAK DAS	97077783876	GIASUDDINAHMED	1/7/2014	9:20:44	0
9085341993	DIPAK DAS	97077783876	GIASUDDINAHMED	1/7/2014	9:19:06	0
9085341993	DIPAK DAS	97077783876	GIASUDDINAHMED	1/7/2014	9:09:31	0
9085341993	DIPAK DAS	97077783876	GIASUDDINAHMED	1/7/2014	7:40:10	0
9085341993	DIPAK DAS	97077783876	GIASUDDINAHMED	1/7/2014	7:12:10	0
9085341993	DIPAK DAS	97077783876	GIASUDDINAHMED	30-06-2014	23:30:16	0
9085341993	DIPAK DAS	97077783876	GIASUDDINAHMED	30-06-2014	23:25:47	0
9085341993	DIPAK DAS	97077783876	GIASUDDINAHMED	30-06-2014	23:25:03	0
9085341993	DIPAK DAS	97077783876	GIASUDDINAHMED	30-06-2014	23:22:56	0
9085341993	DIPAK DAS	97077783876	GIASUDDINAHMED	30-06-2014	23:16:37	0
9085341993	DIPAK DAS	97077783876	GIASUDDINAHMED	30-06-2014	23:15:16	0
9085341993	DIPAK DAS	97077783876	GIASUDDINAHMED	30-06-2014	23:10:09	0
9085341993	DIPAK DAS	97074474658	HITESH KALITA	30-06-2014	23:09:59	0
9085341993	DIPAK DAS	94011165464	HITESWAR KALITA	30-06-2014	23:06:46	139
9085341993	DIPAK DAS	97077783876	GIASUDDINAHMED	30-06-2014	23:05:49	0

Calling (A) Party Telephone Number/MSISDN	Name	Called (B) Party Telephone Number/Access Point Name	Name	Date	Time	Duration In Secs.
9085341993	DIPAK DAS	9707474658	HITESH KALITA	30-06-2014	23:05:22	0
9085341993	DIPAK DAS	9707474658	HITESH KALITA	30-06-2014	23:05:13	0
9085341993	DIPAK DAS	9707783876	GIASUDDINAHMED	30-06-2014	22:58:12	0
9085341993	DIPAK DAS	9707783876	GIASUDDINAHMED	30-06-2014	22:51:44	0
9085341993	DIPAK DAS	9707783876	GIASUDDINAHMED	30-06-2014	22:51:38	0
9085341993	DIPAK DAS	9707783876	GIASUDDINAHMED	30-06-2014	22:35:21	0
9085341993	DIPAK DAS	9707783876	GIASUDDINAHMED	30-06-2014	22:33:46	0
9085341993	DIPAK DAS	9707783876	GIASUDDINAHMED	30-06-2014	22:30:43	0
9085341993	DIPAK DAS	9707783876	GIASUDDINAHMED	30-06-2014	22:29:53	0
9085341993	DIPAK DAS	9707783876	GIASUDDINAHMED	30-06-2014	22:27:04	0
9085341993	DIPAK DAS	9707783876	GIASUDDINAHMED	30-06-2014	22:26:05	0
9085341993	DIPAK DAS	9707783876	GIASUDDINAHMED	30-06-2014	22:24:23	0
9085341993	DIPAK DAS	9707783876	GIASUDDINAHMED	30-06-2014	22:22:15	0
9085341993	DIPAK DAS	9707783876	GIASUDDINAHMED	30-06-2014	22:19:55	0
9085341993	DIPAK DAS	9707783876	GIASUDDINAHMED	30-06-2014	22:18:50	0
9085341993	DIPAK DAS	9707783876	GIASUDDINAHMED	30-06-2014	22:16:33	0
9085341993	DIPAK DAS	9707783876	GIASUDDINAHMED	30-06-2014	22:15:07	0
9085341993	DIPAK DAS	9707783876	GIASUDDINAHMED	30-06-2014	22:13:09	0

Calling (A) Party Telephone Number/MSISDN	Name	Called (B) Party Telephone Number/Access Point Name	Name	Date	Time	Duration In Secs.
9085341993	DIPAK DAS	97077783876	GIASUDDINAHMED	30-06-2014	22:12:16	0
9085341993	DIPAK DAS	97077783876	GIASUDDINAHMED	30-06-2014	22:12:00	0
9085341993	DIPAK DAS	97077783876	GIASUDDINAHMED	30-06-2014	22:10:53	0
9085341993	DIPAK DAS	97077783876	GIASUDDINAHMED	30-06-2014	22:09:45	0
9085341993	DIPAK DAS	97077783876	GIASUDDINAHMED	30-06-2014	22:08:09	0
9085341993	DIPAK DAS	97077783876	GIASUDDINAHMED	30-06-2014	22:05:23	0
9085341993	DIPAK DAS	97077783876	GIASUDDINAHMED	30-06-2014	22:02:42	0
9085341993	DIPAK DAS	97077783876	GIASUDDINAHMED	30-06-2014	21:56:10	0
9085341993	DIPAK DAS	97077783876	GIASUDDINAHMED	30-06-2014	21:55:08	0
9085341993	DIPAK DAS	97077783876	GIASUDDINAHMED	30-06-2014	21:05:22	0
9085341993	DIPAK DAS	97077783876	GIASUDDINAHMED	30-06-2014	21:01:01	0
9085341993	DIPAK DAS	97077783876	GIASUDDINAHMED	30-06-2014	20:53:53	0
9085341993	DIPAK DAS	97074474658	HITESH KALITA	30-06-2014	20:18:36	0
9085341993	DIPAK DAS	97074474658	HITESH KALITA	30-06-2014	20:15:44	0
9085341993	DIPAK DAS	97074474658	HITESH KALITA	30-06-2014	20:13:46	0
9085341993	DIPAK DAS	9401165464	HITESWAR KALITA	30-06-2014	20:10:00	32
9085341993	DIPAK DAS	97074474658	HITESH KALITA	30-06-2014	20:08:26	0
9085341993	DIPAK DAS	97074474658	HITESH KALITA	30-06-2014	20:07:10	0

Calling (A) Party Telephone Number/MSISDN	Name	Called (B) Party Telephone Number/Access Point Name	Name	Date	Time	Duration In Secs.
9085341993	DIPAK DAS	9707474658	HITESH KALITA	30-06-2014	20:06:14	0
9085341993	DIPAK DAS	9707474658	HITESH KALITA	30-06-2014	19:59:18	0
9085341993	DIPAK DAS	9707474658	HITESH KALITA	30-06-2014	19:58:36	0
9085341993	DIPAK DAS	9707474658	HITESH KALITA	30-06-2014	19:57:15	0
9085341993	DIPAK DAS	9707783876	GIASUDDINAHMED	30-06-2014	19:34:32	0
9085341993	DIPAK DAS	9707474658	HITESH KALITA	30-06-2014	19:34:12	0
9085341993	DIPAK DAS	9707783876	GIASUDDINAHMED	30-06-2014	19:33:31	0
9085341993	DIPAK DAS	9707783876	GIASUDDINAHMED	30-06-2014	19:32:42	0
9085341993	DIPAK DAS	9707783876	GIASUDDINAHMED	30-06-2014	19:27:49	0
9085341993	DIPAK DAS	9707783876	GIASUDDINAHMED	30-06-2014	19:20:20	0
9085341993	DIPAK DAS	9707783876	GIASUDDINAHMED	30-06-2014	19:16:57	0
9085341993	DIPAK DAS	9707783876	GIASUDDINAHMED	30-06-2014	19:15:45	0
9085341993	DIPAK DAS	9613521981	MANAS PRATIM DEKA	30-06-2014	18:29:26	0
9085341993	DIPAK DAS	9707474658	HITESH KALITA	30-06-2014	16:53:31	0
9085341993	DIPAK DAS9	9707783876	GIASUDDINAHMED	30-06-2014	16:25:08	0
9085341993	DIPAK DAS	9707783876	GIASUDDINAHMED	30-06-2014	16:18:19	0
9085341993	DIPAK DAS	9707783876	GIASUDDINAHMED	30-06-2014	15:50:45	0
9085341993	DIPAK DAS	9707783876	GIASUDDINAHMED	30-06-2014	15:38:51	0

Calling (A) Party Telephone Number/MSISDN	Name	Called (B) Party Telephone Number/Access Point Name	Name	Date	Time	Duration In Secs.
9085341993	DIPAK DAS	9707783876	GIASUDDINAHMED	30-06-2014	15:34:04	0
9085341993	DIPAK DAS	9707783876	GIASUDDINAHMED	30-06-2014	15:20:42	0
9085341993	DIPAK DAS	9707783876	GIASUDDINAHMED	30-06-2014	15:19:08	0
9085341993	DIPAK DAS	9707783876	GIASUDDINAHMED	30-06-2014	15:10:56	0
9085341993	DIPAK DAS	9707783876	GIASUDDINAHMED	30-06-2014	15:09:16	0
9085341993	DIPAK DAS	9707783876	GIASUDDINAHMED	30-06-2014	15:06:52	0
9085341993	DIPAK DAS	9707783876	GIASUDDINAHMED	30-06-2014	15:04:01	0
9085341993	DIPAK DAS	9707783876	GIASUDDINAHMED	30-06-2014	14:57:38	0
9085341993	DIPAK DAS	9707783876	GIASUDDINAHMED	30-06-2014	14:54:02	0
9085341993	DIPAK DAS	9707783876	GIASUDDINAHMED	30-06-2014	14:52:18	0
9085341993	DIPAK DAS	9707783876	GIASUDDINAHMED	30-06-2014	14:46:21	0
9085341993	DIPAK DAS	9707783876	GIASUDDINAHMED	30-06-2014	13:03:32	0
9085341993	DIPAK DAS	9707783876	GIASUDDINAHMED	30-06-2014	13:02:30	0
9085341993	DIPAK DAS	9707783876	GIASUDDINAHMED	30-06-2014	13:02:28	0
9085341993	DIPAK DAS	9707783876	GIASUDDINAHMED	30-06-2014	11:36:46	0
9085341993	DIPAK DAS	9707783876	GIASUDDINAHMED	30-06-2014	10:34:37	0
9085341993	DIPAK DAS	9707783876	GIASUDDINAHMED	30-06-2014	10:27:37	0
9085341993	DIPAK DAS	9707783876	GIASUDDINAHMED	30-06-2014	10:14:41	0

Calling (A) Party Telephone Number/MSISDN	Name	Called (B) Party Telephone Number/Access Point Name	Name	Date	Time	Duration In Secs.
9085341993	DIPAK DAS	9707783876	GIASUDDINAHMED	30-06-2014	7:12:22	0
9085341993	DIPAK DAS	9707783876	GIASUDDINAHMED	29-06-2014	22:14:03	0
9085341993	DIPAK DAS	9707783876	GIASUDDINAHMED	29-06-2014	22:12:43	0
9085341993	DIPAK DAS	9707783876	GIASUDDINAHMED	29-06-2014	21:28:04	0
9085341993	DIPAK DAS	9401165464	HITESWAR KALITA	29-06-2014	21:25:56	41
9085341993	DIPAK DAS	9401165464	HITESWAR KALITA	29-06-2014	20:56:23	34
9085341993	DIPAK DAS	9707783876	GIASUDDINAHMED	29-06-2014	19:52:53	0
9085341993	DIPAK DAS	9707783876	GIASUDDINAHMED	29-06-2014	19:05:28	0
9085341993	DIPAK DAS	9707783876	GIASUDDINAHMED	29-06-2014	17:17:48	0
9085341993	DIPAK DAS	9707783876	GIASUDDINAHMED	29-06-2014	16:01:57	0
9085341993	DIPAK DAS	9707783876	GIASUDDINAHMED	29-06-2014	7:55:59	0
9085341993	DIPAK DAS	9707783876	GIASUDDINAHMED	29-06-2014	7:54:41	0
9085341993	DIPAK DAS	9707783876	GIASUDDINAHMED	29-06-2014	7:52:37	0
9085341993	DIPAK DAS	9707783876	GIASUDDINAHMED	29-06-2014	7:45:02	0
9085341993	DIPAK DAS	9707783876	GIASUDDINAHMED	28-06-2014	22:48:16	0
9085341993	DIPAK DAS	9707474658	HITESH KALITA	28-06-2014	22:27:07	0
9085341993	DIPAK DAS	9707783876	GIASUDDINAHMED	28-06-2014	22:24:09	0
9085341993	DIPAK DAS	9707474658	HITESH KALITA	28-06-2014	22:21:53	0

Calling (A) Party Telephone Number/MSISDN	Name	Called (B) Party Telephone Number/Access Point Name	Name	Date	Time	Duration In Secs.
9085341993	DIPAK DAS	9707474658	HITESH KALITA	28-06-2014	22:21:33	0
9085341993	DIPAK DAS	9707783876	GIASUDDINAHMED	28-06-2014	22:18:20	0
9085341993	DIPAK DAS	9707783876	GIASUDDINAHMED	28-06-2014	22:15:02	0
9085341993	DIPAK DAS	9707783876	GIASUDDINAHMED	28-06-2014	22:13:40	0
9085341993	DIPAK DAS	9707783876	GIASUDDINAHMED	28-06-2014	22:07:20	51
9085341993	DIPAK DAS	9707783876	GIASUDDINAHMED	28-06-2014	22:04:10	98
9085341993	DIPAK DAS	9707783876	GIASUDDINAHMED	28-06-2014	21:54:49	0
9085341993	DIPAK DAS	9707783876	GIASUDDINAHMED	28-06-2014	21:52:56	0
9085341993	DIPAK DAS	9707783876	GIASUDDINAHMED	28-06-2014	21:50:39	0
9085341993	DIPAK DAS	9707783876	GIASUDDINAHMED	28-06-2014	21:47:09	0
9085341993	DIPAK DAS	9707474658	HITESH KALITA	28-06-2014	21:30:23	0
9085341993	DIPAK DAS	9707474658	HITESH KALITA	28-06-2014	21:26:21	0
9085341993	DIPAK DAS	9707474658	HITESH KALITA	28-06-2014	21:25:06	0
9085341993	DIPAK DAS	9707474658	HITESH KALITA	28-06-2014	21:23:21	0
9085341993	DIPAK DAS	9707783876	GIASUDDINAHMED	28-06-2014	20:51:42	0
9085341993	DIPAK DAS	9707783876	GIASUDDINAHMED	28-06-2014	20:47:54	0
9085341993	DIPAK DAS	9707474658	HITESH KALITA	28-06-2014	20:46:52	0
9085341993	DIPAK DAS	9707783876	GIASUDDINAHMED	28-06-2014	20:44:24	0

Calling (A) Party Telephone Number/MSISDN	Name	Called (B) Party Telephone Number/Access Point Name	Name	Date	Time	Duration In Secs.
9085341993	DIPAK DAS	9707783876	GIASUDDINAHMED	28-06-2014	20:39:32	0
9085341993	DIPAK DAS	9707783876	GIASUDDINAHMED	28-06-2014	20:26:04	0
9085341993	DIPAK DAS	9707783876	GIASUDDINAHMED	28-06-2014	20:20:37	0
9085341993	DIPAK DAS	9707783876	GIASUDDINAHMED	28-06-2014	20:20:34	0
9085341993	DIPAK DAS	9707474658	HITESH KALITA	28-06-2014	19:52:21	0
9085341993	DIPAK DAS	9707783876	GIASUDDINAHMED	28-06-2014	18:34:54	0
9085341993	DIPAK DAS	9707783876	GIASUDDINAHMED	27-06-2014	23:10:51	0
9085341993	DIPAK DAS	9707783876	GIASUDDINAHMED	27-06-2014	23:07:46	0
9085341993	DIPAK DAS	9707783876	GIASUDDINAHMED	27-06-2014	23:06:49	0
9085341993	DIPAK DAS	9707783876	GIASUDDINAHMED	27-06-2014	23:05:02	0
9085341993	DIPAK DAS	9707783876	GIASUDDINAHMED	27-06-2014	22:54:19	0
9085341993	DIPAK DAS	9707783876	GIASUDDINAHMED	27-06-2014	22:28:47	0
9085341993	DIPAK DAS	9707783876	GIASUDDINAHMED	27-06-2014	21:45:52	0
9085341993	DIPAK DAS	9707783876	GIASUDDINAHMED	27-06-2014	21:41:24	0
9085341993	DIPAK DAS	9707783876	GIASUDDINAHMED	27-06-2014	21:39:30	0
9085341993	DIPAK DAS	9707783876	GIASUDDINAHMED	27-06-2014	21:35:05	0
9085341993	DIPAK DAS	9707783876	GIASUDDINAHMED	27-06-2014	21:31:15	0
9085341993	DIPAK DAS	9707783876	GIASUDDINAHMED	27-06-2014	21:16:39	0

Calling (A) Party Telephone Number/MSISDN	Name	Called (B) Party Telephone Number/Access Point Name	Name	Date	Time	Duration In Secs.
9085341993	DIPAK DAS	9707783876	GIASUDDINAHMED	27-06-2014	21:14:59	0
9085341993	DIPAK DAS	9707783876	GIASUDDINAHMED	27-06-2014	20:55:13	0
9085341993	DIPAK DAS	9707783876	GIASUDDINAHMED	27-06-2014	20:47:19	0
9085341993	DIPAK DAS	9707783876	GIASUDDINAHMED	27-06-2014	20:45:27	0
9085341993	DIPAK DAS	9707783876	GIASUDDINAHMED	27-06-2014	20:37:15	0
9085341993	DIPAK DAS	9707783876	GIASUDDINAHMED	27-06-2014	20:33:00	0
9085341993	DIPAK DAS	9707783876	GIASUDDINAHMED	27-06-2014	20:28:01	0
9085341993	DIPAK DAS	9707783876	GIASUDDINAHMED	27-06-2014	20:14:50	0
9085341993	DIPAK DAS	9707783876	GIASUDDINAHMED	27-06-2014	20:13:51	0
9085341993	DIPAK DAS	9707783876	GIASUDDINAHMED	27-06-2014	20:09:44	0
9085341993	DIPAK DAS	9707783876	GIASUDDINAHMED	27-06-2014	20:09:24	0
9085341993	DIPAK DAS	9707783876	GIASUDDINAHMED	27-06-2014	20:04:44	0
9085341993	DIPAK DAS	9707783876	GIASUDDINAHMED	27-06-2014	20:01:16	0
9085341993	DIPAK DAS	9707783876	GIASUDDINAHMED	27-06-2014	19:56:55	0
9085341993	DIPAK DAS	9707783876	GIASUDDINAHMED	27-06-2014	19:56:52	0
9085341993	DIPAK DAS	9707783876	GIASUDDINAHMED	27-06-2014	19:56:49	0
9085341993	DIPAK DAS	9707783876	GIASUDDINAHMED	27-06-2014	19:54:10	0
9085341993	DIPAK DAS	9707783876	GIASUDDINAHMED	27-06-2014	19:24:19	0

Calling (A) Party Telephone Number/MSISDN	Name	Called (B) Party Telephone Number/Access Point Name	Name	Date	Time	Duration In Secs.
9085341993	DIPAK DAS	9707783876	GIASUDDINAHMED	27-06-2014	19:18:36	0
9085341993	DIPAK DAS	9707783876	GIASUDDINAHMED	27-06-2014	19:16:16	0
9085341993	DIPAK DAS	9707783876	GIASUDDINAHMED	27-06-2014	19:12:49	0
9085341993	DIPAK DAS	9707783876	GIASUDDINAHMED	27-06-2014	19:11:48	0
9085341993	DIPAK DAS	9707783876	GIASUDDINAHMED	27-06-2014	19:09:40	0
9085341993	DIPAK DAS	9707783876	GIASUDDINAHMED	27-06-2014	18:10:41	0
9085341993	DIPAK DAS	9707474658	HITESH KALITA	27-06-2014	16:14:09	0
9085341993	DIPAK DAS	9707783876	GIASUDDINAHMED	27-06-2014	15:59:57	0
9085341993	DIPAK DAS	9707783876	GIASUDDINAHMED	27-06-2014	15:57:29	0
9085341993	DIPAK DAS	9707783876	GIASUDDINAHMED	27-06-2014	15:55:08	0
9085341993	DIPAK DAS	9707783876	GIASUDDINAHMED	27-06-2014	10:12:53	0
9085341993	DIPAK DAS	9707783876	GIASUDDINAHMED	27-06-2014	7:41:30	0
9085341993	DIPAK DAS	9707783876	GIASUDDINAHMED	27-06-2014	7:27:27	0
9085341993	DIPAK DAS	9707783876	GIASUDDINAHMED	27-06-2014	2:22:34	0
9085341993	DIPAK DAS	9707783876	GIASUDDINAHMED	26-06-2014	23:23:32	0
9085341993	DIPAK DAS	9707783876	GIASUDDINAHMED	26-06-2014	22:34:58	0
9085341993	DIPAK DAS	9707783876	GIASUDDINAHMED	26-06-2014	22:24:22	0
9085341993	DIPAK DAS	9707783876	GIASUDDINAHMED	26-06-2014	22:23:15	0

Calling (A) Party Telephone Number/MSISDN	Name	Called (B) Party Telephone Number/Access Point Name	Name	Date	Time	Duration In Secs.
9085341993	DIPAK DAS	9707783876	GIASUDDINAHMED	26-06-2014	22:22:38	0
9085341993	DIPAK DAS	9707783876	GIASUDDINAHMED	26-06-2014	22:21:49	0
9085341993	DIPAK DAS	9707783876	GIASUDDINAHMED	26-06-2014	22:20:26	0
9085341993	DIPAK DAS	9707783876	GIASUDDINAHMED	26-06-2014	20:43:05	0
9085341993	DIPAK DAS	9707783876	GIASUDDINAHMED	26-06-2014	20:36:46	0
9085341993	DIPAK DAS	9707783876	GIASUDDINAHMED	26-06-2014	20:17:39	0
9085341993	DIPAK DAS	9707783876	GIASUDDINAHMED	26-06-2014	20:02:06	0
9085341993	DIPAK DAS	9707783876	GIASUDDINAHMED	26-06-2014	19:54:09	0
9085341993	DIPAK DAS	9707783876	GIASUDDINAHMED	26-06-2014	19:52:06	0
9085341993	DIPAK DAS	9707783876	GIASUDDINAHMED	26-06-2014	19:50:27	0
9085341993	DIPAK DAS	9707783876	GIASUDDINAHMED	26-06-2014	19:49:21	0
9085341993	DIPAK DAS	9707783876	GIASUDDINAHMED	26-06-2014	19:48:02	0
9085341993	DIPAK DAS	9707783876	GIASUDDINAHMED	26-06-2014	19:42:08	0
9085341993	DIPAK DAS	9707783876	GIASUDDINAHMED	26-06-2014	19:41:00	0
9085341993	DIPAK DAS	9707783876	GIASUDDINAHMED	26-06-2014	19:40:56	0
9085341993	DIPAK DAS	9707783876	GIASUDDINAHMED	26-06-2014	19:38:11	0
9085341993	DIPAK DAS	9707783876	GIASUDDINAHMED	26-06-2014	19:35:39	0
9085341993	DIPAK DAS	9707783876	GIASUDDINAHMED	26-06-2014	19:33:23	0

Calling (A) Party Telephone Number/MSISDN	Name	Called (B) Party Telephone Number/Access Point Name	Name	Date	Time	Duration In Secs.
9085341993	DIPAK DAS	9707783876	GIASUDDINAHMED	26-06-2014	19:32:34	0
9085341993	DIPAK DAS	9707783876	GIASUDDINAHMED	26-06-2014	19:23:54	0
9085341993	DIPAK DAS	9707783876	GIASUDDINAHMED	26-06-2014	19:20:13	0
9085341993	DIPAK DAS	9707783876	GIASUDDINAHMED	26-06-2014	19:19:08	0
9085341993	DIPAK DAS	9707783876	GIASUDDINAHMED	26-06-2014	19:17:34	0
9085341993	DIPAK DAS	9707783876	GIASUDDINAHMED	26-06-2014	19:15:38	0
9085341993	DIPAK DAS	9707783876	GIASUDDINAHMED	26-06-2014	18:01:55	0
9085341993	DIPAK DAS	9707783876	GIASUDDINAHMED	26-06-2014	17:49:18	0
9085341993	DIPAK DAS	9707783876	GIASUDDINAHMED	26-06-2014	17:48:03	0
9085341993	DIPAK DAS	9707783876	GIASUDDINAHMED	26-06-2014	17:46:06	0
9085341993	DIPAK DAS	9707783876	GIASUDDINAHMED	26-06-2014	17:45:04	0
9085341993	DIPAK DAS	9707783876	GIASUDDINAHMED	26-06-2014	17:43:51	0
9085341993	DIPAK DAS	9707783876	GIASUDDINAHMED	26-06-2014	17:42:23	0
9085341993	DIPAK DAS	9707783876	GIASUDDINAHMED	26-06-2014	17:40:42	0
9085341993	DIPAK DAS	9707783876	GIASUDDINAHMED	26-06-2014	17:36:38	0
9085341993	DIPAK DAS	9707783876	GIASUDDINAHMED	26-06-2014	17:23:48	0
9085341993	DIPAK DAS	9707783876	GIASUDDINAHMED	26-06-2014	17:19:44	0
9085341993	DIPAK DAS	9707783876	GIASUDDINAHMED	26-06-2014	17:15:46	0

Calling (A) Party Telephone Number/MSISDN	Name	Called (B) Party Telephone Number/Access Point Name	Name	Date	Time	Duration In Secs.
9085341993	DIPAK DAS	9707783876	GIASUDDINAHMED	26-06-2014	17:11:27	0
9085341993	DIPAK DAS	9707783876	GIASUDDINAHMED	26-06-2014	17:08:37	0
9085341993	DIPAK DAS	9707783876	GIASUDDINAHMED	26-06-2014	17:06:02	0
9085341993	DIPAK DAS	9707783876	GIASUDDINAHMED	26-06-2014	17:04:06	0
9085341993	DIPAK DAS	9707783876	GIASUDDINAHMED	26-06-2014	17:03:21	0
9085341993	DIPAK DAS	9707783876	GIASUDDINAHMED	26-06-2014	17:03:06	0
9085341993	DIPAK DAS	9707783876	GIASUDDINAHMED	26-06-2014	16:59:28	0
9085341993	DIPAK DAS	9707783876	GIASUDDINAHMED	26-06-2014	16:47:52	0
9085341993	DIPAK DAS	9707783876	GIASUDDINAHMED	26-06-2014	16:38:33	0
9085341993	DIPAK DAS	9707783876	GIASUDDINAHMED	26-06-2014	16:24:41	0
9085341993	DIPAK DAS	9707474658	HITESH KALITA	26-06-2014	16:22:15	0
9085341993	DIPAK DAS	9707783876	GIASUDDINAHMED	26-06-2014	16:02:25	0
9085341993	DIPAK DAS	9707783876	GIASUDDINAHMED	26-06-2014	15:22:56	0
9085341993	DIPAK DAS	9707783876	GIASUDDINAHMED	26-06-2014	15:15:47	0
9085341993	DIPAK DAS	9707783876	GIASUDDINAHMED	26-06-2014	15:14:39	0
9085341993	DIPAK DAS	9707783876	GIASUDDINAHMED	26-06-2014	15:10:20	0
9085341993	DIPAK DAS	9707783876	GIASUDDINAHMED	26-06-2014	15:09:03	40
9085341993	DIPAK DAS	9707783876	GIASUDDINAHMED	26-06-2014	14:55:44	0

Calling (A) Party Telephone Number/MSISDN	Name	Called (B) Party Telephone Number/Access Point Name	Name	Date	Time	Duration In Secs.
9085341993	DIPAK DAS	9707783876	GIASUDDINAHMED	26-06-2014	14:53:07	0
9085341993	DIPAK DAS	9707783876	GIASUDDINAHMED	26-06-2014	13:35:44	0
9085341993	DIPAK DAS	9707783876	GIASUDDINAHMED	26-06-2014	12:21:02	0
9085341993	DIPAK DAS	9707783876	GIASUDDINAHMED	26-06-2014	12:08:38	0
9085341993	DIPAK DAS	9707783876	GIASUDDINAHMED	26-06-2014	9:37:34	0
9085341993	DIPAK DAS	9707783876	GIASUDDINAHMED	26-06-2014	9:17:37	0
9085341993	DIPAK DAS	9707783876	GIASUDDINAHMED	26-06-2014	8:44:59	0
9085341993	DIPAK DAS	9707783876	GIASUDDINAHMED	26-06-2014	8:32:52	0
9085341993	DIPAK DAS	9707783876	GIASUDDINAHMED	26-06-2014	8:30:49	0
9085341993	DIPAK DAS	9707783876	GIASUDDINAHMED	26-06-2014	8:29:46	0
9085341993	DIPAK DAS	9707783876	GIASUDDINAHMED	26-06-2014	6:17:00	0
9085341993	DIPAK DAS	9707783876	GIASUDDINAHMED	25-06-2014	23:05:09	0
9085341993	DIPAK DAS	9707783876	GIASUDDINAHMED	25-06-2014	22:57:29	0
9085341993	DIPAK DAS	9707783876	GIASUDDINAHMED	25-06-2014	22:55:31	0
9085341993	DIPAK DAS	9707783876	GIASUDDINAHMED	25-06-2014	22:52:53	0
9085341993	DIPAK DAS	9085835737	RAMANDRA BARMAN	25-06-2014	22:51:16	0
9085341993	DIPAK DAS	9085835737	RAMANDRA BARMAN	25-06-2014	22:51:07	0
9085341993	DIPAK DAS	9707783876	GIASUDDINAHMED	25-06-2014	22:45:56	0

Calling (A) Party Telephone Number/MSISDN	Name	Called (B) Party Telephone Number/Access Point Name	Name	Date	Time	Duration In Secs.
9085341993	DIPAK DAS	9707783876	GIASUDDINAHMED	25-06-2014	22:30:56	0
9085341993	DIPAK DAS	9707783876	GIASUDDINAHMED	25-06-2014	22:21:34	0
9085341993	DIPAK DAS	9707783876	GIASUDDINAHMED	25-06-2014	19:09:19	0
9085341993	DIPAK DAS	9401165464	HITESWAR KALITA	25-06-2014	19:05:14	18
9085341993	DIPAK DAS	9707783876	GIASUDDINAHMED	25-06-2014	18:54:41	0
9085341993	DIPAK DAS	9707783876	GIASUDDINAHMED	25-06-2014	18:11:27	0
9085341993	DIPAK DAS	9707783876	GIASUDDINAHMED	25-06-2014	18:09:10	0
9085341993	DIPAK DAS	9707783876	GIASUDDINAHMED	25-06-2014	18:07:14	0
9085341993	DIPAK DAS	9707783876	GIASUDDINAHMED	25-06-2014	17:23:29	0
9085341993	DIPAK DAS	9707783876	GIASUDDINAHMED	25-06-2014	17:23:11	0
9085341993	DIPAK DAS	9707783876	GIASUDDINAHMED	25-06-2014	16:19:43	0
9085341993	DIPAK DAS	9707474658	HITESH KALITA	25-06-2014	15:08:43	0
9085341993	DIPAK DAS	9707783876	GIASUDDINAHMED	25-06-2014	13:30:39	0
9085341993	DIPAK DAS	9707783876	GIASUDDINAHMED	25-06-2014	10:02:42	0
9085341993	DIPAK DAS	9707783876	GIASUDDINAHMED	25-06-2014	10:01:52	0
9085341993	DIPAK DAS	9707783876	GIASUDDINAHMED	25-06-2014	9:32:46	0
9085341993	DIPAK DAS	9707783876	GIASUDDINAHMED	25-06-2014	8:09:31	0
9085341993	DIPAK DAS	9707783876	GIASUDDINAHMED	25-06-2014	8:08:43	0

Calling (A) Party Telephone Number/MSISDN	Name	Called (B) Party Telephone Number/Access Point Name	Name	Date	Time	Duration In Secs.
9085341993	DIPAK DAS	9085428530	GIASUDDIN AHMED	25-06-2014	3:09:46	0
9085341993	DIPAK DAS	9085428530	GIASUDDIN AHMED	25-06-2014	3:09:42	0
9085341993	DIPAK DAS	9085428530	GIASUDDIN AHMED	25-06-2014	3:09:38	0
9085341993	DIPAK DAS	9707783876	GIASUDDINAHMED	25-06-2014	1:08:56	0
9085341993	DIPAK DAS	9707783876	GIASUDDINAHMED	24-06-2014	23:07:57	0
9085341993	DIPAK DAS	9707783876	GIASUDDINAHMED	24-06-2014	22:58:03	0
9085341993	DIPAK DAS	9707783876	GIASUDDINAHMED	24-06-2014	22:54:52	0
9085341993	DIPAK DAS	9085428530	GIASUDDIN AHMED	24-06-2014	22:54:20	0
9085341993	DIPAK DAS	9707783876	GIASUDDINAHMED	24-06-2014	22:50:48	0
9085341993	DIPAK DAS	9085428530	GIASUDDIN AHMED	24-06-2014	22:50:06	0
9085341993	DIPAK DAS	9707783876	GIASUDDINAHMED	24-06-2014	22:49:37	0
9085341993	DIPAK DAS	9707783876	GIASUDDINAHMED	24-06-2014	22:49:07	0
9085341993	DIPAK DAS	9707783876	GIASUDDINAHMED	24-06-2014	22:48:18	0
9085341993	DIPAK DAS	9085428530	GIASUDDIN AHMED	24-06-2014	22:47:40	0
9085341993	DIPAK DAS	9707783876	GIASUDDINAHMED	24-06-2014	22:46:02	0
9085341993	DIPAK DAS	9085428530	GIASUDDIN AHMED	24-06-2014	22:45:36	0
9085341993	DIPAK DAS	9085428530	GIASUDDIN AHMED	24-06-2014	22:44:43	0
9085341993	DIPAK DAS	9085428530	GIASUDDIN AHMED	24-06-2014	22:40:32	0

Calling (A) Party Telephone Number/MSISDN	Name	Called (B) Party Telephone Number/Access Point Name	Name	Date	Time	Duration In Secs.
9085341993	DIPAK DAS	9707783876	GIASUDDINAHMED	24-06-2014	22:39:02	0
9085341993	DIPAK DAS	9707783876	GIASUDDINAHMED	24-06-2014	22:38:56	0
9085341993	DIPAK DAS	9085428530	GIASUDDIN AHMED	24-06-2014	22:37:50	0
9085341993	DIPAK DAS	9085428530	GIASUDDIN AHMED	24-06-2014	22:34:02	0
9085341993	DIPAK DAS	9085428530	GIASUDDIN AHMED	24-06-2014	22:33:17	0
9085341993	DIPAK DAS	9707783876	GIASUDDINAHMED	24-06-2014	22:32:01	0
9085341993	DIPAK DAS	9085428530	GIASUDDIN AHMED	24-06-2014	22:31:54	0
9085341993	DIPAK DAS	9085428530	GIASUDDIN AHMED	24-06-2014	22:28:50	0
9085341993	DIPAK DAS	9085428530	GIASUDDIN AHMED	24-06-2014	22:24:53	0
9085341993	DIPAK DAS	9085428530	GIASUDDIN AHMED	24-06-2014	22:23:04	0
9085341993	DIPAK DAS	9085428530	GIASUDDIN AHMED	24-06-2014	22:21:45	0
9085341993	DIPAK DAS	9085428530	GIASUDDIN AHMED	24-06-2014	22:18:46	0
9085341993	DIPAK DAS	9707783876	GIASUDDINAHMED	24-06-2014	22:17:13	0
9085341993	DIPAK DAS	9707783876	GIASUDDINAHMED	24-06-2014	22:15:25	0
9085341993	DIPAK DAS	9085428530	GIASUDDIN AHMED	24-06-2014	21:28:09	0
9085341993	DIPAK DAS	9085428530	GIASUDDIN AHMED	24-06-2014	21:28:03	0
9085341993	DIPAK DAS	9085428530	GIASUDDIN AHMED	24-06-2014	20:58:04	0
9085341993	DIPAK DAS	9085428530	GIASUDDIN AHMED	24-06-2014	20:50:27	0

Calling (A) Party Telephone Number/MSISDN	Name	Called (B) Party Telephone Number/Access Point Name	Name	Date	Time	Duration In Secs.
9085341993	DIPAK DAS	9707783876	GIASUDDINAHMED	24-06-2014	20:13:10	0
9085341993	DIPAK DAS	9707783876	GIASUDDINAHMED	24-06-2014	20:05:31	0
9085341993	DIPAK DAS	9707783876	GIASUDDINAHMED	24-06-2014	20:02:46	0
9085341993	DIPAK DAS	9707783876	GIASUDDINAHMED	24-06-2014	20:00:33	0
9085341993	DIPAK DAS	9707474658	HITESH KALITA	24-06-2014	18:57:14	0
9085341993	DIPAK DAS	9085428530	GIASUDDIN AHMED	24-06-2014	18:44:50	0
9085341993	DIPAK DAS	9085428530	GIASUDDIN AHMED	24-06-2014	18:41:48	0
9085341993	DIPAK DAS	9707783876	GIASUDDINAHMED	24-06-2014	18:36:23	0
9085341993	DIPAK DAS	9707783876	GIASUDDINAHMED	24-06-2014	18:32:03	0
9085341993	DIPAK DAS	9707783876	GIASUDDINAHMED	24-06-2014	17:31:37	0
9085341993	DIPAK DAS	9707783876	GIASUDDINAHMED	24-06-2014	17:01:10	0
9085341993	DIPAK DAS	9707783876	GIASUDDINAHMED	24-06-2014	16:57:05	0
9085341993	DIPAK DAS	9707783876	GIASUDDINAHMED	24-06-2014	16:55:20	0
9085341993	DIPAK DAS	9707783876	GIASUDDINAHMED	24-06-2014	16:53:34	0
9085341993	DIPAK DAS	9707783876	GIASUDDINAHMED	24-06-2014	16:51:22	0
9085341993	DIPAK DAS	9707783876	GIASUDDINAHMED	24-06-2014	16:43:08	0
9085341993	DIPAK DAS	9707783876	GIASUDDINAHMED	24-06-2014	16:41:43	0
9085341993	DIPAK DAS	9707783876	GIASUDDINAHMED	24-06-2014	16:38:51	0

Calling (A) Party Telephone Number/MSISDN	Name	Called (B) Party Telephone Number/Access Point Name	Name	Date	Time	Duration In Secs.
9085341993	DIPAK DAS	9707783876	GIASUDDINAHMED	24-06-2014	16:02:13	0
9085341993	DIPAK DAS	9707783876	GIASUDDINAHMED	24-06-2014	15:31:33	0
9085341993	DIPAK DAS	9707783876	GIASUDDINAHMED	24-06-2014	14:48:53	0
9085341993	DIPAK DAS	9707783876	GIASUDDINAHMED	24-06-2014	9:37:20	0
9085341993	DIPAK DAS	9707783876	GIASUDDINAHMED	24-06-2014	9:20:59	0
9085341993	DIPAK DAS	9707783876	GIASUDDINAHMED	24-06-2014	8:10:23	0
9085341993	DIPAK DAS	9707783876	GIASUDDINAHMED	24-06-2014	8:00:04	0
9085341993	DIPAK DAS	9707783876	GIASUDDINAHMED	24-06-2014	7:47:18	0
9085341993	DIPAK DAS	9707783876	GIASUDDINAHMED	24-06-2014	7:42:19	0
9085341993	DIPAK DAS	9085428530	GIASUDDIN AHMED	23-06-2014	23:39:45	0
9085341993	DIPAK DAS	9707783876	GIASUDDINAHMED	23-06-2014	22:54:14	0
9085341993	DIPAK DAS	9707783876	GIASUDDINAHMED	23-06-2014	22:41:42	0
9085341993	DIPAK DAS	9707474658	HITESH KALITA	23-06-2014	22:35:13	0
9085341993	DIPAK DAS	9707474658	HITESH KALITA	23-06-2014	22:35:12	0
9085341993	DIPAK DAS	9707783876	GIASUDDINAHMED	23-06-2014	22:30:40	0
9085341993	DIPAK DAS	9707783876	GIASUDDINAHMED	23-06-2014	22:26:25	53
9085341993	DIPAK DAS	9707783876	GIASUDDINAHMED	23-06-2014	22:24:47	0
9085341993	DIPAK DAS	9707783876	GIASUDDINAHMED	23-06-2014	22:05:58	0

Calling (A) Party Telephone Number/MSISDN	Name	Called (B) Party Telephone Number/Access Point Name	Name	Date	Time	Duration In Secs.
9085341993	DIPAK DAS	9707474658	HITESH KALITA	23-06-2014	22:03:49	0
9085341993	DIPAK DAS	9707474658	HITESH KALITA	23-06-2014	22:00:26	0
9085341993	DIPAK DAS	9707474658	HITESH KALITA	23-06-2014	21:59:12	0
9085341993	DIPAK DAS	9707783876	GIASUDDINAHMED	23-06-2014	21:47:51	488
9085341993	DIPAK DAS	9707474658	HITESH KALITA	23-06-2014	21:32:11	0
9085341993	DIPAK DAS	9707783876	GIASUDDINAHMED	23-06-2014	21:07:36	0
9085341993	DIPAK DAS	9707783876	GIASUDDINAHMED	23-06-2014	21:01:18	0
9085341993	DIPAK DAS	9707783876	GIASUDDINAHMED	23-06-2014	20:37:41	0
9085341993	DIPAK DAS	9707783876	GIASUDDINAHMED	23-06-2014	20:19:45	602
9085341993	DIPAK DAS	9707783876	GIASUDDINAHMED	23-06-2014	20:07:50	0
9085341993	DIPAK DAS	9401165464	HITESWAR KALITA	23-06-2014	20:06:59	1
9085341993	DIPAK DAS	9707474658	HITESH KALITA	23-06-2014	19:53:57	0
9085341993	DIPAK DAS	9707474658	HITESH KALITA	23-06-2014	19:37:10	0
9085341993	DIPAK DAS	9707783876	GIASUDDINAHMED	23-06-2014	18:50:06	0
9085341993	DIPAK DAS	9707474658	HITESH KALITA	23-06-2014	17:41:45	0
9085341993	DIPAK DAS	9707783876	GIASUDDINAHMED	23-06-2014	16:53:01	0
9085341993	DIPAK DAS	9707783876	GIASUDDINAHMED	23-06-2014	16:47:04	0
9085341993	DIPAK DAS	9401165464	HITESWAR KALITA	23-06-2014	16:39:08	31

Calling (A) Party Telephone Number/MSISDN	Name	Called (B) Party Telephone Number/Access Point Name	Name	Date	Time	Duration In Secs.
9085341993	DIPAK DAS	9707474658		23-06-2014	16:27:36	0
9085341993	DIPAK DAS	9707783876	GIASUDDINAHMED	23-06-2014	14:21:15	0
9085341993	DIPAK DAS	9707783876	GIASUDDINAHMED	23-06-2014	7:10:53	0
9085341993	DIPAK DAS	9707474658	HITESH KALITA	22-06-2014	23:51:03	0
9085341993	DIPAK DAS	9707783876	GIASUDDINAHMED	22-06-2014	23:43:57	0
9085341993	DIPAK DAS	9707783876	GIASUDDINAHMED	22-06-2014	23:42:44	0
9085341993	DIPAK DAS	9707783876	GIASUDDINAHMED	22-06-2014	23:41:50	0
9085341993	DIPAK DAS	9707783876	GIASUDDINAHMED	22-06-2014	23:37:12	0
9085341993	DIPAK DAS	9707783876	GIASUDDINAHMED	22-06-2014	23:24:19	0
9085341993	DIPAK DAS	9707783876	GIASUDDINAHMED	22-06-2014	22:57:22	0
9085341993	DIPAK DAS	9085428530	GIASUDDIN AHMED	22-06-2014	22:40:14	0
9085341993	DIPAK DAS	9707783876	GIASUDDINAHMED	22-06-2014	22:26:17	0
9085341993	DIPAK DAS	9707474658	HITESH KALITA	22-06-2014	22:24:28	0
9085341993	DIPAK DAS	9707783876	GIASUDDINAHMED	22-06-2014	22:23:54	0
9085341993	DIPAK DAS	9707783876	GIASUDDINAHMED	22-06-2014	21:56:56	0
9085341993	DIPAK DAS	9707783876	GIASUDDINAHMED	22-06-2014	21:55:14	0
9085341993	DIPAK DAS	9707783876	GIASUDDINAHMED	22-06-2014	21:41:54	0
9085341993	DIPAK DAS	9707783876	GIASUDDINAHMED	22-06-2014	18:59:02	0

Calling (A) Party Telephone Number/MSISDN	Name	Called (B) Party Telephone Number/Access Point Name	Name	Date	Time	Duration In Secs.
9085341993	DIPAK DAS	9707783876	GIASUDDINAHMED	22-06-2014	15:23:13	12
9085341993	DIPAK DAS	9707783876	GIASUDDINAHMED	22-06-2014	12:32:08	0
9085341993	DIPAK DAS	9085428530	GIASUDDIN AHMED	22-06-2014	9:39:42	0
9085341993	DIPAK DAS	9707474658	HITESH KALITA	22-06-2014	8:23:54	0
9085341993	DIPAK DAS	9085835737	RAMANDRA BARMAN	22-06-2014	8:12:33	0
9085341993	DIPAK DAS	9707474658	HITESH KALITA	22-06-2014	7:32:44	0
9085341993	DIPAK DAS	9707783876	GIASUDDINAHMED	21-06-2014	23:35:13	0
9085341993	DIPAK DAS	9707783876	GIASUDDINAHMED	21-06-2014	23:30:53	0
9085341993	DIPAK DAS	9707783876	GIASUDDINAHMED	21-06-2014	22:50:01	0
9085341993	DIPAK DAS	9707783876	GIASUDDINAHMED	21-06-2014	22:45:57	0
9085341993	DIPAK DAS	9707783876	GIASUDDINAHMED	21-06-2014	22:43:09	0
9085341993	DIPAK DAS	9707474658	HITESH KALITA	21-06-2014	22:41:40	0
9085341993	DIPAK DAS	9707783876	GIASUDDINAHMED	21-06-2014	22:41:15	0
9085341993	DIPAK DAS	9707783876	GIASUDDINAHMED	21-06-2014	22:37:16	0
9085341993	DIPAK DAS	9085428530	GIASUDDIN AHMED	21-06-2014	22:34:12	0
9085341993	DIPAK DAS	9085428530	GIASUDDIN AHMED	21-06-2014	22:32:15	0
9085341993	DIPAK DAS	9707783876	GIASUDDINAHMED	21-06-2014	22:30:39	0
9085341993	DIPAK DAS	9085428530	GIASUDDIN AHMED	21-06-2014	22:24:50	0

Calling (A) Party Telephone Number/MSISDN	Name	Called (B) Party Telephone Number/Access Point Name	Name	Date	Time	Duration In Secs.
9085341993	DIPAK DAS	9707783876	GIASUDDINAHMED	21-06-2014	22:24:07	0
9085341993	DIPAK DAS	9085428530	GIASUDDIN AHMED	21-06-2014	22:23:34	0
9085341993	DIPAK DAS	9401165464	HITESWAR KALITA	21-06-2014	22:23:21	2
9085341993	DIPAK DAS	9707783876	GIASUDDINAHMED	21-06-2014	22:23:02	1
9085341993	DIPAK DAS	9085428530	GIASUDDIN AHMED	21-06-2014	22:22:09	0
9085341993	DIPAK DAS	9085428530	GIASUDDIN AHMED	21-06-2014	22:21:22	0
9085341993	DIPAK DAS	9707783876	GIASUDDINAHMED	21-06-2014	21:43:58	0
9085341993	DIPAK DAS	9707783876	GIASUDDINAHMED	21-06-2014	21:43:06	0
9085341993	DIPAK DAS	9707474658	HITESH KALITA	21-06-2014	21:15:47	0
9085341993	DIPAK DAS	9707474658	HITESH KALITA	21-06-2014	20:35:51	0
9085341993	DIPAK DAS	9707474658	HITESH KALITA	21-06-2014	20:33:43	0
9085341993	DIPAK DAS	9707783876	GIASUDDINAHMED	21-06-2014	20:26:14	0
9085341993	DIPAK DAS	9707783876	GIASUDDINAHMED	21-06-2014	20:13:44	0
9085341993	DIPAK DAS	9707783876	GIASUDDINAHMED	21-06-2014	18:36:11	0
9085341993	DIPAK DAS	9707783876	GIASUDDINAHMED	21-06-2014	18:26:21	0
9085341993	DIPAK DAS	9707474658	HITESH KALITA	21-06-2014	7:51:14	0
9085341993	DIPAK DAS	9707474658	HITESH KALITA	21-06-2014	7:02:19	15
9085341993	DIPAK DAS	9707783876	GIASUDDINAHMED	20-06-2014	23:24:10	0

Calling (A) Party Telephone Number/MSISDN	Name	Called (B) Party Telephone Number/Access Point Name	Name	Date	Time	Duration In Secs.
9085341993	DIPAK DAS	9707783876	GIASUDDINAHMED	20-06-2014	23:01:34	0
9085341993	DIPAK DAS	9707783876	GIASUDDINAHMED	20-06-2014	22:52:44	0
9085341993	DIPAK DAS	9085428530	GIASUDDIN AHMED	20-06-2014	22:47:28	0
9085341993	DIPAK DAS	9085428530	GIASUDDIN AHMED	20-06-2014	22:43:31	0
9085341993	DIPAK DAS	9085428530	GIASUDDIN AHMED	20-06-2014	22:41:48	0
9085341993	DIPAK DAS	9707783876	GIASUDDINAHMED	20-06-2014	22:40:44	0
9085341993	DIPAK DAS	9085428530	GIASUDDIN AHMED	20-06-2014	22:40:17	0
9085341993	DIPAK DAS	9707783876	GIASUDDINAHMED	20-06-2014	22:38:43	0
9085341993	DIPAK DAS	9707474658	HITESH KALITA	20-06-2014	22:36:13	0
9085341993	DIPAK DAS	9085428530	GIASUDDIN AHMED	20-06-2014	22:35:48	0
9085341993	DIPAK DAS	9707783876	GIASUDDINAHMED	20-06-2014	22:34:51	0
9085341993	DIPAK DAS	9707783876	GIASUDDINAHMED	20-06-2014	22:34:48	0
9085341993	DIPAK DAS	9707783876	GIASUDDINAHMED	20-06-2014	21:42:12	0
9085341993	DIPAK DAS	9707783876	GIASUDDINAHMED	20-06-2014	21:35:05	0
9085341993	DIPAK DAS	9707783876	GIASUDDINAHMED	20-06-2014	21:35:03	0
9085341993	DIPAK DAS	9707783876	GIASUDDINAHMED	20-06-2014	21:23:19	0
9085341993	DIPAK DAS	9707783876	GIASUDDINAHMED	20-06-2014	21:20:46	0
9085341993	DIPAK DAS	9707783876	GIASUDDINAHMED	20-06-2014	21:16:56	0

Calling (A) Party Telephone Number/MSISDN	Name	Called (B) Party Telephone Number/Access Point Name	Name	Date	Time	Duration In Secs.
9085341993	DIPAK DAS	9707783876	GIASUDDINAHMED	20-06-2014	21:16:00	0
9085341993	DIPAK DAS	9707474658	HITESH KALITA	20-06-2014	20:55:09	0
9085341993	DIPAK DAS	9707474658	HITESH KALITA	20-06-2014	19:20:07	0
9085341993	DIPAK DAS	9707783876	GIASUDDINAHMED	20-06-2014	17:12:48	563
9085341993	DIPAK DAS	9707783876	GIASUDDINAHMED	20-06-2014	17:09:43	0
9085341993	DIPAK DAS	9707783876	GIASUDDINAHMED	20-06-2014	17:07:29	19
9085341993	DIPAK DAS	9707783876	GIASUDDINAHMED	20-06-2014	17:04:45	61
9085341993	DIPAK DAS	9707474658	HITESH KALITA	20-06-2014	16:00:07	0
9085341993	DIPAK DAS	9707474658	HITESH KALITA	20-06-2014	15:30:58	0
9085341993	DIPAK DAS	9707474658	HITESH KALITA	20-06-2014	9:24:06	0
9085341993	DIPAK DAS	9707474658	HITESH KALITA	20-06-2014	6:50:22	0
9085341993	DIPAK DAS	9707474658	HITESH KALITA	20-06-2014	6:08:05	0
9085341993	DIPAK DAS	9707474658	HITESH KALITA	20-06-2014	5:57:56	0
9085341993	DIPAK DAS	9707783876	GIASUDDINAHMED	20-06-2014	0:11:39	0
9085341993	DIPAK DAS	9707783876	GIASUDDINAHMED	20-06-2014	0:11:37	0
9085341993	DIPAK DAS	9707783876	GIASUDDINAHMED	19-06-2014	20:24:20	0
9085341993	DIPAK DAS	9707783876	GIASUDDINAHMED	19-06-2014	20:21:26	63
9085341993	DIPAK DAS	9707783876	GIASUDDINAHMED	19-06-2014	19:47:44	0

Calling (A) Party Telephone Number/MSISDN	Name	Called (B) Party Telephone Number/Access Point Name	Name	Date	Time	Duration In Secs.
9085341993	DIPAK DAS	9707783876	GIASUDDINAHMED	19-06-2014	19:46:59	0
9085341993	DIPAK DAS	9707474658	HITESH KALITA	19-06-2014	18:56:08	14
9085341993	DIPAK DAS	9707783876	GIASUDDINAHMED	19-06-2014	8:53:47	0
9085341993	DIPAK DAS	9707783876	GIASUDDINAHMED	19-06-2014	8:51:37	0
9085341993	DIPAK DAS	9707783876	GIASUDDINAHMED	19-06-2014	8:48:53	0
9085341993	DIPAK DAS	9707783876	GIASUDDINAHMED	19-06-2014	8:47:02	0
9085341993	DIPAK DAS	9707783876	GIASUDDINAHMED	19-06-2014	8:43:18	0
9085341993	DIPAK DAS	9707783876	GIASUDDINAHMED	19-06-2014	8:41:52	0
9085341993	DIPAK DAS	9707474658	HITESH KALITA	18-06-2014	23:06:40	0
9085341993	DIPAK DAS	9707474658	HITESH KALITA	18-06-2014	22:51:50	0
9085341993	DIPAK DAS	9707474658	HITESH KALITA	18-06-2014	22:46:04	0
9085341993	DIPAK DAS	9707783876	GIASUDDINAHMED	18-06-2014	20:25:54	0
9085341993	DIPAK DAS	9707783876	GIASUDDINAHMED	18-06-2014	20:02:02	0
9085341993	DIPAK DAS	9707783876	GIASUDDINAHMED	18-06-2014	19:53:21	0
9085341993	DIPAK DAS	9707783876	GIASUDDINAHMED	18-06-2014	19:41:08	0
9085341993	DIPAK DAS	9085428530	GIASUDDIN AHMED	18-06-2014	16:51:20	0
9085341993	DIPAK DAS	9085428530	GIASUDDIN AHMED	18-06-2014	16:49:31	0
9085341993	DIPAK DAS	9085428530	GIASUDDIN AHMED	18-06-2014	16:44:01	0

Calling (A) Party Telephone Number/MSISDN	Name	Called (B) Party Telephone Number/Access Point Name	Name	Date	Time	Duration In Secs.
9085341993	DIPAK DAS	9085428530	GIASUDDIN AHMED	18-06-2014	16:39:39	0
9085341993	DIPAK DAS	9707474658	HITESH KALITA	18-06-2014	15:59:36	0
9085341993	DIPAK DAS	9707474658	HITESH KALITA	18-06-2014	15:21:11	0
9085341993	DIPAK DAS	9707474658	HITESH KALITA	18-06-2014	14:49:10	0
9085341993	DIPAK DAS	9707783876	GIASUDDINAHMED	18-06-2014	9:47:08	0
9085341993	DIPAK DAS	9707783876	GIASUDDINAHMED	18-06-2014	8:34:07	0
9085341993	DIPAK DAS	9707474658	HITESH KALITA	18-06-2014	8:29:37	0
9085341993	DIPAK DAS	9707783876	GIASUDDINAHMED	18-06-2014	8:29:12	0
9085341993	DIPAK DAS	9707783876	GIASUDDINAHMED	18-06-2014	8:21:37	0
9085341993	DIPAK DAS	9707783876	GIASUDDINAHMED	18-06-2014	8:17:36	0
9085341993	DIPAK DAS	9707783876	GIASUDDINAHMED	18-06-2014	8:13:56	0
9085341993	DIPAK DAS	9707783876	GIASUDDINAHMED	18-06-2014	8:13:06	0
9085341993	DIPAK DAS	9707783876	GIASUDDINAHMED	18-06-2014	8:08:03	0
9085341993	DIPAK DAS	9707783876	GIASUDDINAHMED	18-06-2014	7:44:29	0
9085341993	DIPAK DAS	9707783876	GIASUDDINAHMED	18-06-2014	7:42:22	0
9085341993	DIPAK DAS	9707783876	GIASUDDINAHMED	18-06-2014	7:41:01	0
9085341993	DIPAK DAS	9707783876	GIASUDDINAHMED	18-06-2014	7:39:07	0
9085341993	DIPAK DAS	9707783876	GIASUDDINAHMED	18-06-2014	7:16:53	0

Calling (A) Party Telephone Number/MSISDN	Name	Called (B) Party Telephone Number/Access Point Name	Name	Date	Time	Duration In Secs.
9085341993	DIPAK DAS	9707783876	GIASUDDINAHMED	18-06-2014	7:10:29	0
9085341993	DIPAK DAS	9707783876	GIASUDDINAHMED	18-06-2014	7:06:50	158
9085341993	DIPAK DAS	9707783876	GIASUDDINAHMED	18-06-2014	7:04:02	0
9085341993	DIPAK DAS	9707783876	GIASUDDINAHMED	18-06-2014	6:55:48	0
9085341993	DIPAK DAS	9707783876	GIASUDDINAHMED	18-06-2014	6:12:43	0
9085341993	DIPAK DAS	9707783876	GIASUDDINAHMED	18-06-2014	5:54:08	0
9085341993	DIPAK DAS	9707783876	GIASUDDINAHMED	18-06-2014	5:46:14	0
9085341993	DIPAK DAS	9707783876	GIASUDDINAHMED	18-06-2014	5:36:09	0
9085341993	DIPAK DAS	9707783876	GIASUDDINAHMED	18-06-2014	5:27:34	418
9085341993	DIPAK DAS	9707783876	GIASUDDINAHMED	18-06-2014	5:14:19	0
9085341993	DIPAK DAS	9707783876	GIASUDDINAHMED	18-06-2014	3:39:46	0
9085341993	DIPAK DAS	9707783876	GIASUDDINAHMED	17-06-2014	22:57:36	0
9085341993	DIPAK DAS	9707783876	GIASUDDINAHMED	17-06-2014	22:54:58	0
9085341993	DIPAK DAS	9707474658	HITESH KALITA	17-06-2014	22:34:27	0
9085341993	DIPAK DAS	9707474658	HITESH KALITA	17-06-2014	22:27:38	0
9085341993	DIPAK DAS	9707474658	HITESH KALITA	17-06-2014	22:23:19	0
9085341993	DIPAK DAS	9707783876	GIASUDDINAHMED	17-06-2014	22:22:14	0
9085341993	DIPAK DAS	9085835737	RAMANDRA BARMAN	17-06-2014	22:20:34	0

Calling (A) Party Telephone Number/MSISDN	Name	Called (B) Party Telephone Number/Access Point Name	Name	Date	Time	Duration In Secs.
9085341993	DIPAK DAS	9707474658	HITESH KALITA	17-06-2014	22:19:09	0
9085341993	DIPAK DAS	9707783876	GIASUDDINAHMED	17-06-2014	22:05:36	0
9085341993	DIPAK DAS	9707783876	GIASUDDINAHMED	17-06-2014	22:04:19	0
9085341993	DIPAK DAS	9707783876	GIASUDDINAHMED	17-06-2014	21:32:33	0
9085341993	DIPAK DAS	9707783876	GIASUDDINAHMED	17-06-2014	21:27:58	234
9085341993	DIPAK DAS	9707474658	HITESH KALITA	17-06-2014	21:27:44	0
9085341993	DIPAK DAS	9707783876	GIASUDDINAHMED	17-06-2014	21:26:59	0
9085341993	DIPAK DAS	9707783876	GIASUDDINAHMED	17-06-2014	21:10:33	0
9085341993	DIPAK DAS	9707783876	GIASUDDINAHMED	17-06-2014	18:46:59	0
9085341993	DIPAK DAS	9707783876	GIASUDDINAHMED	17-06-2014	18:01:07	0
9085341993	DIPAK DAS	9707783876	GIASUDDINAHMED	17-06-2014	17:59:54	0
9085341993	DIPAK DAS	9707783876	GIASUDDINAHMED	17-06-2014	17:10:36	0
9085341993	DIPAK DAS	9707783876	GIASUDDINAHMED	17-06-2014	16:56:39	0
9085341993	DIPAK DAS	9707474658	HITESH KALITA	17-06-2014	16:54:44	0
9085341993	DIPAK DAS	9707783876	GIASUDDINAHMED	17-06-2014	16:15:06	0
9085341993	DIPAK DAS	9707783876	GIASUDDINAHMED	17-06-2014	16:07:54	0
9085341993	DIPAK DAS	9707783876	GIASUDDINAHMED	17-06-2014	16:05:45	0
9085341993	DIPAK DAS	9707474658	HITESH KALITA	17-06-2014	15:53:58	0

Calling (A) Party Telephone Number/MSISDN	Name	Called (B) Party Telephone Number/Access Point Name	Name	Date	Time	Duration In Secs.
9085341993	DIPAK DAS	9707783876	GIASUDDINAHMED	17-06-2014	8:24:59	0
9085341993	DIPAK DAS	9707783876	GIASUDDINAHMED	17-06-2014	8:21:36	0
9085341993	DIPAK DAS	9707783876	GIASUDDINAHMED	17-06-2014	8:02:06	0
9085341993	DIPAK DAS	9401165464	HITESWAR KALITA	17-06-2014	7:04:48	11
9085341993	DIPAK DAS	9401165464	HITESWAR KALITA	17-06-2014	7:03:39	11
9085341993	DIPAK DAS	9401165464	HITESWAR KALITA	17-06-2014	5:03:07	0
9085341993	DIPAK DAS	9707783876	GIASUDDINAHMED	16-06-2014	23:51:52	0
9085341993	DIPAK DAS	9707783876	GIASUDDINAHMED	16-06-2014	23:21:24	0
9085341993	DIPAK DAS	9707783876	GIASUDDINAHMED	16-06-2014	23:19:58	0
9085341993	DIPAK DAS	9707783876	GIASUDDINAHMED	16-06-2014	23:16:40	0
9085341993	DIPAK DAS	9707783876	GIASUDDINAHMED	16-06-2014	23:15:11	0
9085341993	DIPAK DAS	9707783876	GIASUDDINAHMED	16-06-2014	23:13:06	0
9085341993	DIPAK DAS	9707783876	GIASUDDINAHMED	16-06-2014	23:04:15	0
9085341993	DIPAK DAS	9707783876	GIASUDDINAHMED	16-06-2014	22:56:13	0
9085341993	DIPAK DAS	9707783876	GIASUDDINAHMED	16-06-2014	22:51:15	0
9085341993	DIPAK DAS	9707783876	GIASUDDINAHMED	16-06-2014	22:44:56	0
9085341993	DIPAK DAS	9707783876	GIASUDDINAHMED	16-06-2014	22:43:43	0
9085341993	DIPAK DAS	9707783876	GIASUDDINAHMED	16-06-2014	22:42:49	0

Calling (A) Party Telephone Number/MSISDN	Name	Called (B) Party Telephone Number/Access Point Name	Name	Date	Time	Duration In Secs.
9085341993	DIPAK DAS	9707783876	GIASUDDINAHMED	16-06-2014	22:40:30	0
9085341993	DIPAK DAS	9707783876	GIASUDDINAHMED	16-06-2014	22:34:54	293
9085341993	DIPAK DAS	9707783876	GIASUDDINAHMED	16-06-2014	22:32:43	0
9085341993	DIPAK DAS	9085428530	GIASUDDIN AHMED	16-06-2014	22:32:21	0
9085341993	DIPAK DAS	9707783876	GIASUDDINAHMED	16-06-2014	22:22:08	0
9085341993	DIPAK DAS	9707783876	GIASUDDINAHMED	16-06-2014	22:19:20	0
9085341993	DIPAK DAS	9085428530	GIASUDDIN AHMED	16-06-2014	22:13:55	0
9085341993	DIPAK DAS	9707783876	GIASUDDINAHMED	16-06-2014	22:13:43	0
9085341993	DIPAK DAS	9707783876	GIASUDDINAHMED	16-06-2014	21:59:30	0
9085341993	DIPAK DAS	9707474658	HITESH KALITA	16-06-2014	21:39:39	15
9085341993	DIPAK DAS	9707474658	HITESH KALITA	16-06-2014	21:36:54	115
9085341993	DIPAK DAS	9085428530	GIASUDDIN AHMED	16-06-2014	21:36:04	0
9085341993	DIPAK DAS	9401165464	HITESWAR KALITA	16-06-2014	21:35:48	6
9085341993	DIPAK DAS	9085428530	GIASUDDIN AHMED	16-06-2014	21:34:09	0
9085341993	DIPAK DAS	9401165464	HITESWAR KALITA	16-06-2014	21:15:22	0
9085341993	DIPAK DAS	9707474658	HITESH KALITA	16-06-2014	20:36:12	109
9085341993	DIPAK DAS	9707783876	GIASUDDINAHMED	16-06-2014	20:34:54	0
9085341993	DIPAK DAS	9707783876	GIASUDDINAHMED	16-06-2014	20:34:44	0

Calling (A) Party Telephone Number/MSISDN	Name	Called (B) Party Telephone Number/Access Point Name	Name	Date	Time	Duration In Secs.
9085341993	DIPAK DAS	9707783876	GIASUDDINAHMED	16-06-2014	20:34:39	0
9085341993	DIPAK DAS	9707783876	GIASUDDINAHMED	16-06-2014	20:34:35	0
9085341993	DIPAK DAS	9707783876	GIASUDDINAHMED	16-06-2014	20:34:29	0
9085341993	DIPAK DAS	9707783876	GIASUDDINAHMED	16-06-2014	20:34:25	0
9085341993	DIPAK DAS	9707783876	GIASUDDINAHMED	16-06-2014	20:34:20	0
9085341993	DIPAK DAS	9707783876	GIASUDDINAHMED	16-06-2014	20:34:14	0
9085341993	DIPAK DAS	9707783876	GIASUDDINAHMED	16-06-2014	17:53:25	0
9085341993	DIPAK DAS	9085428530	GIASUDDIN AHMED	16-06-2014	17:50:16	0
9085341993	DIPAK DAS	9085428530	GIASUDDIN AHMED	16-06-2014	17:50:14	0
9085341993	DIPAK DAS	9707783876	GIASUDDINAHMED	16-06-2014	14:53:38	0
9085341993	DIPAK DAS	9085428530	GIASUDDIN AHMED	16-06-2014	14:48:02	0
9085341993	DIPAK DAS	9707783876	GIASUDDINAHMED	16-06-2014	14:44:41	0
9085341993	DIPAK DAS	9085428530	GIASUDDIN AHMED	16-06-2014	14:44:11	0
9085341993	DIPAK DAS	9707783876	GIASUDDINAHMED	16-06-2014	14:40:16	113
9085341993	DIPAK DAS	9085428530	GIASUDDIN AHMED	16-06-2014	14:37:41	0
9085341993	DIPAK DAS	9085428530	GIASUDDIN AHMED	16-06-2014	14:35:41	0
9085341993	DIPAK DAS	9707474658	HITESH KALITA	16-06-2014	13:52:46	157
9085341993	DIPAK DAS	9707783876	GIASUDDINAHMED	16-06-2014	13:41:08	0

Calling (A) Party Telephone Number/MSISDN	Name	Called (B) Party Telephone Number/Access Point Name	Name	Date	Time	Duration In Secs.
9085341993	DIPAK DAS	9707783876	GIASUDDINAHMED	16-06-2014	13:32:51	0
9085341993	DIPAK DAS	9085428530	GIASUDDIN AHMED	16-06-2014	13:30:48	0
9085341993	DIPAK DAS	9085428530	GIASUDDIN AHMED	16-06-2014	13:27:06	0
9085341993	DIPAK DAS	9085428530	GIASUDDIN AHMED	16-06-2014	13:27:00	0
9085341993	DIPAK DAS	9707783876	GIASUDDINAHMED	15-06-2014	21:19:33	0
9085341993	DIPAK DAS	9707783876	GIASUDDINAHMED	15-06-2014	21:17:24	0
9085341993	DIPAK DAS	9707783876	GIASUDDINAHMED	15-06-2014	20:39:52	0
9085341993	DIPAK DAS	9707783876	GIASUDDINAHMED	15-06-2014	20:39:46	0
9085341993	DIPAK DAS	9707783876	GIASUDDINAHMED	15-06-2014	20:26:23	0
9085341993	DIPAK DAS	9707783876	GIASUDDINAHMED	15-06-2014	20:24:27	0
9085341993	DIPAK DAS	9707783876	GIASUDDINAHMED	15-06-2014	20:19:21	0
9085341993	DIPAK DAS	9401165464	HITESWAR KALITA	15-06-2014	20:17:49	0
9085341993	DIPAK DAS	9401165464	HITESWAR KALITA	15-06-2014	20:15:46	0
9085341993	DIPAK DAS	9707783876	GIASUDDINAHMED	15-06-2014	20:13:22	0
9085341993	DIPAK DAS	9707783876	GIASUDDINAHMED	15-06-2014	20:12:50	0
9085341993	DIPAK DAS	9707783876	GIASUDDINAHMED	15-06-2014	20:12:48	0
9085341993	DIPAK DAS	9707474658	HITESH KALITA	15-06-2014	20:04:58	241
9085341993	DIPAK DAS	9707783876	GIASUDDINAHMED	15-06-2014	19:54:47	0

Calling (A) Party Telephone Number/MSISDN	Name	Called (B) Party Telephone Number/Access Point Name	Name	Date	Time	Duration In Secs.
9085341993	DIPAK DAS	9707783876	GIASUDDINAHMED	15-06-2014	19:47:23	0
9085341993	DIPAK DAS	9707783876	GIASUDDINAHMED	15-06-2014	19:46:58	0
9085341993	DIPAK DAS	9707783876	GIASUDDINAHMED	15-06-2014	19:38:56	0
9085341993	DIPAK DAS	9707783876	GIASUDDINAHMED	15-06-2014	19:35:01	0
9085341993	DIPAK DAS	9707783876	GIASUDDINAHMED	15-06-2014	19:26:47	0
9085341993	DIPAK DAS	9707783876	GIASUDDINAHMED	15-06-2014	19:23:06	0
9085341993	DIPAK DAS	9707783876	GIASUDDINAHMED	15-06-2014	19:22:43	0
9085341993	DIPAK DAS	9707783876	GIASUDDINAHMED	15-06-2014	15:44:50	0
9085341993	DIPAK DAS	9707474658	HITESH KALITA	15-06-2014	15:25:39	104
9085341993	DIPAK DAS	9707474658	HITESH KALITA	15-06-2014	12:12:49	89
9085341993	DIPAK DAS	9707783876	GIASUDDINAHMED	15-06-2014	12:11:54	0
9085341993	DIPAK DAS	9707783876	GIASUDDINAHMED	15-06-2014	10:23:46	0
9085341993	DIPAK DAS	9707783876	GIASUDDINAHMED	15-06-2014	10:17:54	0
9085341993	DIPAK DAS	9707783876	GIASUDDINAHMED	15-06-2014	10:15:48	0
9085341993	DIPAK DAS	9707783876	GIASUDDINAHMED	15-06-2014	9:57:55	0
9085341993	DIPAK DAS	9707783876	GIASUDDINAHMED	15-06-2014	9:55:39	0
9085341993	DIPAK DAS	9707783876	GIASUDDINAHMED	15-06-2014	9:53:13	0
9085341993	DIPAK DAS	9707783876	GIASUDDINAHMED	15-06-2014	9:50:23	0

Calling (A) Party Telephone Number/MSISDN	Name	Called (B) Party Telephone Number/Access Point Name	Name	Date	Time	Duration In Secs.
9085341993	DIPAK DAS	97077783876	GIASUDDINAHMED	15-06-2014	9:47:04	0
9085341993	DIPAK DAS	97077783876	GIASUDDINAHMED	15-06-2014	9:45:54	0
9085341993	DIPAK DAS	97077783876	GIASUDDINAHMED	15-06-2014	9:40:32	0
9085341993	DIPAK DAS	97077783876	GIASUDDINAHMED	15-06-2014	9:19:03	0
9085341993	DIPAK DAS	9707474658	HITESH KALITA	15-06-2014	9:10:51	250
9085341993	DIPAK DAS	97077783876	GIASUDDINAHMED	15-06-2014	9:07:28	0
9085341993	DIPAK DAS	97077783876	GIASUDDINAHMED	15-06-2014	8:51:24	0
9085341993	DIPAK DAS	97077783876	GIASUDDINAHMED	15-06-2014	8:45:16	0
9085341993	DIPAK DAS	9085428530	GIASUDDIN AHMED	15-06-2014	0:15:34	0
9085341993	DIPAK DAS	9085428530	GIASUDDIN AHMED	15-06-2014	0:13:24	0
9085341993	DIPAK DAS	9085428530	GIASUDDIN AHMED	15-06-2014	0:12:02	0
9085341993	DIPAK DAS	9085428530	GIASUDDIN AHMED	15-06-2014	0:12:00	0
9085341993	DIPAK DAS	9085428530	GIASUDDIN AHMED	14-06-2014	23:48:04	0
9085341993	DIPAK DAS	9085428530	GIASUDDIN AHMED	14-06-2014	23:47:14	0
9085341993	DIPAK DAS	9401165464	HITESWAR KALITA	14-06-2014	23:43:31	0
9085341993	DIPAK DAS	9401165464	HITESWAR KALITA	14-06-2014	23:36:24	0
9085341993	DIPAK DAS	9401165464	HITESWAR KALITA	14-06-2014	23:35:21	0
9085341993	DIPAK DAS	9085428530	GIASUDDIN AHMED	14-06-2014	23:32:35	0

Calling (A) Party Telephone Number/MSISDN	Name	Called (B) Party Telephone Number/Access Point Name	Name	Date	Time	Duration In Secs.
9085341993	DIPAK DAS	9085428530	GIASUDDIN AHMED	14-06-2014	23:31:43	0
9085341993	DIPAK DAS	9401165464	HITESWAR KALITA	14-06-2014	23:31:19	0
9085341993	DIPAK DAS	9085428530	GIASUDDIN AHMED	14-06-2014	23:30:09	0
9085341993	DIPAK DAS	9401165464	HITESWAR KALITA	14-06-2014	23:29:29	0
9085341993	DIPAK DAS	9401165464	HITESWAR KALITA	14-06-2014	23:27:40	0
9085341993	DIPAK DAS	9085428530	GIASUDDIN AHMED	14-06-2014	23:26:30	0
9085341993	DIPAK DAS	9401165464	HITESWAR KALITA	14-06-2014	23:25:28	0
9085341993	DIPAK DAS	9401165464	HITESWAR KALITA	14-06-2014	23:23:43	0
9085341993	DIPAK DAS	9085428530	GIASUDDIN AHMED	14-06-2014	23:22:53	0
9085341993	DIPAK DAS	9401165464	HITESWAR KALITA	14-06-2014	23:21:47	0
9085341993	DIPAK DAS	9401165464	HITESWAR KALITA	14-06-2014	23:20:59	0
9085341993	DIPAK DAS	9085428530	GIASUDDIN AHMED	14-06-2014	23:20:42	0
9085341993	DIPAK DAS	9401165464	HITESWAR KALITA	14-06-2014	23:20:25	0
9085341993	DIPAK DAS	9085428530	GIASUDDIN AHMED	14-06-2014	23:19:11	0
9085341993	DIPAK DAS	9085428530	GIASUDDIN AHMED	14-06-2014	23:16:13	0
9085341993	DIPAK DAS	9707474658	HITESH KALITA	14-06-2014	23:15:51	98
9085341993	DIPAK DAS	9085428530	GIASUDDIN AHMED	14-06-2014	23:13:24	0
9085341993	DIPAK DAS	9085428530	GIASUDDIN AHMED	14-06-2014	23:12:36	0

Calling (A) Party Telephone Number/MSISDN	Name	Called (B) Party Telephone Number/Access Point Name	Name	Date	Time	Duration In Secs.
9085341993	DIPAK DAS	9401165464	HITESWAR KALITA	14-06-2014	23:10:48	0
9085341993	DIPAK DAS	9707783876	GIASUDDINAHMED	14-06-2014	23:04:54	0
9085341993	DIPAK DAS	9707783876	GIASUDDINAHMED	14-06-2014	22:36:28	0
9085341993	DIPAK DAS	9707783876	GIASUDDINAHMED	14-06-2014	22:34:46	0
9085341993	DIPAK DAS	9401165464	HITESWAR KALITA	14-06-2014	22:33:58	0
9085341993	DIPAK DAS	9707783876	GIASUDDINAHMED	14-06-2014	22:31:48	0
9085341993	DIPAK DAS	9707783876	GIASUDDINAHMED	14-06-2014	22:27:53	0
9085341993	DIPAK DAS	9707783876	GIASUDDINAHMED	14-06-2014	22:26:01	0
9085341993	DIPAK DAS	9707783876	GIASUDDINAHMED	14-06-2014	22:25:56	0
9085341993	DIPAK DAS	9707783876	GIASUDDINAHMED	14-06-2014	22:22:43	0
9085341993	DIPAK DAS	9707783876	GIASUDDINAHMED	14-06-2014	22:19:26	0
9085341993	DIPAK DAS	9401165464	HITESWAR KALITA	14-06-2014	22:18:18	0
9085341993	DIPAK DAS	9707783876	GIASUDDINAHMED	14-06-2014	22:18:09	0
9085341993	DIPAK DAS	8255037061	MINATIKALITA	14-06-2014	22:16:44	42
9085341993	DIPAK DAS	9707783876	GIASUDDINAHMED	14-06-2014	22:16:28	0
9085341993	DIPAK DAS	9401165464	HITESWAR KALITA	14-06-2014	22:15:13	60
9085341993	DIPAK DAS	9085428530	GIASUDDIN AHMED	14-06-2014	22:14:34	0
9085341993	DIPAK DAS	9707783876	GIASUDDINAHMED	14-06-2014	22:12:43	0

Calling (A) Party Telephone Number/MSISDN	Name	Called (B) Party Telephone Number/Access Point Name	Name	Date	Time	Duration In Secs.
9085341993	DIPAK DAS	9085428530	GIASUDDIN AHMED	14-06-2014	22:12:38	0
9085341993	DIPAK DAS	9707783876	GIASUDDINAHMED	14-06-2014	22:11:03	0
9085341993	DIPAK DAS	9085428530	GIASUDDIN AHMED	14-06-2014	22:10:46	0
9085341993	DIPAK DAS	9707783876	GIASUDDINAHMED	14-06-2014	21:32:34	0
9085341993	DIPAK DAS	9085428530	GIASUDDIN AHMED	14-06-2014	20:55:09	0
9085341993	DIPAK DAS	9085428530	GIASUDDIN AHMED	14-06-2014	20:50:51	0
9085341993	DIPAK DAS	9085428530	GIASUDDIN AHMED	14-06-2014	20:49:53	0
9085341993	DIPAK DAS	9085428530	GIASUDDIN AHMED	14-06-2014	20:49:23	0
9085341993	DIPAK DAS	9085428530	GIASUDDIN AHMED	14-06-2014	20:48:40	0
9085341993	DIPAK DAS	9085428530	GIASUDDIN AHMED	14-06-2014	20:46:08	0
9085341993	DIPAK DAS	9085428530	GIASUDDIN AHMED	14-06-2014	20:43:16	0
9085341993	DIPAK DAS	9707783876	GIASUDDINAHMED	14-06-2014	20:35:33	0
9085341993	DIPAK DAS	9707474658	HITESH KALITA	14-06-2014	20:29:22	48
9085341993	DIPAK DAS	9707783876	GIASUDDINAHMED	14-06-2014	20:26:52	25
9085341993	DIPAK DAS	9707783876	GIASUDDINAHMED	14-06-2014	20:25:43	32
9085341993	DIPAK DAS	9707783876	GIASUDDINAHMED	14-06-2014	20:08:47	0
9085341993	DIPAK DAS	9577672921	DHANMONI DEKA	14-06-2014	19:39:28	80
9085341993	DIPAK DAS	9707783876	GIASUDDINAHMED	14-06-2014	19:27:42	0

Calling (A) Party Telephone Number/MSISDN	Name	Called (B) Party Telephone Number/Access Point Name	Name	Date	Time	Duration In Secs.
9085341993	DIPAK DAS	9707783876	GIASUDDINAHMED	14-06-2014	19:23:01	0
9085341993	DIPAK DAS	9707783876	GIASUDDINAHMED	14-06-2014	19:22:57	0
9085341993	DIPAK DAS	9707783876	GIASUDDINAHMED	14-06-2014	19:16:33	0
9085341993	DIPAK DAS	9401165464	HITESWAR KALITA	14-06-2014	19:11:25	0
9085341993	DIPAK DAS	9401165464	HITESWAR KALITA	14-06-2014	19:09:37	0
9085341993	DIPAK DAS	9707783876	GIASUDDINAHMED	14-06-2014	19:08:22	0
9085341993	DIPAK DAS	9707783876	GIASUDDINAHMED	14-06-2014	19:06:25	0
9085341993	DIPAK DAS	9707783876	GIASUDDINAHMED	14-06-2014	19:05:15	0
9085341993	DIPAK DAS	9707783876	GIASUDDINAHMED	14-06-2014	19:04:20	0
9085341993	DIPAK DAS	9707783876	GIASUDDINAHMED	14-06-2014	19:01:11	0
9085341993	DIPAK DAS	9707783876	GIASUDDINAHMED	14-06-2014	18:59:19	0
9085341993	DIPAK DAS	9707783876	GIASUDDINAHMED	14-06-2014	18:49:32	0
9085341993	DIPAK DAS	9085428530	GIASUDDIN AHMED	14-06-2014	18:48:27	0
9085341993	DIPAK DAS	9707783876	GIASUDDINAHMED	14-06-2014	18:37:33	0
9085341993	DIPAK DAS	9707783876	GIASUDDINAHMED	14-06-2014	17:51:40	0
9085341993	DIPAK DAS	9707474658	HITESH KALITA	14-06-2014	16:25:17	284
9085341993	DIPAK DAS	9401165464	HITESWAR KALITA	14-06-2014	15:47:36	0
9085341993	DIPAK DAS	9707783876	GIASUDDINAHMED	14-06-2014	15:25:57	0

Calling (A) Party Telephone Number/MSISDN	Name	Called (B) Party Telephone Number/Access Point Name	Name	Date	Time	Duration In Secs.
9085341993	DIPAK DAS	9401165464	HITESWAR KALITA	14-06-2014	14:57:20	0
9085341993	DIPAK DAS	9401165464	HITESWAR KALITA	14-06-2014	14:57:11	0
9085341993	DIPAK DAS	9707474658	HITESH KALITA	14-06-2014	14:27:19	220
9085341993	DIPAK DAS	9707474658	HITESH KALITA	14-06-2014	14:25:34	76
9085341993	DIPAK DAS	9707783876	GIASUDDINAHMED	14-06-2014	14:24:06	0
9085341993	DIPAK DAS	9707474658	HITESH KALITA	14-06-2014	13:24:21	247
9085341993	DIPAK DAS	9707783876	GIASUDDINAHMED	14-06-2014	13:09:06	0
9085341993	DIPAK DAS	9707783876	GIASUDDINAHMED	14-06-2014	13:08:15	0
9085341993	DIPAK DAS	9401165464	HITESWAR KALITA	14-06-2014	8:45:08	129
9085341993	DIPAK DAS	9707783876	GIASUDDINAHMED	14-06-2014	8:32:20	150
9085341993	DIPAK DAS	9401165464	HITESWAR KALITA	14-06-2014	8:08:24	0
9085341993	DIPAK DAS	9707783876	GIASUDDINAHMED	14-06-2014	7:02:45	0
9085341993	DIPAK DAS	9707783876	GIASUDDINAHMED	14-06-2014	0:55:44	0
9085341993	DIPAK DAS	9707783876	GIASUDDINAHMED	14-06-2014	0:01:33	0
9085341993	DIPAK DAS	9401165464	HITESWAR KALITA	13-06-2014	23:04:35	0
9085341993	DIPAK DAS	9401165464	HITESWAR KALITA	13-06-2014	23:02:41	0
9085341993	DIPAK DAS	9401165464	HITESWAR KALITA	13-06-2014	22:58:13	244
9085341993	DIPAK DAS	9401165464	HITESWAR KALITA	13-06-2014	22:31:18	0

Calling (A) Party Telephone Number/MSISDN	Name	Called (B) Party Telephone Number/Access Point Name	Name	Date	Time	Duration In Secs.
9085341993	DIPAK DAS	9401165464	HITESWAR KALITA	13-06-2014	22:29:55	0
9085341993	DIPAK DAS	9401165464	HITESWAR KALITA	13-06-2014	22:22:36	0
9085341993	DIPAK DAS	9401165464	HITESWAR KALITA	13-06-2014	21:38:51	733
9085341993	DIPAK DAS	9707783876	GIASUDDINAHMED	13-06-2014	21:36:20	0
9085341993	DIPAK DAS	9707783876	GIASUDDINAHMED	13-06-2014	21:26:04	0
9085341993	DIPAK DAS	9707783876	GIASUDDINAHMED	13-06-2014	21:22:25	0
9085341993	DIPAK DAS	9707783876	GIASUDDINAHMED	13-06-2014	21:13:33	0
9085341993	DIPAK DAS	9707783876	GIASUDDINAHMED	13-06-2014	21:09:42	0
9085341993	DIPAK DAS	9707783876	GIASUDDINAHMED	13-06-2014	21:09:03	0
9085341993	DIPAK DAS	9707783876	GIASUDDINAHMED	13-06-2014	21:07:40	0
9085341993	DIPAK DAS	9707783876	GIASUDDINAHMED	13-06-2014	21:06:03	0
9085341993	DIPAK DAS	9085428530	GIASUDDIN AHMED	13-06-2014	21:00:30	0
9085341993	DIPAK DAS	9085428530	GIASUDDIN AHMED	13-06-2014	20:59:19	0
9085341993	DIPAK DAS	9085428530	GIASUDDIN AHMED	13-06-2014	20:56:34	0
9085341993	DIPAK DAS	9707783876	GIASUDDINAHMED	13-06-2014	20:55:18	0
9085341993	DIPAK DAS	9085428530	GIASUDDIN AHMED	13-06-2014	20:47:28	0
9085341993	DIPAK DAS	9707783876	GIASUDDINAHMED	13-06-2014	20:40:23	0
9085341993	DIPAK DAS	9707783876	GIASUDDINAHMED	13-06-2014	20:23:29	0

Calling (A) Party Telephone Number/MSISDN	Name	Called (B) Party Telephone Number/Access Point Name	Name	Date	Time	Duration In Secs.
9085341993	DIPAK DAS	9707783876	GIASUDDINAHMED	13-06-2014	20:20:57	0
9085341993	DIPAK DAS	9707783876	GIASUDDINAHMED	13-06-2014	20:18:14	0
9085341993	DIPAK DAS	9707783876	GIASUDDINAHMED	13-06-2014	20:16:53	0
9085341993	DIPAK DAS	9707783876	GIASUDDINAHMED	13-06-2014	20:14:47	0
9085341993	DIPAK DAS	9707783876	GIASUDDINAHMED	13-06-2014	19:54:36	0
9085341993	DIPAK DAS	9707783876	GIASUDDINAHMED	13-06-2014	19:50:09	153
9085341993	DIPAK DAS	9401165464	HITESWAR KALITA	13-06-2014	19:45:28	154
9085341993	DIPAK DAS	9707783876	GIASUDDINAHMED	13-06-2014	19:40:20	0
9085341993	DIPAK DAS	9707783876	GIASUDDINAHMED	13-06-2014	19:37:55	0
9085341993	DIPAK DAS	9707783876	GIASUDDINAHMED	13-06-2014	18:55:56	0
9085341993	DIPAK DAS	9085428530	GIASUDDIN AHMED	13-06-2014	18:51:28	0
9085341993	DIPAK DAS	9401165464	HITESWAR KALITA	13-06-2014	17:15:03	0
9085341993	DIPAK DAS	9401165464	HITESWAR KALITA	13-06-2014	17:11:42	107
9085341993	DIPAK DAS	9707474658	HITESH KALITA	13-06-2014	17:06:30	171
9085341993	DIPAK DAS	9401165464	HITESWAR KALITA	13-06-2014	17:04:40	0
9085341993	DIPAK DAS	9401165464	HITESWAR KALITA	13-06-2014	17:04:30	0
9085341993	DIPAK DAS	9707474658	HITESH KALITA	13-06-2014	17:04:12	2
9085341993	DIPAK DAS	9707783876	GIASUDDINAHMED	13-06-2014	16:37:06	0

Calling (A) Party Telephone Number/MSISDN	Name	Called (B) Party Telephone Number/Access Point Name	Name	Date	Time	Duration In Secs.
9085341993	DIPAK DAS	9707783876	GIASUDDINAHMED	13-06-2014	16:35:22	38
9085341993	DIPAK DAS	9707783876	GIASUDDINAHMED	13-06-2014	16:30:57	0
9085341993	DIPAK DAS	9707783876	GIASUDDINAHMED	13-06-2014	16:24:53	0
9085341993	DIPAK DAS	9707783876	GIASUDDINAHMED	13-06-2014	16:23:00	0
9085341993	DIPAK DAS	9401165464	HITESWAR KALITA	13-06-2014	16:22:05	0
9085341993	DIPAK DAS	9707783876	GIASUDDINAHMED	13-06-2014	16:21:18	0
9085341993	DIPAK DAS	9707783876	GIASUDDINAHMED	13-06-2014	16:20:25	0
9085341993	DIPAK DAS	9401165464	HITESWAR KALITA	13-06-2014	16:19:17	0
9085341993	DIPAK DAS	9401165464	HITESWAR KALITA	13-06-2014	16:19:12	32
9085341993	DIPAK DAS	9401165464	HITESWAR KALITA	13-06-2014	16:18:31	0
9085341993	DIPAK DAS	9401165464	HITESWAR KALITA	13-06-2014	16:17:54	0
9085341993	DIPAK DAS	9707783876	GIASUDDINAHMED	13-06-2014	16:12:58	0
9085341993	DIPAK DAS	9707474658	HITESH KALITA	13-06-2014	16:09:34	55
9085341993	DIPAK DAS	9707783876	GIASUDDINAHMED	13-06-2014	16:09:07	75
9085341993	DIPAK DAS	9707474658	HITESH KALITA	13-06-2014	16:02:18	215
9085341993	DIPAK DAS	9707783876	GIASUDDINAHMED	13-06-2014	15:56:59	156
9085341993	DIPAK DAS	9707783876	GIASUDDINAHMED	13-06-2014	15:36:22	0
9085341993	DIPAK DAS	9707783876	GIASUDDINAHMED	13-06-2014	15:34:27	0

Calling (A) Party Telephone Number/MSISDN	Name	Called (B) Party Telephone Number/Access Point Name	Name	Date	Time	Duration In Secs.
9085341993	DIPAK DAS	9401165464	HITESWAR KALITA	13-06-2014	15:33:25	0
9085341993	DIPAK DAS	9707783876	GIASUDDINAHMED	13-06-2014	15:27:52	0
9085341993	DIPAK DAS	9707783876	GIASUDDINAHMED	13-06-2014	15:27:33	0
9085341993	DIPAK DAS	9401165464	HITESWAR KALITA	13-06-2014	15:22:49	207
9085341993	DIPAK DAS	9707783876	GIASUDDINAHMED	13-06-2014	14:59:22	0
9085341993	DIPAK DAS	9707783876	GIASUDDINAHMED	13-06-2014	14:50:59	0
9085341993	DIPAK DAS	9707783876	GIASUDDINAHMED	13-06-2014	14:33:49	0
9085341993	DIPAK DAS	9707783876	GIASUDDINAHMED	13-06-2014	13:42:01	0
9085341993	DIPAK DAS	9707474658	HITESH KALITA	13-06-2014	13:41:16	40
9085341993	DIPAK DAS	9707783876	GIASUDDINAHMED	13-06-2014	13:35:24	0
9085341993	DIPAK DAS	9707783876	GIASUDDINAHMED	13-06-2014	13:31:47	0
9085341993	DIPAK DAS	9707783876	GIASUDDINAHMED	13-06-2014	13:17:55	0
9085341993	DIPAK DAS	9707783876	GIASUDDINAHMED	13-06-2014	13:05:36	0
9085341993	DIPAK DAS	9085428530	GIASUDDIN AHMED	13-06-2014	12:57:04	0
9085341993	DIPAK DAS	9707783876	GIASUDDINAHMED	13-06-2014	12:54:51	0
9085341993	DIPAK DAS	9707783876	GIASUDDINAHMED	13-06-2014	12:54:50	0
9085341993	DIPAK DAS	9085428530	GIASUDDIN AHMED	12/6/2014	22:30:23	0
9085341993	DIPAK DAS	9085428530	GIASUDDIN AHMED	12/6/2014	22:17:56	0

Calling (A) Party Telephone Number/MSISDN	Name	Called (B) Party Telephone Number/Access Point Name	Name	Date	Time	Duration In Secs.
9085341993	DIPAK DAS	9085428530	GIASUDDIN AHMED	12/6/2014	22:15:27	0
9085341993	DIPAK DAS	9085428530	GIASUDDIN AHMED	12/6/2014	22:15:04	0
9085341993	DIPAK DAS	9401165464	HITESWAR KALITA	12/6/2014	22:07:36	0
9085341993	DIPAK DAS	9401165464	HITESWAR KALITA	12/6/2014	22:02:35	73
9085341993	DIPAK DAS	9401165464	HITESWAR KALITA	12/6/2014	22:02:20	0
9085341993	DIPAK DAS	9401165464	HITESWAR KALITA	12/6/2014	22:01:42	0
9085341993	DIPAK DAS	9707783876	GIASUDDINAHMED	12/6/2014	22:01:28	0
9085341993	DIPAK DAS	9401165464	HITESWAR KALITA	12/6/2014	22:01:18	0
9085341993	DIPAK DAS	9085428530	GIASUDDIN AHMED	12/6/2014	22:00:35	0
9085341993	DIPAK DAS	9401165464	HITESWAR KALITA	12/6/2014	21:59:53	0
9085341993	DIPAK DAS	9401165464	HITESWAR KALITA	12/6/2014	21:57:57	0
9085341993	DIPAK DAS	9401165464	HITESWAR KALITA	12/6/2014	21:55:58	0
9085341993	DIPAK DAS	9401165464	HITESWAR KALITA	12/6/2014	21:55:26	0
9085341993	DIPAK DAS	9401165464	HITESWAR KALITA	12/6/2014	21:37:55	967
9085341993	DIPAK DAS	9085428530	GIASUDDIN AHMED	12/6/2014	21:37:21	0
9085341993	DIPAK DAS	9401165464	HITESWAR KALITA	12/6/2014	21:03:01	488
9085341993	DIPAK DAS	9401165464	HITESWAR KALITA	12/6/2014	21:00:23	84
9085341993	DIPAK DAS	9401165464	HITESWAR KALITA	12/6/2014	20:38:59	1266

Calling (A) Party Telephone Number/MSISDN	Name	Called (B) Party Telephone Number/Access Point Name	Name	Date	Time	Duration In Secs.
9085341993	DIPAK DAS	9707783876	GIASUDDINAHMED	12/6/2014	19:25:08	0
9085341993	DIPAK DAS	9707783876	GIASUDDINAHMED	12/6/2014	19:02:56	0
9085341993	DIPAK DAS	9401165464	HITESWAR KALITA	12/6/2014	18:52:37	89
9085341993	DIPAK DAS	9085428530	GIASUDDIN AHMED	12/6/2014	18:02:30	0
9085341993	DIPAK DAS	9085428530	GIASUDDIN AHMED	12/6/2014	17:40:22	0
9085341993	DIPAK DAS	9085428530	GIASUDDIN AHMED	12/6/2014	17:37:02	0
9085341993	DIPAK DAS	9085428530	GIASUDDIN AHMED	12/6/2014	17:31:55	0
9085341993	DIPAK DAS	9707783876	GIASUDDINAHMED	12/6/2014	17:30:07	0
9085341993	DIPAK DAS	9707783876	GIASUDDINAHMED	12/6/2014	15:24:06	0
9085341993	DIPAK DAS	9707783876	GIASUDDINAHMED	12/6/2014	9:56:15	0
9085341993	DIPAK DAS	9707783876	GIASUDDINAHMED	12/6/2014	9:55:19	0
9085341993	DIPAK DAS	9707783876	GIASUDDINAHMED	12/6/2014	9:14:17	0
9085341993	DIPAK DAS	9707783876	GIASUDDINAHMED	12/6/2014	9:01:41	0
9085341993	DIPAK DAS	9707783876	GIASUDDINAHMED	12/6/2014	8:53:52	0
9085341993	DIPAK DAS	9707783876	GIASUDDINAHMED	12/6/2014	8:51:42	0
9085341993	DIPAK DAS	9707783876	GIASUDDINAHMED	12/6/2014	8:50:35	0
9085341993	DIPAK DAS	9707783876	GIASUDDINAHMED	12/6/2014	8:48:20	0
9085341993	DIPAK DAS	9707474658	HITESH KALITA	12/6/2014	8:46:49	77

Calling (A) Party Telephone Number/MSISDN	Name	Called (B) Party Telephone Number/Access Point Name	Name	Date	Time	Duration In Secs.
9085341993	DIPAK DAS	9707783876	GIASUDDINAHMED	12/6/2014	8:45:45	0
9085341993	DIPAK DAS	9707783876	GIASUDDINAHMED	12/6/2014	8:44:51	0
9085341993	DIPAK DAS	9085428530	GIASUDDIN AHMED	12/6/2014	6:17:34	0
9085341993	DIPAK DAS	9085428530	GIASUDDIN AHMED	12/6/2014	4:39:02	0
9085341993	DIPAK DAS	9085428530	GIASUDDIN AHMED	12/6/2014	4:37:07	0
9085341993	DIPAK DAS	9085428530	GIASUDDIN AHMED	12/6/2014	4:37:04	0
9085341993	DIPAK DAS	9085428530	GIASUDDIN AHMED	12/6/2014	4:37:02	0
9085341993	DIPAK DAS	9085428530	GIASUDDIN AHMED	11/6/2014	23:14:27	0
9085341993	DIPAK DAS	9085428530	GIASUDDIN AHMED	11/6/2014	23:14:23	0
9085341993	DIPAK DAS	9085428530	GIASUDDIN AHMED	11/6/2014	23:11:49	0
9085341993	DIPAK DAS	9085428530	GIASUDDIN AHMED	11/6/2014	23:09:36	0
9085341993	DIPAK DAS	9085428530	GIASUDDIN AHMED	11/6/2014	23:09:31	0
9085341993	DIPAK DAS	9085428530	GIASUDDIN AHMED	11/6/2014	23:09:25	0
9085341993	DIPAK DAS	9707783876	GIASUDDINAHMED	11/6/2014	23:06:36	0
9085341993	DIPAK DAS	9707474658	HITESH KALITA	11/6/2014	23:05:34	0
9085341993	DIPAK DAS	9707783876	GIASUDDINAHMED	11/6/2014	23:05:20	0
9085341993	DIPAK DAS	9085428530	GIASUDDIN AHMED	11/6/2014	23:04:28	0
9085341993	DIPAK DAS	9707783876	GIASUDDINAHMED	11/6/2014	23:03:49	0

Calling (A) Party Telephone Number/MSISDN	Name	Called (B) Party Telephone Number/Access Point Name	Name	Date	Time	Duration In Secs.
9085341993	DIPAK DAS	9707783876	GIASUDDINAHMED	11/6/2014	23:02:02	0
9085341993	DIPAK DAS	9085428530	GIASUDDIN AHMED	11/6/2014	22:59:36	0
9085341993	DIPAK DAS	9085428530	GIASUDDIN AHMED	11/6/2014	22:59:30	0
9085341993	DIPAK DAS	9707783876	GIASUDDINAHMED	11/6/2014	22:56:18	0
9085341993	DIPAK DAS	9707783876	GIASUDDINAHMED	11/6/2014	22:56:16	0
9085341993	DIPAK DAS	9707783876	GIASUDDINAHMED	11/6/2014	22:56:14	0
9085341993	DIPAK DAS	9085428530	GIASUDDIN AHMED	11/6/2014	22:54:11	0
9085341993	DIPAK DAS	9085428530	GIASUDDIN AHMED	11/6/2014	22:54:06	0
9085341993	DIPAK DAS	9085428530	GIASUDDIN AHMED	11/6/2014	22:50:46	0
9085341993	DIPAK DAS	9085428530	GIASUDDIN AHMED	11/6/2014	22:49:41	0
9085341993	DIPAK DAS	9085428530	GIASUDDIN AHMED	11/6/2014	22:49:04	0
9085341993	DIPAK DAS	9085428530	GIASUDDIN AHMED	11/6/2014	22:48:12	0
9085341993	DIPAK DAS	9085428530	GIASUDDIN AHMED	11/6/2014	22:47:27	0
9085341993	DIPAK DAS	9707783876	GIASUDDINAHMED	11/6/2014	22:34:23	0
9085341993	DIPAK DAS	9707783876	GIASUDDINAHMED	11/6/2014	22:34:17	0
9085341993	DIPAK DAS	9707783876	GIASUDDINAHMED	11/6/2014	22:33:09	0
9085341993	DIPAK DAS	9707783876	GIASUDDINAHMED	11/6/2014	22:31:44	0
9085341993	DIPAK DAS	9707783876	GIASUDDINAHMED	11/6/2014	22:27:53	0

Calling (A) Party Telephone Number/MSISDN	Name	Called (B) Party Telephone Number/Access Point Name	Name	Date	Time	Duration In Secs.
9085341993	DIPAK DAS	9707783876	GIASUDDINAHMED	11/6/2014	22:25:39	0
9085341993	DIPAK DAS	9707783876	GIASUDDINAHMED	11/6/2014	22:25:37	0
9085341993	DIPAK DAS	9707783876	GIASUDDINAHMED	11/6/2014	22:23:39	0
9085341993	DIPAK DAS	9707783876	GIASUDDINAHMED	11/6/2014	22:22:16	0
9085341993	DIPAK DAS	9707783876	GIASUDDINAHMED	11/6/2014	22:18:14	0
9085341993	DIPAK DAS	9085428530	GIASUDDIN AHMED	11/6/2014	22:17:05	0
9085341993	DIPAK DAS	9707783876	GIASUDDINAHMED	11/6/2014	22:16:31	0
9085341993	DIPAK DAS	9707783876	GIASUDDINAHMED	11/6/2014	22:16:28	0
9085341993	DIPAK DAS	9707783876	GIASUDDINAHMED	11/6/2014	22:15:12	23
9085341993	DIPAK DAS	9707783876	GIASUDDINAHMED	11/6/2014	22:13:02	0
9085341993	DIPAK DAS	9085428530	GIASUDDIN AHMED	11/6/2014	22:06:24	0
9085341993	DIPAK DAS	9085428530	GIASUDDIN AHMED	11/6/2014	21:57:42	0
9085341993	DIPAK DAS	9085428530	GIASUDDIN AHMED	11/6/2014	21:54:39	0
9085341993	DIPAK DAS	9085428530	GIASUDDIN AHMED	11/6/2014	21:54:34	0
9085341993	DIPAK DAS	9707783876	GIASUDDINAHMED	11/6/2014	21:51:28	0
9085341993	DIPAK DAS	9707783876	GIASUDDINAHMED	11/6/2014	21:49:57	0
9085341993	DIPAK DAS	9707783876	GIASUDDINAHMED	11/6/2014	21:49:46	0
9085341993	DIPAK DAS	9085428530	GIASUDDIN AHMED	11/6/2014	21:49:29	0

Calling (A) Party Telephone Number/MSISDN	Name	Called (B) Party Telephone Number/Access Point Name	Name	Date	Time	Duration In Secs.
9085341993	DIPAK DAS	9085428530	GIASUDDIN AHMED	11/6/2014	21:37:58	0
9085341993	DIPAK DAS	9085428530	GIASUDDIN AHMED	11/6/2014	21:37:48	0
9085341993	DIPAK DAS	9707783876	GIASUDDINAHMED	11/6/2014	21:34:53	206
9085341993	DIPAK DAS	9707783876	GIASUDDINAHMED	11/6/2014	21:34:45	0
9085341993	DIPAK DAS	9707783876	GIASUDDINAHMED	11/6/2014	21:33:46	12
9085341993	DIPAK DAS	9707783876	GIASUDDINAHMED	11/6/2014	21:30:12	197
9085341993	DIPAK DAS	9707783876	GIASUDDINAHMED	11/6/2014	21:12:30	416
9085341993	DIPAK DAS	9085428530	GIASUDDIN AHMED	11/6/2014	20:54:34	0
9085341993	DIPAK DAS	9085428530	GIASUDDIN AHMED	11/6/2014	20:54:22	0
9085341993	DIPAK DAS	9085428530	GIASUDDIN AHMED	11/6/2014	20:47:22	0
9085341993	DIPAK DAS	9707783876	GIASUDDINAHMED	11/6/2014	20:43:38	0
9085341993	DIPAK DAS	9707783876	GIASUDDINAHMED	11/6/2014	20:39:26	0
9085341993	DIPAK DAS	9707783876	GIASUDDINAHMED	11/6/2014	20:38:00	0
9085341993	DIPAK DAS	9085428530	GIASUDDIN AHMED	11/6/2014	20:34:14	0
9085341993	DIPAK DAS	9085428530	GIASUDDIN AHMED	11/6/2014	20:32:23	0
9085341993	DIPAK DAS	9085428530	GIASUDDIN AHMED	11/6/2014	20:24:44	0
9085341993	DIPAK DAS	9085428530	GIASUDDIN AHMED	11/6/2014	20:18:44	0
9085341993	DIPAK DAS	9085428530	GIASUDDIN AHMED	11/6/2014	19:54:20	0

Calling (A) Party Telephone Number/MSISDN	Name	Called (B) Party Telephone Number/Access Point Name	Name	Date	Time	Duration In Secs.
9085341993	DIPAK DAS	9707783876	GIASUDDINAHMED	11/6/2014	19:15:36	0
9085341993	DIPAK DAS	9707783876	GIASUDDINAHMED	11/6/2014	19:13:46	0
9085341993	DIPAK DAS	9707783876	GIASUDDINAHMED	11/6/2014	19:12:28	0
9085341993	DIPAK DAS	9707474658	HITESH KALITA	11/6/2014	18:49:24	0
9085341993	DIPAK DAS	9707783876	GIASUDDINAHMED	11/6/2014	18:36:54	0
9085341993	DIPAK DAS	9707783876	GIASUDDINAHMED	11/6/2014	18:32:45	0
9085341993	DIPAK DAS	9707783876	GIASUDDINAHMED	11/6/2014	18:27:36	0
9085341993	DIPAK DAS	9707783876	GIASUDDINAHMED	11/6/2014	18:07:22	0
9085341993	DIPAK DAS	9707783876	GIASUDDINAHMED	11/6/2014	17:59:04	0
9085341993	DIPAK DAS	9401165464	HITESWAR KALITA	11/6/2014	17:58:53	69
9085341993	DIPAK DAS	9707474658	HITESH KALITA	11/6/2014	17:56:36	0
9085341993	DIPAK DAS	9707783876	GIASUDDINAHMED	11/6/2014	17:54:29	0
9085341993	DIPAK DAS	9707783876	GIASUDDINAHMED	11/6/2014	17:52:51	0
9085341993	DIPAK DAS	9707783876	GIASUDDINAHMED	11/6/2014	17:52:40	0
9085341993	DIPAK DAS	9707783876	GIASUDDINAHMED	11/6/2014	17:52:31	0
9085341993	DIPAK DAS	9707783876	GIASUDDINAHMED	11/6/2014	17:38:10	0
9085341993	DIPAK DAS	9707783876	GIASUDDINAHMED	11/6/2014	17:36:39	0
9085341993	DIPAK DAS	9707783876	GIASUDDINAHMED	11/6/2014	17:24:17	0

Calling (A) Party Telephone Number/MSISDN	Name	Called (B) Party Telephone Number/Access Point Name	Name	Date	Time	Duration In Secs.
9085341993	DIPAK DAS	9707474658	HITESH KALITA	11/6/2014	17:16:33	0
9085341993	DIPAK DAS	9707783876	GIASUDDINAHMED	11/6/2014	16:41:51	0
9085341993	DIPAK DAS	9707783876	GIASUDDINAHMED	11/6/2014	16:26:41	0
9085341993	DIPAK DAS	9707783876	GIASUDDINAHMED	11/6/2014	16:24:39	0
9085341993	DIPAK DAS	9707783876	GIASUDDINAHMED	11/6/2014	16:23:21	0
9085341993	DIPAK DAS	9707783876	GIASUDDINAHMED	11/6/2014	16:10:37	0
9085341993	DIPAK DAS	9707474658	HITESH KALITA	11/6/2014	16:02:55	0
9085341993	DIPAK DAS	9707783876	GIASUDDINAHMED	11/6/2014	16:02:03	0
9085341993	DIPAK DAS	9707474658	HITESH KALITA	11/6/2014	16:00:41	0
9085341993	DIPAK DAS	9707474658	HITESH KALITA	11/6/2014	15:58:20	0
9085341993	DIPAK DAS	9707783876	GIASUDDINAHMED	11/6/2014	15:50:27	0
9085341993	DIPAK DAS	9707783876	GIASUDDINAHMED	11/6/2014	15:49:50	0
9085341993	DIPAK DAS	9707783876	GIASUDDINAHMED	11/6/2014	15:40:03	0
9085341993	DIPAK DAS	9707783876	GIASUDDINAHMED	11/6/2014	15:32:36	0
9085341993	DIPAK DAS	9707783876	GIASUDDINAHMED	11/6/2014	15:22:19	0
9085341993	DIPAK DAS	9707783876	GIASUDDINAHMED	11/6/2014	15:11:33	0
9085341993	DIPAK DAS	9707783876	GIASUDDINAHMED	11/6/2014	15:09:13	0
9085341993	DIPAK DAS	9707783876	GIASUDDINAHMED	11/6/2014	14:56:15	0

Calling (A) Party Telephone Number/MSISDN	Name	Called (B) Party Telephone Number/Access Point Name	Name	Date	Time	Duration In Secs.
9085341993	DIPAK DAS	9707783876	GIASUDDINAHMED	11/6/2014	14:54:49	0
9085341993	DIPAK DAS	9707783876	GIASUDDINAHMED	11/6/2014	14:52:29	0
9085341993	DIPAK DAS	9707783876	GIASUDDINAHMED	11/6/2014	14:49:54	0
9085341993	DIPAK DAS	9707783876	GIASUDDINAHMED	11/6/2014	14:49:49	0
9085341993	DIPAK DAS	9707783876	GIASUDDINAHMED	11/6/2014	14:46:11	0
9085341993	DIPAK DAS	9707474658	HITESH KALITA	11/6/2014	14:45:40	0
9085341993	DIPAK DAS	9707783876	GIASUDDINAHMED	11/6/2014	14:38:15	0
9085341993	DIPAK DAS	9707783876	GIASUDDINAHMED	11/6/2014	14:36:49	0
9085341993	DIPAK DAS	9707783876	GIASUDDINAHMED	11/6/2014	14:30:14	0
9085341993	DIPAK DAS	9401165464	HITESWAR KALITA	11/6/2014	14:23:36	86
9085341993	DIPAK DAS	9707783876	GIASUDDINAHMED	10/6/2014	20:21:14	0
9085341993	DIPAK DAS	9707783876	GIASUDDINAHMED	10/6/2014	20:04:00	0
9085341993	DIPAK DAS	9707783876	GIASUDDINAHMED	10/6/2014	19:58:19	0
9085341993	DIPAK DAS	9707783876	GIASUDDINAHMED	10/6/2014	19:53:02	0
9085341993	DIPAK DAS	9707783876	GIASUDDINAHMED	10/6/2014	19:23:52	0
9085341993	DIPAK DAS	9707783876	GIASUDDINAHMED	10/6/2014	19:14:51	0
9085341993	DIPAK DAS	9401165464	HITESWAR KALITA	10/6/2014	19:11:21	0
9085341993	DIPAK DAS	9085428530	GIASUDDIN AHMED	10/6/2014	18:56:18	0

Calling (A) Party Telephone Number/MSISDN	Name	Called (B) Party Telephone Number/Access Point Name	Name	Date	Time	Duration In Secs.
9085341993	DIPAK DAS	9707783876	GIASUDDINAHMED	10/6/2014	18:52:26	0
9085341993	DIPAK DAS	9707783876	GIASUDDINAHMED	10/6/2014	18:40:22	0
9085341993	DIPAK DAS	9707783876	GIASUDDINAHMED	10/6/2014	18:15:57	0
9085341993	DIPAK DAS	9707783876	GIASUDDINAHMED	10/6/2014	15:22:12	0
9085341993	DIPAK DAS	9707783876	GIASUDDINAHMED	10/6/2014	14:21:58	0
9085341993	DIPAK DAS	9707783876	GIASUDDINAHMED	10/6/2014	14:20:20	0
9085341993	DIPAK DAS	9707783876	GIASUDDINAHMED	10/6/2014	9:40:50	0
9085341993	DIPAK DAS	9707783876	GIASUDDINAHMED	10/6/2014	9:16:59	0
9085341993	DIPAK DAS	9707783876	GIASUDDINAHMED	10/6/2014	9:14:57	0
9085341993	DIPAK DAS	9707783876	GIASUDDINAHMED	10/6/2014	8:38:26	0
9085341993	DIPAK DAS	9401165464	HITESWAR KALITA	10/6/2014	8:01:26	26
9085341993	DIPAK DAS	9707783876	GIASUDDINAHMED	9/6/2014	23:12:43	0
9085341993	DIPAK DAS	9085428530	GIASUDDIN AHMED	9/6/2014	23:07:13	0
9085341993	DIPAK DAS	9707783876	GIASUDDINAHMED	9/6/2014	23:05:10	0
9085341993	DIPAK DAS	9085428530	GIASUDDIN AHMED	9/6/2014	23:04:00	0
9085341993	DIPAK DAS	9707783876	GIASUDDINAHMED	9/6/2014	23:02:48	0
9085341993	DIPAK DAS	9085428530	GIASUDDIN AHMED	9/6/2014	23:02:19	0
9085341993	DIPAK DAS	9085428530	GIASUDDIN AHMED	9/6/2014	23:02:15	0

Calling (A) Party Telephone Number/MSISDN	Name	Called (B) Party Telephone Number/Access Point Name	Name	Date	Time	Duration In Secs.
9085341993	DIPAK DAS	9707783876	GIASUDDINAHMED	9/6/2014	22:59:54	0
9085341993	DIPAK DAS	9707783876	GIASUDDINAHMED	9/6/2014	22:57:55	0
9085341993	DIPAK DAS	9707783876	GIASUDDINAHMED	9/6/2014	22:56:11	0
9085341993	DIPAK DAS	9707783876	GIASUDDINAHMED	9/6/2014	22:55:04	0
9085341993	DIPAK DAS	9707783876	GIASUDDINAHMED	9/6/2014	22:52:52	0
9085341993	DIPAK DAS	9707783876	GIASUDDINAHMED	9/6/2014	22:51:50	0
9085341993	DIPAK DAS	9085428530	GIASUDDIN AHMED	9/6/2014	22:50:06	0
9085341993	DIPAK DAS	9085428530	GIASUDDIN AHMED	9/6/2014	22:49:57	0
9085341993	DIPAK DAS	9707783876	GIASUDDINAHMED	9/6/2014	22:46:14	0
9085341993	DIPAK DAS	9707783876	GIASUDDINAHMED	9/6/2014	22:42:55	0
9085341993	DIPAK DAS	9707783876	GIASUDDINAHMED	9/6/2014	22:42:16	0
9085341993	DIPAK DAS	9085428530	GIASUDDIN AHMED	9/6/2014	22:41:53	0
9085341993	DIPAK DAS	9707783876	GIASUDDINAHMED	9/6/2014	22:39:22	0
9085341993	DIPAK DAS	9085428530	GIASUDDIN AHMED	9/6/2014	22:37:33	0
9085341993	DIPAK DAS	9707783876	GIASUDDINAHMED	9/6/2014	22:37:16	0
9085341993	DIPAK DAS	9707783876	GIASUDDINAHMED	9/6/2014	22:33:39	0
9085341993	DIPAK DAS	9085428530	GIASUDDIN AHMED	9/6/2014	22:30:44	0
9085341993	DIPAK DAS	9707783876	GIASUDDINAHMED	9/6/2014	22:28:22	0

Calling (A) Party Telephone Number/MSISDN	Name	Called (B) Party Telephone Number/Access Point Name	Name	Date	Time	Duration In Secs.
9085341993	DIPAK DAS	97077783876	GIASUDDINAHMED	9/6/2014	22:16:36	0
9085341993	DIPAK DAS	97077783876	GIASUDDINAHMED	9/6/2014	22:11:51	0
9085341993	DIPAK DAS	9085428530	GIASUDDIN AHMED	9/6/2014	22:09:34	0
9085341993	DIPAK DAS	97077783876	GIASUDDINAHMED	9/6/2014	22:07:02	0
9085341993	DIPAK DAS	9085428530	GIASUDDIN AHMED	9/6/2014	22:06:07	0
9085341993	DIPAK DAS	9085428530	GIASUDDIN AHMED	9/6/2014	22:04:48	0
9085341993	DIPAK DAS	9085428530	GIASUDDIN AHMED	9/6/2014	22:01:37	0
9085341993	DIPAK DAS	9085428530	GIASUDDIN AHMED	9/6/2014	21:56:25	0
9085341993	DIPAK DAS	9085428530	GIASUDDIN AHMED	9/6/2014	21:53:45	0
9085341993	DIPAK DAS	9085428530	GIASUDDIN AHMED	9/6/2014	21:53:41	0
9085341993	DIPAK DAS	97077783876	GIASUDDINAHMED	9/6/2014	21:19:33	0
9085341993	DIPAK DAS	97077783876	GIASUDDINAHMED	9/6/2014	21:18:09	0
9085341993	DIPAK DAS	97077783876	GIASUDDINAHMED	9/6/2014	21:16:01	0
9085341993	DIPAK DAS	97077783876	GIASUDDINAHMED	9/6/2014	21:14:01	0
9085341993	DIPAK DAS	97077783876	GIASUDDINAHMED	9/6/2014	21:12:13	0
9085341993	DIPAK DAS	97077783876	GIASUDDINAHMED	9/6/2014	21:12:08	0
9085341993	DIPAK DAS	9085428530	GIASUDDIN AHMED	9/6/2014	21:06:11	0
9085341993	DIPAK DAS	9085428530	GIASUDDIN AHMED	9/6/2014	21:06:05	0

Calling (A) Party Telephone Number/MSISDN	Name	Called (B) Party Telephone Number/Access Point Name	Name	Date	Time	Duration In Secs.
9085341993	DIPAK DAS	9707783876	GIASUDDINAHMED	9/6/2014	21:05:47	0
9085341993	DIPAK DAS	9085428530	GIASUDDIN AHMED	9/6/2014	20:59:58	0
9085341993	DIPAK DAS	9085428530	GIASUDDIN AHMED	9/6/2014	20:59:52	0
9085341993	DIPAK DAS	9085428530	GIASUDDIN AHMED	9/6/2014	20:48:13	0
9085341993	DIPAK DAS	9085428530	GIASUDDIN AHMED	9/6/2014	20:45:36	0
9085341993	DIPAK DAS	9085428530	GIASUDDIN AHMED	9/6/2014	20:43:14	0
9085341993	DIPAK DAS	9707783876	GIASUDDINAHMED	9/6/2014	20:12:23	0
9085341993	DIPAK DAS	9707783876	GIASUDDINAHMED	9/6/2014	19:59:54	0
9085341993	DIPAK DAS	9707783876	GIASUDDINAHMED	9/6/2014	19:59:48	0
9085341993	DIPAK DAS	9707783876	GIASUDDINAHMED	9/6/2014	19:51:57	0
9085341993	DIPAK DAS	9707783876	GIASUDDINAHMED	9/6/2014	19:48:34	0
9085341993	DIPAK DAS	9707783876	GIASUDDINAHMED	9/6/2014	19:33:20	0
9085341993	DIPAK DAS	9707783876	GIASUDDINAHMED	9/6/2014	19:27:59	0
9085341993	DIPAK DAS	9707783876	GIASUDDINAHMED	9/6/2014	19:27:05	0
9085341993	DIPAK DAS	9707783876	GIASUDDINAHMED	9/6/2014	19:15:08	0
9085341993	DIPAK DAS	9707783876	GIASUDDINAHMED	9/6/2014	19:13:13	0
9085341993	DIPAK DAS	9401165464	HITESWAR KALITA	9/6/2014	19:12:24	13
9085341993	DIPAK DAS	9707783876	GIASUDDINAHMED	9/6/2014	19:09:29	0

Calling (A) Party Telephone Number/MSISDN	Name	Called (B) Party Telephone Number/Access Point Name	Name	Date	Time	Duration In Secs.
9085341993	DIPAK DAS	9707783876	GIASUDDINAHMED	9/6/2014	18:58:02	0
9085341993	DIPAK DAS	9707783876	GIASUDDINAHMED	9/6/2014	18:56:22	0
9085341993	DIPAK DAS	9401165464	HITESWAR KALITA	9/6/2014	17:02:18	9
9085341993	DIPAK DAS	9085428530	GIASUDDIN AHMED	9/6/2014	16:52:30	0
9085341993	DIPAK DAS	9085428530	GIASUDDIN AHMED	9/6/2014	16:41:06	0
9085341993	DIPAK DAS	9085428530	GIASUDDIN AHMED	9/6/2014	16:37:13	0
9085341993	DIPAK DAS	9085428530	GIASUDDIN AHMED	9/6/2014	16:23:55	0
9085341993	DIPAK DAS	9085428530	GIASUDDIN AHMED	9/6/2014	16:22:32	0
9085341993	DIPAK DAS	9085428530	GIASUDDIN AHMED	9/6/2014	16:19:32	0
9085341993	DIPAK DAS	9707783876	GIASUDDINAHMED	9/6/2014	15:57:18	0
9085341993	DIPAK DAS	9707783876	GIASUDDINAHMED	9/6/2014	15:54:50	0
9085341993	DIPAK DAS	9707783876	GIASUDDINAHMED	9/6/2014	15:53:51	0
9085341993	DIPAK DAS	9707783876	GIASUDDINAHMED	9/6/2014	15:43:05	0
9085341993	DIPAK DAS	9707783876	GIASUDDINAHMED	9/6/2014	15:40:58	0
9085341993	DIPAK DAS	9707783876	GIASUDDINAHMED	9/6/2014	15:38:46	0
9085341993	DIPAK DAS	9707783876	GIASUDDINAHMED	9/6/2014	15:25:03	0
9085341993	DIPAK DAS	9401165464	HITESWAR KALITA	9/6/2014	15:20:40	10
9085341993	DIPAK DAS	9707783876	GIASUDDINAHMED	9/6/2014	15:20:27	0

Calling (A) Party Telephone Number/MSISDN	Name	Called (B) Party Telephone Number/Access Point Name	Name	Date	Time	Duration In Secs.
9085341993	DIPAK DAS	9707783876	GIASUDDINAHMED	9/6/2014	8:18:57	0
9085341993	DIPAK DAS	9707783876	GIASUDDINAHMED	9/6/2014	8:14:53	0
9085341993	DIPAK DAS	9707783876	GIASUDDINAHMED	9/6/2014	8:14:34	0
9085341993	DIPAK DAS	9707783876	GIASUDDINAHMED	9/6/2014	8:09:22	0
9085341993	DIPAK DAS	9707783876	GIASUDDINAHMED	9/6/2014	7:35:23	0
9085341993	DIPAK DAS	9707783876	GIASUDDINAHMED	9/6/2014	7:25:18	0
9085341993	DIPAK DAS	9707783876	GIASUDDINAHMED	9/6/2014	0:45:20	0
9085341993	DIPAK DAS	9707783876	GIASUDDINAHMED	8/6/2014	23:27:54	0
9085341993	DIPAK DAS	9707783876	GIASUDDINAHMED	8/6/2014	23:18:21	0
9085341993	DIPAK DAS	9707783876	GIASUDDINAHMED	8/6/2014	23:17:14	0
9085341993	DIPAK DAS	9707783876	GIASUDDINAHMED	8/6/2014	23:16:22	0
9085341993	DIPAK DAS	9707783876	GIASUDDINAHMED	8/6/2014	21:07:00	0
9085341993	DIPAK DAS	9707783876	GIASUDDINAHMED	8/6/2014	19:56:53	0
9085341993	DIPAK DAS	9707783876	GIASUDDINAHMED	8/6/2014	19:54:03	25
9085341993	DIPAK DAS	9707783876	GIASUDDINAHMED	8/6/2014	16:44:27	0
9085341993	DIPAK DAS	9707783876	GIASUDDINAHMED	8/6/2014	16:32:16	0
9085341993	DIPAK DAS	9707783876	GIASUDDINAHMED	8/6/2014	15:33:21	0
9085341993	DIPAK DAS	9707783876	GIASUDDINAHMED	8/6/2014	15:15:53	0

Calling (A) Party Telephone Number/MSISDN	Name	Called (B) Party Telephone Number/Access Point Name	Name	Date	Time	Duration In Secs.
9085341993	DIPAK DAS	9707783876	GIASUDDINAHMED	8/6/2014	14:32:46	0
9085341993	DIPAK DAS	9707783876	GIASUDDINAHMED	8/6/2014	14:26:44	0
9085341993	DIPAK DAS	9707783876	GIASUDDINAHMED	8/6/2014	14:14:53	0
9085341993	DIPAK DAS	9707783876	GIASUDDINAHMED	8/6/2014	13:34:41	250
9085341993	DIPAK DAS	9707783876	GIASUDDINAHMED	8/6/2014	11:19:17	292
9085341993	DIPAK DAS	9707783876	GIASUDDINAHMED	7/6/2014	23:53:22	0
9085341993	DIPAK DAS	9707783876	GIASUDDINAHMED	7/6/2014	23:14:53	0
9085341993	DIPAK DAS	9707783876	GIASUDDINAHMED	7/6/2014	23:09:32	0
9085341993	DIPAK DAS	9707783876	GIASUDDINAHMED	7/6/2014	23:07:53	0
9085341993	DIPAK DAS	9707783876	GIASUDDINAHMED	7/6/2014	22:56:29	0
9085341993	DIPAK DAS	9707783876	GIASUDDINAHMED	7/6/2014	22:36:44	292
9085341993	DIPAK DAS	9707783876	GIASUDDINAHMED	7/6/2014	22:06:48	0
9085341993	DIPAK DAS	9707783876	GIASUDDINAHMED	7/6/2014	18:38:48	0
9085341993	DIPAK DAS	9707783876	GIASUDDINAHMED	7/6/2014	11:17:23	0
9085341993	DIPAK DAS	9707783876	GIASUDDINAHMED	6/6/2014	23:26:39	0
9085341993	DIPAK DAS	9707783876	GIASUDDINAHMED	6/6/2014	23:21:04	0
9085341993	DIPAK DAS	9707783876	GIASUDDINAHMED	6/6/2014	23:16:37	0
9085341993	DIPAK DAS	9707783876	GIASUDDINAHMED	6/6/2014	23:13:00	156

Calling (A) Party Telephone Number/MSISDN	Name	Called (B) Party Telephone Number/Access Point Name	Name	Date	Time	Duration In Secs.
9085341993	DIPAK DAS	9707783876	GIASUDDINAHMED	6/6/2014	22:42:22	0
9085341993	DIPAK DAS	9707783876	GIASUDDINAHMED	6/6/2014	21:34:44	0
9085341993	DIPAK DAS	9707783876	GIASUDDINAHMED	6/6/2014	16:39:25	0
9085341993	DIPAK DAS	9707783876	GIASUDDINAHMED	6/6/2014	8:20:08	0
9085341993	DIPAK DAS	9707783876	GIASUDDINAHMED	6/6/2014	7:34:35	50
9085341993	DIPAK DAS	9707474658	HITESH KALITA	6/6/2014	6:47:35	75
9085341993	DIPAK DAS	9707783876	GIASUDDINAHMED	5/6/2014	23:19:05	0
9085341993	DIPAK DAS	9707783876	GIASUDDINAHMED	5/6/2014	23:07:03	0
9085341993	DIPAK DAS	9707783876	GIASUDDINAHMED	5/6/2014	23:04:23	0
9085341993	DIPAK DAS	9707783876	GIASUDDINAHMED	5/6/2014	23:01:06	85
9085341993	DIPAK DAS	9707783876	GIASUDDINAHMED	5/6/2014	22:35:47	0
9085341993	DIPAK DAS	9707783876	GIASUDDINAHMED	5/6/2014	21:48:36	0
9085341993	DIPAK DAS	9707783876	GIASUDDINAHMED	5/6/2014	21:47:14	8
9085341993	DIPAK DAS	9707783876	GIASUDDINAHMED	5/6/2014	21:45:01	73
9085341993	DIPAK DAS	9707783876	GIASUDDINAHMED	5/6/2014	21:35:32	12
9085341993	DIPAK DAS	9707783876	GIASUDDINAHMED	5/6/2014	21:33:32	0
9085341993	DIPAK DAS	9707783876	GIASUDDINAHMED	5/6/2014	21:21:36	315
9085341993	DIPAK DAS	9707783876	GIASUDDINAHMED	5/6/2014	21:02:20	0

Calling (A) Party Telephone Number/MSISDN	Name	Called (B) Party Telephone Number/Access Point Name	Name	Date	Time	Duration In Secs.
9085341993	DIPAK DAS	9707783876	GIASUDDINAHMED	5/6/2014	19:54:41	0
9085341993	DIPAK DAS	9707783876	GIASUDDINAHMED	5/6/2014	19:50:53	20
9085341993	DIPAK DAS	9707474658	HITESH KALITA	5/6/2014	18:23:13	35
9085341993	DIPAK DAS	9707783876	GIASUDDINAHMED	5/6/2014	16:24:58	0
9085341993	DIPAK DAS	9707783876	GIASUDDINAHMED	5/6/2014	16:11:16	0
9085341993	DIPAK DAS	9707783876	GIASUDDINAHMED	5/6/2014	16:07:29	99
9085341993	DIPAK DAS	9707783876	GIASUDDINAHMED	5/6/2014	14:46:29	0
9085341993	DIPAK DAS	9707783876	GIASUDDINAHMED	5/6/2014	9:45:15	0
9085341993	DIPAK DAS	9707783876	GIASUDDINAHMED	5/6/2014	9:45:13	0
9085341993	DIPAK DAS	9707783876	GIASUDDINAHMED	5/6/2014	9:45:11	0
9085341993	DIPAK DAS	9707783876	GIASUDDINAHMED	4/6/2014	23:42:18	76
9085341993	DIPAK DAS	9707783876	GIASUDDINAHMED	4/6/2014	23:05:34	0
9085341993	DIPAK DAS	9707783876	GIASUDDINAHMED	4/6/2014	18:37:45	39
9085341993	DIPAK DAS	9707783876	GIASUDDINAHMED	4/6/2014	18:34:27	0
9085341993	DIPAK DAS	9707783876	GIASUDDINAHMED	4/6/2014	17:21:43	0
9085341993	DIPAK DAS	9707783876	GIASUDDINAHMED	4/6/2014	17:20:32	0
9085341993	DIPAK DAS	9707783876	GIASUDDINAHMED	4/6/2014	16:40:12	3
9085341993	DIPAK DAS	9707783876	GIASUDDINAHMED	4/6/2014	15:38:48	0

Calling (A) Party Telephone Number/MSISDN	Name	Called (B) Party Telephone Number/Access Point Name	Name	Date	Time	Duration In Secs.
9085341993	DIPAK DAS	9707783876	GIASUDDINAHMED	4/6/2014	15:34:32	0
9085341993	DIPAK DAS	9707783876	GIASUDDINAHMED	4/6/2014	8:16:46	0
9085341993	DIPAK DAS	9707783876	GIASUDDINAHMED	3/6/2014	22:40:20	0
9085341993	DIPAK DAS	9707783876	GIASUDDINAHMED	3/6/2014	22:30:35	0
9085341993	DIPAK DAS	9707783876	GIASUDDINAHMED	3/6/2014	22:27:39	0
9085341993	DIPAK DAS	9707783876	GIASUDDINAHMED	3/6/2014	20:52:36	0
9085341993	DIPAK DAS	9707783876	GIASUDDINAHMED	3/6/2014	20:51:45	0
9085341993	DIPAK DAS	9707783876	GIASUDDINAHMED	3/6/2014	20:14:21	436
9085341993	DIPAK DAS	9707783876	GIASUDDINAHMED	3/6/2014	20:13:27	25
9085341993	DIPAK DAS	9707783876	GIASUDDINAHMED	3/6/2014	20:01:44	0
9085341993	DIPAK DAS	9707783876	GIASUDDINAHMED	3/6/2014	19:50:47	0
9085341993	DIPAK DAS	9707474658	HITESH KALITA	3/6/2014	19:46:41	66
9085341993	DIPAK DAS	9707783876	GIASUDDINAHMED	3/6/2014	19:25:02	0
9085341993	DIPAK DAS	9707783876	GIASUDDINAHMED	3/6/2014	19:09:23	1
9085341993	DIPAK DAS	9707783876	GIASUDDINAHMED	3/6/2014	17:52:03	0
9085341993	DIPAK DAS	9707783876	GIASUDDINAHMED	3/6/2014	17:49:32	0
9085341993	DIPAK DAS	9707474658	HITESH KALITA	3/6/2014	17:04:08	25
9085341993	DIPAK DAS	9707474658	HITESH KALITA	3/6/2014	16:33:11	0

Calling (A) Party Telephone Number/MSISDN	Name	Called (B) Party Telephone Number/Access Point Name	Name	Date	Time	Duration In Secs.
9085341993	DIPAK DAS	9707783876	GIASUDDINAHMED	3/6/2014	16:24:18	0
9085341993	DIPAK DAS	9707783876	GIASUDDINAHMED	3/6/2014	16:20:00	0
9085341993	DIPAK DAS	9707474658	HITESH KALITA	3/6/2014	14:49:36	26
9085341993	DIPAK DAS	9707474658	HITESH KALITA	3/6/2014	8:08:24	0
9085341993	DIPAK DAS	9707783876	GIASUDDINAHMED	3/6/2014	8:06:42	0
9085341993	DIPAK DAS	9707783876	GIASUDDINAHMED	3/6/2014	7:39:39	0
9085341993	DIPAK DAS	9707783876	GIASUDDINAHMED	3/6/2014	7:27:30	0
9085341993	DIPAK DAS	9707783876	GIASUDDINAHMED	3/6/2014	7:09:28	0
9085341993	DIPAK DAS	9707783876	GIASUDDINAHMED	3/6/2014	6:14:01	0
9085341993	DIPAK DAS	9707783876	GIASUDDINAHMED	3/6/2014	0:20:11	0
9085341993	DIPAK DAS	9707783876	GIASUDDINAHMED	3/6/2014	0:11:12	0
9085341993	DIPAK DAS	9707783876	GIASUDDINAHMED	3/6/2014	0:06:29	0
9085341993	DIPAK DAS	9707783876	GIASUDDINAHMED	3/6/2014	0:03:37	0
9085341993	DIPAK DAS	9707783876	GIASUDDINAHMED	3/6/2014	0:01:54	0
9085341993	DIPAK DAS	9707783876	GIASUDDINAHMED	3/6/2014	0:01:37	0
9085341993	DIPAK DAS	9707783876	GIASUDDINAHMED	3/6/2014	0:00:07	0
9085341993	DIPAK DAS	9707783876	GIASUDDINAHMED	2/6/2014	23:58:34	0
9085341993	DIPAK DAS	9707783876	GIASUDDINAHMED	2/6/2014	23:57:49	0

Calling (A) Party Telephone Number/MSISDN	Name	Called (B) Party Telephone Number/Access Point Name	Name	Date	Time	Duration In Secs.
9085341993	DIPAK DAS	9707783876	GIASUDDINAHMED	2/6/2014	23:56:08	0
9085341993	DIPAK DAS	9707783876	GIASUDDINAHMED	2/6/2014	23:54:13	0
9085341993	DIPAK DAS	9707783876	GIASUDDINAHMED	2/6/2014	23:43:32	499
9085341993	DIPAK DAS	9707783876	GIASUDDINAHMED	2/6/2014	23:42:57	0
9085341993	DIPAK DAS	9707783876	GIASUDDINAHMED	2/6/2014	23:42:55	0
9085341993	DIPAK DAS	9707783876	GIASUDDINAHMED	2/6/2014	23:42:41	0
9085341993	DIPAK DAS	9707783876	GIASUDDINAHMED	2/6/2014	23:41:59	0
9085341993	DIPAK DAS	9707783876	GIASUDDINAHMED	2/6/2014	23:35:48	0
9085341993	DIPAK DAS	9707783876	GIASUDDINAHMED	2/6/2014	23:35:19	0
9085341993	DIPAK DAS	9707783876	GIASUDDINAHMED	2/6/2014	23:33:12	0
9085341993	DIPAK DAS	9707783876	GIASUDDINAHMED	2/6/2014	23:33:10	0
9085341993	DIPAK DAS	9707783876	GIASUDDINAHMED	2/6/2014	23:33:07	0
9085341993	DIPAK DAS	9707783876	GIASUDDINAHMED	2/6/2014	23:26:09	0
9085341993	DIPAK DAS	9707783876	GIASUDDINAHMED	2/6/2014	23:25:50	0
9085341993	DIPAK DAS	9707783876	GIASUDDINAHMED	2/6/2014	23:23:35	0
9085341993	DIPAK DAS	9707783876	GIASUDDINAHMED	2/6/2014	23:19:41	0
9085341993	DIPAK DAS	9707783876	GIASUDDINAHMED	2/6/2014	23:19:32	0
9085341993	DIPAK DAS	9707783876	GIASUDDINAHMED	2/6/2014	23:16:21	0

Calling (A) Party Telephone Number/MSISDN	Name	Called (B) Party Telephone Number/Access Point Name	Name	Date	Time	Duration In Secs.
9085341993	DIPAK DAS	9707783876	GIASUDDINAHMED	2/6/2014	23:13:45	0
9085341993	DIPAK DAS	9707783876	GIASUDDINAHMED	2/6/2014	23:10:22	0
9085341993	DIPAK DAS	9707783876	GIASUDDINAHMED	2/6/2014	23:10:18	0
9085341993	DIPAK DAS	9707783876	GIASUDDINAHMED	2/6/2014	22:56:57	0
9085341993	DIPAK DAS	9707783876	GIASUDDINAHMED	2/6/2014	22:52:51	0
9085341993	DIPAK DAS	9707783876	GIASUDDINAHMED	2/6/2014	22:46:22	0
9085341993	DIPAK DAS	9707783876	GIASUDDINAHMED	2/6/2014	22:39:55	135
9085341993	DIPAK DAS	9707474658	HITESH KALITA	2/6/2014	20:01:52	30
9085341993	DIPAK DAS	9707783876	GIASUDDINAHMED	2/6/2014	19:54:39	0
9085341993	DIPAK DAS	9707783876	GIASUDDINAHMED	2/6/2014	19:53:14	0
9085341993	DIPAK DAS	9707474658	HITESH KALITA	2/6/2014	19:09:09	33
9085341993	DIPAK DAS	9707783876	GIASUDDINAHMED	2/6/2014	18:44:45	29
9085341993	DIPAK DAS	9707474658	HITESH KALITA	2/6/2014	17:49:47	28
9085341993	DIPAK DAS	9707783876	GIASUDDINAHMED	2/6/2014	8:27:51	0
9085341993	DIPAK DAS	9707783876	GIASUDDINAHMED	2/6/2014	8:14:18	261
9085341993	DIPAK DAS	9707783876	GIASUDDINAHMED	1/6/2014	22:55:10	0
9085341993	DIPAK DAS	9707783876	GIASUDDINAHMED	1/6/2014	22:29:35	0
9085341993	DIPAK DAS	9707783876	GIASUDDINAHMED	1/6/2014	22:27:27	0

Calling (A) Party Telephone Number/MSISDN	Name	Called (B) Party Telephone Number/Access Point Name	Name	Date	Time	Duration In Secs.
9085341993	DIPAK DAS	9707783876	GIASUDDINAHMED	1/6/2014	22:25:53	0
9085341993	DIPAK DAS	9707783876	GIASUDDINAHMED	1/6/2014	22:10:27	0
9085341993	DIPAK DAS	9707783876	GIASUDDINAHMED	1/6/2014	21:29:01	0
9085341993	DIPAK DAS	9707783876	GIASUDDINAHMED	1/6/2014	21:06:23	0
9085341993	DIPAK DAS	9707474658	HITESH KALITA	1/6/2014	21:01:35	0
9085341993	DIPAK DAS	9707783876	GIASUDDINAHMED	1/6/2014	20:38:32	0
9085341993	DIPAK DAS	9707474658	HITESH KALITA	1/6/2014	20:38:16	0
9085341993	DIPAK DAS	9707783876	GIASUDDINAHMED	1/6/2014	20:28:58	59
9085341993	DIPAK DAS	9707783876	GIASUDDINAHMED	1/6/2014	20:25:47	0
9085341993	DIPAK DAS	9707783876	GIASUDDINAHMED	1/6/2014	20:21:15	0
9085341993	DIPAK DAS	9707783876	GIASUDDINAHMED	1/6/2014	18:48:02	0
9085341993	DIPAK DAS	9707474658	HITESH KALITA	1/6/2014	17:26:56	0
9085341993	DIPAK DAS	9707474658	HITESH KALITA	1/6/2014	16:51:30	0
9085341993	DIPAK DAS	9707474658	HITESH KALITA	1/6/2014	15:11:21	0
9085341993	DIPAK DAS	9707474658	HITESH KALITA	1/6/2014	10:04:06	52
9085341993	DIPAK DAS	9707474658	HITESH KALITA	1/6/2014	10:03:36	10
9085341993	DIPAK DAS	9707783876	GIASUDDINAHMED	1/6/2014	9:06:51	0
9085341993	DIPAK DAS	9707783876	GIASUDDINAHMED	1/6/2014	9:02:47	0

Calling (A) Party Telephone Number/MSISDN	Name	Called (B) Party Telephone Number/Access Point Name	Name	Date	Time	Duration In Secs.
9085341993	DIPAK DAS	9707783876	GIASUDDINAHMED	1/6/2014	9:01:32	0
9085341993	DIPAK DAS	9707474658	HITESH KALITA	31-05-2014	23:34:47	0
9085341993	DIPAK DAS	9707783876	GIASUDDINAHMED	31-05-2014	23:14:26	0
9085341993	DIPAK DAS	9707783876	GIASUDDINAHMED	31-05-2014	23:03:10	0
9085341993	DIPAK DAS	9707783876	GIASUDDINAHMED	31-05-2014	22:50:09	0
9085341993	DIPAK DAS	9707783876	GIASUDDINAHMED	31-05-2014	22:12:43	0
9085341993	DIPAK DAS	9864754773	GIASUDDINAHMED	31-05-2014	22:00:46	0
9085341993	DIPAK DAS	9707474658	HITESH KALITA	31-05-2014	21:52:58	0
9085341993	DIPAK DAS	9707783876	GIASUDDINAHMED	31-05-2014	21:39:02	0
9085341993	DIPAK DAS	9707783876	GIASUDDINAHMED	31-05-2014	21:24:43	0
9085341993	DIPAK DAS	9707783876	GIASUDDINAHMED	31-05-2014	21:22:54	0
9085341993	DIPAK DAS	9707783876	GIASUDDINAHMED	31-05-2014	21:19:15	0
9085341993	DIPAK DAS	9707783876	GIASUDDINAHMED	31-05-2014	21:16:29	0
9085341993	DIPAK DAS	9707783876	GIASUDDINAHMED	31-05-2014	21:14:00	0
9085341993	DIPAK DAS	9707474658	HITESH KALITA	31-05-2014	20:12:19	0
9085341993	DIPAK DAS	9707474658	HITESH KALITA	31-05-2014	19:51:16	0
9085341993	DIPAK DAS	9707474658	HITESH KALITA	31-05-2014	19:46:46	0
9085341993	DIPAK DAS	9707474658	HITESH KALITA	31-05-2014	19:44:16	0

Calling (A) Party Telephone Number/MSISDN	Name	Called (B) Party Telephone Number/Access Point Name	Name	Date	Time	Duration In Secs.
9085341993	DIPAK DAS	9707783876	GIASUDDINAHMED	31-05-2014	15:52:22	571
9085341993	DIPAK DAS	9707474658	HITESH KALITA	31-05-2014	7:55:50	52
9085341993	DIPAK DAS	9707783876	GIASUDDINAHMED	31-05-2014	7:17:04	429
9085341993	DIPAK DAS	9707783876	GIASUDDINAHMED	30-05-2014	23:13:00	0
9085341993	DIPAK DAS	9707783876	GIASUDDINAHMED	30-05-2014	23:10:07	0
9085341993	DIPAK DAS	9707783876	GIASUDDINAHMED	30-05-2014	22:02:39	0
9085341993	DIPAK DAS	9707783876	GIASUDDINAHMED	30-05-2014	21:59:57	66
9085341993	DIPAK DAS	9707783876	GIASUDDINAHMED	30-05-2014	13:11:07	0
9085341993	DIPAK DAS	9707783876	GIASUDDINAHMED	30-05-2014	13:05:25	0